CAPITAL DILEMMA

Capital Dilemma: Growth and Inequality in Washington, DC uncovers and explains the dynamics that have influenced the contemporary economic advancement of Washington, DC. This volume's unique interdisciplinary perspective, using historical, sociological, anthropological, economic, geographic, political, and linguistic theories and approaches, captures the comprehensive factors related to changes taking place in one of the world's most important cities.

Capital Dilemma clarifies how preexisting urban social hierarchies, established mainly along race and class lines but also along national and local interests, are linked with the city's contemporary inequitable growth. While accounting for historic disparities, this book reveals how more recent federal and city political decisions and circumstances shape contemporary neighborhood gentrification patterns, highlighting the layered complexities of the modern national capital and connecting these considerations to Washington, DC's past as well as to present-day policy choices.

As we enter a period when advanced service-sector cities prosper, Washington, DC's changing landscape illustrates important processes and outcomes critical to other US cities and national capitals throughout the world. The *Capital Dilemma* for DC, and other major cities, is how to produce sustainable equitable economic growth. This volume expands our understanding of the contradictions, challenges, and opportunities associated with contemporary urban development.

Derek Hyra is an associate professor in the School of Public Affairs and founding director of the Metropolitan Policy Center at American University. His research focuses on processes of neighborhood change, with an emphasis on housing, urban politics, and race. Dr. Hyra is the author of *The New Urban Renewal: The Economic Transformation of Harlem and Bronzeville* (The University of Chicago Press, 2008) and recently completed his second book, *Making the Gilded Ghetto: Race, Class, and Politics in the Cappuccino City* (The University of Chicago Press, forthcoming), which investigates the redevelopment of Washington, DC's Shaw/U Street neighborhood. He received his BA from Colgate University and his PhD from the University of Chicago.

Native Washingtonian **Sabiyha Prince** is an anthropologist, author, researcher, and qualitative data analyst. Her work has focused on the ways class, race, and other aspects of status and identity overlap to shape the condition and experience of African Americans in cities, topics she has explored in her books *African Americans and Gentrification in Washington, DC: Race, Class, and Social Justice in the Nation's Capital* (2014) and *Constructing Belonging: Race, Class, and Harlem's Professional Workers* (2004). A proponent of an engaged anthropology, Prince has worked with community groups in Washington, DC and appeared on MSNBC, NPR, the Pacifica Radio Network, and Al Jazeera English as a key contributor to the award-winning documentary *There Goes the Neighborhood* (2010).

CAPITAL DILEMMA

Growth and Inequality in Washington, DC

Edited by
Derek Hyra and Sabiyha Prince

Routledge
Taylor & Francis Group

NEW YORK AND LONDON

First published 2016
by Routledge
711 Third Avenue, New York, NY 10017

and by Routledge
2 Park Square, Milton Park, Abingdon, Oxon OX14 4RN

Routledge is an imprint of the Taylor & Francis Group, an informa business.

Library of Congress Cataloging-in-Publication Data
Capital dilemma : growth and inequality in Washington, D.C. / edited by
    Derek Hyra and Sabiyha Prince. — 1 Edition.
        pages cm
  1. Washington (D.C.)—Social conditions.   2. Equality—Washington (D.C.)
3. Gentrification—Washington (D.C.)   4. Cities and towns—Growth.
I. Hyra, Derek S., editor.   II. Prince, Sabiyha, 1959– editor.
    HN80.W3C37 2016
    307.7609753—dc23
    2015020618

ISBN: 978-1-138-88690-2 (hbk)
ISBN: 978-1-138-88692-6 (pbk)
ISBN: 978-1-315-71448-6 (ebk)

Typeset in Bembo
by Apex CoVantage, LLC

Printed and bound in Great Britain by
TJ International Ltd, Padstow, Cornwall

This volume is dedicated to all those working to make the nation's capital a city where equitable growth takes place.

CONTENTS

TABLES AND FIGURES

Tables

Figures

PREFACE

Washington, DC is a 21st-century urban powerhouse. While other municipalities have contended with decline or economic stagnation during the Great Recession of 2008, the nation's capital and its metropolitan region have boomed. Its recent rise in global stature and increased population have thrust DC into discussions as one of America's most appealing and prosperous cities. It is also the case that while this city has become reconstituted into a neo-urban dynamo, inequalities have become stark. Fissures of class, race, and other variables foster uneven development and influence social relations in assorted ways (Hyra, forthcoming; Prince, 2014).

Capital Dilemma uncovers, highlights, and explains the factors that have influenced DC's advancement over the past 20 years. It also explores the formation of hierarchies and how diverse populations have been differentially impacted during these decades of marked change. As such this volume introduces readers to the layered complexities of the new national capital and connects these circumstances to DC's past by exploring histories that are intrinsically linked to contemporary conditions. This book reflects an interdisciplinary combination of research methodologies and findings and presents contributions on urban planning, demographic change, racial formation, community destruction, and large economic and political trends, among other wide-ranging topics. *Capital Dilemma* also conveys the idea that DC's contemporary developmental trajectory, both its economic growth and rising inequality, illustrates important change processes and outcomes critical to other US cities and national capitals throughout the world.

During the past two decades, monumental changes have taken place in DC's economic, political, and sociocultural landscapes. Once unfairly characterized as a murder capital and poster child for governmental corruption and mismanagement, national media are now celebrating today's DC as a rejuvenated city to which enthusiastic, more "diverse" populations are relocating. Descriptions such as *up and coming* and other code words have been deployed to imply something may have been remiss before, but now DC is offering those amenities upwardly mobile urbanites so heartily look for in today's urban settings.

Proof of these changes comes in a variety of forms. The Washington, DC Economic Partnership (2014) issued a report that found the city averaged 10.2 million square feet of development groundbreakings between 2010 and 2013 and has 1.8 million square feet of retail space currently under construction. Big-box stores, small coffee shops, vintage furniture boutiques, and an assortment of bars and restaurants accompany bike lanes and gleaming new condominiums as physical evidence of these numbers. As these transitions become more visible and commonplace, however, stark social disparities have also grown. Increasingly dismal indicators of inequality show that ambitious building projects and a seemingly strong post-recession recovery in jobs have led to mixed results for the residents of America's capital.

With an area median household income of $90,149, Washington, DC's household income is the highest among large US cities, including San Francisco, Boston, and New York (US Bureau of the Census, 2013). Job growth indicators are also up, supporting the idea that DC is in the midst of a notable economic boom; however, census data also present contrasting views by showing that one in five Washingtonians lives in poverty (US Bureau of the Census, 2013). The economic recovery has had its greatest advantageous effect on residents holding advanced degrees. At the other end of the spectrum are low-wage workers facing stagnant growth in earnings and high rates of unemployment during this much-celebrated period of DC's economic advancement (Lazere & Guzman, 2015).

A 2014 Urban Institute study linked chronic homelessness to the profound dearth of affordable rental units available for DC residents (Hendey, Tatian, & MacDonald, 2014). This same report asserted that a lack of reasonably priced housing affects people of all income levels, with some heads of household devoting more than 30% of their incomes toward this expense. That being said, soaring costs are particularly difficult to contend with for members of low-income households. In a 2014 report titled *Out of Reach*, the National Low Income Housing Coalition listed DC among the top 10 states requiring residents earn the highest hourly wages to rent a median-priced two-bedroom apartment. In the nation's capital, a $28.25 hourly wage rate is needed to afford a typical two-bedroom unit (Arnold, Crowley, Bravve, Brundage, & Biddlecombe, 2014).

Another notable shift connected to the economic changes occurring in America's capital is the decreasing number of Black residents in DC. Once standing at 71% of the populace, African Americans now constitute less than 49% of the people living in the city (US Bureau of the Census, 2013). Blacks and Latinos have felt the brunt of low job attainment rates and slow or nonexistent wage growth, but vulnerable populations have not been passive in the face of these socioeconomic challenges. Grassroots organizing to counter gentrification, and its attendant cycles of neglect and abandonment, for example, has mobilized working-class people, the poor, people of color, and their allies to push back against policies that overlook their particular needs and standpoints. In doing so these populations are coming together in various locations across the city to address disadvantages that reflect historical inequalities. Community activists' efforts show that an inclusive, rather than strictly top-down, approach to advocating for and understanding urban development generates overlooked insights. A broader vantage point draws attention to the struggles and susceptibilities many residents grapple with in the face of unprecedented growth and prosperity in DC.

Taking these complexities into consideration, this edited volume presents the research of anthropologists, geographers, historians, sociolinguists, sociologists, and urban planners who engage in a broad and thorough examination of the links between advancement for some and inequality for others in DC—a dynamic witnessed in the nation's capital since its founding (Gillette, 1995). The following pages provide readers with an opportunity to connect the implementation of contemporary policies with the outgrowths of structural disparities over time. This volume reveals that the dilemma confronting the people living in and governing the nation's capital is one the United States faces as a whole—meeting the challenge of fostering urban revitalization while directly and simultaneously addressing the problem of existing social hierarchies. This book examines the tension between growth and inequality and offers solutions to the myriad and long-standing problems accompanying the process of uneven development.

This volume also attempts to build on and advance a "DC school" of knowledge. There have been three primary US schools of urbanism: the Chicago, the New York, and the Los Angeles schools (Halle, 2003; Shearmur, 2008). Each of these cities inspired theoretical and empirical studies of urban development patterns that served as models for understanding development patterns within and beyond these particular cities. DC was typically passed by as an important urban research site because many scholars viewed it as a federal government company town rather than a municipality that could potentially generalize to other cities. While the federal government remains important, today's DC economy is more diverse and dynamic and represents an advanced service sector economy, which might be very telling of future urban growth throughout the country. Rather than framing a particular DC model of urban growth, this volume contributes to building a DC school by showcasing various studies, with different theoretical approaches, undertaken in a particular service sector–dominated city. The comprehensiveness and nuanced approach of this volume will differentiate this book from other DC investigations by showcasing the complex impact of the recent economic changes taking place throughout this vital city.

This volume begins with chapters that describe and explain some of Washington, DC's early context. While DC has always been primarily a service-sector economy revolving around the federal government, it has a unique racial and political history tied to discrimination and White-dominated congressional oversight that has greatly contributed to the city's social hierarchy. The initial section of this book examines the formation and resistance to these hierarchies primarily, but not exclusively, during the 20th century. These historical chapters are followed by a set of readings that give insight into DC's contemporary urban and economic policies. The four chapters within this part of this book highlight how business improvement districts (BIDs), budget decisions, biking, and big real estate developments have contributed to DC's economic revitalization. The third and final section investigates how the city's recent economic transformation has impacted its neighborhoods, particularly the low- and moderate-income areas just outside of Washington, DC's central business district (CBD). As one moves through this book, it becomes clear DC is experiencing a 21st-century economic development boom with growing inequalities and racial disparities. DC's rising tide is not lifting all boats equally. The mid-20th century American Dilemma, highlighted by Swedish scholar Gunnar Myrdal (1944), is today's *Capital Dilemma*, and we hope this volume provokes thoughts and actions geared toward social justice and equitable development.

References

Arnold, A., Crowley, S., Bravve, E., Brundage, S., & Biddlecombe, C. (2014). *Out of reach.* Washington, DC: The National Low Income Housing Coalition.

Gillette, H., Jr. (1995). *Between justice and beauty: Race, planning, and the failure of urban policy in Washington, DC.* Baltimore, MD: The Johns Hopkins University Press.

Halle, D. (2003). *New York and Los Angeles: Politics, society, and culture—a comparative view.* Chicago, IL: The University of Chicago Press.

Hendey, L., Tatian, P., & MacDonald, G. (2014). *Housing security in the Washington region.* Washington, DC: The Urban Institute.

Hyra, D. (forthcoming). *Making the gilded ghetto: Race, class and politics in the cappuccino city.* Chicago, IL: The University of Chicago Press.

Lazare, E., & Guzman, M. (2015). *Left behind: DC's economic recovery is not reaching all residents.* Washington, DC: The DC Fiscal Policy Institute.

Myrdal, G. (1944). *An American dilemma: The Negro problem and modern democracy.* New York, NY: Harper & Brothers.

Prince, S. (2014). *African Americans and gentrification in Washington, DC: Race, class and social justice in the nation's capital.* Burlington, VT: Ashgate Publishing Company.

Shearmur, R. (2008). Chicago and L.A.: A clash of epistemologies. *Urban Geography, 29*(2), pp. 167–176.

US Bureau of the Census. (2013). *Median Household Income: 25 Most Populous Metro Areas Sorted by Median Income.* Washington, DC: Author.

Washington DC Economic Partnership. (2014). *DC development report.* Washington, DC: Author.

ACKNOWLEDGMENTS

This volume attempts to advance a DC SCHOOL of knowledge, but it was conceived in Chicago. After we presented on an American Anthropological Association gentrification panel in 2013, we met the next day for breakfast along Michigan Avenue. Over French toast, bacon, and eggs, we discussed pulling together our networks of DC scholars for a comprehensive volume on the nation's capital. Both of us were completing our own books about gentrification and redevelopment in DC, but we felt, beyond our individual offerings, there was much more to communicate about the city and many people conducting extraordinary DC research. We thank Jesse Mumm, who brought us together for that panel, as well as the spirits of the Chicago School for inspiring this DC volume.

This book is the result of the dedication and hard work of many individuals and several institutions. We thank the contributing authors for all their hard work and dedication in preparing this volume. In particular, we would like to thank Howard Gillette, Gabriella Modan, Blair Ruble, and Brett Williams. Not only have they written new material for this volume but their incredible books, *Between Justice and Beauty*, *Turf Wars*, *Washington's U Street*, and *Upscaling Downtown*, have inspired us and set a solid scholarly foundation on which contemporary research on the city rests. While these authors do not appear in this book, we also thank Carl Abbott, Michael Fauntroy, Dennis Gale, Constance Green, Charles Harris, Stephen Fuller, C.R. Gibbs, Harry Jaffe, Tom Sherwood, Gregory Squires, and Ronald Walters for their motivating work on the history of inequality and/or the political economy of the nation's capital.

Two institutions were critical in fostering this book's completion. We thank the Woodrow Wilson International Center for Scholars (the Wilson Center) for hosting a one-day conference that brought the participating authors together in

2014 to present their work. The Wilson Center's Thea Cooke was instrumental in coordinating this mini-conference and we thank her for her effort. We also thank the Metropolitan Policy Center and the School of Public Affairs at American University for assisting this project with both financial and intellectual support.

Meghan Doughty, an outstanding graduate assistant at the Metropolitan Policy Center, deserves much of the credit for seeing this project through to publication. Meghan helped in so many ways. She managed the early editorial work and kept the authors and us on task throughout the rounds of revisions. Her consistent and steadfast enthusiasm and effort improved this manuscript and made it a much more pleasant and manageable endeavor. We also thank Allison Hyra, Autumn Spalding, and Brandie Williams for their fantastic assistance in organizing and managing the review of the page proofs.

As an editorial team, our authors inspired us, but we were also motivated by those engaged with making DC a more equitable place to live. Much of our understanding of how the city changed and the ways development forces were impacting people stems from grassroots community organizations located in the low- and moderate-income areas where many long-term residents face what Brett Williams has identified as the "churn." We deeply admire these local organizations that tirelessly toil to make DC a place where people of various races, ethnicities, and backgrounds can live and prosper. To assist these grassroots efforts, we respectfully dedicate a portion of this volume's royalties to two organizations: Empower DC and ONE DC. While several DC advocacy organizations are performing great work, these two have been central to assisting low- and moderate individuals who struggle amidst DC's growing economic prosperity.

The Routledge team was exceptional in understanding the merits and importance of this volume to the field of urban studies. We sincerely thank Nicole Solano for her dedication and support of the manuscript and for her belief that a DC volume was needed to move urban thought forward. We also thank Routledge's Judith Newlin for pulling all the volume's pieces together and seeing that they effectively crystallized during the production process. We are so pleased with the final product and your consistent oversight made it happen.

Finally, we thank our families—those who are with us today and those who are with us in spirit. A manuscript, even an edited one, takes considerable inspiration, time, effort, and dedication. We thank our present-day families and friends for providing us enormous love, support, and understanding that allowed us to accomplish this volume. We also acknowledge those who are not with us today but who helped pave the way for our successes.

INTRODUCTION

For a City in Transition, Questions of Social Justice and Economic Viability Remain

Howard Gillette

In 1975, my wife and I, five years into our 30-year stay in Washington, DC, sold a modest home we had recently bought in Cleveland Park for a three-story row house overlooking Rock Creek Park in the city's Mount Pleasant neighborhood. A larger house, in a cheaper area, we thought, would support the children we were expecting while remaining within our income as fledgling academics. The choice of the new location was not entirely random. One of my graduate students lived on the block, and although the neighborhood as a whole had the reputation of declining precipitously after the 1968 riots, the housing stock was solid, and our block on Park Road had a distinct level of cohesion, dominated as it was by a cluster of households occupied by refugees from postwar Czechoslovakia. Eight years after the riots, Washington, DC was far from recovered. Corridors of devastation remained virtually untouched to remind residents of the physical damage. More deeply, psychological scars infused even the most common of social interactions with suspicion if not outright hostility, especially when such exchanges involved relations between those of different races.

It was hard not to be aware of the political dimensions of such relations in the mid-1970s. Having been governed by a federally appointed commission since the close of Reconstruction, Washington, DC residents had increasingly made home rule a civil rights objective in the years after the city had become the first in the nation with a Black majority in the mid-1950s. Under recommendations made by a commission chaired by former congressman Ancher Nelson, they secured in 1973 the right to elect a mayor and city council, although not the right to be represented in Congress. The 1978 election as mayor of Marion Barry, whose long tenure in Washington, DC had started with his role as an organizer for the Student Nonviolent Coordinating Committee in 1965, marked the triumph of local Black activist leadership that has lasted most of 40 years.

In Mount Pleasant, whose dominant White majority had fled the area after the 1968 riots to leave African Americans as a substantial majority of its 10,000 residents, Whites like myself were acutely aware of our minority position. We made an effort to participate in the local neighbors' association, not as leaders but as foot soldiers, and we made a point of exchanging greetings with others we met on walks through the neighborhood. At least that was the pattern for our first years in the area.

As Washington, DC underwent a cyclical real estate revival in ensuing years, property values rose. More Whites discovered housing value along Mount Pleasant's tree-lined streets. Suddenly, the neighborhood was the object of contests between historic preservationists and developers after years when neither group would have paid the area the least bit of attention (Low & Cherkasky, 2010). And, over time, those formal but necessary greetings between strangers to acknowledge their common neighborhood identity ceased. As they grew in number, some Whites even seemed to disavow the possibility that this was someone else's neighborhood, as they set about establishing their own presence and the norms they expected to rule both the physical place and the social relations that defined it.

American University anthropologist Brett Williams captured this moment in *Upscaling Downtown: Stalled Gentrification in Washington, D.C.* Williams's careful ethnographic work focused particularly on ways native Black Washingtonians were offended by newcomers to Mount Pleasant. At the time, I believed that Williams overstated the clash of attitudes, given the area's history as a predominantly White streetcar suburb before being so thoroughly recast in the 1960s. But given patterns of demographic change in the years since, I believe the changing social relations that I witnessed personally and that Williams wrote about in the 1980s were especially telling.

Gentrification, the process where affluent residents replace those of more modest means, especially as housing markets heat up, proceeded apace in the years I continued to live in Mount Pleasant. By the time I left the city in 1999, Whites were surging into a majority in the neighborhood, and the number of Black residents had sharply declined. A considerable Hispanic presence, concentrated between Mount Pleasant Street and 16th Street, was dissipating. Indeed, several years later, my son moved into an apartment complex that had once been a Hispanic stronghold, finding not just many peers among the residents but his future wife. In the years since, whole neighborhoods further to the east have gentrified, bringing young people back to areas their parents would never have considered inhabiting. As neighborhood demography changed, home prices escalated in Mount Pleasant and adjacent Adams Morgan, from a median sales price of $200,000 in 2000 to $530,000 in 2012. Further to the east, in Brightwood Park, Crestwood, and Petworth, median home sales prices more than doubled in the same period, from $186,000 to $455,000.[1]

Most of these changes have been reported, sometimes breathlessly, in the mainstream media, and they attract considerable attention from contributors to this book. A clear driver in such narratives, as has been the case in much of Washington, DC's history, has been the growth of the federal government and associated activities—lobbying, public relations, and contracting (Fuller, 2014; Leonhardt, 2012; Lowrey, 2013). There is a good deal of truth in this, but there is also a temptation to oversimplify the axiom that government growth determines the fate of greater Washington, DC's local communities. Such equations threaten to obscure underlying social dimensions that could prove even more influential and enduring.

Even as Washington, DC languished in the 1970s, even as it became the object of critical evaluation for its poverty, its crime, and its strained finances, to say nothing of its uneasy race relations, a powerful fear emerged that anticipated much that was to come. A number of Black Washingtonians called it "The Plan." Yes, Washington, DC had achieved majority Black status. It had even achieved a modicum of home rule. Still, the suspicion existed that Whites were determined to take control of the city again. That was "the plan," and it was going to be done with government support, to remake the downtown and whole neighborhoods, elevating their value for the managers of the government-related work that dominated the capital area and pushing city residents to both the social and geographic periphery (Jaffe and Sherwood, 1994: 132). Although Tom Toles later noted that he was not aware of the particular controversy building in Washington, DC, his 1998 cartoon titled "The Plan" for the *Buffalo News* captured perfectly the argument being made in the nation's capital.[2]

Fears that materialized in Washington, DC were not unique to the capital city. As Susan Fainstein (2011) argues persuasively, redevelopment has been a primary tool for raising revenue for cities across the country for much of a generation. Facing the loss of both human and monetary capital in the aftermath of economic restructuring after World War II, cities first sought federal funding for reinvestment, then turned to the private sector after national assistance for redevelopment greatly reduced. When such efforts were not complemented by associated programs for improved wages, housing, and social services, she notes, the result of upgrading residential and commercial areas was displacement.

Washington, DC's pattern of redevelopment, and fears of its consequences, was well established even before the issue gained national prominence. As early as the mid-1940s, as Congress debated the first major federal programs to upgrade cities through a sustained program in "urban renewal," representatives of Washington, DC's all-Black citizens' associations testified to their fears of displacement, calling the proposed plan to remake the Southwest sector of the city "a shameful un-American displacement program" (Gillette, 1995, pp. 149, 163).[3] Their concerns proved well founded, as virtually the entire Southwest was razed to make way for new buildings, parks, institutions—besides federal facilities to

FIGURE 0.1 The Plan.

accommodate an ever-expanding federal presence—and other citywide facilities, such as Arena Theater. As much as the press liked to tout the elimination of areas once deemed slums in the shadow of the Capitol, the social effect was profound on the displaced majority Black population. News of their discontent extended well beyond the bars, beauty parlors, and churches in the new neighborhoods where they relocated. A social survey, *Where Are They Now?* (Thursz, 1966), reported that if many former Southwest residents lived in better physical conditions, they nonetheless expressed high levels of alienation and regret over the loss of their old neighborhood. A documentary film, *Southwest Remembered*, narrated by popular television personality Renee Chenault, circulated in the 1990s to bring that sense of anger over displacement to a wide audience.

As redevelopment plans extended to other areas, such as the Shaw neighborhood bordering the historic U Street entertainment corridor, local Black leadership made every effort to ensure that new investment would benefit current residents. But even as some political control shifted from federal to local agencies, national funding for redevelopment dried up. Washington, DC retained from years of federal governance a substantial payment meant to cover the costs of national business in the city (Fauntroy, 2003). The amount of that payment fluctuated over the years before it was eliminated entirely, and while it existed it fell well short of compensating the District government for costs associated with the federal presence. Denied any prospect of taxing commuters or the many tax-exempt buildings that drew them into the city, local officials were left with the unsavory prospect of meeting the city's needs, including its considerable social costs, largely from the taxes drawn from residential and commercial properties. Inevitably, they looked to rising property values and their returns to local government to meet those needs.

For several decades, DC's mayor, Marion Barry, was the primary voice for Washington, DC's dispossessed, favoring investments in social welfare over physical redevelopment. But Barry too had to meet financial obligations, and his record in securing social justice was mixed as he made his own deals and formed his own alliances with members of the city's business establishment. His arrest for use of crack cocaine in 1990 and his subsequent controversial tenure as mayor and city councilman after he served time in jail kept him in public view but weakened the credibility of the early social causes that had elevated him to prominence in the city.[4] Recent land-use decisions for redeveloping even the poorest areas east of the Anacostia River raise further fears of displacement without, as yet, assuring effective means for upholding social welfare priorities. They further heightened in Washington, DC in 2011 especially, as news circulated that the city had lost its Black majority. Some have blamed gentrification (Asch & Musgrove, 2012; Tavernise, 2011).

Critics of current policies and population trends raise the specter of Washington, DC becoming another San Francisco, where high costs, not the least for housing, close out middle- as well as lower-income residents. Washington, DC is a long way from that condition, but its status as a political anomaly makes the city vulnerable to the worst possible set of outcomes: high levels of displacement without means of exercising control over the allocation of the city's own finances and its equable deployment to the benefit of the whole range of its current and future residents.

Neal Peirce (1993) has been just one of many observers who make the case that metropolitan regions are the engines of the modern US economy. Undoubtedly there have been times when the entire Washington, DC area has benefited from its special status as the heart of the federal government. As defense expenditures, both direct and through a host of contractors, expanded after the 9/11 attacks, and rose even higher to meet the crisis ignited by the most recent recession, the region profited (Fuller, 2014). But the effects of those investments were uneven, and politics had a lot to do with that. Not only have Washington, DC's finances remained under federal supervision, the city's anomalous status prevents it from dealing with surrounding states as an equal partner in the allocation of resources to maximize area assets.

Given the depth of the historically grounded racial divide in the city, suspicions are bound to continue about policy decisions that favor one race or income group over another. That is an issue that requires leadership that is sensitive to the concerns Marion Barry championed over decades but is not bound by their polarizing premises. Advisory neighborhood commissions that were introduced with preliminary home rule in the 1970s can play a role in mediating misunderstandings in changing neighborhoods. It is hard to conceive the city ever reaching a position of equilibrium, however, without assuring its residents representation in a federal government that has so much to do with their personal as well as collective fortunes.

If there ever was an anachronism in American politics it is the denial of the right of representation to the more than 600,000 people living in Washington, DC. For several decades, city activists have sought statehood for Washington, DC without, however, gaining the support either of Republicans who oppose adding two US senators sure to be Democrats, or of the courts. The alternative of allowing the portion of Washington, DC originally ceded by Maryland to return to that state, leaving, as statehood would, a small core area as the operating federal capital, lacks popular support, although history suggests such action would be legally acceptable and legislatively simple.[5]

Washington, DC's exclusion from the full rights of citizenship continues to fuel resentment in the city, not the least among African Americans. One could hear such sentiment in the tributes offered to Marion Barry at the time of his death in November 2014. Among the thousands of citizens who poured out to witness the funeral procession for the self-proclaimed "Mayor for Life" was Felicia Gregory, 57, of Mount Pleasant. No one's perfect, she told a *Washington Post* reporter, but Barry "communicated with the people. That's what we wanted: Just be fair" (Davis and DeBonis, 2014).

Fairness seems to have been in short supply over the life of Washington, DC's political subordination to the federal government. Whatever steps have been taken toward establishing self-governance, they remain incomplete, thus helping sustain suspicions, if not of planned conspiracies, at the very least of external hostility to the aspirations of longtime Washington, DC residents. It is unlikely, however, that such sentiments have resonated with young Whites flocking to the city to capitalize on the opportunities a vital city can provide. For a good many newcomers, old resentments could seem out of place, as suggested in the array of caustic comments that appeared on the *Washington Post*'s Web site about Barry's funeral, including one that suggested what was being mourned was the passing not just of an individual but of "Chocolate City" itself. The very presence of such newcomers, however, could have the effect of further heightening antagonism to the accompanying gentrifying process.

Any evidence of a conscious plan to remake the District of Columbia remains speculative at best. Nonetheless dramatic change is under way, even if the boom that marked the most substantial changes in the area as government contracting expanded dramatically in the years after 9/11 appears to be over. How growth proceeds and at what pace remains to be seen. That story might seem particular to the District of Columbia, given the federal presence as crucible for what happens in the city and region. Because fiscal as well as social progress in Washington, DC represents a clear contest for resolving long-term issues of social justice, however, that process should be followed with interest not just in the nation's capital but in metropolitan areas across the country where similar dramas are taking place.

Notes

1 www.neighborhoodinfodc.org/nclusters/nclusters.html. Such changes are analyzed across the city in Sturtevant (2013) and Prince (2014).
2 www.washingtonpost.com/blogs/tom-toles/post/blast-from-the-past/2011/03/29/AFQQjIvB_blog.html.
3 Years after he spoke out against federal renewal legislation for Washington, DC, Joseph Curtis, who lived in Anacostia for some 20 years before returning to the new Southwest, maintained his anger over the process, describing the neighborhood he once cherished as "gone, vanished, bulldozed into eternity." Do-gooders, he claimed, "assumed that a sound community was a group of antiseptic buildings and not a collection of people and memories" (Green & Green, 1989: 44–45).
4 David Remnick's posting for the *New Yorker*, November 23, 2014, marking Barry's death, at www.newyorker.com/news/news-desk/postscript-marion-barry-1936–2014, captured well the former mayor's mixed legacy. For my own assessment of Barry's years in public office through the 1990s, see Gillette (2001).
5 During the mid-1990s, a local group, the Committee for the Capital City, headed by a former general counsel to the DC City Council, Lawrence Mirel, pressed the case for retrocession, without building much of a positive response. See Mirel (1995) and Janofsky (1996). Since that time Republicans have been the prime supporters of retrocession, although William Donald Schaefer endorsed the idea when he was governor of Maryland. Democrats not only prefer statehood and the boost it would provide to their membership in the Senate, they fear the loss with retrocession of the three electoral votes awarded the District by a 1961 constitutional amendment.

References

Asch, C. M., & Musgrove, G. D. (2012, October 19). Not gone, not forgotten: Struggling over history in a gentrifying D.C. *The Washington Post.*
Davis, A. C., & DeBonis, M. (2014, December 5). Rollicking funeral procession a fitting coda for former D.C. mayor Marion Barry. *The Washington Post.*
Fainstein, S. S. (2011). Redevelopment planning and distributive justice in the American metropolis. In C. R. Hayward & T. Swanstrom (Eds.), *Justice and the American metropolis* (pp. 149–176). Minneapolis, MN: University of Minneapolis Press.
Fauntroy, M. (2003). *Home rule or house rule: Congress and the erosion of local governance in the District of Columbia.* Lanham, MD: University Press of America.

Fuller, S. (Presenter) (2014, October 7). Federal spending fuels the Washington region's new economy. Conference on a post-industrial powerhouse: Growth and inequality in our nation's capital. Lecture conducted from American University Metropolitan Policy Center and Woodrow Wilson Center Urban Sustainability Laboratory. Washington, DC.

Gillette, H., Jr. (1995). *Between justice and beauty: Race, planning, and the failure of urban policy in Washington, D.C.* Baltimore, MD: The Johns Hopkins University Press.

Gillette, H., Jr. (2001). Protest and power in Washington, D.C.: The troubled legacy of Marion Barry. In D. R. Colburn & J. S. Adler (Eds.), *African-American mayors: Race, politics, and the American city* (pp. 200–222). Urbana, IL: University of Illinois Press.

Green, P. S., & Green, S. L. (1989). Old Southwest remembered: The photographs of Joseph Owen Curtis. *Washington History, 1*, 44–45.

Jaffe, H. S., & Sherwood, T. (1994). *Dream city: Race, power, and the decline of Washington, D.C.* New York, NY: Simon & Schuster.

Janofsky, M. (1996, February 7). A plan to put Washington in Maryland. *The New York Times.*

Leonhardt, D. (2012, August 5). Why is D.C. doing so well? *The New York Times.*

Low, L., & Cherkasky, M. (2010). Mount Pleasant. In K. Smith (Ed.), *Washington at home.* 2nd ed. (pp. 213–227). Baltimore, MD: The Johns Hopkins University Press.

Lowrey, A. (2013, January 10). The bucks stopped here. *The New York Times Magazine.*

Mirel, L. H. (1995, February 13). Retroceding to Maryland. *The Legal Times.*

Peirce, N. R. (1993). *Citistates: How urban America can prosper in a competitive world.* Washington, DC: Seven Locks Press.

Prince, S. (2014). *African Americans and gentrification in Washington, D.C.: Race, class, and social justice in the nation's capital.* Burlington, VT: Ashgate Publishing Company.

Sturtevant, L. (2013). The new District of Columbia: What population growth and demographic change mean for the city. *Journal of Urban Affairs, 36*(2), 276–299.

Tavernise, S. (2011, July 17). A population changes, uneasily. *The New York Times.*

Thursz, D. (1966). *Where are they now?* Washington, DC: Health and Welfare Council of the National Capital Area.

Williams, B. (1988). *Upscaling downtown: Stalled gentrification in Washington, D.C.* Ithaca, NY: Cornell University Press.

20th-Century Development, Social Inequality, and Change

PART I

20th-Century
Development, Social
Inequality, and Change

1

EXCEPTIONALISM AND THE NATIONAL CAPITAL IN LATE 20TH-CENTURY PARIS AND WASHINGTON, DC

Christopher Klemek

For more than 100 years—including the first three-quarters of the 20th century—the French and American republics denied the most basic democratic rights to all the citizens living in their capital cities. As French filmmaker Chris Marker declared tartly in his provocative 1962 cinematic essay, *Le Joli Mai:* "Le maire de Paris aurait du pain sur la planche, mais il n'y a pas de maire à Paris" ("The mayor of Paris would have a lot to do, but there isn't a mayor in Paris"). Surprisingly, urban historians have largely avoided Paris and Washington, DC, considered either too unrepresentative—or just too unwieldy—to fit into the field's established interpretations. And more generally, capital cities have occupied their own distinct niche of scholarship, segregated even from the mainstream narratives of relevant subdisciplines like urban planning, urban political theory, or urban history.

Add to this the largely insular frame for US urban analysis. American cities, so the arguments go, are not comparable to others in the industrialized world—because of their car-centric transport, sprawling unregulated land use, racial/political/economic balkanization, or some combination thereof. Furthermore, Washington, DC is supposedly exceptional even among US cities, a unique administrative district relatively insulated from market forces. Thus DC history is commonly understood, or more often dismissed, with an extreme formulation of the attitudes broadly afflicting US urban history, a strong sense of exceptionalism. But perhaps the frame of reference dictated by that US urban context is misleading. Just how distinctive is Washington, DC among the major global capitals? How uniquely American were the movements and outcomes witnessed there? And what is the particular role of any urban capital's population within the modern nation-state?

While long a hallmark of colonial "Atlantic" history, scholars of modern America have recently joined in the effort to place aspects of the US experience in a broader, global context (Klemek, 2011; Wagner, 2012). It's a good time to add two congruent capital cities to that comparative mix. While Paris and Washington, DC will ultimately remain special-status communities, unique in many ways, they are simultaneously urban crucibles of volatile inequalities—not only economic, but also of status, power, and identities—in ostensibly egalitarian republics.

Dangerous Classes and Disenfranchised Capitals in the Age(s) of Revolution

The City of Light has long functioned as a bloody civic theater of battle. Absolutist Louis XIV moved the seat of power from Paris to Versailles to insulate his court from the intrigues of the capital. A century later, in one of the watershed events of the Age of Revolutions, Parisian women marched his grandson all the way back to the city in a demonstration rich with symbolism—but also with very real consequences—culminating in his public execution there. Over the 19th century, the relationship between the French nation-state and its capital city would be characterized by several more rounds of authoritarian assertion punctuated by revolutionary mobilization. The Second Empire renovation of Paris's iconic *grands boulevards* represented an unprecedentedly ambitious attempt by Napoleon III's prefect Georges-Eugène Haussmann to bring an unruly industrial city to heel, economically, politically, and urbanistically. The ultimate confrontation came when the Versailles-based government of Adolphe Thiers launched a *semaine sanglante* to liquidate the Paris Commune in late May 1871. In its bloody wake, Thiers set up a durable republican constitutional order that simultaneously obviated Parisian self-governance. The capital city's "dangerous classes" had been definitively put down and disenfranchised, but, as military historian John Keegan notes: "The repression of the Paris Commune in 1871 undoubtedly left scars on the psyche of working class Paris which ache to this day" (Keegan, 1978, p. 75).

With some analogies to Versailles, it could be argued that Washington, DC's origins lay in a reaction against the dangerous classes who harassed late colonial and early republican elites in Philadelphia, New York, Boston, and Charleston. John Adams—the only chief executive, after all, to preside over both the old capital and the new—would subsequently take pains to remind his successor, Thomas Jefferson, about the "terrorism" of 1793 "when ten thousand People in the Streets of Philadelphia, day after day, threatened to drag Washington out of his House, and effect a Revolution in the Government, or compel it to declare War in favour of the French Revolution" (John Adams to Thomas Jefferson). But rather than rejecting such a volatile setting for mass democracy, George Washington's actions around the establishment of his namesake city bespeak the clear goal of a thriving political and economic capital in his native tidewater. Planned streets and public works of grand European scale paired with his personal advocacy of private canal improvements to catalyze a major maritime port, one certainly intended to support a large urban population (Achenbach, 2004). One of Jefferson's many contradictions was how he romanticized the revolutionary Parisian mobs (watering the tree of liberty with blood, etc.), but yet dissented from the Federalists' vision of a strong urban capital. This ambivalence further complicates his contentious supervision of the city planning efforts by the Frenchman L'Enfant (whose father had been no less than a member of the *ancien regime*'s royal academy) (Berg, 2009).

Through the first half of the 19th century, Washingtonians proved a far smaller and less restive population, especially in comparison with the revolution-prone Parisians, or even the riotous denizens of other American cities. Washingtonians were consistently denied real congressional representation. This issue came to a head over inadequate appropriations for regional transportation infrastructure (the canals), and resulted in the retrocession of the lands Virginia granted to the District. But Washingtonians did enjoy self-governance in the form of a council (after 1802) and a mayor directly elected by citizens (at least White, male, property-owning ones, from 1820 onward).

The great destabilizer of this status quo for DC, as for the entire nation, was slavery and abolition. Civic unrest, such as it was during the antebellum years, sprang from this issue, reflecting anxieties about free people of color, antislavery agitators, escapees, and other challenges to "the peculiar institution." National and local elites were acutely aware of DC's tenuous position, located in the heart of the largest slave states, yet with a concentrated and steadily growing free Black population. Unparalleled opportunities for African Americans coexisted with draconian Black codes and the city's high profile made its conditions an object lesson for both sides of the national debate (Brown, 1972). The Civil War exploded these tense dynamics, with Washington, DC leading the charge not only on the military battlefields of the surrounding countryside, but also by example on the urban home front.

A surge of Civil War refugees and grassroots agitation in the wartime capital produced trailblazing emancipation policies—the "first freed" phenomenon—and this momentum extended through Reconstruction enfranchisement, a Radical Republican mayoral administration, and a short-lived experiment with territorial status (Masur, 2012). But the 1870s suppression of this Black power specter, even Congress' pretext of government scandal, suggested not a victorious Union capital so much as the rollback of civil rights in "redeemed" areas of the former Confederacy. If anything, DC's fate was even more severe; its disenfranchisement covered not only freedmen but extended to Whites as well, for a century hence.

The Urban Crucible Cools?

The French state shunned *problèmes urbains* throughout the Third Republic (1870–1940) so as to avoid waking Paris's destabilizing demons (Oblet, 2005). At the same time, French urbanism, in concert with other European movements, exhibited real dynamism during the interwar period. This encompassed not only internationally prominent urban development figures like Charles-Édouard "Le Corbusier" Jeanneret-Gris, but also locally influential practitioners such as Maurice Rotival. In terms of statutory structures, in 1919 the government mandated development plans for all towns in France with a population over 10,000, an impetus growing out of the Musée Social (a sort of belle époque think tank for progressive reform) (see Hein, 2002; Rodgers, 2009).

In the ensuing Gaullist state that emerged following World War II, French civil society generally evinced little of the Habermasean "public sphere" debate found among neighboring West German planners; instead, a paternalistic or downright authoritarian strain characterized postwar French planning (urban and otherwise) (Newsome, 2009). In the face of this, however, Paris emerged from occupation manifesting a feisty yet vibrant "democracy of the streets" (Wakeman, 2009). The tension between those two trajectories would build to a crisis point over the ensuing decades.

In 20th-century America, by contrast, cities were the consummate crucibles of liberal policy. With roots going back to Progressive Era reform movements and policy precedents inherited from New Deal programs, federal lawmakers and policy makers gave urban affairs a consistent priority from the late 1940s to the early 1970s, alongside (and often entangled with) the perennial crises of the Cold War and civil rights. Urban renewal—a portmanteau for large-scale, postwar projects in cities that ranged from Title I slum clearance to subsidized business redevelopment and from public housing provision to federal highway construction—engendered relatively little partisan contention. Yet it eventually became a lightning rod for dissent from outside the political elite. With Vietnam-era quagmire analogies seeming uncannily apt, domestic liberalism met its demise in large part when ambitious (and primarily urban) programs like Model Cities and affirmative action lost the battle for hearts and minds among rapidly polarizing constituencies. An open historical question remains whether this arc of events was driven more from the top down or the bottom up (see Clement, 2014; Sugrue, 2004; Von Hoffman, 2014).

Over the first half of the 20th century, the US capital offered a showy canvas for successive generations of urbanists, from Daniel Burnham and Frederick Law Olmstead Jr. to Harland Bartholomew and Louis Justement. In the second half, it would become an important crucible for the grassroots backlash against urban renewal projects in the city's core, particularly the "freeway revolts," which occurred in Paris as well. But this was just one of the key dynamics roiling the postwar city, or more accurately, the segregated metropolitan region.

Grassroots and Periphery in Capital Regions

The significance of the urban periphery in both France and the United States had been largely negative, that is, déclassé, through the first half of the 19th century

(Blumin, 1989; Merriman, 1991). American cities underwent a rapid inversion of this pattern in the two or three decades preceding 1900, which spilled out into the "streetcar suburbs" and beyond (Schnore & Knights, 1969; Warner, 1962). Paris developed an aggressive private real estate sector during the same period, but it did not produce the radiating zones of affluent neighborhoods described in the Chicago school of sociology's model of American spatial succession (Yates, 2012). Instead, the *banlieue* periphery remained largely a working-class "red belt" into the post–World War II period (Fourcaut, Bellanger, & Flonneau, 2007). Eventually, these industrial suburbs would provide foot soldiers for riots in the streets of central Paris (Seidman, 2004).

In 1961, Jane Jacobs endorsed "the wry remark that 'a region is an area safely larger than the last one to whose problems we found no solution'" (Jacobs, 1961). Rather cynical, perhaps, but at that moment Paris and Washington, DC could have offered her rich fodder for such an assertion. Both experienced a move toward reform of regional governance two decades before Home Rule was granted within the municipal boundaries. Both reforms grew out of regional planning impulses and institutions that went back generations. Both responded to suburban growth patterns, and both played out most acutely around the question of transportation (Schrag, 2006). Washington, DC planners began to reconsider their suburban growth strategy by the mid-1950s, shifting emphasis from decentralization toward a recentering of the region in an attempt to reestablish the core as its center of gravity (Gillette, 2011). In practice, aside from the Metro rail system, most public policies through the 1950s and 1960s continued to reinforce patterns of suburban White affluence segregated from Black urban poverty. Parisian regional planning largely had the inverse effect: public housing projects concentrated disproportionately at the periphery.

New metropolitan dynamics were palpable in the Washington, DC urban region as early as World War II, most notably when downtown office crowding resulted in a Pentagon site across the Potomac River (Carroll, 2006). After the war, as Andrew Friedman has emphasized, the US global "empire" was ruled inconspicuously from the Virginia suburbs by a Cold War military and intelligence community who lived and worked there (Friedman, 2013). In 1950, the US National Capital Park and Planning Commission published a "Comprehensive Plan for the National Capital and Its Environs" with an emphasis on regional aspects of development (US National Capital Park and Planning Commission, 1950). And from 1957 to 1960, Congress convened a Joint Committee on Washington Metropolitan Problems, whose recommendations spurred John Kennedy's appointment of the "first Presidential Advisor for National Capital Affairs in 1962, Charles A. Horsky" (Thornell, 1990, p. 49; Joint Committee on Washington Metropolitan Problems). Louis Justement, as a leader in the professional community of architects around Washington, DC, endorsed large-scale redevelopment toward a car-friendly city, via a series of influential modernist proposals and commissions, testimony, and publications, beginning in the late 1940s and continuing through the 1960s (Justement, 1946a, 1946b). Most consequentially, planner Harland Bartholomew spearheaded a regional transportation study that, following its 1959 publication, yielded the federal creation of a National Capital Transportation Agency (soon replaced in 1967 by the current Washington Metropolitan Area Transit Authority) (Schrag, 2006 and Gillette, 1985).

These centrifugal forces also strongly reflected Washington, DC's racial dynamics. The DC metro area averaged 300% population growth between 1940 and 1970, but the growth was not spread evenly: its suburbs grew 700% while the District's growth averaged only 14% over the same decades. Correspondingly the city went from about three quarters to one quarter of the regional population share. And these trends were even more uneven in racial terms. While some African Americans acted on suburban impulses (particularly toward Prince George's County, MD), the vast majority lived within the city limits, essentially concentrated in the core of the region's White suburban majority. Thus in 1957, Washington, DC became "the first major city in the country with a majority black population" (Gillette, 2011, pp. 153–154).

It was a fitting milestone for the nation's increasingly Black capital—or else an irony in its rapidly segregating capital region—that 1957 was also the year Congress passed a civil rights act and the president sent federal troops to enforce civil rights in the South for the first time since Reconstruction. As during that previous era, the District's (now dominant) African American population was at the vanguard of the movement, even if attentions focused further south. The DC civil rights community pioneered successful antidiscrimination strategies on battlegrounds and test cases, including public pools and playgrounds (1945–1954), restrictive covenants (1946–1950), schools (1947–1952), private restaurants (1949–1953), and amusement parks (1960–1961). Additionally, a formidable network of DC activists and legal strategists linked Howard University and the NAACP, neighborhood organizations were vigorous, and the Urban League, CORE, SCLC, and SNCC each maintained important DC chapters (led by Sterling Tucker, Julius Hobson, Walter Fauntroy, and Marion Barry, respectively).

Race was nowhere near as dominant an issue in Paris during "Les Trente Glorieuses" (1945–1975). But regional restructuring and physical redevelopment loomed large. Restructuring the governance of Paris and its region was enacted, following the false start of an ineffectual 1959 decree, with the passage of legislation in 1961 and 1964, the latter of which finally took effect on New Year's Day 1968.[1] First as a *District* and then as the *Préfecture de la région de Paris*, the metropolitan region thus came under the control of Paul Delouvrier, a powerful French hybrid of Robert Moses and Robert McNamara, in his capacity as *délégué général* from 1961, and then from 1966–1969 simultaneously as *préfet*.

The reorganization of Paris accompanied an extensive federal program of redevelopment for modernization, particularly in the areas of housing and transportation. Some critics decried the erasure of older forms of urban living or the anomie associated with the new ones. Such a dim view was first vividly captured by Jean-Luc Godard's 1967 film *2 ou 3 choses que je sais d'elle* (trans: *Two or Three Things I Know About Her*), whose settings contrast traditional neighborhoods with so-called HLM (for *Habitation à Loyer Modéré*, or moderate-rent housing projects) on the outskirts of Paris—the city itself being the "her" of the movie's title. Subsequent print critiques would lament the "assassination" of a city immortalized by Henri Cartier-Bresson and generations of other artists, writers, and lovers (Chevalier, 1994).

Chris Marker ominously concludes his 1962 Paris documentary, *Le Joli Mai*, with the implication that Algerian and other colonial populations represented a fifth column of sorts, hidden in plain sight within the capital. In this respect, the immigrant population's status is comparable to that of the contraband, runaways, and freedmen who flooded into Washington, DC during the Civil War and whose citizenship was not yet clearly established at the time. Eventually, they would recast the Parisian *banlieues* from one bourgeois anxiety-inducing hue to another: the "red belt" became a "black belt" (Stovall, 2003).

Decolonization, particularly the Algerian War (1954–1962), induced seismic shakeups of the French cultural and political order. Drawing a direct causal link to the street clashes of May 1968, Kristin Ross argues that this earlier ordeal formed the deep, psychological underpinning of student and worker mobilization because it estranged those domestic groups' sympathies from the forceful exercise of state power, even before the government's violence was directed at them (Ross, 2008). Such arguments could be extended to the brutal repression of American civil rights activists, as shown on television sets around the world. Scholars have identified police brutality as a common provocation for revolts across the long, transatlantic 1960s (see Marwick, 2011; Seidman, 2004; Sugrue, 2008). Indeed, in what was probably the most direct case of a systemic consequence, the Paris police crackdown on students in May 1968 precipitated a general strike by French workers.

Flashpoint and Blowback: The Ironic Legacies of 1968

The grassroots in both capitals proved incendiary in the spring of 1968. Overnight on April 4, a peaceful memorial march for Martin Luther King Jr. on Washington, DC's U Street, NW, steadily escalated into an expression of mass vandalism against private buildings. It eventually grew into a pitched riot drawing in police, national guards, and finally regular military units entailing 15,500 soldiers. By the time calm returned, the casualties included 13 civilians dead, 1,200 injured, 7,600 arrested, and broad swaths of the Shaw and U Street neighborhoods damaged by roughly 1,200 fires. Strangely, no violence was directed at the capital city's prominent symbols of state power. General Ralph Haines, the army vice chief of staff and Washington Task Force commander during the unrest, "observed that rioters made no attempts to damage federal buildings, foreign embassies and residences; and that no calls for help had come from the police concerning government buildings" (Price, 1997, p. 88).

If this episode is understood to have any larger significance, it is usually as part of the nationwide expression of violent frustration upon King's assassination (engulfing 72 cities in 29 states), as well as the final conflagration culminating a series of "long hot summers" of conflict in impoverished African American city neighborhoods. In addition to the frustrations these actions expressed for many Black residents in such communities, the resulting images also crystalized a loss of faith in the Great Society domestic agenda, both within the Johnson administration, and among an electorate turning toward Nixonite neoconservatism (see Moynihan, 1969). For decades, many Washingtonians' local narratives, as in other American cities, would invoke 1968 as the watershed moment of urban decline, lamenting inner-city neighborhoods that "never recovered after the riots."

In 1968, though, nationally significant developments on the DC streets went considerably beyond the April riots. Gordon Mantler highlights the SCLC-led Poor People's Campaign and its Resurrection City encampment on the Mall through May and June of that year, noting:

> Only in Washington in the spring of 1968 did local, regional, and national activists of so many different backgrounds—from veterans of the labor and southern civil rights movements to activists of the newer Chicano, American Indian, antiwar, and welfare rights struggles—attempt to construct a physical and spiritual community explicitly about justice and poverty that went beyond a one-day rally.
>
> (Mantler, 2013, p. 5)

Such interpretations of 1968, emphasizing the national significance of grassroots events in the US capital, nevertheless remain the exception rather than the rule.

The meaning of Paris 1968 is, by contrast, explicitly central to France's national political narrative (see Le Goff, 2002; Vigna, 2007, 2011). Even historians who underrate the significance of 1968 in French life admit events in the streets of the capital that year constituted "the precipitating factor" for major political changes (Christofferson, 2008; Marwick, 2011). This is not to say that its legacies are uncomplicated or settled. For instance, received popular wisdom about the "68ers" foregrounds the radical "student commune" and sloganeering youth movements, as well as their ultimate dissipation over subsequent years. But more scholarly analysis identifies workers' strikes as the key to Parisian mobilization in May and June 1968, reflecting the frustration of the politically marginalized working class in de Gaulle's Cold War France (not to speak of Keegan's older scars). Another concrete result was the creation of a durable "union of the left" for the opposition parties, lasting through the 1970s, to underpin the subsequent Mitterrand era of socialist dominance (Christofferson, 2008).

The Parisian riot casualties of May 1968 were about half that of DC (despite having triple the regional population); most of those who died in the violence were factory workers. Notwithstanding de Gaulle's dramatic retreat to Germany for consultation with his military advisors during the height of the May crisis, the French state was never seriously at risk of losing control of either basic logistics or public opinion—a conclusion shared by scholars of both the French and American riots (Price, 1997; Seidman, 2004). Nevertheless, also common to both cases was the political success of law-and-order rhetoric, a backlash visible in that year's reactionary rise of French interior minister Raymond Marcellin or American presidential candidate Richard Nixon.

The Belatedly Swift Return(s) of Home Rule

Counterintuitively, it was in the midst of this post-1968 rightward turn that home rule finally rematerialized for these disorderly capitals. To be sure, momentum was building well before 1968. In fact, the US Congress had held hearings, produced studies, and even made some reforms toward local self-governance in 1939, 1949, and 1952. Growing out of a poll tax debate, the 23rd Amendment, granting Washingtonians electoral college votes for presidential elections beginning in 1964, passed the 86th Congress in 1960 and was ratified in 1961 by 39 states (albeit only one from the former Confederacy: Tennessee). In 1967, Joseph Tydings, a White senator from Maryland, called for "political justice" in restoring home rule to DC. That same year, Lyndon Johnson replaced the appointed three-member commission that had governed the District since 1873 with a presidentially appointed mayor and council (Acosta, 2004; Tydings, 1967).

Most White liberal institutions in the city—notably the *Washington Post*, the Central Labor Council, and the Democratic Party—were supportive of DC self-determination, while local opposition was anchored by the *Evening Star* and the White businessmen's Board of Trade. The latter institution, having successfully lobbied for the town's de facto power elite since the end of Reconstruction, continued to hold the unsurprising view in the 1960s that there was "not a thing wrong with having Congress as our city council" (Derthick, 1963, p. 94). With echoes of the 1870s, nationally prominent segregationists—and even some liberals—argued that the absence of home rule in DC prevented the development of an electoral machine styled on ethno-racial recognition and advancement, and thus enabled a more "substantive" politics (Derthick, 1963, p. 106). In the mid-1960s, West Virginia senator Robert Byrd, a former Klansman who filibustered the 1964 Civil Rights Act, publicly assailed home rule (Byrd, 1967).

Crucially, South Carolina representative John McMillan blocked any home rule legislation via the House Committee of the District of Columbia he chaired.

Having already successfully challenged many institutionalized forms of bigotry in the DC community, the local branches of the civil rights movement eventually seized upon home rule as a civil rights issue. Urban planning became racially politicized in DC after about 1964, primarily upon the advent of major federal highway demolitions, with Marion Barry and others organizing to stop "white men's roads through black men's homes"—a local analog of the nationwide backlash known as "freeway revolts" (Schrag, 2006, p. 119). Such slogans, as well as posters and actions from the period, reveal how the politicization of planning and urban (re)development decision making acted as a lightning rod for local control questions. (Similarly, the Parisians' "*sous les pavés la plage!*" was both a street battle cry as well as an ideological challenge to the meaning of urban space.)

After a century's delay, home rule ultimately returned to the American capital in a swift cascade of political events, culminating in the rise of African American populist Marion Barry to become the city's "mayor for life." This chain reaction began when Walter Fauntroy, elected DC's non-voting delegate to Congress in 1970, targeted Rep. McMillan's district with voter registration drives that successfully "primaried" the segregationist Democrat out of office in 1972 (Fauntroy, 2010). Soon after, McMillan's replacement as chair of the House DC committee, Congressional Black Caucus founder Rep. Charles Diggs (D-Detroit), opened the floodgates and Congress enacted the District of Columbia Self-Rule and Governmental Reorganization Act, signed by Richard Nixon on December 24, 1973. Finally, in the first direct mayoral election since the ballot of 1870, Walter Washington bested Clifford Alexander; Supreme Court Justice Thurgood Marshall swore him into office on January 2, 1975. But then Marion Barry upset the incumbent in 1978's three-way primary with the mayor and Sterling Tucker. Ironically, with Afrocentric and Black pride associations lingering from his 1960s activism, Barry was largely suspect to DC's Black bourgeoisie, and he relied primarily on White middle-class support for the first of his four mayoral wins (Jaffe & Sherwood, 2014).

Over the same period, national political shifts brought electoral reform and a charismatic mayor to the French capital, as well. Within a year of the 1968 uprising, de Gaulle's power finally foundered on the rock of a failed national referendum that proposed, among other reforms, the reorganization of local governments. Return of home rule for Paris subsequently occurred with the passage of legislation by the (still conservative) French Parliament on New Year's Eve 1975, stipulating a newly elected mayor to take office in 1977.[2] On March 25, 1977, 45-year-old Jacques Chirac won the first mayoral elections since the 1870 siege of Paris. Chirac was the leader of a new Gaullist conservative party, the RPR, which held the largest national assembly bloc during the 1970s. He rose to prime minister between 1974 and 1976, but when he fell out of favor with centrist president Valéry Giscard d'Estaing, Chirac turned his ambitions toward the capital city. And as he secured reelection in 1983, then again in 1989, the Paris mayoralty provided Chirac with a chic political *pied-à-terre* to wait out the socialist dominance of François Mitterrand, whom he ultimately succeeded as president in 1995 (Lançon, 1997; Lidgi, 2001; Renaud, 1997).

This was no accident. Chirac had actively engineered the resurrection of a Paris mayoralty as a parachute for his career. But it also set in motion reforms that transcended his personal ends. The restoration of home rule in the capital coincided with further metropolitan reorganization. In 1976, the name and structure of the Paris region were changed to Préfecture de L'Île-de-France, accompanied by the abolition of the delegate general and other changes in governance. The official region now encompasses, in addition to the *départment* of Paris proper, seven other neighboring *départments* (Essonne, Hauts-de-Seine, Seine-Saint-Denis, Seine-et-Marne, Val-de-Marne, Val-d'Oise, and Yvelines), collectively corresponding more or less to the metropolitan area.

Conclusions

Neither the French nor the American national narrative gives the return of home rule in the capital much notice, not to speak of their suburban contexts. Yet both episodes marked epochal changes at the heart of their democracies. After a full century of disenfranchisement—and almost exactly the same one—citizens in the shadow of the patriotic monuments to republicanism obtained the most basic self-government. And unless we are to dismiss it as sheer coincidence, their correspondence belies causal explanations that rely on particular dynamics of the ideological or racial politics of either city or nation. In fact, these final developments marked an important, if overlooked, dénouement to the long 1960s, completing a story arc that finds its proximate roots in the metropolitan regional growing pains that stretch back to the early postwar years, and reached their climaxes in the sometimes violent mobilizations that came to a head in the central cities during 1968. Correspondingly, by the mid-1970s, new national political orders had been established on either side of the Atlantic.

Seen within an even longer arc, stretching over decades or even centuries, the residents of these capital cities experienced the top-down, centralizing impulses of the nation-state to a far greater degree than the citizens of other regions or urban communities. Paris, more than any other part of modern France, bore the brunt of a French political culture Tocqueville noted for its administrative centralization and authoritarianism. Remarkably, the US capital, boxed out of the American federal system that Tocqueville found so distinctive, was no less subject to despotism from its national government. Moreover, such parallels, given how unmediated and often undemocratic the governance of Paris and Washington, DC proved to be, reflect largely unfiltered components of national regimes.

At the same time, an absence of mediation meant that large urban capitals were also the sites where governing elites were most directly exposed to popular protest. Most recently, grassroots mobilization in the 1960s precipitated outward changes by the 1970s. Of course, these governments' embrace of reinstated home rule could be dismissed as little more than superficial attempts to blunt such protest ("riot insurance") without substantive, structural concessions. That case can certainly be made circa 1969 when, with questionable sincerity, Nixon preached "black capitalism" and de Gaulle embraced decentralization. But by the mid-1970s, when home rule initiatives finally carried and took effect, those heavy-handed conservatives had fallen from favor. The democracy of the streets seems to have echoed through the corridors of power.

Nevertheless, dreams of self-governance were not necessarily realized in ways that capital citizens or their allies had hoped for or anticipated. The center-right coalition in the French Parliament returned more comprehensive autonomy to its capital city in 1975 than did the Democratic US Congress in 1973. Moreover, the dictatorial directives Congress has imposed on Washington, DC, even since the passage of the DC Home Rule Act, belie a widespread assumption that strains of authoritarianism are stronger in France than the United States. After a century of disenfranchisement, and despite seemingly greater odds against them, Parisians achieved a substantially new intergovernmental order. Washingtonians, who to this day enjoy neither unrestricted home rule nor full participation in the national government, still have not.

After 1975, nominal Black power returned to local government in Washington, DC for the first time since it was squashed during the first Reconstruction. In practical terms, fiscal, judicial, and legislative prerogatives of the DC municipal government remained unusually circumscribed. As the charismatic African American mayor of the emblematic "chocolate city" during the 1980s and early 1990s, Marion Barry became a whipping boy for Reaganite America, facing years of aggressive federal investigation, prosecution, and ultimately a 1990 conviction for his indiscretion. Congress also regularly overruled the DC Council's laws, and stripped its budgetary control completely in 1995. The District also continued to feel like a blockaded island even closer at hand, given DC's suburban patterns, where administratively conservative (i.e., unregulated) regional development emplaced economic and racial segregation on a metropolitan scale.

In many respects, the Parisian experience since home rule offers a parallel case—albeit an inverted one. Conservative center city elites controlled Paris's revived Hôtel de Ville and Paris essentially provided an exile-at-home for Mayor Chirac throughout the Mitterrand socialist heyday of the 1980s and early 1990s. Meanwhile, at the metropolitan scale, regional government commanded strong state-planning authorities, but their effect was the ongoing concentration of poor and minority groups on the periphery.

Which of these newer disalignments of local and federal power will prove more volatile remains an open and constantly evolving question. Just since the 1990s, much has changed. Even as the first Black president inhabits the White House, vigorous gentrification in central Washington, DC suggests an eventual convergence with the Parisian economic geography of suburban marginalization. Meanwhile, riots in the French suburbs have recently revealed the long-simmering frustration of racially and economically marginalized communities there. So for these crucible capitals, it is hardly *plus ça change*; but maybe, if we admit some transatlantic transpositions, we continue to recognize some of *les mêmes choses*. And while it is untenable to flatly suggest that "as the capital goes, so goes the nation-state," a comparative examination of their "exceptional" urban histories reveals key junctures when each country's rulers had to vigilantly attend to how power is rooted in those most special of cities.

Acknowledgments

Thanks to Derek Hyra, Howard Gillette, and Meghan Doughty for their helpful suggestions.

Notes

1 *Loin° 61–845 du 2 août 1961 relative a l'organisation de la region de Paris, abrogeant l'ordonnance 59272 du 4 février 1959 relative a la creation d'un district de la region de Paris*, accessed September 28, 2014, http://legifrance.gouv.fr/affichTexteArticle.do?cidTexte=JORFTEXT000000874933&idArticle=JORFARTI000001867533&dateTexte=19610803&categorieLien=cid; *Loi n° 64–707 du 10 juillet 1964 portant réorganisation de la région parisienne*, accessed September 28, 2014, http://legifrance.gouv.fr/jo_pdf.do?cidTexte=JORFTEXT000000319965.

2 *Loin° 75–1331 du 31 décembre 1975 portant réforme du régime administratif de la ville de Paris*, accessed September 28, 2014, www.legifrance.gouv.fr/affichTexte.do;jsessionid=3F681D7AD13CFE59720188AA3869CB53.tpdjo16v_1?cidTexte=JORFTEXT000000699208&dateTexte=19760103.

References

Achenbach, J. (2004). *The grand idea: George Washington's Potomac and the race to the West*. New York, NY: Simon & Schuster.

Acosta, L. M. (2004, October). The legal history of the District of Columbia prior to home rule: A bibliographic essay. *Legal Reference Services Quarterly*, 23(4), 43–74.

Bell, J. C. (2014). *Creative federalism and urban policy: Placing the city in the Great Society* (Doctoral dissertation, George Washington University).

Berg, S. W. (2009). *Grand avenues: The story of Pierre Charles L'Enfant, the French visionary who designed Washington*. New York, NY: Knopf Doubleday.

Blumin, S. M. (1989). *The emergence of the middle class: Social experience in the American city, 1760–1900*. Cambridge, UK: Cambridge University Press.

Brown, L. W. (1972). *Free Negroes in the District of Columbia, 1790–1846*. Oxford, UK: Oxford University Press.

Byrd, R. (1966). The case against home rule. *Legal Issues, 6*.

Byrd, R. (1967, March). District of Columbia "home rule." *American University Law Review, 16*, 254–270.

Carroll, J. (2006). *House of war: The Pentagon and the disastrous rise of American power*. Boston, MA: Houghton Mifflin Harcourt.

Chevalier, L. (1977). *L'assassinat de Paris*. Paris, France: Calmann-Lévy.

Chevalier, L. (1994). *The assassination of Paris*. Chicago, IL: The University of Chicago Press.

Christofferson, M. S. (2008, December 1). The French "Sixties." *French Politics, Culture & Society, 26*(3), 123–140.

Derthick, M. (1963, January). Politics in voteless Washington. *Journal of Politics, 25*(1), 97–99.

Fauntroy, M. K. (2010). Home rule for the District of Columbia. In T. M. Travis & R. Walters (Eds.), *Democratic destiny and the District of Columbia: Federal politics and public policy* (p. 26). Lanham, MD: Lexington Books.

Fourcaut, A., Bellanger, E., & Flonneau, M. (2007). *Paris/banlieues, conflits et solidarités: Historiographie, anthologie, chronologie, 1788–2006*. Paris, France: Creaphis Editions.

Friedman, A. (2013). *Covert capital: Landscapes of denial and the making of U.S. empire in the suburbs of northern Virginia*. Berkeley, CA: University of California Press.

Gillette, H. (1985). A national workshop for urban policy: The metropolitanization of Washington, 1946–1968. *The Public Historian*, 7–27.

Gillette, H. (2011). *Between justice and beauty: Race, planning, and the failure of urban policy in Washington*. Philadelphia, PA: University of Pennsylvania Press.

Hein, C. (2002). Maurice Rotival: French planning on a world-scale (part I). *Planning Perspectives, 3*(17), 247–265.

Jacobs, J. (1961). *The death and life of great American cities*. New York, NY: Random House.

Jaffe, H. S., & Sherwood, T. (2014). *Dream city: Race, power, and the decline of Washington, D.C.* New York: Argo-Navis.

John Adams to Thomas Jefferson, 30 June 1813. (2009). In *The papers of Thomas Jefferson*, vol. 6, Retirement Series. Princeton, NJ: Princeton University Press, 254, http://founders.archives.gov/documents/Jefferson/03-06-02-0216.

Joint Committee on Washington Metropolitan Problems (1957–1960). (n.d.). Records of the Joint Committees of Congress 1789–1989 (Record Group 128, JC 130–132), US National Archives, www.archives.gov/legislative/guide/house/chapter-23-joint-washington.html.

Justement, L. (1946a). *New cities for old: City building in terms of space, time, and money*. New York, NY: McGraw-Hill.

Justement, L. (1946b). Urban planning in a democracy. *Journal of the American Institute of Architects, 5*(6) (June), 299–308.

Keegan, J. (1978). *The face of battle*. New York, NY, and London: Penguin.

Klemek, C. (2011). *The transatlantic collapse of urban renewal: Postwar urbanism from New York to Berlin*. Chicago, IL: The University of Chicago Press.

Lançon, C. (1997). *Une Taupe Chez Chirac: La Vie Secrète de La Mairie de Paris*. Paris, France: Les Belles Lettres.

Le Goff, J.-P. (2002). *Mai 68, L'Héritage impossible*. Paris, France: La Découverte.

Lidgi, S. (2001). *Paris-Gouvernance Ou, Les Malices Des Politiques Urbaines: J. Chirac / J. Tibéri*. Paris, France: L'Harmattan.

Louis Justement Papers, 1946–1968. George Washington University, Gelman Library Special Collections. https://library.gwu.edu/ead/ms2045.xml.

Mantler, G. K. (2013). *Power to the poor: Black-brown coalition and the fight for economic justice, 1960–1974.* Chapel Hill, NC: University of North Carolina Press.

Marwick, A. (2011). *The sixties: Cultural revolution in Britain, France, Italy, and the United States, c.1958–c.1974.* London: Bloomsbury Publishing.

Masur, K. (2012). *An example for all the land: Emancipation and the struggle over equality in Washington, D.C.* Chapel Hill, NC: University of North Carolina Press.

Meriman, J. M. (1991). *The margins of city life: Explorations on the French urban frontier, 1815–1851.* Oxford, UK: Oxford University Press.

Moynihan, D. P. (1969). *Maximum feasible misunderstanding: Community action in the war on poverty.* New York, NY: Free Press.

Newman, S. P. (1999). *Parades and the politics of the street: Festive culture in the early American republic.* Philadelphia, PA: University of Pennsylvania Press.

Newsome, W. B. (2009). *French urban planning, 1940–1968: The construction and deconstruction of an authoritarian system.* New York, NY: Peter Lang.

Nightingale, C. H. (2012). *Segregation: A global history of divided cities.* Chicago, IL: The University of Chicago Press.

Oblet, T. (2005). *Gouverner la ville : Les voies urbaines de la démocratie modern.* Paris, France: Presses Universitaires de France.

Price, B. L. T. (1997). *King to king: A study of civil unrest and federal intervention from 1968 to 1992* (Doctoral dissertation, Texas A&M University), 88.

Renaud, J. P. (1997). *La methode Chirac: De la mairie de Paris a l'Elysee : essai.* Paris, France: La Longue vue.

Rodgers, D. T. (2009). *Atlantic crossings: Social politics in a progressive age.* Cambridge, MA: Harvard University Press.

Ross, K. (2008). *May '68 and its afterlives.* Chicago, IL: The University of Chicago Press.

Schnore, L. F., & Knights, P. R. (1969). Residence and social structure: Boston in the ante-bellum period. In S. Thernstrom & R. Sennett (Eds.), *Nineteenth-century cities: Essays in the new urban history* (pp. 247–256). New Haven, CT: Yale University Press.

Schrag, Z. M. (2006). *The great society subway: A history of the Washington metro.* Baltimore, MD: The Johns Hopkins University Press.

Seidman, M. (2004). *The imaginary revolution: Parisian students and workers in 1968.* New York, NY: Berghahn Books.

Stovall, T. E. (2003). From red belt to black belt: Race, class, and urban marginality in twentieth-century Paris. In S. Peabody & T. E. Stovall (Eds.), *The color of liberty: Histories of race in France* (pp. 351–370). Durham, NC: Duke University Press.

Sugrue, T. J. (2004, June). Affirmative action from below: Civil rights, the building trades, and the politics of racial equality in the urban north, 1945–1969. *Journal of American History, 91*(1), 145–173.

Sugrue, T. J. (2008). *Sweet land of liberty: The forgotten struggle for civil rights in the north.* New York, NY: Random House.

Thornell, J. T. (1990). *Governance of the nation's capital: A summary history of the forms and powers of local government for the District of Columbia, 1790 to 1973,* US House, Committee on the District of Columbia, 101 Cong., 2. Sess. US Government Printing Office, 49.

Tydings, J. D. (1967, March). Home rule for the District of Columbia: The case for political justice. *American University Law Review, 16,* 271–277.

US National Capital Park and Planning Commission. (1950). *Regional aspects of the comprehensive plan: A portion of the comprehensive plan for the national capital and its environs.* Washington, DC: Government Printing Office.

Vigna, X. (2007). *L'insubordination ouvrière dans les années 68 : Essai d'histoire politique des usines.* Rennes, France: Presses Universitaires de Rennes.

Vigna, X. (2011). Beyond tradition: The strikes of May–June 1968. In J. Jackson, A. L. Milne, & J. S. Williams (Eds.), *May 68: Rethinking France's last revolution* (pp. 47–57). London: Palgrave Macmillan.

Von Hoffman, A. (Ed.) (2014, July 1). Forum: Urban renewal. *Journal of Urban History, 40*(4), 631–647.

Wagner, K. (2012). The transnational significance of the American Civil War: A global history. *Bulletin of the German Historical Institute, 50,* 124–130.

Wakeman, R. (2009). *The heroic city: Paris, 1945–1958.* Chicago, IL: The University of Chicago Press.

Warner, S. B., Jr. (1962). *Streetcar suburbs: The process of growth in Boston, 1870–1900.* Cambridge, MA: Harvard University Press and The M.I.T. Press.

Yates, A. (2012). Selling Paris: The real estate market and commercial culture in the fin-de-siècle capital. *Enterprise and Society, 13*(4), 773–789.

2

MUSIC, RACE, DESEGREGATION, AND THE FIGHT FOR EQUALITY IN THE NATION'S CAPITAL

Maurice Jackson

Between 1890 and 1918, the African American population in Washington, DC grew dramatically as Blacks moved to the city to flee the lynch mobs, political and economic oppression, and poverty of the South.[1] The prospect of employment in the federal government provided opportunities for Blacks and contributed to the emergence of a Black "middle class" who generally lived near Howard University. As Paul Dunbar wrote, "here comes together the flower of colored citizenship from all over the country . . . the breeziness of the West here meets the refinement of the East, the warmth and grace of the South, the culture and fine reserve of the North" (1901, p. 9).

One who moved to DC was James Reese Europe, who was born in Mobile, Alabama, in 1880 and came with his family to Washington, DC when he was 10. They settled at 308 B Street, SE, not far from where his father worked at the post office, first as a clerk and later as a supervisor. By coincidence, John Philip Sousa, the famed director of the US Marine Corps band, and his family moved a few doors down the street, at 318 B Street. Reid Badger noted that "the Marine Band itself had a long standing relationship with the African American community in Washington" and "regularly took part in such important events in the black community as Howard University's commencement ceremonies, and band members often provided musical instruction to promising black children. One of these young men was Jim Europe," who took lessons in piano and violin from the assistant bandmaster of the US Marine Corps (1995, p. 20). March music, performed by military bands and in parades, had long played a role in New Orleans, where it combined with African and Creole rhythms. Marches were also a big part of the annual DC Emancipation Day parades, so it was not unusual for youngsters to hear and enjoy it. Years later, W.E.B. Du Bois wrote appreciatively in *The Crisis* that Europe had a "genius for organization" and that his marches "all in all . . . are worthy of the pen of Sousa" (1912, pp. 66–67).

For two years, Europe attended the M Street High School, founded in 1870 as the Preparatory High School for Colored Youth, the first public high school for Blacks in the country. He was recruited to the school's new cadet corps, started by Major Christian A. Fleetwood, a recipient of the Medal of Honor for his Civil War services. The Cadet Corps and bands attracted many outstanding students, including "historian Rayford L. Logan, poet Sterling Brown, scholar and diplomat Mercer Cook (son of Will Marion Cook), Army Lieutenant Colonel West Hamilton, federal judge William H. Hastie, and blood-plasma researcher Dr. Charles H. Drew" (Tucker, 1995, p. 7). Mercer Cook's "cadet training would later prove useful when he sought to organize the black musicians of New York; it was undoubtedly helpful to him as an officer in the 15th New York Infantry Regiment in World War I" (Badger, 1995, p. 22). M Street was renamed the Paul Lawrence Dunbar High School in 1916 and had "a remarkable history which chronicles the achievements of an underprivileged people" (Hundley, 1965, p. 20).

After his father died in 1899, Europe dropped out of M Street School and in 1904 he headed to New York City to escape the District's crippling discrimination and to make his name in music. Many artists preferred Harlem, where, as Langston Hughes wrote, "people are not so ostentatiously proud of themselves, and where one's family background is not much of a concern," as he believed the Black elite of Washington, DC held it to be (1927, pp. 226–227). In 1910, Europe founded the Clef Club in New York and its DC affiliate as "a combination musicians' hangout, labor exchange, fraternity club, and concert hall," while also serving as a contracting agency for Black musicians (Lewis, 1979, p. 31). Du Bois noted the significance of the Clef Club: "Before [Black musicians] were prey to scheming head waiters and booking agents, now they are performers whose salaries and hours are fixed by contracts" (1912, pp. 66–67). Europe formed the 125-strong Clef Club Symphony Orchestra and on May 2, 1912, musicians presented "A Concert of Negro Music" at Carnegie Hall. With songs all by Black composers, it was "the first performance ever given by a black orchestra at the famous bastion of white musical establishment" (Gates & Higginbotham, 2004, p. 350).

The election of Woodrow Wilson marked a turning point for the Black population. In 1912, before Wilson's inauguration, Tuskegee Institute's Booker T. Washington believed that "the eyes of the entire country are upon the 100,000 Negroes in the District of Columbia" (1901, p. 1). But the next year, after Wilson became president, Washington was less optimistic, telling a colleague: "I have recently spent several days in Washington and I have never seen the colored people so discouraged and bitter as they are at the present time" (1913, pp. 186–187). Wilson had set policies that separated Blacks within the federal government and between 1910 and 1918, the proportion of Black employees there declined.

At the time, racial lines hardened in Washington, DC in other ways. Despite the presence of a Black middle class, the overwhelming majority of Washington, DC's Black population was poor. Most lived in crowded neighborhoods and slum-like alley dwellings because of racially restrictive housing and economic segregation. The Alley Dwelling Act of 1918 (and later of 1934) condemned the small hovels and ultimately forced entire Black neighborhoods to relocate to the Southeast quadrant of the District, across the Anacostia River. Most Blacks worked as domestic and low-skilled laborers with little hope of advancement. Labor unions resisted Black membership so there were few ways to escape poverty.

When the United States entered World War I, Europe served among the 325,000 Blacks in the segregated military. He saw action with Harlem's famed 369th Regiment and organized its regimental band. The 369th was originally the 15th Infantry Regiment of the New York National Guard (Harris, 2003, p. 31). Europe did not join the 15th simply out of patriotism. He told one of his friends, composer and bandleader Noble Sissle, who also joined the 15th, that "there has never been such an organization of Negro men that will bring together all classes of men for a common good." He added, "Our race will never amount to anything, politically or economically, in New York or anywhere else unless there are strong organizations of men who stand for something in the community" (Badger, 1995, p. 142). Europe was commissioned as an officer and conductor and Sissle enlisted as a private, playing violin and becoming the drum major. Of the four Black regiments under the American Expeditionary Force led by General John J. "Black Jack" Pershing, three, including Europe's, were put under French command. As Gail Buckley wrote, "They weren't really *American*, anyway, so giving them to the French seemed to satisfy both Wilson's expressed desire to serve humanity and his racism. They would be adopted with fulsome gratitude by the French Fourth Army" (2001, p. 165).

Although the men preferred to call themselves "Men of Bronze," they were nicknamed the "Enfant Perdus" (the lost or abandoned children) by the French and the "Hellfighters" by the Germans. The band's performances helped introduce European audiences to African American musicians, the blues, and jazz. When they played a snazzy rendition of the "Marseillaise," the French crowd did not at first recognize their national anthem, but then, according to Sissle, "there came over their faces an astonished look, quickly alert, snap-into-attention and salute by every French soldier and sailor present" (Badger, 1995, p. 163). At performances at a Nantes opera house to honor Abraham Lincoln's birthday, Europe said, "We played to 50,000 people at least, and had we wished it we might be playing yet" (Ward & Burns, 2000, p. 68). Europe became the first African American officer to experience combat, on April 20, 1918. By war's end, the unit had amassed 191 combat days without loss of life or an inch of ground. For their valor, the French government awarded the unit's soldiers the Croix-de-Guerre, the French Army's highest honor. They also won 171 decorations for bravery, the most of any US regiment. On their return on February 17, 1919, the regiment marched up 5th Avenue in New York City to thunderous applause.

We Return Fighting

Du Bois wrote of African American bravery in war and of the racism the men came home to in his article "Returning Soldiers." There he declared: "We return. We return from fighting. We return fighting. Make way for Democracy! We saved it in France, and by the Great Jehovah, we will save it in the United States of America, or know the reason why" (Du Bois, 1919, pp. 13–14). Returning Black soldiers seldom found the respect and benefits they had been promised. While overseas many Black soldiers, like Europe, experienced a bit of equality. Some were influenced by the pan-Africanist ideas of Du Bois or by socialism. By the "Red Summer" of 1919, postwar ethnic and economic tensions following demobilization combined with fear of Bolshevism and flared into violence in US cities, including Washington, DC. Returning White soldiers believed they were competing with Blacks for the jobs they had left to go to war.

On Friday, July 18, 1919, Elsie Stephnick, the wife of a Naval Aviation Department employee, was allegedly assaulted by a Black man on D Street, SW. Several hundred angry White soldiers, sailors, and marines, recently returned from the war, gathered in Southwest Washington, DC armed with clubs, pipes, and pistols and began attacking African Americans (*Washington Post*, July 21, 1919). Both the *Washington Post* and the *New York Times* reported with incendiary headlines the alleged sex crime by a "negro fiend." Headlines read, "Armed and Defiant Negroes Roam About Shooting at Whites," "Negro Runs Amuck, Wounding Many in Flight," and "Race War in Washington" (*New York Times*, July 22, 1919).

On Sunday, July 20, 1919, more than 1,000 civilians and several hundred soldiers and marines resumed the riots, attacking Black pedestrians and dragging others from their cars. Then on Monday afternoon, Superintendent of Police Major Pullman and District Commissioner Louis Brownlow called up all police officers, reserve soldiers, and 400 regular army troops recruited from Fort Myer cavalry, and order was gradually restored. Although President Wilson was "greatly concerned," he never made any public comment on the matter nor did he declare martial law (as some congressmen desired). Of the nearly 100 people arrested, only eight or nine were White. In the end, at least four Blacks and three Whites died (Green, 1967, p. 192).

African Americans, however, did not perceive the violence in the same manner as the *New York Times* and the *Washington Post*. Former diplomat and NAACP president James Weldon Johnson warned America that Blacks would not sit silent in the face of White violence. "[T]he Negroes saved themselves and saved

Washington by their determination not to run, but to fight, fight in defense of their lives and their homes" (Johnson, 1919). This riot marked a milestone for Black citizens as they banded together and fought the White oppression that had come to define DC's social dynamic. Shocked when African Americans began to fight back in defense of their communities, White mobs retreated. Unwilling to see racism as the cause of violence, Whites blamed criminals, outside agitators, and socialist and Bolshevik propaganda. Blacks in DC adopted the words of poet Claude McKay, who captured their spirit and determination in his poem, "If We Must Die." "Like men we'll face the murderous pack, Pressed to the wall, dying, but fighting back!" (1919, p. 21).

Over the next decade, Howard University scholar Alain Locke advocated the development of the "New Negro," with a new self-awareness and confidence in racial identity. Locke noted "a renewed race-spirit that consciously and proudly sets itself apart," a result of the "ripening forces as culled from the first fruits of the Negro Renaissance" (1925, pp. xvii, 9). Coming amidst what he saw as a new intellectual and cultural identity, he believed that the "New Negro is keenly responsive as an augury of a new democracy in American culture," who is "contributing his share to the new social understanding" (Locke, 1925, pp. xvii, 9). This "Washington Renaissance" in many ways preceded the better-known Harlem Renaissance (Williams, 2004).

A New Era of Cultural Protests

The new racial solidarity Locke promoted was tested in June 1922. Robert Russa Moton, the successor to Booker T. Washington at Tuskegee, was a featured speaker at the dedication of the Lincoln Memorial. Although his name was listed on the official invitation and program, Moton and other Blacks were cordoned off in a segregated section far from the dais. Responding to this indignity, the *Baltimore African American* reported, "twenty-one distinguished guests of the nation at the dedication of the Lincoln Memorial yesterday got up from their seats and left the exercises when they found they had been jimcrowed." The paper on June 2, 1922, speculated that Dr. Moton referred to this incident, saying in his address that he hoped "black and white, North and South are going to strive to finish the work Lincoln so nobly began—to make America an example for the world of equal justice, and equal opportunity for all who strive and are willing to serve under the flag that makes men free."

Marian Anderson

A 1939 concert by internationally celebrated contralto Marion Anderson exposed Washington, DC's segregated society to the rest of the country. For several years, the Howard University Music Department had presented an annual concert featuring Anderson, using space at Dunbar High and local auditoriums. In 1939, Anderson was fresh off a successful European tour and her promoters, along with Howard officials, decided to move the event to Constitution Hall, owned by the Daughters of the American Revolution (DAR), not realizing that the DAR had in its leasing agreements a "white artist only" clause. Unlike the National Theatre, which denied Black audience admittance but allowed Black performers, Constitution Hall allowed Black patrons to sit in roped-off areas, but did not allow African American performers (Pelacanos, 2008, pp. 45–52).

When denied the use of Constitution Hall, the newly formed Marian Anderson Citizens Committee (MACC) tried to reserve the White-only Central High School (now Cardoza High), but the school board denied the auditorium to events with African American performers or audience members.[2] With the support of First Lady Eleanor Roosevelt, who resigned her DAR membership over the issue, Secretary of the Interior Harold Ickes made arrangements for Anderson to perform. On Easter Sunday, April 9, 1939, the concert was held on the steps of the Lincoln Memorial with more than 75,000 in attendance. Anderson sang Negro spirituals such as "Nobody Knows the Trouble I've Seen" and "Gospel Train," arranged by her old friend Harry Burleigh, as well as Franz Schubert's "Ave Maria." The program was broadcast over NBC Radio to millions and the world heard it live and in rebroadcasts in newsreels at movie houses.

Mary McLeod Bethune, head of the National Council of Negro Women, an appointee to the National Youth Administration, and a member of Roosevelt's Kitchen Cabinet, wrote to Charles Hamilton Houston, special counsel of the NAACP and dean of Howard Law School, that "through the Marion Anderson Protest Concert we made our triumphant entry into the democratic spirit of American life" (Arsenault, 2009, p. 163). Historian Constance McLaughlin Green wrote that "it was no longer a local affair only. Race relations in the nation's capital thenceforward were a matter of interest to Americans everywhere" (1967, p. 249).

The MACC also decided to challenge the school board's decision to deny Anderson the right to sing at Central High. At a mass meeting on March 26, a few days before the scheduled concert, Herbert Marshall, head of the DC branch of the NAACP, declared that "the denial of the use of the Central High School auditorium is the very antithesis of democracy." Their appeal was denied. Historian Raymond Arsenault noted that, while the DAR battle had been won, "the battle over racial justice in the nation's capital was just beginning" and "it would be years before black Washingtonians achieved anything approaching fundamental reform in the District's schools" (2009, p. 174).

Billie Holiday

That same April 1939 when Ms. Anderson performed at the Lincoln Memorial, Billie Holiday first performed "Strange Fruit" at New York's Café Society, a midtown club that attracted a varied audience, from Nelson Rockefeller to Lillian Hellman and Langston Hughes. The song was then studio-recorded on April 20 and released a few months later. "Strange Fruit" had a profound riveting effect on jazz and on the struggle against lynching (Margolick, 2000, p. 42). The *Baltimore African American* reported in March 1940 that "Miss Holiday recently sang ['Strange Fruit'] at the Howard Theatre in Washington" and "speculation became rife as to whether it actually will incite or condemn mob action," but the paper said the song "immediately won praise from both the hot and classical schools." The paper also speculated "that Holiday might have even won the NAACP's prestigious Spingarn Medal, given annually to blacks for special achievements, had the black church not disapproved of entertainers at the time." She often performed in Washington, DC and was especially fond of playing at Club Bali, staying at the Dunbar Hotel. In 1949, she had a three-week engagement, breaking the club record, which ended on April 7, her birthday (Blackburn, 2005, p. 228). Georgianne Williamson of the *Washington Post* said, "Billie is earthy, but with complete good grace. More factual than suggestive, still she's got a gallop that has the bar sitters, around her in a semi circle at her feet, supplying a chorus of adulation" (De Ferrari, 2013, p. 100). Ahmet Ertegun later wrote, from DC, that the song deeply moved his entire family.

Duke Ellington

Washington, DC–born Duke Ellington also made a contribution to the desegregation of his native city. He knew well the works of prolific African American historian Rayford Logan, an old family friend, who in 1941 published *The Diplomatic Relations of the United States with Haiti*, and, according to Ellington biographer John Edward Hasse, he "owned 800 books on black history, and had underlined passages about Denmark Vesey and Nat Turner" (Hasse, 1993, p. 254). Ellington was also familiar with the art of Jacob Lawrence, the poetry of Langston Hughes, and the prose of Du Bois related to the Haitian Revolution and Toussaint L'Ouverture. Although some writers emphasize Ellington's social conservatism, Terry Teachout offers another view of Duke: "Ellington, like many other blacks, appreciated the Communist Party's stance against racism, and his sentiments were widely shared in Harlem," while noting that the maestro, like many of his generation, was a Republican. Teachout points out that Ellington "himself would actively support the candidacy of Benjamin J. Davis Jr., when he ran for New York's city council" in 1943, siding with a Black man he admired for openly fighting racism (2013, p. 226).

On January 23, 1943, Duke Ellington's *Black, Brown and Beige* premiered at New York's Carnegie Hall. Count Basie, Jimmy Lunceford, and Benny Goodman attended the performance, as did First Lady Eleanor Roosevelt and Leopold Stokowski. According to the *Washington African American*, "Frank Sinatra left his engagement at the Paramount to visit backstage." Among the African American celebrities in attendance were Marian Anderson, Langston Hughes, and Alain Locke. Tickets to the concert sold out two weeks before the premiere and "an overflow crowd of about 2,000 persons milled about the sidewalks and lobby of [the 3,000-person capacity] Carnegie Hall . . . in the hopes of securing tickets" (Cohen, 2004, pp. 1010–1011). The concert, which was done in support of Russian War Relief, grossed $7,000 and netted $5,000. The concert was repeated in Boston on January 28, 1943, and in Cleveland on February 20, 1943, all for integrated audiences (Jackson, 2010, pp. 154–156). The set was influenced by the Blacks who fought at the Battle of Savannah and by Ellington's appreciation of the Haitian Revolution. "I have gone back to the history of my race and tried to express it in rhythm," Ellington wrote. "We used to have a little something in Africa, something we have lost. One day we shall get it again" (Collier, 1987, p. 216).

Ahmet Ertegun

Ahmet and Nesuhi Ertegun, sons of the Turkish ambassador to the United States, had a profound impact on the Washington, DC jazz scene. Arriving in Washington, DC in 1935, the young men and their sister Selma quickly developed a love and appreciation of African American music of all kinds: blues, spirituals, gospels, jazz, and later rhythm and blues. They learned about the city and about African Americans from the embassy's custodian, Cleo Payne, an ex-prizefighter who taught Ahmet Ertegun to box and took him to boxing matches, "introduced him to beer joints, and . . . gave him an appetite for soul food" (Wade & Picardie, 1990, p. 29). Often they travelled the streets of Washington, DC, driven by the embassy's African American chauffeur, spending long hours going to record stores, and visiting the homes of Blacks to listen to and purchase jazz recordings.

Despite segregation, the Erteguns socialized with the African American community. "In the forties, Washington was like a Southern town," Ahmet later wrote. "There was total segregation. Black people had their own movie theatres in their own section of town and were not allowed in the white movie theatres." Except, that is, for the burlesque shows where Whites sat downstairs and Blacks in the balcony. "Black and white musicians did play together, but it was not easy. It was more possible in New York, particularly Harlem, but in Washington at that time it was virtually impossible" (Ertegun et al., 2001, p. 12). They began to meet "the black professors at Howard University, especially the Dean of the School of English Literature, Sterling Brown," and others in "the black intelligentsia and members of the Washington black society. Our common interest in jazz brought all of us together." He said, "We had a lot of friends in Washington, and we could never go to a restaurant together, never go to a movie, or to the theater with them. . . . It was impossible to go out. I couldn't even take Duke Ellington, who is one of the geniuses of our country, to a restaurant. Or Count Basie. That's how it was and we could not accept it" (Wade & Picardie, 1990, pp. 30–31).

Beginning in 1940, the brothers began to invite musicians they had seen play on Saturday nights at the Howard Theatre and elsewhere to the embassy for Sunday lunches. Their jazz-loving friends and whichever band was in town would play, including Duke Ellington, Louis Armstrong, Johnny Hodges, Benny Carter, Rex Stuart, Joe Marsala, Lester Young, and Meade Lux Lewis.[3] White Washingtonians with strong Southern sensibilities were disturbed to see Blacks entering the embassy by the front door. Ertegun often told the story of a Southern senator who lived nearby complaining to his father, Mehmet, about African Americans entering the embassy through the front door. Ahmet said, "My father would respond with a terse one-sentence reply such as: 'In my home, friends enter by the front door—however, we can arrange for you to enter from the back" (Ertegun et al., 2001, p. 7). Frustrated by the racism of White society, the Ertegun brothers decided to hold jazz concerts open to integrated audiences in 1942. While Whites had long gone to U Street and the Howard Theatre, there had not been events that promoted Blacks and Whites listening to music together. Ahmet Ertegun wrote that:

> We decided to put on the first integrated concert in Washington. We had black and white musicians onstage, people like Sidney Bechet, Joe Turner, Pete Johnson, Pee Wee Russell, and others—and also we had an integrated audience. We had a lot of trouble finding a place in Washington where we could stage this event. The first concert we held was at the Jewish community center, which was the only place that would allow a mixed audience and a mixed band. After that the National Press Club broke down and let us to use their auditorium. Leadbelly used to come to some of our open jam sessions at the embassy and he sang at the first concert we gave at the National Press Club. When he peeked out from the wings backstage and saw the size of the crowd, he said, 'Man, you gotta give me double the price, otherwise I'm not going on.' So of course we did—we gave him everything we could, and you know, we certainly weren't pretending to be experienced promoters, we were just doing it for the love of the music.
>
> (Ertegun et al., 2001, p. 12)

The Erteguns also dented racial boundaries when they organized this first interracial concert in Washington, DC, located on 16th Street about a mile north of the White House. As Nesuhi remembered in a 1979 interview with the *Washington Post*, "Blacks and whites couldn't sit together in most places. So we put on concerts . . . jazz was our weapon for social action" (du Lac, 2011). Ahmet recalled later that many who came to the Jewish Community Center "did not know it would be integrated" and that the Press Club relented and allowed their next concert because he promised "to make a big scene out of it if they didn't let us rent it"

(Greenfield, 2011, p. 32). The music was played by a racially mixed jazz orchestra for a mixed audience and interracial audiences began to be more common in the DC jazz clubs (Jackson, 2013). Soon the Erteguns were known throughout the city's jazz scene. In a *Washington Post* article on May 16, 1943, titled "Two Turks, Hot for U.S. Swing," William Gottlieb wrote, "the young Erteguns treated the music of Morton, Armstrong, Oliver, Ellington and the rest with sincere enthusiasm and scholarly discrimination, an attitude that, strangely enough, is more typical of Europeans than Americans."

When Lead Belly performed in the Erteguns' second concert, he was familiar with the realities of segregation in Washington, DC. Born Huddie Ledbetter, he was initially brought to the city to record at the Library of Congress by folklorist Alan Lomax. According to John Szwed, "the Ledbetters were to have stayed with the Lomaxes in their apartment, but when the landlord got word that they had Negroes as guests he threatened to call the police and, under Washington's segregated housing laws, have them all put out of the building" (Swed, 2010, p. 105). The next day Lomax and Lead Belly searched for a Black hotel or rooming house. Then, with their wives, they sought a place to eat together, and were denied entrance to restaurants. So Lead Belly wrote "Bourgeois Blues" to reflect his views of race and class in the city: "Me and my wife went all over town, And everywhere we went people turned us down. Lord in a bourgeois town." Over the years, this song has been used to unflatteringly describe the city's "black bourgeoisie."

Ahmet and Nesuhi Ertegun moved to New York and in September 1947 founded Atlantic Records, where they worked with the greats of American music of all colors, races, and religions. Noted pianist, composer, jazz educator, and Dunbar graduate Dr. Billy Taylor later wrote in appreciation that, "in their own way, the Erteguns defied segregation to frequent our neighborhood and patronize our music. They also produced Jazz concerts that featured racially mixed groups, shocking the Washington, D.C. establishment and delighting their friends" (Taylor & Reed, 2013, p. 29). In a 2007 PBS documentary about Atlantic Records, Ahmet commented, "All popular music stems from black music, be it jazz or rock and roll." Reflecting on his career, he added, "I'd be happy if people said that I did a little bit to raise the dignity and recognition of the greatness of African American music" (Atlantic Records, 2007). The Erteguns left Washington, DC a different city. Through their insistence on breaking racial barriers, they had cracked open a door to greater integration in entertainment venues and, ultimately, much more.

A New Push

The 1940s brought the emergence of the modern civil rights movement, as African Americans worked more aggressively for equality through the courts, the federal government, unions, and civic organizations. Many regard a planned march on Washington, DC in June 1941 by labor leader A. Philip Randolph as its beginning.

Randolph had threatened to bring 100,000 people to Washington, DC to protest discrimination in federal agencies, but agreed to call off the march when President Roosevelt issued Executive Order 8802, which prohibited such discrimination. Roosevelt also established the Fair Employment Practices Committee in 1942 to address some of the same issues. When African Americans began returning home from the war, they brought expectations that the idea of "Double V"—Victory against fascism abroad and Victory against racism and injustice at home—meant they would return to a more equitable Washington, DC.

In 1946, David Rosenberg, the owner of Club Bali, where Lester Young, Billie Holiday, Louis Armstrong, and Sarah Vaughan had appeared, made news with plans to build a space where there would be a nondiscrimination policy for both musicians and audiences. On January 12, 1947, Rosenberg opened the Music Hall—one of the first professional venues in Washington, DC that allowed mixed-race bands and audiences—with great fanfare at 9th and V Streets, NW. It featured a one-week engagement by Louis Armstrong. By late April, the Music Hall had hosted Billy Eckstine, Ella Fitzgerald, Cootie Williams, Lionel Hampton, Tony Pastor, Cab Calloway, Rex Stewart, Jimmy Lunceford, Illinois Jacquet, Erskine Hawkins, Andy Kirk, Dizzy Gillespie, Art Tatum, and Sam Donahue. Charlie "Yardbird" Parker also performed there, while he and Dizzy Gillespie were leading the new bebop revolution in jazz.

Jazz continued to weaken segregation's hold through concerts promoted by Willis Conover, a popular disc jockey on radio station WWDC. "During his military service, he acted to desegregate Washington. His part in this effort was to present musicians in nightclubs, insisting that blacks be admitted. He also produced a series of Saturday midnight concerts at the Howard Theatre. His opposition to racism was lifelong, and deeply felt" (Lees, 2003, p. 253). Conover held the first of many integrated jazz concerts on Saturday, April 24, 1948, at the All Souls Unitarian Church on 16th Street, NW, a fitting place to hold a socially pioneering performance. Long a bastion of social liberalism, the church's bell rang on Emancipation Day, January 1, 1863, and would again during the March on Washington on August 28, 1963. Among its founders in 1821 was John Quincy Adams, called by some "the Abolitionist" for his role arguing the *Amistad* case before the US Supreme Court (Rediker, 2012). The church has continued its activism to this day.

With the success of the first "jam session" at All Souls Church, "Willis Conover Presents Jam Session No. 2" was held on May 9, 1948, at the National Press Club, which by then had adopted a policy of nondiscrimination, in part because of the efforts of the Ertegun brothers, journalist and photographer William Gottlieb, and Conover. The third of that first series of concerts was held two weeks later, on Sunday afternoon, May 23, at the Music Hall. It was advertised that day in the *Washington Daily News* as Dixieland vs. Bebop, featuring Charlie Parker. Ron Frits writes that the Music Hall was a good choice: "Venues in the Washington area that would accommodate patrons regardless of race and charge reasonable rent, while offering amenities far and above the standard in 1948, [were] few and far between" (Frits, 1948). Conover later became famous internationally as a jazz broadcaster for the Voice of America (Davenport, 2009, p. 133).

Newly emboldened African Americans sought the integration of cultural venues beyond jazz clubs. The Actors' Equity, representing thousands of actors and stage managers, took a stand against segregation at theatres such as the National in 1947. The actors' union issued a statement that read, "We state now to the National Theatre—and to a public which is looking to us to do what is just and humanitarian—that unless the situation is remedied, we will be forced to forbid our members to play there" (Lightman, 2009). Rather than integrate, the National Theatre closed in 1948 and stayed shut until 1952, when new owners agreed to allow interracial audiences.

Late in 1947, the President's Committee on Civil Rights, appointed by President Harry S. Truman, issued a report titled "To Secure These Rights," which "shocked the nation with its revelations of how deeply racial segregation and discrimination were rooted" in the city and the nation (Caplan, 1989, p. 31). Within a year, Truman issued Executive Order 9981, which desegregated the military and other areas of federal employment (Jackson, 2013, p. A16). This was particularly significant for Washington, DC, with its thousands of federal employees and military personnel, many of them Black.

Another 1948 milestone was the Supreme Court's ruling in *Shelly v. Kraemer*, which stated that racially restrictive housing covenants were not enforceable. As a result, some middle-class Blacks moved into neighborhoods where they had been barred before, such as Shepherd Park, Brightwood, and Brookland near Catholic University. One of the four cases joined to *Brown v. Board of Education, Bolling v. Sharpe*, originated in Washington, DC. That same year a report titled "Segregation in Washington" was published with the endorsement of some 90 prominent Americans, including Eleanor Roosevelt, Hubert Humphrey, and Walter Reuther.

The Lost Laws

In 1949, the Coordinating Committee for the Enforcement of D.C. Anti-Discrimination Laws began a campaign against segregation in restaurants and public facilities. Longtime resident and activist Marvin Caplan described the city at mid-century:

> By 1950, segregation by law and by custom was firmly entrenched in Washington. Segregated restaurants were only one reflection of a racially divided city. Black Washingtonians encountered segregation in the most fundamental aspects of their daily lives. . . . Blacks who ventured downtown found most hotels and movie houses closed to them.
>
> (Caplan, 1989, p. 26)

The Coordinating Committee focused on certain antidiscriminatory "lost laws" passed in 1872 and 1873. Although never repealed, as were many such laws after Reconstruction, the laws were not enforced. On January 27, 1950, 86-year-old Mary Church Terrell and three others entered Thompson's Cafeteria on 14th Street downtown and tried to purchase food. The restaurant's refusal to serve them formed the basis of the suit in the *District of Columbia v. Thompson Co.* First the municipal court (1950) and then the appellate courts (1951) ruled against their complaint, and the case went on to the Supreme Court. Picket lines and marches began in downtown DC as the boycott spread to other restaurants and to People's Drug Store and the Hecht Company department store on 7th Street and G.C. Murphy's on F Street. On one occasion, "Josephine Baker, the celebrated singer and dancer and friend of Mrs. Terrell (who seemed to know everyone), spared a moment during a visit to the capital to come down to Hecht's, and when she was refused service, took a turn on the picket line" (Caplan, 1989, p. 34).

Entertainers and public citizens also played another role. The Coordinating Committee began publishing a list of eating establishments "which are reported to serve meals to well behaved persons irrespective of race." The headline of the January 24, 1951, *Afro American Newspaper* read, "List Published of the 36 White-Owned Restaurants in D.C. Serving All Comers," as well as "All Federal Building Cafeterias." The paper reported that foreign embassies and the US State Department kept updated lists of places that served all races.[4] This policy no doubt was reflective of larger number of diplomats of color coming to the city. In fact some years later, during the height of the civil rights struggles, African Americans were known to wear African dresses, headdresses, Dashikis, kufi hats and caps, and other African-themed attire, hoping to escape discrimination by "passing" as diplomats in DC or in their travels south to visit relatives. Some believed that Blacks from Africa, the Caribbean, or Latin America or those who spoke another language were treated better. Finally, in 1953, Justice William O. Douglas wrote in the majority opinion in the *Thompson* case "that we find no other intervening act which would effect repeal of the [lost laws]." As the Coordinating Committee successfully tested the laws, movie theatres, hotels, public facilities, and restaurants were integrated.

As the civil rights movement grew stronger in the 1950s, the federal government responded. President Dwight D. Eisenhower, in his first State of the Union Address in 1953, said that Washington, DC must be an "honored example for all communities of our nation" and declared that "not one single penny of federal money should be spent in a way that would discriminate against anyone" (Eisenhower, 1953). Over the next several years he ordered the integration of all US military academies and the end of segregated schools on military bases, as well as the elimination of the all-Black military units not yet integrated under President Truman. In his 1956 State of the Union Address, Eisenhower described the low Black voter turnout as "disturbing," speculating that it was because of intimidation at the polls (Eisenhower, 1956). Then in September 1957, nine African

American students were blocked from entering the all-White Central High School in Little Rock, Arkansas. Defying federal law, Governor Orval Faubus stationed National Guard troops around the school to prevent their entry (Von Eschen, 2004, p. 63).

Louis Armstrong, who had been approached by the State Department to visit the Soviet Union as part of the Jazz Ambassadors program, was angered (Teachout, 2009, pp. 314, 336). After seeing pictures of White mobs throwing objects at young Black girls, Armstrong told a reporter, "My people—the Negroes—are not looking for anything—we just want a square shake. But when I see on television and read about a crowd in Arkansas spitting and cursing at a little colored girl—I think I have a right to get sore—and say something about it" (*Chicago Defender*, September 28, 1957). Referring to his trips abroad representing the United States, he told another reporter on September 19, "The way they are treating my people in the South the Government can go to hell. The people over there ask me what's wrong with my country. What am I supposed to say?" Accusing the president of being "two faced" and having "no guts," he added, "It's getting so bad a colored man hasn't got any country" (*Pittsburgh Courier*, September 28, 1957).

Because of his outspokenness, some concerts and TV appearances were cancelled, but Armstrong found a new appreciation among Black Americans and throughout the world. In September, perhaps affected by the man known throughout the world as Satchmo, Eisenhower sent 1,200 paratroopers from the 101st Airborne to Little Rock to escort the Little Rock Nine into Central High. Satchmo then sent a message to Ike: "If you decide to walk into the schools with the little colored kids, take me along, daddy. God Bless You" (Margolick, September 23, 2007). This had a tremendous impact in Washington, DC in the same year that African Americans became the majority population. In his own way "ole Satch" had reached the president, not just with his trumpet or his singing, but with his spoken word. And his actions directly contributed to democracy in the nation's capital.

Conclusion

Lawrence Levine has observed that "culture is not a fixed condition but a process, the product of interaction between the past and the present. Its toughness and resiliency are determined not by a culture's ability to withstand change, which indeed may be a sign of stagnation not life, but by its ability to reach creatively and responsively to the realities of the new situation" (1977, p. 5). The music Washingtonians created advanced society and helped to bring the races together in the fight for equality. By the 1960s, Washington, DC was moving slowly, if not to a city of "equals," then at least to a place where "equal rights" were the law. By this time, Washington, DC had become the first major city in the country with a majority Black population. The 23rd Amendment was ratified in 1961, allowing

Black and White Washington, DC residents to vote in a presidential election. The following year at Pierce Hall in All Souls Church on February 13, 1962, guitarist Charlie Byrd, tenor sax giant Stan Getz, and bassist Keter Betts recorded their groundbreaking session, *Jazz Samba*, bringing multiethnic Brazilian sounds to the nation.[5]

The 1964 Civil Rights Act was passed the same year Washingtonians voted for president for the first time since 1800. That same year, the Ramsey Lewis Trio recorded *The Ramsey Lewis Trio at the Bohemian Caverns* and repeated its success there with the Grammy-winning *The In Crowd with the Ramsey Lewis Trio* in 1965. Al Clarke of WOOK Radio wrote in the liner notes, "Nowhere in the country has the trio been more enthusiastically received than in the nation's capital, where they enjoy the praise of fans of all nations" (Clarke, 1965). That year, the 1965 Voting Rights Act was also passed.

Washington, DC–born musicians continued to express their desire for equality. Billy Taylor, who graduated from Dunbar High in 1939, reflected on his years in Washington, DC and the racial situation in America when he recorded "I Wish That I Knew How It Would Feel to Be Free," in 1963, two weeks before the assassination of President John Kennedy. "The lyrics were about freedom, which for African Americans was the clarion cry of that era." He believed that the song "captured the essence of the Civil Rights Movement" and that Martin Luther King was especially fond of Nina Simone's popular 1967 recording of it. Taylor noted that King "was a lover of Jazz," but because he could never remember the title he always asked him to play "that Baptists sounding song" (Taylor & Reed, 2013, p. 148).

In May 1971, the largest demonstration in US history, the May Day Peace protest against the war in Vietnam, was held in the nation's capital. That was also the year Washington, DC native Marvin Gaye released one of the biggest-selling albums in history. "What's Going On" also ranks among the top as music of social protest. Gaye was deeply moved by the letters his brother had sent from Vietnam and the conditions of Black people in America. One of the songs on the album, "Inner City Blues, Makes Me Wanna Holler," is a song reflecting the chaos of the times and with it violence, poverty, and the plight of ghetto youth, who took the song as their own. The beginning words, "Rockets moon shots/Spend it on the have not's," took "the government to task for probing outer space while leaving the poor to fend for themselves" (Dyson, 2004, p. 66). The song is about inequality and the denial of democratic rights. Gaye said that "what mattered was the message. For the first time I felt like I had something to say" (Gaye, 2001).

Gil Scott-Heron, who had lived in DC and once taught at Federal City College, also wrote songs about life in Washington, DC, his most famous being "the H20Gate Blues." He said that many of his "songs began taking shape in DC" as he observed the Black condition, and, "instead of just glossing over the problem," he generally used an individual or an individual's circumstances as an example of a larger thing, the "plight of impoverished Black Washingtonians" (Scott-Heron, 2012, p. 177).

Washingtonians still do not have a voting representative in the US Congress, so the struggle for democracy and equal rights continues. Scott-Heron said it best in a song on his 1982 album *Moving Target*. Titled "Washington, D.C.," a key verse reflects the city in 2015. "It's a mass of irony for all the world to see, It's the nation's capital, It's Washington, DC."

Notes

1 Some material in this chapter first appeared in Jackson, M. (Spring 2014). Great Black Music and the Desegregation of Washington, D.C., Washington History, 26(1): 13–36.
2 Central High School, at 13th and Clifton Streets, NW, was later renamed Cardozo. Pulitzer Prize–winning author Edward P. Jones is a 1968 graduate.
3 In the past two years, a series of jazz events was held at the Turkish Embassy to commemorate the 1940s events, sponsored by the embassy and by Jazz at the Lincoln Center.
4 John Kelley wrote that the list appears to have grown out of the sermon by Rev. A. Powell Davies of All Souls Unitarian Church on February 1, 1953, when Powell said that he would not "knowingly eat a meal in any restaurant in the District of Columbia that will not serve meals to Negroes," and called on "all who truly believe in human brotherhood" to join him. Started in 1951, the list was constantly updated, in the end comprising 60 establishments. Kelley, "D.C. restaurant list is a relic from a painful past," *Washington Post*, October 5, 2011.
5 James Reeb, the White assistant minister of All Souls Unitarian Church, where John Quincy Adams worshiped and Blacks and Whites like Keter Betts and Charlie Byrd performed, was murdered by a gang of White men in Selma, Alabama, in 1965 because of his efforts to win equality for African Americans.

References

Arsenault, R. (2009). *The sound of freedom: Marian Anderson, the Lincoln Memorial and the concert that awakened America*. New York, NY: Bloomsbury Press.

Atlantic Records. (2007). *The house that Ahmet built*. PBS.

Baltimore African American. (1922, June 2). Colored folk defy Jim Crow: Near riots marks enforcement of segregation by soldiers with guns and bayonets.

Badger, R. (1995). *A life in ragtime: A biography of James Reese Europe*. New York, NY: Oxford University Press.

Blackburn J. (2005). *With Billie: A new look at the unforgettable Lady Day*. New York, NY: Vintage.

Buckley, G. (2001). *And American patriots: The story of blacks in the military from the Revolution to Desert Storm*. New York, NY: Random House.

Caplan, M. (1989). "Eat Anywhere!" *Washington History*, 1 (Spring).

Caplan, M. (1999). *Farther along: A civil rights memoir*. Baton Rouge, LA: Louisiana State University Press.

Chicago Defender. (1957, September 28). Satch blasts echoed by top performers: Nixes tour, raps Ike and Faubus, 53.

Clarke, A. (1965). WOOK Radio, liner notes *The In Crowd with the Ramsey Lewis Trio*, Chess Records.

Cohen, H. G. (2004). Duke Ellington and *Black, Brown and Beige:* The composer as historian at Carnegie Hall. *American Quarterly* (Winter).

Collier, J. L. (1987). *Duke Ellington*. New York, NY: Oxford University Press.

Davenport, L. (2009). *Jazz diplomacy; Promoting America in the Cold War era*. Jackson, MI: University of Mississippi Press.

De Ferrari, J. (2013). *Historic restaurants of Washington, D.C.* Charleston, NC: The History Press.

Du Bois, W.E.B. (1912, May). The Negro Church. *The Crisis: A Record of Darker Races. 24*.

Du Bois, W.E.B. (1919, May). Returning soldiers. *The Crisis, 18*.

Du Bois, W.E.B. (1961). *The souls of black folk*. Greenwich, CT: Fawcett.

du Lac, J. (2011, February 3). A chord of jazz history to echo at Turkish embassy. *The Washington Post*.

Dunbar, P. L. (1901, December). Negro society in Washington. *The Saturday Evening Post*, 9.

Dyson, M. E. (2004). *Mercy, mercy me: The art, loves and demons of Marvin Gaye*. New York, NY: Basis Civitas Books.

Ellington, D. (1943, January). *The Duke Ellington Carnegie Hall concerts*. Prestige Records.

Ertegun, A., et al. (2001). *"What'd I say": The Atlantic story, 50 years of music*. New York, NY: Welcome Rain Publishers.

Europe, J. R. (1914, March 15). Interview with the *New York Evening Post*.

Frits, R. (1948). Liner notes to *Charlie Parker: Washington, D.C., 1948*. Plattsburg, NY: Uptown Records.

Gates, H. L., & Higginbotham, E. B. (Eds.). (2004). *African American lives*. Oxford, UK: Oxford University Press.

Gaye, M. (2001). *The very best of Motown*. UTV Records. Liner notes David Ritz.

Gottlieb, W. (1943, May 16). Two Turks, hot for U.S. swing. *The Washington Post*, L2.

Green, C. M. (1967). *The secret city: A history of race relations in the nation's capital*. Princeton, NJ: Princeton University Press.

Greenfield, R. (2011). *The last sultan: The life and times of Ahmet Ertegun*. New York, NY: Simon & Schuster.

Harlan, L. R. (1983). *The Booker T. Washington papers, Volume 12, 1912–1914*. Urbana, IL: The University of Illinois Press.

Harris, S. L. (2003). *Harlem's Hell Fighters: The African-American 369th Infantry in World War I*. Washington, DC: Brassey's.

Hasse, J. E. (1993). *Beyond category: The life and genius of Duke Ellington*. New York, NY: Simon & Schuster.

Hughes, L. (2008). Trouble with angels: National Theater (1935). In G. Pelecanos (Ed.), *D.C. Noir 2: The Classics* (pp. 45–52). Washington, DC: Akahashic Classics.

Hughes, L. (1927, August). Our wonderful society: Washington. *Opportunity*, 5.

Hundley, M. G. (1965). *The Dunbar story, 1870–1955*. New York, NY: Vantage Press.

Jackson, M. (2013, May). Washington, D.C.: From the founding of a slaveholding capital to a center of abolitionism. *Journal of African Diaspora Archeology and Heritage*, special issue, "Atlantic Approaches on Slave Resistance in the Americas."

Jackson, M. *The Washington Post* (2013, August 23). 50 years after the march, the fight for equality isn't over: Addressing income disparities in income and housing is next for the district, p. A16.

Jackson, M. *The Hill* (2013, November 12). Remembering the Turkish brothers who helped change race relations in America, Congressional Record, Volume 159, Issue 160. Washington, DC: U.S. Government Publishing Office.

Jackson, M. (2010). No man could hinder him: Remembering Toussaint L'Ouverture and the Haitian revolution in the history and culture of the African American people. In M. Jackson & J. Bacon (Eds.), *African Americans and the Haitian Revolution* (pp. 141–164). New York: Routledge.

Johnson, J. W. (1919). *The Washington riots: An N.A.A.C.P. investigation.* Washington, DC: National Association for the Advancement of Colored People.

Lees, G. (2003). *Friends along the way: A journey through jazz.* New Haven, CT: Yale University Press.

Levine, L. W. (1977). *Black culture and Black consciousness.* New York, NY: Oxford University Press.

Lewis, D. L. (1979). *When Harlem was in vogue.* New York, NY: Penguin.

Lightman, D. (2009, January 16). Racial barriers fell slowly in capital. *McClatchy News Service.*

Locke, A. (Ed.). (1925). *The new Negro: An interpretation.* New York, NY: Albert & Charles Bonni.

Lomax, A. (1950). *Mister Jelly Roll: The fortunes of Jelly Roll Morton, New Orleans Creole and "inventor of jazz."* New York, NY: Pantheon Div., Random House.

Margolick, D. (2000). *Strange fruit: Café society and the early cry for civil rights.* Philadelphia, PA: Running Press.

Margolick, D. (2007, September 23). The day Louis Armstrong made noise. *New York Times,* retrieved from www.nytimes.com/2007/09/23/opinion/23margolick.html?pagewanted=all

McKay, C. (1919, July). If we must die. *The Liberator, 2.*

Munson, I. (2007). *Freedom sounds: Civil rights call out to jazz and Africa.* Cambridge, MA: Harvard University Press.

Perl, Peter. (2007, October 29). Race riots of 1919 gave glimpse of future struggles. *The Washington Post.*

Pittsburgh Courier (1957, September 28). Satchmo tells off U.S.

Rediker, M. (2012). *The Amistad rebellion: An Atlantic odyssey of slavery and freedom.* New York, NY: Viking.

Ruble, B. A. (2010). *Washington's U Street: A biography.* Washington, DC and Baltimore, MD: Woodrow Wilson Center Press and the Johns Hopkins University Press.

Schaffer, M. (1998, April 3). Lost riot. *Washington City Paper.*

Scott-Heron, G. (2012). *The last holiday: A memoir.* New York, NY: Grove Press.

Southern, E. (Ed.). (1971). *Readings in black American music.* New York, NY: W. W. Norton.

Stewart, A. (2013). *First class: The legacy of Dunbar, America's first black public high school.* New York, NY: Lawrence Hill.

Szwed, J. (2010). *Alan Lomax: The man who recorded the world.* New York, NY: Penguin.

Taylor, B., with Reed, T. L. (2013). *The jazz life of Dr. Billy Taylor.* Bloomington, IN: Indiana University Press.

Teachout, T. (2013). *Duke: The life of Duke Ellington.* New York, NY: Gotham Books.

Tolney, S. E., & Beck, E. M. (1992). Racial violence and black migration in the American South. *American Sociological Review, 57*(1), 103–116.

Tucker, M. (1995). *Ellington: The early years.* Urbana, IL: The University of Illinois Press.

Von Eschen, P. M. (2004). *Satchmo blows up the world: Jazz ambassadors play the Cold War.* Cambridge, MA: Harvard University Press.

Wade, D., & Picardie, J. (1990). *Music man: Ahmet Ertegun, Atlantic Records and the triumph of rock 'n roll.* New York, NY: W. W. Norton.

Ward, G. C., & Burns, K. (2000). *Jazz: A history of America's music.* New York, NY: Alfred A. Knopf.

Washington, Booker T. "Booker T. Washington to Oswald Garrison Villard, "Aug. 10, 1913, Washington Papers 28: 186-187, Library of Congress, The Booker *T. Washington Papers, Volume 12,* 1912-1914. Urbana; University of Illinois Press, 1983, 248.

The Washington Bee (1919, August 2). The rights of the black man.

The Washington Post (1919, July 21b). Servicemen beat Negroes in race riot at capital.

The Washington Post (1919, July 22). Race war in Washington. July 23, 1919.

The Washington Post (1919, July 25). Riots elsewhere, forecast by Negro.

Williams, E. C. (2004). *When Washington was in vogue.* New York, NY: Amistad.

3

PRIMED FOR DEVELOPMENT

Washington, DC's Great Society Transitions, 1964–1974

Bell Julian Clement

Friday morning, January 31, 1969, found Richard M. Nixon at the intersection of 7th and T Streets in Washington, DC's Shaw neighborhood, surveying the blasted hulk of Waxie Maxie Discount Records—gutted in the riots of the previous spring—and contemplating the wreckage of Lyndon Johnson's Great Society dreams (Fiske, 1969). Nixon, who had been inaugurated 11 days prior as the 37th president of the United States, was using the visit to signal his own plans for the nation's capital. He was announcing his commitment to getting the still-stalled post-riot reconstruction moving in time to deliver a remade city as host for what he could hope would be the glorious national bicentennial gala crowning his successful two-term presidency.

For Johnson and Nixon, as for all presidents of the mid-20th century, the American city claimed a central place in domestic policy thinking. Starting with the 1949 creation of the urban redevelopment program and reaching the height of its intensity in Johnson's Great Society initiatives, this focus reframed a wide range of domestic challenges as "urban" issues, elements in a rising "urban crisis."

The city of Washington, DC is a prism of national politics, reflecting and refracting the nation's aspirations and anxieties. No surprise, then, that Washington, DC was a prime object—victim or beneficiary—of this national urban policy activism. While the nature of Washington, DC's relationship to federal social policy deliberations is open to discussion—some argue for its particular significance as a national laboratory, while others forward similar claims for other cities (Gillette, 1995; Hirsch, 1983)—the fact is that the federal public housing, urban redevelopment, and Model Cities programs were each piloted in Washington, DC before being launched nationally. These programs' Washington, DC successes and shortfalls were closely monitored by members of Congress and the executive branch, serving as fuel for ideological fires in debates over American urban governance.

National urban policy interventions in the nation's capital thus have been high-stakes and particularly energetic. Federal policy efforts have had a larger role in shaping Washington, DC than any other city. During the Great Society era, this federal influence is traceable in changes in the District's civic organization, in the tenor of its economic development approach, and in the structure and priorities of local government itself. Together, these three factors frame the context in which present-day battles over social equity and economic development occur.

Federal City

The 1960s were a period of radical expansion of the American body politic, accomplished through both formal and informal modifications to the terms of citizenship (Keyssar, 2000). The decade opened with the 1961 ratification of the 23rd Amendment, recognizing Washingtonians' right to vote in presidential elections. There followed the vote reapportionment battles waged in federal courts, starting with 1962's *Baker v. Carr*, which overthrew the nationwide rotten borough system and addressed the grievances of the nation's largest class of underrepresented voters, urban residents (Graham, 1972). Next came the 24th Amendment, which in 1964 prohibited the poll taxes long used to disenfranchise the poor and people of color, and in 1965, the Voting Rights Act empowering federal government intervention in state affairs to protect access to the ballot. Johnson's dogged commitment to home rule for Washington, DC aimed to complete this program of national enfranchisement.

These formal changes to the constitutional framework of citizenship were amplified by the citizen engagement focus of the Johnson domestic program, the War on Poverty requirement of "maximum feasible participation" by citizens (Davies, 1996; Marris & Rein, 1982). War on Poverty initiatives responded to and were supported by rising citizen activism, prominently including the Black freedom struggle. Washington, DC was a key node in the dense, nationwide, network of association that leveraged the strength of this movement for full African American citizenship. Locally, Washington, DC hosted the era's iconic 1963 March for Jobs and Justice. Malcolm X arrived that same year to establish Nation of Islam Mosque No. 4 (Marable, 2011). The Southern Christian Leadership Conference was represented in the District through New Bethel Baptist minister Walter Fauntroy, a Martin Luther King Jr. lieutenant and leading local activist (Garrow, 1999). Marion Barry, who in 1960 had served as first chair of the Student Nonviolent Coordinating Committee, relocated to Washington, DC in 1965 to open its local chapter (Carson, 1981). This surge of activism fed the Johnson administration's energetic prosecution of the War on Poverty in the Federal City.

A second aspect of the national policy approach to the cities visible in 1960s Washington, DC was decision makers' continued reliance on social program interventions intended to improve governance or community quality of life in preference to interventions addressed to the growing precariousness of the city's place in the national economy. Great Society urban policy making took place at the cusp of a transition in the nation's approach to its cities. Mid-century liberal thought understood the city as first and foremost a civic community, a part of the public sphere that required and merited public investment. Johnson administration urban experts viewed the city as an essential mechanism of American democracy: it was in cities that diverse citizens mingled, argued, bargained, and made political decisions (Weaver, 1964; Wood, 1958, 1977). In the years between Lyndon Baines Johnson's (LBJ) arrival in the Oval Office and Richard Nixon's (RN) departure from it, this view of the city as fundamentally a civic place shifted toward a new "growth machine" concept that understood the city as an enterprise, one that ought to be made to pay for itself (Logan & Molotch, 1987). The difficulty of this transition was reflected in the choices federal decision makers made for Washington, DC. In 1960s DC, federal policy offered resources for the betterment of the city as a civic community, but failed to grapple with the looming problem of its viability as an economic enterprise.

National policy concerns were also reflected in a third development, that of an aggressive push by federal officials for local government reform. A recalibration of federal system relations was being forced by Americans' demands for increases in the quantity and quality of public services; the growing disparity between ample federal tax revenues and meager state and local receipts; the demonstrated fecklessness of state governments as stewards of their cities; and growing public support for national policy goals and the federal action necessary to achieve them. The resulting federal system reform efforts—LBJ's "Creative Federalism" and RN's "New Federalism" initiatives—aimed at bettering the woeful condition of municipal government administrative competence and at assimilating cities into direct partnership with the federal government in the implementation of national policy. In DC, these efforts led to a series of administrative reforms, culminating in the reorganization provisions included in the 1973 federal grant of limited home rule. Although celebrated largely as steps toward self-government, these measures were also important advances in removing obstacles in government structure to the economic development process (Clement, 2014).

Citizen Participation

Johnson-era funding built a network of grassroots organizations in Washington, DC. The Great Society initiatives worked in space that had been cleared by earlier rounds of national policy intervention in the city—federally mandated desegregation, urban renewal, and highway building—which had toppled a previous generation of civic associations. The new organizations were jerrybuilt and collapsed as federal funding ebbed, but by the time they fell they had remade DC's civic climate.

The rapid demographic shifts of the mid-20th century wracked the District of Columbia with special force. Wartime Washington, DC had grown by more than 20%, from 663,000 residents in 1940 to just more than 800,000 in 1950, with one estimate pegging peak population at 899,000, in 1946.[1] Decline was equally precipitous. In each decennial census after 1950, Washington, DC lost population, until bottoming out in 2000 at 572,000. The steepest drop, 15%, came during the 1970s (US Bureau of the Census, 2012). However, simple population tallies mask the significant socioeconomic change then under way in the nation's capital. The District was experiencing not only the stresses of rapidly fluctuating population levels but also the stresses of socioeconomic transition. During the 1950s, Washington, DC lost 173,000 White residents and gained 131,000 Black residents (US Bureau of the Census, 1960). Many of the newcomers were poor, and social welfare costs increased markedly. DC appropriations for public welfare operating expenses stood at $17.5 million in 1960, and at $32 million in 1967. The welfare department served an average of 23,347 residents per month in 1959; in 1967, it served 47,878 (Washington Board of Trade Economic Development Committee, 1968).

Added to this demographic tumult were the impacts of the new federal engagement with the city. No municipality was more thoroughly roiled by federal policy makers than Washington, DC, the Federal City. In a mere half-dozen years, 1948–1954, the *de jure* scaffolding of DC segregation was entirely stripped away. In 1948, *Hurd v. Hodge* denied District homeowners the use of racially restrictive covenants. The 1953 Thompson's Restaurant case resurrected the city's "Lost Laws," ending discrimination in public accommodations (District of Columbia v. John R. Thompson Co., Inc., 1953). Washington, DC's segregated school system fell immediately with the Supreme Court's May 1954 decision in *Bolling v. Sharpe* (one of the five cases collected as *Brown v. Board of Education*), since the Eisenhower administration insisted on action in time for that school year's autumn term. Simultaneous with these recalibrations of Washingtonians' civil rights, federal urban renewal began its disruption of city dwellers' property rights. *Berman v. Parker*, challenging urban redevelopment in Southwest DC, was decided by the Court just six months after *Bolling*, and validated the public taking of private property for urban redevelopment. Together, desegregation and the federal reworking of urban land use exploded the foundations of traditional Washington, DC civil society (Pritchett, 2003).

The results of this turmoil were reflected in the withering away of the civic organizations that had once regulated life in the nation's capital. The authority of the Federation of Citizens Associations collapsed under the heap of derision that mounted as it stoutly refused to disavow its "Whites-only" policy well into the 1960s. The Black Federation of Civic Associations also was undermined. Its membership, made up of longtime residents and homeowners, was too conservative to lead the Black freedom activism then emerging in DC (Clement, 2004).

There were losses associated with these sweeping renovations of the 1950s and early 1960s, but the transition opened space in the District's social terrain into which rising constituencies and their organizations moved rapidly. A lush crop of new community organizations blossomed, watered by War on Poverty resources (Paka, 1970). The United Planning Organization (UPO), formed in 1962 to steward the Kennedy administration anti-juvenile delinquency initiatives being piloted in the Cardozo neighborhood, was designated to administer War on Poverty funding for the entire metropolitan area (Gilliam, 1964a; Schuette, 1962). In 1965, as Sargent Shriver's Office of Economic Opportunity (OEO) geared up War on Poverty programs in earnest, UPO outreach spawned a network of community centers. Some of these, like CHANGE, Inc., in Columbia Heights, soon demanded autonomy and spun themselves off as independent community development organizations (Gilliam, 1964b; Lewis, 1966). Another layer of organization followed in 1966, based on President Johnson's instruction to HUD Secretary Robert Weaver to see to "the establishment . . . of a neighborhood center" in "every ghetto of America" (Johnson, 1966, p. 585). Neighborhood centers were succeeded shortly by the Model Cities Ward Councils and the Model Cities Commission (Bernstein, 1968b; Levey, 1968), to which Commissioner-Mayor Walter Washington's administration quickly added a citywide set of "service area councils" (Moore, 1970) and, in the rebuilding effort after the 1968 riot, a network of "project area committees" (Meyer, 1972). As neighborhood activist and future DC Councilmember Nadine Winter observed at the time, the field was crowded. "We have groups to do physical planning and other groups to chop up, criticize and destroy the planners. We get dizzy trying to relate to a NCPC, a RLA, a CIP, a SAC, a PAC, and others, all working in Near Northeast within 30 blocks to do planning" (Aubin, 1971).

Great Society activism was not a substitute for democratic self-government. For one, the breadth of its outreach was questionable. One skeptical member of Congress conducted a survey and reported that most residents of targeted District neighborhoods were not even aware that a War on Poverty was going on (Weil, 1968). But even the more robust of the Great Society–funded newcomers faced challenges to their authority to speak for the community.

A case in point is MICCO, the Model Inner City Community Organization, formed as a dry run of the Model Cities program in Washington, DC's Shaw neighborhood a few months in advance of the launch of the national program, and shepherded by Reverend Walter E. Fauntroy. Using the federal grant for which Fauntroy, an LBJ advisor on African American affairs, had won the president's support, MICCO planners produced a neighborhood-wide plan for Shaw (Cohen, 1969; MICCO Inc., 1967). The group also began positioning itself to control potentially profitable development projects. In the process, MICCO activity began to draw together a network of Black Washingtonian entrepreneurs and professionals—people like developer Ted Hagans and attorney (later judge) Marjorie McKenzie Lawson (Braestrup, 1969b; Meyer, 1971). This machine building had the potential to create a foundation of locally based, mainstream

Black power—and in fact, it did serve as a foundation for Reverend Fauntroy's successful 1971 bid to become DC's first congressional delegate, a position he held for 20 years.

But MICCO's prominence also drew opposition. Although MICCO claimed it was a consortium made up of 150 Shaw-based organizations, rival community groups disputed its grassroots authenticity and its authority to speak for the neighborhood (Kaiser, 1968b; Meyer & Smith, 1972). The attempt to use grassroots planning efforts to stand in for democratically elected decision makers led down a troubled path. MICCO exacerbated the friction by siding with more powerful Black business interests against struggling Shaw merchants. For example, it backed the African American entrepreneurs operating together as "Uptown Progress" in their bid to control the 14th and U Street site of the present-day Reeves Center. Ella Jean Brown, whose carry-out restaurant at that corner was slated for demolition, organized her small business neighbors as NICCO—the Neighborhood Inner-City Community Organization—to resist the move, but was unable to muster resources equal to those of MICCO and Uptown Progress (Braestrup, 1969a).

But if the role of specific Great Society–funded organizations was controversial, there was nonetheless agreement that these community initiatives altered Washington, DC civics. Great Society resources—rhetoric as well as dollars—jolted awake the District's long-comatose political scene. The effort "unleashed pent-up energy at the grassroots level, spun off new organizations, spurred protest movements and set in motion a new activist way of getting things done in Washington," observed one *Washington Post* reporter. "Call it what you will," opined another, "the fact is that thousands of Washingtonians are beginning to take a meaningful part ... in bringing about change." "The most significant work" of the OEO-spawned grassroots organizations was "their role in sparking citizen interest" (Clopton, 1968; Morgan, 1966b).

The new activism spawned "an interesting crop of new and surprisingly sophisticated political leaders," and a citywide corps "of community workers, with channels into the poorest slums." Some of these activists operated through the War on Poverty–funded organizations themselves, but others were "emerging as leaders less through the poverty program than through the poverty program doctrine of action and change" and tended "to be more militant, more change-minded, more interested in tactics" (Clopton, 1968; Morgan, 1966b).

This "creeping democracy" was seen as "having a ripple effect," catalyzing a new structure of grassroots organization in the city. The city's veteran political professionals saw "in the recent stirrings the makings of a viable party system." Contemporaries observed that the new activism had "already produced ... the start of what could become a system of patronage," and noted that some activists "go so far as to call the new force 'our own machine'" and that the efforts had the "potential for creating the city's first grassroots power structure." Smiled the

Washington Post editors, "The ghosts of the bosses would be vastly amused to see the reformers sweating now to rebuild what they spent 50 years tearing down" (Clopton, 1968; Morgan, 1966b; Politics of poverty, 1965).

The new organizations, based on neighborhood convening rather than citywide balloting, and operating through planning rather than politics, failed to provide a widely acceptable substitute for representative government. But although the Great Society proved unable to deliver self-government for the District, its programs did succeed in the important task of engaging Washingtonians in democratic action. Great Society programs left their imprint in the new limited home rule government's provisions for citizen participation, in their success in making grassroots input into development decisions part of the District's civic ideology, and in training the cadre of managers who would staff the new District government under mayors Walter Washington and Marion Barry.

Urban Economic Viability

While providing separate pools of funding both to Washington, DC neighborhoods and to DC's downtown, Great Society efforts did not yield an integrated approach to the city's economic woes nor address its precarious position in the metropolitan economy. Johnson's major urban initiative, the Model Cities program, addressed itself narrowly to distressed neighborhoods. The approach was based on the view that the American economy, then at its postwar zenith, was powerful enough to provide for the well-being of all and that equitable distribution of benefits could be ensured simply by guaranteeing that all citizens had access to economic and political participation. The Great Society's bifurcated approach to DC's marginalized neighborhoods and its financial stakeholders was insufficient to connect the two.

In the decade during which the American concept of the city transitioned from one of "civic community" to one of "economic enterprise," Washington, DC business stakeholders kept a foot in each camp. The city's business leaders recognized and took seriously their duties of community stewardship. But it was the specter of urban economic collapse that absorbed their attention.

The importance of the local business establishment is amplified in a city denied self-government. The Washington Board of Trade, founded in 1889, operated as a shadow government. It pursued its stewardship of local interests through direct dealings with the congressional committees that had legal control of the District, circumventing citizens' groups and even the three presidentially appointed DC commissioners charged with day-to-day operations. A second, even more reclusive and powerful organization, the Federal City Council, had been formed in 1954, on the model of the Pittsburgh Alleghany Conference, to champion urban renewal in Washington, DC. In 1959, the Council had in turn organized

Downtown Progress, Inc., a coalition of DC bankers, downtown department stores, and public utilities, tasking it with reviving the city's faltering downtown. Among them, these three groups championed economic development, sought to protect the DC tax base, and attempted to forward the interests of the District in its heated competition with suburban jurisdictions (Allen, 1973; Brown, 2004; Elfenbein, 1989; McArdle, 1973).

The Board of Trade provided a handy target for DC's increasingly vociferous Black power activists and statehood advocates seeking to heighten the contradictions between their own positions and that of the establishment in the ongoing battles for African American empowerment and home rule in Washington, DC. The reality of the business stakeholders' day-to-day operations was less sinister than it was made to appear. Like the social activists, these business activists, if operating with less-than-perfect information, nonetheless were deeply concerned about the state of their city and took seriously the responsibilities of stewardship that they claimed for themselves. Members were receptive to the plight of the District's marginalized citizens. The Board recognized that "the problem of housing for low and moderate income groups" was "without question, the most serious human and economic problem facing our City today" (Kreimann, 1965b; Washington Board of Trade, 1965).[2] The organization advocated public workforce development programs for the District's unemployed and sponsored annual campaigns to identify summer jobs for disadvantaged youth (Strengthen youth program, 1967, 1968; Sullivan & GWBOT Task Force for Community Development, 1966; Valentine, 1969; Washington Board of Trade Economic Development Committee, n.d.). By 1970, the Board of Trade's president-elect, Giant Food's Joseph Danzansky, was advocating a merger including the majority-Black DC Chamber of Commerce, the Board, and other area business groups (Danzansky, 1970; Elfenbein, 1989). Although the Board had long opposed home rule for Washington, DC—warning it was a sham that would leave real power with the Congress and might endanger the annual federal payment to the District—by 1972 it had joined the rest of the District in support (Elfenbein, 1989; Washington Board of Trade Economic Development Bureau, 1972).

But although business stakeholders were concerned about conditions in Washington, DC's poor neighborhoods, they saw city challenges from a perspective different from that of impoverished residents. For Board of Trade members, the key problem for Washington, DC, one that would determine the city's ability to provide for the welfare of any of its citizens, was that of sustaining economic development. In their view, the major challenge to the city's economic viability lay in competition from the suburbs. The District, Board members observed, was at the "verge of a potentially dangerous egress of capital" from the downtown in favor of outlying jurisdictions (Washington Board of Realtors Legislation and Taxation Committee, 1968; Washington Board of Trade Economic Development Bureau, 1972).

From the business perspective, the District's problem boiled down to figuring out how to maximize central business district development and thus strengthen the tax base. Business stakeholders worried over the inadequacy of the District's rickety public development arrangements and urged reform of the government process. The Board of Trade identified the scarcity of downtown land as another obstacle, and argued for zoning for increased density and raising the District's traditional height limitation as means of making room for continued growth (Rosinski & Washington Board of Trade Community Planning Committee, 1965). To further expand the downtown area available for commercial development and fortify the District's anemic tax base, the Board advocated the use of urban renewal to clear blighted central city property for redevelopment (Washington Board of Trade Economic Development Bureau, 1971). The Board supported a speed-up in low-cost housing development, but proposed that such housing be sited in outlying areas, to preserve central city sites for taxable commercial development (Kreimann, 1965a). High on the business community's agenda was the promotion of major projects to spur economic development that would give the central city a leg up on its suburban competition. These included construction of a subway system and a convention center and revitalization of Pennsylvania Avenue in preparation for the national bicentennial in 1976 (Brown, 2004).

The major Great Society initiative for cities, the Model Cities program, did not speak to these business concerns. Model Cities altered the method for distributing federal resources within ghetto neighborhoods by giving control over the process to mayors, acting in conjunction with neighborhood groups. But it did nothing to alter the way resources were distributed in the metropolitan area as a whole by the existing processes of economic development (Demonstration Cities and Metropolitan Development Act, 1966). Nor did it challenge the interests of Washington, DC's business stakeholders in a way that might have forced them to engage with distressed neighborhoods. The interests of low-income residents had few points of connection with those of the elite business community. That low-income residents were not in high demand as members of the workforce is evidenced by the lengths to which the Board of Trade went each year to drum up summer jobs for disadvantaged youth. Nor did the inner city offer an attractive retail market. The April 1968 looting and arson that followed Martin Luther King Jr.'s assassination forced out the small businesses that had operated there; the heightened street tensions of the period and the unavailability of insurance kept them from returning (Asher and Kaiser, 1968; Bernstein, 1968a; Kaiser, 1968a). Sites in those neighborhoods were not yet prized for their development potential despite their central location. This lack of shared interest between the District's distressed neighborhoods and the business stakeholders struggling to keep the city economically viable in a competitive metropolitan environment meant that while inner-city communities may have had the empathy of elements of the business establishment, they did not engage its energies.

Those business energies were focused instead on winning congressional approval for projects to fortify the District's tax base, for example the drive to win the use of federal urban renewal funds for downtown redevelopment. Unlike any other city in the country, the District had been excluded from downtown urban renewal by a quirk in the program's statutory framework (Housing Act, 1954). The 1954 overhaul that had remade the national "urban redevelopment" program into "urban renewal" had expanded nonresidential use of federal renewal funding; but the amendment had been held not to include Washington, DC, and the House District Committee had been cold to local pleas that the oversight be repaired (Carper, 1964).[3]

Pressure intensified with Downtown Progress's 1961 completion of a revitalization plan for the central business district. The group, hoping to give the central city a leg up in its competition with the booming suburbs, began lobbying Congress for an amendment to permit use of federal urban renewal funds in the project. Much of the DC business community, as well as the *Washington Post* editorial board, strongly favored the proposal (Schuette, 1964; Politics of poverty, 1965). The local interests aligned in opposition were downtown leaseholders—businesses who would not be compensated for their loss of location if their buildings were condemned by the District as part of an urban renewal plan. These leaseholders included smaller downtown merchants (Businessmen's group, 1964) and, more tellingly, DC's parking lot magnates. It was the parking barons who could claim credit for the House District Committee's foot-dragging on the issue. Parking lot owners had cultivated close relations with the Committee. They had previously used their influence to win federal legislation banning the District from developing public parking lots and hoped now to protect their valuable holdings from the public planning process (Lardner, 1965; Morgan, 1966a). Hill intransigence was overwhelmed only by the Great Society exuberance of the 89th Congress. The necessary language was tacked onto the Johnson administration's 1965 omnibus housing act, circumventing the House District Committee (Housing and Urban Development Act, 1965). With the clarifying language in place, an initial federal planning grant for the downtown renewal project was immediately approved (Raspberry, 1965).

Mid-century optimism about the ability of the American system to provide for all, obviating the need for fundamental economic system reforms, along with a view of the city as a civic and political rather than an economic problem, circumscribed the Great Society's urban policy response. Johnson's signature urban effort, the Model Cities program, focused narrowly on improving conditions in distressed neighborhoods and failed to engage the efforts of the DC business community. The Johnson administration did deliver major benefits to the District's economic stakeholders, including resources for downtown renewal. But responses to the most pressing question confronting the city, that of its continued viability in the evolving American economy, remained beyond the limits of the Great Society strategy.

Administrative Redevelopment

Less remarked at the time, or since, than its conspicuous impacts in reconfiguring local civic organization and in intervening in economic development were the changes the Great Society made in the structure of District government. These changes, called for from all quarters, granted a modicum of local self-rule but were also necessary first steps toward remaking District government as a competent economic development partner.

The disruptions of federal desegregation orders, urban renewal, and highway building shone a spotlight on the limited administrative capability of American municipal government. In this, Washington, DC was, if not unique, an extreme case, snarled in the bureaucratic accretions of its 100 years as a federal agency. Congress's discretion in the District of Columbia was nearly absolute. From the institution of commissioner government in 1874, the city was treated as an "agency" of the federal government—utterly voteless, without representation of any kind at the local or national level, "administered," not governed (Fauntroy, 2010; Lessoff, 1994; Rimensnyder, 1975).

The most debilitating flaw in DC's commissioner government was the lack of an executive authority. Executive power assigned to a board of three commissioners was not likely to be exercised decisively, especially since the board operated as a committee. Although one of the commissioners was designated board president, his powers were in no way superior to those of his two colleagues (Grier, 1967; Hanson, 1971). In addition, commissioners were pinned, uncomfortably, between the Washington, DC agendas of the White House and the Hill, which grew increasingly divergent during the postwar period. As presidential appointees, commissioners were expected to administer the District in line with the chief executive's program for the city. As the national government was drawn more deeply into regulating the day-to-day lives of American citizens, presidents used directives for the District of Columbia to signal their positions on national policy matters.

But commissioners were also directly accountable to Congress, and in attempting to forward the White House agenda they risked running afoul of the House District Committee, the congressional body that most closely concerned itself with District affairs and whose policy positions generally stood in opposition to those of the executive. This committee set policy for the District and, in conjunction with District appropriations subcommittees, controlled the DC budget. Issues likely to come before the Committee were generally of peripheral importance in the national political conversation and unlikely to generate much legislative leverage for the lawmakers engaged with them. For that reason, House leadership used District Committee assignments to provide a fleeting first assignment to congressional freshmen, or for the longer-term shelving of mediocrities. This is not to say that appointment to the House District Committee lacked its attractions. Representatives, whose limited political ambitions were appropriately tailored to their limited political talents, flocked there. For them, District Committee rewards, which included both control of District patronage (city jobs and contracts) and political contributions from District Democratic and Republican party fundraisers (who lacked candidates of their own), were ample (Albrook, 1956b).

Even if executive authority for the District had been workably consolidated in a single officeholder and executive and legislative preferences harmonized, other features of the city's administrative terrain would have obstructed effective management. Perhaps because of the lack of a municipal executive able to initiate responses to public needs, Congress frequently addressed a new need by the creation of a new, special-purpose commission.[4] The proliferating boards and commissions were not directly responsible to the commissioners. Some board members were appointed by the commissioners, some by the president. While the commissioners were charged with negotiating the agencies' budgets with Congress, policy decisions, and authority over the District departments tasked with implementing them, frequently came under the purview of the boards, not the commissioners (Nelson Commission, 1972).

Largely unworkable from its beginnings, this DC administrative regime was overwhelmed by the demands for effective process and efficient decision making placed on Washington, DC's public agencies during the postwar period. Attempts to move plans for interstate highway connections, federal enclave extensions, Southwest urban redevelopment, a massive, 10-year public works program initiated in 1954, or the long-awaited cultural center, among other projects, highlighted District administrative gridlock.[5]

Enactment of Model Cities forced a first step toward reorganization of DC government development agencies. A chief objective of the legislation was to strengthen local governments in order to make them capable partners in the implementation of national urban policy (Clement, 2014). The statute made the demonstration of the ability to administer the complex Model Cities program—designed to coordinate the full range of social welfare as well as physical redevelopment initiatives for an all-out attack on slum conditions—a prerequisite for Model Cities funding (Demonstration Cities, §103(a)(4)).

Schuyler Lowe, who as the DC director of general administration was widely recognized as the *eminence grise* behind the management of local Washington, DC, seized on the Model Cities directive as an opportunity to consolidate District development functions under the purview of one general manager reporting to the commissioners (Kaiser, 1967b). In addition to rationalizing District management of development processes, the plan Lowe submitted in the spring of 1967 had the advantage of moving control of land-use decisions out from under the engineer-commissioner, a position filled by an officer in the Army Corps of Engineers detailed by the president (An Act, 1878, §2). Washingtonians had long chafed under this "military rule," reasoning that whatever the caliber of the individual appointed he was likely to have greater sympathy for military protocol than for the complex social problems of the city (Lessoff, 1994). Although Lowe was forced out of office in his struggle with Engineer-Commissioner Robert E. Mathe, resigning abruptly in May 1967, the commissioners adopted a form of his plan, consolidating renewal and Model Cities functions and moving them into civilian control (Kaiser, 1967a, 1967c).

By the time of Director Lowe's departure, the prospect of further reform was visible on the horizon. Lyndon Johnson had made an all-out push for a DC Home Rule Act in 1965, but had been beaten back by Congress—the first substantive defeat for his Great Society agenda (Califano, 1991). LBJ had refused to abandon the cause. DC Home Rule was part of the general movement of the period to expand the franchise, especially on behalf of urban dwellers and African Americans. In addition, Johnson viewed home rule for DC, then a majority-Black city, as the capstone of his contribution to the Black freedom movement. Disappointed in his legislative effort, Johnson moved to reform District government using his executive authority, sending a reorganization plan to the Hill in June 1967 (Reorganization, 1967). Legislators debated the measure during July—the examples of riot-engulfed Newark and Detroit flickering before their eyes—and allowed it to go into effect.

Contemporaries celebrated this move as a step toward home rule, but it had granted only the form, not the substance of self-government (Grier, 1967). Patterned on a proposal made by the Truman administration, and thereafter promoted by the federal Bureau of the Budget, Johnson's Reorganization Plan No. 3 of 1967 gave Washington, DC a "commissioner-mayor" and a nine-member Council to replace its three-commissioner government. But the officials would still be appointed by the president, not elected by locals (D.C. reform, 1967). The significance of this plan for DC governance was that it at last consolidated executive authority in one official, ending the fragmentation that had bedeviled District program administration (Johnson, 1967). DC native Walter E. Washington, recalled to the District from his post as head of the New York City Housing Authority, was sworn in as commissioner-mayor, and local businessman John Hechinger as Council chair, in November 1967.

A third major reform entailed reorganization of District government's development apparatus, long a chief desideratum of the Washington, DC business community (Albrook, 1960; Scharfenberg, 1972). Board of Trade representatives pointed out that the hopeless snarls in the District's planning and development labyrinth were sending development projects, desperately needed by the District's flagging tax base, over the border into suburban Maryland and Virginia (Washington Board of Trade, 1963). The Federal City Council had submitted a reorganization proposal as recently as 1961, only to see it dead-end in Congress (Schuette, 1964). The District's entrepreneurs were not the sole complainants:

pleas for reform came from citizens whose community development plans were stymied, and from District government itself. With these concerns in mind, the president fortified his 1967 reorganization of DC government with a series of orders in the spring of 1968 that transferred to the commissioner-mayor the authority to carry out the functions of the National Capital Housing Authority, the Redevelopment Land Agency, and the Board of Recreation (Executive Order 11,401; Reorganization Plan No. 4 of 1968; Reorganization Plan No. 3 of 1968).

Enactment of the limited Home Rule bill, finally passed by the 93rd Congress in autumn 1973 and signed into law by President Nixon that Christmas Eve (District, 1973), capped this phase of DC governance reform. Working from the findings of the Nelson Commission that Congress established in 1970 to make recommendations for DC government restructuring, the DC Self-Government and Governmental Reorganization Act of 1973 merged the National Capital Housing Authority and the Redevelopment Land Agency into DC government proper (An Act, 1970; District, 1973, §§ 201, 202; Nelson Commission, 1972). The act also tussled with the vexed question of the separation of federal and local interests in administration of DC planning, assigning initial authority for the latter to the new DC government (District, 1973, § 203).

Taken together, the modifications required by the Model Cities program and the restructuring brought about by Johnson's reorganization and the Nixon administration's limited Home Rule Act had begun the process of converting District government into a competent public partner in urban economic development efforts.

Moving Forward

By the time Richard Nixon left office in August 1974, Washington, DC was a city transformed. The decade 1964–1974 had altered the pattern of civic participation, experimented with responses to the growing problem of urban economic viability, and remade governance structures.

Great Society funding and ethos had called forth civic activism, trained organizers, and left a legacy of grassroots organizational structures and statutory citizen participation requirements. Going forward, the issue was whether newly empowered citizens could maintain momentum, locating the resources and innovating the organizational forms to sustain participation and give it impact. Civic exuberance would have to find ways of translating itself into permanent government process if its benefits were to be preserved.

Great Society initiatives had made bold steps to address one existential challenge to urban viability—that of Washington, DC's glaring social inequities—but had side-stepped the equally pressing problem of urban economic sustainability. War on Poverty and Model Cities programs had aimed to stabilize and strengthen impoverished city neighborhoods, but did not offer the means of assimilating them into the economic life of the District as a whole. Sustaining the economic life of the District as a whole had been left to the aging urban renewal workhorse. The repositioning of Washington, DC in the economy of the greater metropolitan area presented a looming challenge that was as yet unaddressed.

Great Society efforts had also restructured DC governance. Most conspicuously, the changes had extended self-government, culminating in the 1973 limited Home Rule bill. More subtle, but significant, were reforms aimed at improving administrative competence. The consolidation of the municipal executive power, creation of local planning capacity, and repositioning of formerly independent land-use agencies under direct mayoral control were first steps toward recreating DC government as a competent economic development actor.

The result was, in sum, a civic landscape of opportunity and challenge. The 1960s left Washington, DC a city full of progressive promise, teetering hopefully on uncertain foundations.

Acknowledgments

The author gratefully acknowledges the U.S. Department of Housing and Urban Development and the Lyndon B. Johnson Presidential Library, which provided support for the research on which this essay is based.

Notes

1 Peak population estimate by Ludivine Gilli, Centre de recherches d'histoire nord-américaine, Sorbonne, December 2011. H-Urban discussion. http://h-net.msu.edu/cgi-bin/logbrowse.pl?trx=vx&list=H-Urban&month=1112&week=d&msg=2/YKxXt01ISY1B%2bIKyKkLA&user=&pw=.
2 The Board dabbled in low-cost housing production with the 468-unit Belford Towers development in Prince George's County, completed in 1969 (Elfenbein, 1989, p. 88).
3 The prohibition was the result of a statutory anomaly. The District's urban renewal program operated under the authority of the DC Redevelopment Land Act of 1945 (Pub. L. No. 79–592, 60 Stat. 790, August 2, 1946), a predecessor to the 1949 Housing Act (Pub. L. No. 81–171, 63 Stat. 413, July 15, 1949) that created the national urban redevelopment program. Like the DC act, the 1949 statute had provided only for redevelopment directed to residential uses. In 1954, Congress had amended the national program to allow for use of redevelopment funds in cities' commercial districts. (Housing Act of 1954, Pub. L. No. 83–560, 68 Stat. 590, August 2, 1954). In the view of some, the 1954 amendment applied to the District, but others argued to the contrary and DC corporation counsel ruled in favor of the latter, leaving Washington, DC the only major US city without a downtown urban renewal program.
4 The National Capital Parks and Planning Commission (1926); the National Capital Housing Authority (created as the DC Alley Dwelling Authority in 1934); the Board

of Recreation (1942); the Redevelopment Land Agency (1946); the National Capital Transportation Agency (1960) were among the results.

5 In addition to the physical redevelopment efforts taxing municipal capacity, these years witnessed administrative growing pains in the District, including creation of a comprehensive plan for the city (1950); reorganization of its administrative structure (1952); institution of the city's first housing code (1955); and revision of the DC zoning ordinance (1958).

References

Action at last. (1965, July 30). *The Washington Post, Times Herald (1959–1973)*, p. A20.

Albrook, R. C. (1956, November 18). A cure for all jealous constituents. *The Washington Post and Times Herald (1954–1959)*, p. E8.

Albrook, R. C. (1960, October 2). Some changes may be in the offing. *The Washington Post, Times Herald (1959–1973)*, p. E2.

Allen, R. W. (1973, January). A summary of twentieth century economic development of the District of Columbia and the Washington metropolitan area. *Records of the Columbia Historical Society, Washington, D.C., 49*, 532–555.

An Act Providing a Permanent Form of Government for the District of Columbia, 20 Stat. 102 (June 11, 1878).

An Act to Establish a Commission on the Organization of the Government of the District of Columbia and to Provide for a Delegate to the House of Representatives from the District of Columbia. Pub. L. No. 91–405, 84 Stat. 845 (September 22, 1970).

Asher, R. L., & Kaiser, R. G. (1968, December 29). Broken promises line riot area streets. *The Washington Post, Times Herald (1959–1973)*, p. B1.

Aubin, H. (1971, August 17). Urban agencies plan proposed by council. *The Washington Post, Times Herald (1959–1973)*, p. B4.

Baker v. Carr. 1962, 369 U.S. 186.

Berman v. Parker. 1954, 348 U.S. 26.

Bernstein, C. (1968a, June 15). Insurance, tourism: Business still suffers: Cancellations go on despite reassurances costs up five fold. *The Washington Post, Times Herald (1959–1973)*, p. B1.

Bernstein, C. (1968b, October 29). Citizens get model cities plan role. *The Washington Post, Times Herald (1959–1973)*, p. B1.

Bolling et al. v. Sharpe et al. 1954, 347 U.S. 497.

Braestrup, P. (1969a, June 8). Office building foes stage rally. *The Washington Post, Times Herald (1959–1973)*, p. 25.

Braestrup, P. (1969b, December 31). Political fight stalls NW renewal plan. *The Washington Post, Times Herald (1959–1973)*, p. B1.

Brown, K. A. (2004). *Make no little plans: The first 50 years of the Federal City Council.* Charlottesville, VA: Milestones Historical Consultants.

Brown v. Board of Education of Topeka, Kansas. 1954, 347 U.S. 483.

Businessmen seek 4600 youth jobs. (1968, April 3). *The Washington Post, Times Herald (1959–1973)*, p. B3.

Businessmen's group opposes urban renewal. (1964, September 14). *The Washington Post, Times Herald (1959–1973)*, p. D9.

Califano, J. A. (1991). *The triumph & tragedy of Lyndon Johnson: The White House years.* New York, NY: Simon & Schuster.

Carper, E. (1964, August 1). Senate votes renewal of downtown: Provision carried in $1.2 billion housing measure has been in question. *The Washington Post, Times Herald (1959–1973)*, p. A1.

Carson, C. (1981). *In struggle: SNCC and the black awakening of the 1960s.* Cambridge, MA: Harvard University Press.

Clement, B. J. (2004). Pushback: The white community's dissent from "Bolling." *Washington History, 16*(2).

Clement, B. J. (2014). Creative federalism and urban policy: Placing the city in the Great Society. Washington, DC: George Washington University.

Clopton, W., Jr. (1968, December 1). A new thing for district—political spirit: News analysis a new thing for D.C., political awareness. *The Washington Post, Times Herald (1959–1973)*, p. B1.

Cohen, V. (1969, January 6). Final MICCO plan filed. *The Washington Post, Times Herald (1959–1973)*, p. C2.

Danzansky, J. B. (1970, December 26). Pool area resources, Danzansky suggests. *The Washington Post, Times Herald (1959–1973)*, p. C4.

Davies, G. (1996). *From opportunity to entitlement: The transformation and decline of Great Society liberalism.* Lawrence, KS: University Press of Kansas.

D.C. reform: An old problem. (1967, June 1). *The Washington Post, Times Herald (1959–1973)*, p. F1.

Demonstration Cities and Metropolitan Development Act. Pub. L. No. 89–754, 80 Stat. 1255 (November 3, 1966).

District of Columbia Self-Government and Governmental Reorganization Act. 1973. Pub. L. No. 93–198, 87 Stat. 774 (December 24, 1973).

District of Columbia v. John R. Thompson Co., Inc., 203 F.2d 579 (D.C. Cir.), reversed and remanded, 346 U.S. 100 (June 8, 1953).

Elfenbein, J. I. (1989). *Civics, commerce, and community: The history of the greater Washington Board of Trade, 1889–1989.* Washington, DC: Center for Washington Area Studies of the George Washington University.

Executive Order 11,401, "Modifying Executive Order No. 6868 of October 9, 1934, as Amended, Designating the Authority to Carry Out the Provisions of the District of Columbia Alley Dwelling Act," 33 F.R. 4559, 3 C.F.R., 1968 Comp., p. 106 (March 13, 1968).

Fauntroy, M. K. (2010). Home rule for the District of Columbia. In R. W. Walters & T. M. Travis (Eds.), *Democratic destiny and the District of Columbia: Federal politics and public policy.* Lanham, MD: Lexington Books, 21–43.

Fiske, P. R. (1969, February 1). President visits riot site: Work begun on small park in ruined area; shaking hands. *The Washington Post, Times Herald (1959–1973)*. P. A1.

Garrow, D. J. (1999). *Bearing the cross: Martin Luther King, Jr., and the Southern Christian Leadership Conference.* New York, NY: Quill.

Gillette, H. (1995). *Between justice and beauty: Race, planning, and the failure of urban policy in Washington, D.C.* Baltimore, MD: The Johns Hopkins University Press.

Gilliam, D. (1964a, August 16). D.C. to get $7.5 million for anti-poverty work. *The Washington Post*, p. B6.

Gilliam, D. (1964b, November 25). Bulk of $1.4 million set for centers in 4 neighborhoods: Expects more funds pleased with grant district gets $1,455,980 for attack on poverty. *The Washington Post, Times Herald (1959–1973)*, p. A1.

Graham, G. S. (1972). *One man, one vote: Baker v. Carr and the American levellers.* Boston, MA: Little Brown.

Grier, G.W. (1967). *D.C. reorganization: Making it work. Improving the government of the national capital, report no. 2.* Washington, DC: Washington Center for Metropolitan Studies.

Hanson, R. (1971). *Governing the District of Columbia.* Community Governance, no. 3. Washington, DC: Washington Center for Metropolitan Studies.

Hirsch, A. R. (1983). *Making the second ghetto: Race and housing in Chicago, 1940–1960.* Historical Studies of Urban America. Chicago, IL: The University of Chicago Press.

Housing Act of 1954, Pub. L. No. 83–560, 68 Stat. 590 (August 2, 1954).

Housing and Urban Development Act of 1965, Pub. L. No. 89–117, 79 Stat. 451 (August 10, 1965).

Hurd et ux. v. Hodge et al. 1948, 334 U.S. 24.

Johnson, L. B. (1966). Remarks at Columbus Circle, Syracuse, New York, August 19, 1966. In *Public papers of the president—Lyndon B. Johnson, 1966, Book II,* 844. Washington, DC: US Government Printing Office.

Johnson, L. B. (1967). Special message to the Congress transmitting Reorganization Plan 3 of 1967: Government of the District of Columbia. In *Public papers of the President—Lyndon B. Johnson, 1966, Book I,* 585–89. Washington, DC: US Government Printing Office.

Kaiser, R. G. (1967a, May 12). Schuyler Lowe to quit as District's top aide. *The Washington Post, Times Herald (1959–1973),* p. A1.

Kaiser, R. G. (1967b, May 21). D.C. officials in confusion: News analysis extra effort exerted District confused on reorganization model city needs personnel needs. *The Washington Post, Times Herald (1959–1973),* p. B1.

Kaiser, R. G. (1967c, June 28). D.C. to hire super grade city planner. *The Washington Post, Times Herald (1959–1973),* p. A1.

Kaiser, R. G. (1968a, August 1). Burned out in riot, many owners won't reopen. *The Washington Post, Times Herald (1959–1973),* p. H3.

Kaiser, R. G. (1968b, August 31). City generates ideas but little action—red tape snarls agencies' projects: News analysis. *The Washington Post, Times Herald (1959–1973),* B1.

Keyssar, A. (2000). *The right to vote: The contested history of democracy in the United States.* New York, NY: Basic Books.

Kreimann, W. V. (1965a). Memo to: Members, Community Planning Committee; In Re: meeting for Tuesday, April 13, 1965; agenda, April 6, 1965. Greater Washington Board of Trade Papers, Box 148, Folder 12 — Regional / City Planning & Development, Housing. George Washington University, GLSC.

Kreimann, W. V. (1965b). Memo to: Members, Community Planning Committee; In Re: Housing problems in the District of Columbia ["information only—not adopted"], May 14, 1965. Greater Washington Board of Trade Papers, Box 148, Folder 12—Regional / City Planning & Development, Housing. George Washington University, GLSC.

Lardner, G., Jr. (1965, September 30). Group tries to maim downtown renewal. *The Washington Post, Times Herald (1959–1973),* p. A23.

Lessoff, A. (1994). *The nation and its city: Politics, corruption, and progress in Washington, D.C., 1861–1902.* Baltimore, MD: The Johns Hopkins University Press.

Levey, R. F. (1968, December 23). Model cities panel installed, mayor's 5 appointees named. *The Washington Post, Times Herald (1959–1973),* p. C1.

Lewis, J. W. (1966, February 9). Antipoverty agency taking steps to split away from UPO: Called CHANGE. *The Washington Post, Times Herald (1959–1973),* p. B1.

Logan, J. R., & Molotch, H. L. (1987). *Urban fortunes: The political economy of place.* Berkeley, CA: University of California Press.

Marable, M. (2011). *Malcolm X: A life of reinvention.* New York, NY: Viking.

Marris, P., & Rein, M. (1982). *Dilemmas of social reform: Poverty and community action in the United States.* Chicago, IL: The University of Chicago Press.

McArdle, W. F. (1973). The development of the business sector in Washington, D.C., 1800–1973. *Records of the Columbia Historical Society, Washington, D.C., 49* (January), 556–594.

Meyer, E. (1971, September 5). Shaw area proposals create rift: Talked to several. *The Washington Post, Times Herald (1959–1973)*, p. A1.

Meyer, E. (1972, May 28). 14th St. corridor gets renewal unit. *The Washington Post, Times Herald (1959–1973)*, p. D11.

Meyer, E. L., & Smith, J. Y. (1972, February 21). MICCO's Critics: Shaw Agency Said to Benefit Fauntroy, Not 'Little Guy'. *The Washington Post, Times Herald (1959–1973)*, p. A1.

MICCO, Inc. (1967). MICCO annual report—planning for Shaw: with the people, by the people, for the people. Fauntroy Papers I, Box 25, Folder 18. George Washington University, GLSC.

Moore, I. (1970, January 3). Mayor to split city into service areas: Decentralization of services planned in D.C. *The Washington Post, Times Herald (1959–1973)*, p. 1.

Morgan, D. (1966a, March 20). Two Men Build Fortune on Need for Parking: Names Seldom Seen. *The Washington Post, Times Herald (1959–1973)*, p. A1.

Morgan, D. (1966b, June 16). Poverty war voice is heard: Gains semblance of political organization here. *The Washington Post, Times Herald (1959–1973)*, p. F1.

Nelson Commission [Commission on the Organization of the Government of the District of Columbia]. (1972). *Report of the Commission on the Organization of the Government of the District of Columbia.* Washington, DC: US Government Printing Office.

Paka, V. (1970, January 2). The new politics of poverty and renewal: A new style of big-city politics is rising in central Washington. Six years of federal grants have created overlapping layers of street-level organizations now energetically seeking the support of the inner city's long-neglected citizen. *The Washington Post, Times Herald (1959–1973)*, p. B1.

Pritchett, W. E. (2003). The "public menace" of blight: Urban renewal and the private uses of eminent domain. *Yale Law & Policy Review, 21*(1), 1–52.

Raspberry, W. J. (1965, October 30). $1 million granted to launch study of downtown renewal. *The Washington Post, Times Herald (1959–1973)*, p. B1.

Reorganization Plan No. 3 of 1967. 1967. Vol. 32 F.R. 11669, 81 Stat. 948, as amended Pub. L. No. 90–623, Sec. 7(b), Oct. 22, 1968, 82 Stat. 1315.

Reorganization Plan No. 3 of 1968, eff. May 23, 1968. 33 F.R. 7747, 82 Stat. 1370 (March 13, 1968).

Reorganization Plan No. 4 of 1968, eff. June 30, 1968. 33 F.R. 7749, 82 Stat. 1371 (March 13, 1968).

Rimensnyder, N. F. (1975). *The political evolution of the District of Columbia: Current status and proposed alternatives.* Washington, DC: Library of Congress Congressional Research Service.

Rosinski, D. C., & Washington Board of Trade Community Planning Committee. (1965). National Capital Planning Commission report 1965/1985 — proposed physical development policies for Washington, D.C., December 1, 1965. Greater Washington Board of Trade Papers, Box 148, Folder 13 — Regional / City Planning & Development, Policy 1964–67. George Washington University, GLSC.

Scharfenberg, K. (1972, May 18). Super unit held vital to renewal. *The Washington Post, Times Herald (1959–1973)*, p. A6.

Schuette, P. A. (1962, December 16). New agency to combat delinquency: President's Committee Grant. *The Washington Post, Times Herald (1959–1973)*, p. A25.

Schuette, P.A. (1964, October 11). Urban renewal needs renewing: Shopper-pleasing plan. *The Washington Post, Times Herald (1959–1973)*, p. E1.

Strengthen youth program, D.C. Board of Trade urges: Funds cut in half board steps noted. (1967, April 20). *The Washington Post, Times Herald (1959–1973)*, p. B1.

Sullivan, Mark, Jr., & GWBOT Task Force for Community Development. (1966). Recommendations to the Board of Directors of the Metropolitan Washington Board of Trade with respect to the Community Renewal Program for the District of Columbia. November 21, 1966. Greater Washington Board of Trade Papers, Box 148, Folder 13—Regional / City Planning & Development, Policy 1964–67. George Washington University, GLSC.

The politics of poverty. (1965, April 27). *The Washington Post, Times Herald (1959–1973)*, p. A16.

US Bureau of the Census. (1960). Table 39: State of birth of the native population, by color, for the District of Columbia, 1900–1960. In *General Social and Economic Characteristics—District of Columbia*.

US Bureau of the Census. n.d. *Historical Data, Washington, D.C.*

US Bureau of the Census. (2012) Historical Statistics - The 2012 Statistical Abstract, "No. HS-4, Resident Population by State: 1900 to 2002". Retrieved September 19, 2015, from http://www.census.gov/compendia/statab/hist_stats.html.

Valentine, P. W. (1969, June 16). Businessmen top quota on jobs for poor: Businessmen exceed quota on jobs for poor. *The Washington Post, Times Herald (1959–1973)*, p. C1.

Voting Rights Act of 1965, Pub. L. No. 89–110, 79 Stat. 437 (August 6, 1965).

Washington Board of Realtors Legislation and Taxation Committee. (1968). Commentary on real estate taxation in the District of Columbia. Greater Washington Board of Trade Papers, Box 85, Folder 33 — Economic Development Committee—Research & Information Council—1968. George Washington University, GLSC.

Washington Board of Trade. (1963). A report of the Metropolitan Washington Board of Trade—Program for the reorganization of planning in the District of Columbia and the Washington Metropolitan Area. Greater Washington Board of Trade Papers, Box 148, Folder 14 — Regional / City Planning & Development, Policy 1968–1970. George Washington University, Gelman Library, Special Collections (hereinafter "GLSC").

Washington Board of Trade. (1965). Memo to: Community Planning Committee; In Re: District of Columbia Renewal Program—Policy Review—Final; Recommendation, November 19, 1965. Greater Washington Board of Trade Papers, Box 84, Folder 27—Community Planning. George Washington University, GLSC.

Washington Board of Trade. (1972, April). Board supports local self-government for D.C. *Board of Trade News*, 27(4). Greater Washington Board of Trade Papers, Box 184, Publications—Board of Trade News. George Washington University, GLSC.

Washington Board of Trade Economic Development Bureau. (1971). The 1972 Economic Development Program, January 4, 1971. Greater Washington Board of Trade Papers, Box 135, Folder 6—Economic Development Bureau—Program of Work. George Washington University, GLSC.

Washington Board of Trade Economic Development Bureau. (1972). Metropolitan Washington municipal budgets: How they work, Fall 1972. Greater Washington Board of

Trade Papers, Box 135, Folder 9—Economic Development Bureau—Municipal Budget. George Washington University, GLSC.

Washington Board of Trade Economic Development Committee. n.d. The Economic Development Program for 1970. Greater Washington Board of Trade Papers, Box 48, Folder 33—Economic Development Committee—1971. George Washington University, GLSC.

Washington Board of Trade Economic Development Committee. (1968). D.C. Appropriations—Public Welfare. Greater Washington Board of Trade Papers, Box 85, Folder 29—Economic Development Committee—Research & Information Council—1968. George Washington University, GLSC.

Weaver, R. C. (1964). *The urban complex: Human values in urban life.* Garden City, NY: Doubleday.

Weil, M. (1968, October 4). Poor "never heard" of antipoverty war. *The Washington Post, Times Herald (1959–1973)*, p. A9.

Wood, R. C. (1958). Metropolitan government, 1975: An extrapolation of trends—the new metropolis: Green belts, grass roots or gargantua? *The American Political Science Review, 52*(1), 108–122.

Wood, R. C. (1977). A matter of national urgency. *National Civic Review, 66*(1), 15–18.

4

HOME RULE FROM BELOW

The Cooperative Movement in Washington, DC

Johanna Bockman

In 1975, the District of Columbia formally began home rule. During the previous 100 years, the US Congress directly governed DC through the House and Senate Committees on the District of Columbia and through an appointed Board of Commissioners.[1] For many of those years, segregationist congressmen, like John L. McMillan of South Carolina, chair of the House Committee almost continuously from 1948 to 1972 (Fauntroy, 2003), dominated these committees. In addition, neighborhood associations composed mostly of White residents made local community decisions in the District (Travis, 2010). Rather than wait for society to change and offer equal participation in political and economic life, DC residents, in particular African Americans, excluded from these institutions built autonomous spheres to gain control over their lives and forged new resources in the District beyond formal government. When formal home rule did come to the District, it built on and expanded many of these already existing grassroots strategies to create areas of autonomy and local control in DC. Specifically, I argue that DC residents used the cooperative movement as a form of "home rule from below."

Long before formal home rule began, DC residents established consumer, worker, financial, purchasing, and housing cooperatives. African Americans had long supported cooperatives as a means to create economic wealth, political power, and cultural freedom.[2] Cooperatives proliferated throughout the city under Mayor Marion Barry, whose tenure from 1979 to 1991 brought home rule from below into the formal government and created new structures to support citywide community development based on cooperatives. Cooperatives represented one way to forge a new society, a society in which all members might be equal.

Cooperatives are just one part of "the common," resources held in common, such as nature, but also collective spaces, social activities involved in production and community building, and experiments in living that we create together. According to Hardt and Negri (2009), capitalists live off the common by privatizing it to make profits, thus destroying the common in the process. Private property is fundamentally different from the common. For Hardt and Negri, public property is also fundamentally different from the common because public property held by the government represents state domination and constituted power from above, "which not only guarantees capitalist exploitation and defends the rule of property but also maintains and polices all identity hierarchies" (2009, p. 355). In contrast to the constituted power of state sovereignty, the common expresses constitutive power, which can create autonomous spaces outside of private property and capital, and which can maintain equality and democracy through horizontal organizational structures. As a form of constitutive power, cooperatives in DC provided an avenue for residents to create a new social world of emergent home rule from below, at a time when Washington, DC lacked formal home rule. To realize home rule fully, even after formal home rule was implemented, DC residents needed to maintain and expand the common.

As Hardt and Negri predicted, however, the constituted powers of formal government over time undermined this home rule from below. This chapter explores the history of cooperatives in Washington, DC in the 20th century and how real estate agents, developers, and politicians were able to exploit these structures for their own benefit, fundamentally altering home rule from below into a more limited home rule from above.

Cooperatives Before Home Rule

Washington, DC has a long history of cooperatives. In 1880, the Rochdale Co-operative Society of the District of Columbia began, and by 1894 had 6,000 members. This consumer cooperative provided members access to low-priced goods through contracted dealers. Later, it ran a number of stores (Cooperative Society, 1894). The name came from the Rochdale Society of Equitable Pioneers founded in England in 1844 by a group of handloom weavers put out of work by machines (Conover, 1959). The Rochdale Society of Equitable Pioneers operated according to principles now called Rochdale Principles and practiced worldwide, including democratic control based on equality ("one member, one vote"), open membership, and equal rights for men and women in all membership affairs (Conover, 1959). Later principles included requirements that cooperatives provide assistance to already existing cooperatives and help to create new cooperatives. Cooperatives, it was hoped, might spread to create a new kind of society.[3]

Across the United States, from the 1870s to the 1890s, cooperatives were very popular. Cooperatives formed primarily among farmers, most famously assisted by the National Grange Association, which supported the use of the Rochdale Principles (Chaddad & Cook, 2012). In tandem, the Knights of Labor organized workers' cooperatives and the Sovereigns of Industry began organizing consumer cooperatives for urban workers. However, the District lacked cooperative laws that might allow cooperatives to incorporate as cooperatives, control who could use the name "cooperative," and encourage new cooperatives to form. As a result, any cooperatives functioning in DC had to incorporate in another state, most often in Virginia, or register as a corporation. If DC cooperatives incorporated in Virginia, they were required to hold their meetings there, and Virginia law recognized only farm cooperatives. Any nonfarm cooperatives were not allowed to use the word "cooperative" in their names (US Congress, 1940).[4] The expansion of cooperatives would have to wait for further developments.

The DC cooperative movement gained support from people like Kansas senator Arthur Capper, who headed the Senate Committee on the District of Columbia. Before his arrival in DC in 1919, he was a national supporter of cooperatives.[5] Capper successfully sponsored the 1922 Capper-Volstead Act and later laws allowing farmers to form cooperatives to process and market their products, rather than leaving farmers at the whim of larger corporate distributors.[6] Capper also sought to encourage nonfarm cooperatives. Once he arrived in DC, he submitted a Senate bill (S. 3066) to allow the formation and incorporation of cooperatives in DC itself. In his report accompanying the bill, Capper wrote, "The organizations, cooperative in character, in the whole United States run up in number into the thousands, and 33 of the States of the Union have provided special laws facilitating their institution, the District of Columbia being one of the relatively few backward jurisdictions."[7] He also voiced his hope that Congress would allow DC residents to create cooperatives functioning according to the Rochdale Principles. Unfortunately, while Capper successfully helped farming cooperatives across the country, Senate Bill S. 3066 did not pass until 1940.

In spite of these legal setbacks, cooperatives spread widely in DC because of the collapse of the economy during the Great Depression.[8] The 1933 Federal Emergency Relief Act encouraged the formation of cooperative and self-help associations "for the barter of goods and services."[9] The Federal Emergency Relief Agency also provided grants and surplus government buildings and materials to these associations. By 1935, the Division of Self-Help within the District of Columbia Emergency Relief Administration helped establish 13 self-help cooperatives with 722 members, predominately African Americans and women (Parker, 1935). The majority of the cooperatives sewed bed and bath linens, while some also provided other services, such as shoe repair, barbering, and building. The members could use labor credits to purchase items or services. Thus, the members produced for each other and exchanged their surpluses with other cooperatives. In the words of one observer at the time, "It is the general practice among self-help associations not to sell their products for cash nor in such a way as to bring them onto the competitive market" (Parker, 1935, p. 606). Most famously, civil rights activist Nannie Helen Burroughs set up the Northeast Self-Help Cooperative, later renamed Cooperative Industries, Inc., in Lincoln Heights. This cooperative served approximately 6,000 people in far Northeast DC between 1934 and 1938.[10] The government additionally supported the Greenbelt cities and their cooperatives (MacKean, 2013).

The cooperative movement developed a momentum of its own. In 1934, a group of DC residents formed the Washington Consumers' League, which two years later created two cooperative groups. The first was Rochdale Stores, Inc., a group of cooperative groceries located in Takoma Park, Bethesda, Georgetown, Cleveland Park, Mount Pleasant, and Falls Church (US Congress, 1940). It sold 400 Co-op branded foods and had 700 members. The second, Konsum, was a gasoline and oil cooperative that started as a single rented pump at a private gas station and became a cooperative gas station at 21st and Virginia Avenue, NW.[11] African Americans also pushed forward the cooperative movement during the 1930s. In 1934, African Americans formed the Capitol Cab Company, which, according to *Ebony* in 1962, was "the largest cooperatively owned taxi fleet in the world" with 1,500 taxicabs (p. 48). According to the author of *Negro Business and Business Education*, Joseph A. Pierce, African Americans in DC formed branches of the Rochdale Stores, which provided them jobs and brought them into large interracial groups: "To Negroes, who are usually excluded from business ventures of more than very small local value, the prospect of finding employment in the large and growing co-operative movement offers a definite hope for the future" (1947/1995, p. 178). In 1938, the Washington Bookshop, also called The Bookshop or the Bookshop Association, formed as a cooperative that sold books and phonograph records at a discount, and also functioned as an interracial social club, art gallery, and lecture hall (McReynolds & Robbins, 2009). During the 1930s, cooperatives flourished in DC as a means to cope with the massive unemployment and economic crisis caused by the Great Depression, and as a public space for interracial sociability.

In 1941, the Washington Bookshop could change its name to the Washington Cooperative Bookshop because, just a year earlier, Congress (with the help of Senator Capper) passed the DC Cooperative Association Act (S. 2013). The DC Cooperative Association Act provided cooperatives with a legal structure, including one vote for every member, and allowed cooperatives from across the country to register in DC. However, the Washington Cooperative Bookshop soon came under attack by the House Un-American Activities Committee, allegedly for being subversive (McReynolds & Robbins, 2009). In 1945, the House held hearings on whether cooperatives were un-American and a "threat to private enterprise in the United States."[12] Because of the increasingly oppressive political environment of the 1950s, very few cooperatives formed in the District.

The 1960s brought an upswing in cooperative formation. At this time, many food cooperatives and buying clubs formed because inflation made food too expensive for many low-income people and many grocery stores had moved out of the city, leaving what we now call "food deserts." However, community organizers were motivated by much more than inflation. For example, in 1966, community organizers on Capitol Hill worked with Greenbelt Consumer Co-op, and later with the Anacostia Buyers Club, to create a food-buying club involving the poor.[13] In 1970, community organizers at the Friendship House, with the help of Black Markets, Inc., turned the buying club into the nation's first food co-op in public housing, MLK Cooperative Store No. 1 (see Figure 4.1). While concerned about inflation, these organizers believed "in the co-operative idea" that would help "Black progress" in DC, especially among the poorest residents.[14] Significantly, MLK Cooperative Store No. 1 was located in the Arthur Capper public housing project, named after the now deceased Kansas senator who had helped DC legally recognize cooperatives.

By 1975, this broad range of cooperatives provided DC residents spaces for autonomy and control, a form of home rule. This home rule from below did not merely recreate an individualistic consumer society, but rather imagined a new society based on the common. The civil rights movement supported a wide variety of cooperatives because people, especially those marginalized from mainstream White society, could take control of their economic lives and create an alternative to individualist consumer society (Gordon Nembhard, 2014; Ransby,

FIGURE 4.1 Martin Luther King Food Co-op. From: © 2015 Roland L. Freeman.

2003). The proliferation of different kinds of cooperatives in the District could forge a new kind of society based on broad civil, political, and economic equality. Home rule in District government would complement and build on this home rule from below.

Cooperative-Based Home Rule

Starting from his first days as mayor in 1979, Marion Barry brought home rule from below into the DC government.[15] In the Mayor's Office, Barry established the Energy Office, which brought in people like Jack Werner from United Planning Organization (UPO) to set up energy cooperatives and support food cooperatives around urban gardening.[16] He brought Jerome S. Paige, who worked on housing cooperatives, into the DC Department of Housing. Barry also appointed Cornelius "Cornbread" Givens, who moved to DC when Barry became mayor, to head the umbrella organization for cooperatives, the Mayor's Commission for Cooperative Economic Development.

Cornbread Givens was a civil rights leader and a national advocate for cooperatives. Givens was born in Newark, NJ. He worked in unions and owned his own construction company. In 1965, he was one of the first African Americans to run for mayor in a major city, Jersey City. In the late 1960s, he also became a leader in the Poor People's Campaign, which he helped transform into the Poor People's Development Foundation (PPDF).[17] Incorporated in the District in October 1968, the PPDF sought to help poor communities develop cooperatives.[18]

The PPDF began working with farmer cooperatives of Southern tenant farmers in 1971. These cooperatives formed in response to the backlash against the Voting Rights Act of 1965. Southern tenant farmers who decided to register to vote were, in retaliation, evicted from their tenant farms. Cooperatives were seen as a means to help these tenant farmers survive and exercise their right to vote, as well as realize civil rights more generally. Cornbread Givens worked to connect Southern farmers' cooperatives with consumer food cooperatives, farmers' markets, health food stores, and collective warehouses, which he set up around Newark, NJ and New York City. Members of the PPDF trucked food up to Newark and New York City to be sold in farmers' markets and health food stores.[19]

During the 1970s, Cornbread Givens helped to put cooperatives on the national Democratic Party platform and on "The National Black Agenda for the '80s."[20] Givens envisioned an entire development plan in which each community would integrate:

- producer cooperatives (particularly important for job creation)
- consumer cooperatives
- credit unions
- low-income housing cooperatives

- a local charity (funded by profits from the other cooperatives to develop social action programs like schools, hospitals, and child development centers) all organized by a community-wide cooperative.[21]

Givens understood these cooperatives as necessarily working together, thus forming an integrated model of community development. In addition, institutions at the national level, such as the National Consumer Cooperative Bank, for which Givens successfully advocated in 1978, would assist in implementing these community plans.[22]

Mayor Marion Barry supported Givens' vision as a model for DC. Barry made Givens the chairperson of the Commission for Cooperative Economic Development. According to the PPDF records, Barry "indicated that he will use his good offices to establish Washington, D.C. as [a] 'demonstration' city for cooperative development."[23] At a February 1980 conference, Barry said:

> In Washington, as in every other major urban center in America, we have entire sections of our city which have been abandoned and neglected by the mainstream of economic activity. . . . Although private enterprise has neglected or abandoned some areas of our city, we must not give up the fight. It is time for the citizens of these areas themselves to become owners and providers of the basic services needed for daily life. The cooperative movement is just what is needed to provide this opportunity.[24]

By May, Barry had established his Commission for Cooperative Economic Development and enlisted others in his program to use cooperatives to create jobs and solve the inner-city food crisis.[25] According to Givens, the Commission was "the very first Commission of this kind anywhere in the nation."[26] As chairperson of the Commission, Givens gained the opportunity to realize his community development model based on cooperatives throughout DC.

Givens interpreted his mandate as broadly as possible. Barry declared that the Commission should identify needs for cooperatives in different parts of the District, provide technical support, and develop legislation and support structures for cooperative economic development. Barry also established the Commission specifically to support the formation of cooperatives in housing, food, and home heating oil (Consumer Cooperatives, 1980). Givens sought to go far beyond this mandate. For example, at a public hearing in 1981, Givens suggested an enormous range of cooperatives:

1. Food stores, supermarkets, clothing and furniture stores, shopping centers, drugstores, gas stations, auto repair shops, home heating oil cooperatives, energy conservation materials cooperatives, construction rehabilitation cooperatives, insurance companies, etc.

2. Light industries: clothing factories, shoe and furniture factories, machine shops, industries to supply federal and District government needs, etc.
3. Services cooperatives: neighborhood health services, hospitals, child care centers, schools, all forms of recreation, including bowling, skating, cable TV, major league baseball, basketball and football teams, etc.[27]

Givens thus imagined that the DC economy might be run entirely on cooperative principles. Reflecting his earlier commitment to PPDF, Givens continually emphasized that the Commission must assist low- and moderate-income residents in establishing cooperatives, especially cooperatives that created jobs.[28] Givens envisioned the proliferation of cooperatives as a way to forge economic and political power among low- and moderate-income residents.

The District government's support of cooperative development spurred the growth of new DC food cooperatives during the 1980s. In 1980, seven families began the Shepherd Street Collective, a food-buying club, which expanded and formed into the Community Based Buying Clubs (CBBC) to help similar groups form and improve their buying power (McCall, 1982). CBBC held People's Market Days, during which Agricultural Teams, Inc., an African American–owned agricultural cooperative in North Carolina, brought food directly from its farms to sell at different locations in DC. As can be seen in Table 4.1, many new food cooperatives formed.[29] By 1986, the Arthur Capper public housing project was no longer the only project with a food cooperative; at least five other projects had food cooperatives all run by their residents, most supported by PPDF. These included: Arthur Capper, Barry Farms,[30] Kenilworth Parkside (Sugarman, 1986), senior public housing buildings Horizon House (Eisen, 1982) and Judiciary House (NCHA, 1984), and Sursum Corda.[31] Figure 4.2 shows the Judiciary Homes Senior Citizens Food Co-op.

TABLE 4.1 Home Rule–Era New Food Cooperatives

Name	Year Started	Location
City Garden	1975	Mount Pleasant
Fields of Plenty	1977	Adams Morgan
Shepherd Street	1980	NW, DC
Chakula	1981	Howard University
Fort Davis	1981	Fort Davis
Cornucopia	1981	Capitol Hill (Walter Street, SE)
Barry Farms	1982★	Anacostia
Horizon House	1982	12th and M Streets, NW
Takoma Park-Silver Spring	1982	Takoma Park, Silver Spring
Judiciary House	1984★	Judiciary Square
Kenilworth Parkside	1986★	Ward 7
Earlier food co-ops		
Glut	1969	Mt. Rainier
MLK No. 1	1970	Capitol Hill/Navy Yard

Note: The dates with an ★ are approximate years.

FIGURE 4.2 Judiciary Homes Senior Citizens Food Co-op. From: NCHA 1985 Annual Report, p. 18.

The Commission was also mandated to encourage the development of housing co-ops. DC had long experienced gentrification and displacement, from the 1930s and 1940s in Georgetown and the 1950s on Capitol Hill to the economic crisis of the 1970s that brought large-scale evictions and homelessness in DC. In response, the new District government passed some of its earliest laws to stop displacement (Huron, 2012; Wells, 2013). The Condominium Act of 1976 required that developers stop the conversion of affordable apartments into condominiums, which led to a complete moratorium on conversions in 1978. The Real Property Transfer Excise Tax of 1978 was the country's first urban tax on land speculation (Huron, 2012). The Rental Housing Sale and Conversion Act of 1980, more popularly called the Tenant Opportunity to Purchase Act or TOPA, gave tenants the right to purchase their buildings if they went on the market (Huron, 2012).

With home rule, housing activists put forth cooperatives as a means to end displacement. They specifically advocated limited-equity cooperatives (LEC). LECs set limits on the resale value of cooperative units, so that they remained affordable, and/or involved shares in the cooperative, rather than private ownership of units, and required tenant participation in management.[32] In 1979, the Metropolitan Washington Planning and Housing Association (MWPHA) set up a Coop Housing Services Program to assist apartment tenants in the conversion process to cooperatives and set up a revolving loan fund for these conversions. Low-income residents soon began to use TOPA to buy their buildings and create long-term affordable cooperative housing. MWPHA also helped develop a network of tenant groups and housing cooperatives, such as the Columbia Heights Federation of Housing Cooperatives and the Sojourners Housing Ministry, both in the 14th Street area. Additionally, Ministries United to Support Community Life (MUSCLE) formed in 1977 and began to provide similar assistance to buildings where at least 50% of the tenants qualified for Section 8 housing (Paige & Reuss, 1983). Already by late 1980, DC tenants' associations had created 17 LECs with 1,000 units and 20 more tenants' associations were in the process of buying their buildings to turn into LECs. The numbers continued to increase. By the late 1990s, while New York City had more LECs in absolute numbers, Washington, DC had more proportional to its population (Huron, 2012).

DC residents also started other kinds of cooperatives. In 1979, the Women's Community Bakery Collective moved from Hyattsville, MD, to Capitol Hill. The workers' cooperative made about 500 loaves of bread per day, as well as rolls, granola, cookies, muffins, and cakes, which resulted in a half million dollars in business each year (Landman, 1993). Three years later, the DC Urban Produce Cooperative registered as a cooperative on North Capitol Street near L Street. In 1984, the DC Federation of Cooperative Associations officially registered on 14th Street, NW, near R Street.[33] And credit unions continued to expand during home rule.

Home rule provided an environment open to expanding the social, political, and economic world of the common. DC residents created new cooperatives and other experiments in common property. However, at the same time, home rule remained limited for a variety of reasons. One, Congress continually intervened in DC government, which limited home rule. Two, during the 1970s and 1980s, the nature of city governance changed across the United States. The 1973 economic crisis and then the Reagan administration's federal budget cuts significantly reduced city budgets. Thus, cooperative economic development had to compete for a shrinking pot of money with many other programs and priorities. Then the cooperative movement also suffered from the problems of the Barry administration.

The Cooptation of Cooperatives and Home Rule from Above

In 1985, Ivanhoe Donaldson, a high-level District government official and close colleague of Barry, plead guilty to embezzling DC government funds. Some of these embezzled funds had moved through Cornbread Givens' PPDF and, while Givens did not go to jail, he did lose citywide support for cooperatives and the momentum of the PPDF (Jaffe & Sherwood, 1994). "It knocked us out. . . . It set back the whole effort. We were on a roll. It just winded down. . . . I'm still disappointed in Donaldson. He has never apologized," Givens later remembered (Cherkis, 1999). At the same time, elites worldwide implemented neoliberal policies, which increasingly relied on private business motivated by profits to provide—or not—public goods and services. In this environment shifting away from a political order–based cooperation and the common and toward one created by the privatization of the public and the common, cooperatives began to be used in isolation from Givens' broader community model to dismantle home rule from below and to support a new kind of political order, home rule from above.

The redevelopment of the Ellen Wilson public housing project, located on Capitol Hill at 7th and I Streets, SE, demonstrates this shifting environment. In 1988, the DC Department of Public and Assisted Housing closed Ellen Wilson for major renovations and moved out all of the 129 families living there (Lang, 1999).[34] In 1992, homeless veterans occupied the vacated buildings and began renovating the languishing public housing project. Interestingly, 10 years earlier, one of the veterans occupying Ellen Wilson, Cecil Byrd, had proposed to Cornbread Givens' Commission on Cooperative Economic Development that it form a Housing Rehabilitation and Energy Training Cooperative for Vietnam Veterans.[35] Within six months, Mayor Sharon Pratt Kelly evicted the veterans from Ellen Wilson, which would allow for the privatization of this space (Naylor, 1992; Rosenbaum, 1992).[36]

From all accounts, the Ellen Wilson redevelopment started out quite inclusively, although the veterans were not included. The main organizational groups—the Ellen Wilson Neighborhood Redevelopment Corporation (a Community Development Corporation [CDC]) and the Ellen Wilson Community Advisory Council—brought public housing residents from Ellen Wilson and from the neighboring Arthur Capper and Carrollsburg projects to the table with homeowners and business owners. Ellen Wilson residents enthusiastically supported the possibility of housing cooperatives because they might allow them to own their own housing, although they feared they would not be allowed to live in the new development. Church leaders and members understood the redevelopment of Ellen Wilson as a step toward social justice that would also improve the lives of individual Ellen Wilson residents (Blagburn, n.d.). These groups put together a plan to use federal HOPE VI funds for Ellen Wilson's redevelopment. While at least public housing residents had fears that the promises might not be realized, residents across Capitol Hill took part in the planning for a new Ellen Wilson housing development.

Once the plans were submitted to the US Department of Housing and Urban Development (HUD), however, the situation changed dramatically. As one newspaper article noted in 1995, "The size of the grant has increased as plans have changed. And the income levels are much, much higher than those of the people who used to live at Ellen Wilson or of D.C. public housing residents in general, which are generally below 12 percent of the median income" (Haggerty, 1995). Many homeowners and business owners rejected the redevelopment plan, sought to eradicate the cooperative housing plan, and pressed to reduce the number of units for low-income residents.[37] In the end, it is not clear that any former Ellen Wilson residents were allowed to return to the development.[38] According to Blagburn (n.d.), Ellen Wilson residents were displaced because, while they were organized, they were not connected to influential elites, who could make certain the plans were realized and the promises kept.

In this transitional period in DC, housing cooperatives were implemented in isolation from Givens' integrated community model and could be used to displace the poor. HUD had long supported limited-equity cooperatives. In 1985, a former HUD employee, Marilyn Melkonian, created the non-profit development firm

Telesis, which soon specialized in converting public housing to limited-equity cooperatives. In contrast to calls for cooperatives as a way to create real home rule, Telesis understood limited-equity cooperatives in a very specific sense. One journalist summarized the Telesis plan: "While there will be a 'homeowners' cooperative board' of residents, neighbors and public agency representatives, the on-site management company will dominate, choosing 'tenants' and enforcing so-called proper conduct."[39] A group calling themselves the "Coalition to Save Ellen Wilson," argued for a cooperative tenant council that would organize "housekeeping-type chores."[40] No one spoke about these cooperatives as part of the broader community model Cornbread Givens had envisioned. Cooperatives primarily functioned as a means to push through the demolition of Ellen Wilson and the displacement of its residents.

In contrast to public housing residents, the Capitol Hill business community could realize its neighborhood vision without public housing. The business community was organized and had connections to realize its interests. President George Bush's HUD secretary from 1989 to 1993, Jack Kemp, sought to realize his conservative libertarian views through his programs to sell public housing to its tenants and create so-called enterprise zones. In 1989, a neighbor of the Ellen Wilson project, Karl Zinsmeister, wrote a letter to Capitol Hill Restoration Society president:

> I think a meeting with Kemp and assistants is probably the most important step for us (though I think we ought to meet with the DC people first). I've worked a lot in the Kemp wing of politics and I can tell you this project ought to ring all the right bells for him right now: private sector involvement in solving social problems, fostering tenant empowerment and demanding individual responsibility, using market-based solutions to minister to human needs, property privatization, etc. etc. This makes a lovely little test case on its merits, and being located so conveniently for presidential walk-throughs. We ought to start thinking about a strong meeting with Kemp soon. . ..We should also start thinking about economics soon. *My back-of-the-envelope tells me the Ellen Wilson site is worth maybe 15 million dollars.*[41]

A small group organized around the local National Capital Bank, the Capitol Hill Restoration Society, local real estate agents and businesses, as well as politically connected neighbors like Zinsmeister, to realize a neighborhood without the public housing residents. They used narrowly understood housing cooperatives to displace these residents.

Changes in city finances also helped this small group. With fiscal crises and reduced federal funds, cities even more desperately relied upon private investors to fund city projects. By the 1980s, unprecedented levels of foreign capital flowed into the US economy due to worldwide deregulation and removal of restraints on the flow of credit, and due to high US interest rates, which lured these funds into the United States (Krippner, 2011). Then, the 1986 revision of the federal tax code introduced the Low-Income Housing Tax Credit (LIHTC). Soon, Wall Street investment houses invented tax-credit investment tools to draw thousands of affluent investors to finance low- and moderate-income housing, especially projects that would dismantle public housing and replace it with mixed-income housing (Gallagher, 1990; Komen, 1988). The availability of investment funds made the redevelopment of housing projects like Ellen Wilson imaginable to, and very lucrative for, organized local developers, real estate agents, banks, and investors.

In 1995, the Congress created the District of Columbia Financial Responsibility and Management Assistance Authority (the Control Board), which officially dismantled home rule from below. The Control Board was organized because "[a] combination of accumulated operating deficits, cash shortages, management inefficiencies, and deficit spending in the current fiscal year have created a fiscal emergency in the District of Columbia."[42] The five-person Control Board could override decisions by the elected Mayor and the City Council and implement its own policies. The Control Board reorganized the District government and implemented significant budget cuts.

The Commission on Cooperative Economic Development had not regularly met since 1986. The Control Board abolished it in 1998 and thus officially ended the integration of Cornbread Givens' cooperative vision into the DC government. By this point, several cooperatives had already closed. In 1992, the Women's Community Bakery Collective on Capitol Hill shut its doors.[43] Many of the food cooperatives had closed. The DC Housing Authority went into a receivership, headed by David Gilmore. Gilmore had the sole right to transfer property and negotiate the terms without public hearings (Fehr, 1998). Gilmore closed the Arthur Capper public housing project, thus also shuttering the MLK food cooperative inside. Gilmore also removed the obstacles to the Ellen Wilson plan, maintaining the cooperatives in their limited form (Van Den Toorn, 1995). Through these and other strategies, DC political and economic elites turned democratic home rule from below into technocratic home rule from above.

Conclusions

Before formal home rule, DC residents sought to build autonomous spheres, gain control over life, and forge new resources in the District beyond formal government, what I call "home rule from below." As part of the common with its constitutive power, cooperatives were autonomous spaces outside private property and capital in which DC residents could realize and expand equality and democracy. According to Cornbread Givens' vision, adopted by the Barry administration, communities should develop integrated systems of different types of cooperatives—producer cooperatives, consumer cooperatives, credit unions, low-income housing cooperatives, and so on—that might provide jobs, democratic control of life, equality, and community wealth. Givens understood the cooperative movement as particularly significant for African Americans and for poor residents of DC. DC residents struggled continually to maintain a broader sense of home rule than that imagined by many DC elites. With the economic and governmental crises of the 1970s and 1980s, however, home rule from below was undermined, replaced by limited forms of governmental rule, or limited home rule from above. In 1995, the DC Control Board removed vestiges of home rule from below within DC government, including using elements like housing cooperatives in isolation and in extremely limited form to realize this removal.

However, the cooperative movement continues today in Washington, DC. In 2012, a group of people interested in cooperatives put on a day-long conference on cooperatives with about 200 participants. The group maintains a Web site with a co-op directory, showing the wide range of cooperatives in DC today and announcing more cooperatives to come: http://coopdc.org/. It is not clear whether these cooperatives view themselves as part of a project of home rule from below, as part of broader community model like that of Cornbread Givens, or as part of the long history of cooperatives in DC. It is hoped that this chapter may provide a history to link today's cooperatives with a broader form of home rule from below.

Appendix I

Mayor's Commission on Cooperative Economic Development

Originating Agency: Office of the Mayor

1) These people will serve until June 1, 1983: Cornbread Givens, Emma C. Mimms, James D. Vitarello, Bruce Bryan, Ruth Jordan, Sylvia Correa, Caroline Cullen Ramsay, George Clarke.

2) These people will serve until June 1, 1982: G. Mujahid, A. Beyah, Stam Straughter, Hank Albarelli, George A. Didden, Carol Ann Phillips, Larry F. Weston, William Washburn III, Leo M. Bernstein.

3) These people will serve until June 1, 1981: Sterling Green, Gwendolyn King, Richard Tolliver, William J. Barrow III, Bettye J. Mobley-Washington, Toni D. Schmiegelow, Raymond H. Brown, Blenna A. Cunningham.

4) These people are government members and serve at the pleasure of the mayor: Julian C. Nicholas, Edward Meyers, Jack Werner, Herbert Simmons, Marie Nahikian.

Cornbread Givens is Chairperson and serves at the pleasure of the Mayor. *District of Columbia Register*, Mayor's Order 80–260, October 22, 1980.

Notes

1 In 1973, Congress passed the Home Rule Act, which led to elections for mayor and city council in November 1974 and the swearing in of the new government in January 1975. The Home Rule Act also allowed for the election of advisory neighborhood commissioners. DC-based political scientist Michael Fauntroy has defined home rule as "a government status in which authority and responsibility for management of a unit of government (e.g., state, city, county, territorial) falls to that unit of government, subject to the parameters set by a superior unit of government" (2010, p. 23). Home rule thus assured DC some level of self-government. However, congressional intervention in DC government continues today, thus limiting home rule and leading Fauntroy (2003) to ask whether DC has home rule or house rule, rule by the US Congress.

2 As Jessica Gordon Nembhard has argued, "African Americans have used cooperative economic development as a strategy in the struggle for economic stability and independence" (2009, p. 186). For more extensive discussion of African American participation in the cooperative movement, see Gordon Nembhard (2014).

3 For the original 1844 Rochdale Principles, see The Rochdale Principles. The Rochdale Pioneers Museum. Accessed January 23, 2015, www.rochdalepioneersmuseum. coop/about-us/the-rochdale-principles/. For a more recent, official interpretation of these principles, see Co-operative identity, values & principles. International Cooperative Alliance. Accessed January 23, 2015, http://ica.coop/en/whats-co-op/co-operative-identity-values-principles.

4 Housing cooperatives often incorporated in Delaware. Michigan enacted the first cooperative law in 1886, followed by Wisconsin, Kansas, and Pennsylvania in 1887 (Chaddad & Cook, 2012, p. 177).

5 Arthur Capper differed significantly from the later, segregationist chairmen of the House and Senate DC committees. For example, Capper was the first president of the Topeka branch of the National Association for the Advancement of Colored People (NAACP) and on the national board of the NAACP for more than 30 years.

6 The Capper-Volstead Act of 1922 and of 1926 provided for cooperative marketing and producers' associations. These acts have been called "the Magna Carta of Cooperative Marketing" (Socolofsky, 1962, p. 151), which brings to mind Linebaugh's later view about the commons in his *The Magna Carta Manifesto: Liberties and Commons for All*.

7 Mr. Capper submitted the "Incorporation of Cooperative Associations in the District of Columbia," Senate Report No. 310, which accompanied S. 3066, on December 2, 1919 (US Congress, 1919).

8 The federal government's Emergency Relief Administration supported some cooperatives, which could exchange but not sell their goods (US Congress, 1940).

9 Library of Congress manuscripts, Nannie Helen Burroughs Papers, MSS57026, Box 52, Folder 2, "Administrative and Financial File, Cooperative Industries, Constitution, Articles of Incorporation, etc. . .," Division of Self-Help Cooperatives, Federal Emergency Relief Administration, "Manual of Rules and Policies Concerning Self-Help and Non-Profit Cooperatives Eligible to Federal Aid," Revised—Dec. 1934.

10 Nannie Helen Burroughs. 2001. *A Register of Her Papers in the Library of Congress*. Accessed January 23, 2015, http://lcweb2.loc.gov/service/mss/eadxmlmss/eadpdfmss/2003/ms003010.pdf. For more details on these cooperatives, see Gordon Nembhard (2014).

11 Konsum had a second gas station in Mount Pleasant, but it soon went out of business.

12 The hearings began in April 1945 (US Congress, 1946).

13 Over several decades, Greenbelt, MD, had developed an extensive cooperative system that helped to form new cooperatives. For more information on Greenbelt cooperatives, see MacKean (2013).

14 "Food Co-Op" (1970) and GWU Special Collections, Friendship House Association Records, MS2142, Box 60, File 1, "Arthur Capper Consumers' Fed., 1969," "The Arthur Capper Consumer Federation: History and Developments," October 1969. Another MLK Food Cooperative existed on North Capitol Street, near the Central Post Office, maybe within Sursum Corda public housing (Green, 1972).

15 I have no information about any cooperative policies by the first mayor, Walter Washington.

16 Personal conversation with Jack Werner.

17 Library of Congress, Manuscript Room, Civil Rights during the Carter Administration, 1977–1981, Part: 1 Papers of the Special Assistant for Black Affairs, Section B, Microfilm: 23,401, Reel 17. Letter from Cornbread Givens of PPDF to Mr. Hamilton Jordan, White House Chief of Staff, August 17, 1979.

18 Ibid., Reel 11. "Statement of Capability," PPDF, February 12, 1980, p. 1.

19 PPDF worked with the Archer County Small Farmers Cooperative Association of Archer County, Florida; the New Communities Farm in Leesberg, Georgia, a land trust of more than 4,000 acres; the Eastern Georgia Small Farmers Cooperative Association in Waynesboro, Georgia; and the Sea Island Small Farmers Cooperative Association on John's Island, South Carolina. PPDF then helped set up a natural food store, The Urban Vegetable, in New York City. Ibid., "Statement of Capability," PPDF, February 12, 1980, p. 2.

20 Ibid., Reel 11. Workpaper on the National Task Force for Cooperative Economic Development, Prepared by Cornbread Givens, PPDF, 1328 NY Avenue, DC., March 5, 1980. The 1976 Democratic Party Platform stated, "We shall encourage consumer groups to establish and operate consumer cooperatives that will enable consumers to provide themselves marketplace alternatives and to provide a competitive spur to profit-oriented enterprises." "Democratic Party Platform of 1976," The American Presidency. Accessed January 23, 2015, www.presidency.ucsb.edu/ws/?pid=29606.

21 Library of Congress, Manuscript Room, Civil Rights during the Carter Administration, 1977–1981, Part: 1 Papers of the Special Assistant for Black Affairs, Section C, Microfilm: 23,472, Reel 17. File: Poor Peoples Development Foundation, Inc. [O/A 6493], Statement of Testimony by the Poor Peoples Development Foundation, Inc. and the Poor Peoples' Cooperative Bank Implementation Commission on the National Consumer Cooperative Bank before the Inter-Agency Task Force on the National Consumer Cooperative Bank Act, January 9, 10, 11. Presented by Mr. Cornbread Givens, Mr. Frank Shaffer Corona, Ms. Ennis Frances, Ms. Phyllis Brooks. February 9, 1979. Appendix.

22 In 1978, Congress passed a law to create the National Consumer Cooperative Bank, for which Givens had advocated and which exists today as the NCB.

23 Library of Congress, Manuscript Room, Civil Rights during the Carter Administration, 1977–1981, Part: 1 Papers of the Special Assistant for Black Affairs, Section B, Microfilm: 23,401, Reel 11. "Statement of Capability," PPDF, February 12, 1980, p. 3.

24 Ibid., Reel 11. *PPDF newsletter*, *1*(1), March 1980.

25 An amended Mayor's Order (Appendix I) lists who was on the Commission, including Cornbread Givens.

26 DC Archives, DCA 08–010 [Committees], Box 2/7 Coops, File "Commission for Cooperative Econ Dev.," "Community Cooperative Economic Development, 'Blueprint for Action,'" 1981–1983.

27 DC Archives, DCA 08–010 [Committees], Box 2/7 Coops, File "Commission for Cooperative Econ Dev.," "Opening Statement of Cornbread Givens," Commission's Public Hearings, Establishing Community Owned Cooperatives in the District of Columbia, May 9, 1981.

28 DC Archives, DCA 08–010 [Committees], Box 2/7 Coops, File "Commission for Cooperative Econ Dev.," "Community Cooperative Economic Development, 'Blueprint for Action' 1981–1983," November 1981, pp. 8, 11, 17.

29 I have included two Maryland-based cooperatives because they were important participants in the broader DC cooperative movement.

30 The co-op accepted food stamps (Sugarman, 1986).

31 It is unclear whether a food cooperative existed within Sursum Corda. An MLK Food Cooperative was supposed to exist on North Capitol Street, near the Central Post Office (Green, 1972).

32 In 1983, the city passed an emergency bill to legalize housing cooperatives with non-Rochdale voting. The original DC Cooperative Association Act required one person, one vote, according to Rochdale Principles. The emergency act allowed proportional voting, rather than Rochdale voting. The 1983 DC Cooperative Housing Association Proportionate Voting Emergency Act permits proportional voting. November 1983, "Emergency action averts co-op housing voting crisis," p. 3.

33 For a list of DC cooperatives, see http://coopdc.org/coop-directory/.

34 In 1987, the National Capital Housing Authority (NCHA) was abolished. The DC Department of Public and Assisted Housing took over many of its activities and then was replaced by the DC Housing Authority (DCHA) in 1994.

35 DC Archives, Minutes of MCCED meeting, January 14, 1981 and March 19, 1981, as well as DC Archives, DCA 08–010 [Committees], Box 2/7 Coops, File "Commission for Cooperative Econ Dev.," "Community Cooperative Economic Development, 'Blueprint for Action' 1981–1983." In 1992, these veterans may have discussed creating a Cooperative Builders Yard, a cooperative that would train veterans in construction in Southeast DC. Personal conversation with Dominic Moulden.

36 In addition, personal conversation with Cecil Byrd.

37 For example, the Sousa Neighborhood Association and National Capital Bank's James Didden both rejected the proposals (Haggerty, 1995; Van Den Toorn, 1995).

38 "Although the original project planners intended to give priority to those who lived in the former Ellen Wilson dwellings, the Townhomes was not completed until more than a decade after Ellen Wilson was abandoned. By then, most former residents could not be located or had moved on. Invitations were then extended to people living in the nearby Arthur Capper project. However, Jones was one of the few Arthur Capper residents who was able to pass the Townhomes's screening process and save enough money for the initial down payment" (Schulberg, 2013).

39 Meeting with developer Marilyn Melkonian reported in Rice (1995).

40 "Statement of the Coalition to Save Ellen Wilson," probably attached to "Letter from Karl Zinsmeister to Jim, April 3, 1989" in footnote 41.

41 Emphasis inserted. GWU Special Collections, Capitol Hill Restoration Society, MS2009, Box 70, File 16, "Ellen Wilson Correspondence, 1989–1990," Pat Schauer. Letter from Karl Zinsmeister to Jim, April 3, 1989.

42 The Control Board's official name was the District of Columbia Financial Responsibility and Management Assistance Authority. For the entire text of the bill that created the Control Board: H.R.1345, District of Columbia Financial Responsibility and Management Assistance Act of 1995 (Enrolled as Agreed to or Passed by Both House and Senate), http://thomas.loc.gov/cgi-bin/query/z?c104:h.r.1345.enr.

43 According to Landman (1993), the main members closed it in 1992 because they wanted to try something else.

References

Blagburn, M. (n.d.). Ellen Wilson dwellings: Clergy and community activists' reaction to the mixed income revitalization development.

Chaddad, F., & Cook, M. L. (2012). Legal frameworks and property rights in U.S. agricultural cooperatives: The hybridization of cooperative structures. In P. Battilani & H. G. Schröter (Eds.), *The cooperative business movement, 1950 to the present* (pp. 175–194). Cambridge, UK: Cambridge University Press.

Cherkis, J. (1999, November 5). Dreams and cornbread: This civil rights movement legend has never left the grass roots. *Washington City Paper.* Accessed February 27, 2015, www.washingtoncitypaper.com/articles/18433/dreams-and-cornbread/.

Conover, M. (1959). The Rochdale Principles in American co-operative associations. *The Western Political Quarterly, 12*(1), 111–122.

Consumer Cooperatives Commission. (1980, June 26). *The Washington Post,* p. DC2.

Cooperative society, one that is successful in the District of Columbia. [Editorial]. (1894). *Sacramento Daily Union, 87*(99).

Eisen, J. (1982, December 21). Co-op food market opens. *The Washington Post,* p. B6.

Fauntroy, M. K. (2003). *Home rule or house rule: Congress and the erosion of local governance in the District of Columbia.* Lanham, MD: University Press of America.

Fauntroy, M. K. (2010). Home rule for the District of Columbia. In R. W. Walters & T. M. Travis (Eds.), *Democratic destiny and the District of Columbia: Federal politics and public policy* (pp. 21–44). Lanham, MD: Lexington Books.

Fehr, S. C. (1998, November 7). D.C. wants marines to take site of failed SE complex. *The Washington Post,* p. B1.

Gallagher, J. (1990, February 12). Survival: Inner city's last developer. *St. Louis Post-Dispatch.*

Gordon Nembhard, J. (2009). Cooperative economics education. In K. Lomotey (Ed.), *Encyclopedia of African American education* (pp. 186–188). Los Angeles, CA: Sage Publications.

Gordon Nembhard, J. (2014). *Collective courage: A history of African American cooperative economic thought and practice.* University Park. PA: The Pennsylvania State University Press.

Green, E. (1972). Some co-ops make it, some don't. *DC Gazette, 3*(16), 13.

Haggerty, M. (1995, September 23). Public housing renewal plan strikes a nerve. *The Washington Post,* p. E1.

Hardt, M., & Negri, A. (2009). *Commonwealth.* Cambridge, MA: Belknap Press of Harvard University Press.

Huron, A. (2012). The work of the urban commons: Limited-equity cooperatives in Washington, D.C. (Doctoral dissertation, Department of Earth and Environmental Sciences, City University of New York Graduate Center).

Jaffe, H., & Sherwood, T. (1994). *Dream city: Race, power, and the decline of Washington, D.C.* New York, NY: Simon & Schuster.

Koman, K. L. (1988, February 8). Renovation drops by 50 here since new tax changes. *St. Louis Post-Dispatch.*

Krippner, G. R. (2011). *Capitalizing on crisis: The political origins of the rise of finance.* Cambridge, MA: Harvard University Press.

Landman, R. H. (1993). *Creating community in the city: Cooperatives and community gardens in Washington, D.C.* Westport, CT: Bergin & Garvey.

Lang, L. (1999, April 16). Dream city. *Washington City Paper.* Accessed February 27, 2015, www.washingtoncitypaper.com/articles/17108/dream-city.

MacKean, M. T. (2013). Greenbelt America: A New Deal vision for suburban public housing. (Doctoral dissertation, Department of History, Northwestern University).

McCall, J. (1982, December 22). Co-op way to stalking cheaper produce. *The Washington Post,* pp. DC1–DC2.

McReynolds, R., & Robbins, L. S. (2009). *The librarian spies: Philip and Mary Jane Keeney and Cold War espionage.* Westport, CT: Praeger Security International.

National Capital Housing Authority (NCHA). (1984). *Annual report.* Washington, DC: National Capital Housing Authority.

Naylor, J. (1992, June 1). Homeless vets have strategy, take complex. *Washington Times,* p. B1.

Paige, J. S., & Reuss, M. M. (1983). *Safe, decent, and affordable: Citizen struggles to improve housing in the District of Columbia, 1890–1982.* Washington, DC: Department of Urban Studies, University of the District of Columbia.

Parker, F. E. (1935). Self-help activities among the unemployed in Washington, D.C. *Monthly Labor Review, 40*(3), 604–611.

Pierce, J. A. (1995). *Negro business and business education: Their present and prospective development.* New York, NY: Plenum Press. (Original work published 1947).

Ransby, B. (2003). *Ella Baker and the black freedom movement: A radical democratic vision.* Chapel Hill, NC: University of North Carolina Press.

Rice, B. (1995, September 6). Impossible dream for Ellen Wilson public-housing site. *The Hill.*

Rosenbaum, C. (1992, October 14). Mayor vows help, homes for squatters appoints task force after meeting. *Washington Times,* p. B3.

Schulberg, J. (2013, November 4). A model for mixed-income living. *The Washington Post,* p. B1.

Socolofsky, H. E. (1962). *Arthur Capper, publisher, politician, and philanthropist.* Lawrence, KS: University of Kansas Press.

Sugarman, C. (1986, December 10). Gladys Bunker & the fresh ideal: Co-op brings fruit & vegetables to low-income in Anacostia. *The Washington Post,* pp. E1, E10.

Travis, T.-M. C. (2010). Walter Washington: Mayor of the last colony. In R. W. Walters & T.-M. Travis (Eds.), *Democratic destiny and the District of Columbia: Federal politics and public policy* (pp. 45–60). Lanham, MD: Lexington Books.

US Congress, House, Select Committee on Small Business. (1946). *The competition of cooperatives with other forms of business enterprise.* Washington, DC: US Government Printing Office.

US Congress, Senate. (1919). *Incorporation of cooperative associations in the District of Columbia.* Senate Report No. 310 accompanying S. 3066, submitted by Mr. Capper, December 2, 1919. Washington, DC: US Government Printing Office.

US Congress, Senate. (1940). *District of Columbia cooperative associations.* Hearings before a Subcommittee of the Committee on the District of Columbia, United States Senate, Seventy-Sixth Congress, Third Session, on S. 2013, a Bill to Amend the Code of the District of Columbia to Provide for the Organization and Regulation of Cooperative Associations, and for Other Purposes. April 16, 18–19, 1940. Washington, DC: US Government Printing Office.

Van Den Toorn, B. (1995, September 22). Ellen Wilson developers grilled. *Washington's Hill Rag.*

Wells, K. (2013). A decent place to stay: Housing crises, failed laws, and property conflicts in Washington, D.C. (Doctoral dissertation, Department of Geography, Syracuse University).

World's largest co-op cab co. [Editorial]. (1962). *Ebony, 17*(5), 48–54.

5

STRUGGLING FOR HOUSING, FROM DC TO JOHANNESBURG

Washington Innercity Self Help Goes to South Africa

Amanda Huron

Introduction

In the early 1990s, a group of Washington, DC housing activists traveled to Johannesburg to help start the first housing cooperatives in South Africa's history. These activists were from Washington Innercity Self Help, or WISH, a community-based group organized around issues of concern to low- and moderate-income people. WISH had been founded in 1978, and by the early 1990s, much of its work was directed toward helping low-income tenants purchase their buildings from their landlords and form limited-equity housing cooperatives—collectively owned housing that, because of restrictions placed on resale prices, would be affordable to poor people for years to come. WISH thought limited-equity co-ops were one solution to the displacement and unaffordability wracking Washington, DC. And it also thought these co-ops served as a structure within which people could become involved in their housing, an experiment in small-scale democracy that could pulse out into their surrounding neighborhoods, and enable local people to be empowered in their city at a larger scale. For WISH, housing co-ops represented affordability, collective control, and democratic participation. So when a group of Johannesburg tenants requested WISH's assistance in starting their own housing co-ops in the immediate wake of apartheid, WISH was eager to help.

In the late 1980s, comparisons between Washington, DC and South Africa were easy to find, from the corridors of power to the cities' punk undergrounds. In 1986, Washington, DC's delegate to Congress, Walter E. Fauntroy, declared that his threefold mission was to "Free South Africa, free Haiti, free D.C." (Fauntroy, 1986). A couple years later, DC punk band Soul Side sang, "Nation's capital like little South Africa/Look further on down the road/Every major city pushing down the poor" (Soul Side, 1989). Anti-apartheid organizing was strong in Washington, DC, where years of daily protests outside the South African embassy provided the opportunity for a wide variety of people to demonstrate against the regime. The similarities between DC and South Africa stirred the public imagination. Both were majority-Black places that had been ruled for years by a powerful White minority, places where democracy was denied and the poor suffered. Although Washingtonians finally won the right to elect their own local representation in 1974, for 100 years the city had been directly ruled by members of Congress from other states—many of whom were outright racists (Fauntroy, 2003; Jaffe & Sherwood, 1994). There was a similarity, too, to the racial geographies of the DC neighborhoods in which WISH concentrated its efforts and the Johannesburg neighborhoods where the tenants who requested WISH's help lived. In both cities, these were centrally located areas that had been built for Whites, but later abandoned by Whites and by capital. In DC, the abandonment began in the 1950s; in South Africa, the 1980s. By the early 1990s, in some ways the context in the two cities was very different: Johannesburg was suffering continuing disinvestment, while in DC, tenants were concerned about gentrification. But in both cities, home ownership for low-income people of color was equated with stability and with political power.

For WISH, going to South Africa was a political project. Ultimately, I argue, what WISH and its South African counterparts were together constructing was what geographer Cindi Katz (2001) would call a countertopography. A countertopography, for Katz, is a way of drawing lines of connection to understand how similar processes affect different places. Through back-and-forth visits, the Washingtonians and Johannesburgers realized the similarities between their two cities. And in both places, they reckoned with the sometimes impossible difficulty of forging more equal cities in the context of capitalist real estate markets.

The Origins of Washington Innercity Self Help

Washington, DC in 1978, the year WISH was founded, was a city rife with contradiction. On one hand was massive poverty and disinvestment. 1978 marked the 10-year anniversary of the civil disturbances that exploded in the wake of the assassination of Martin Luther King, Jr., which destroyed several of the city's commercial corridors. Those areas—upper 14th Street, NW, 7th Street, NW, H Street, NE—were still, 10 years later, largely abandoned by capital. And the people who lived in those areas—most of whom were African American—were still largely poor. In fact, many African Americans who could afford to move to the suburbs in the 1970s did so, leaving behind people who could not afford to leave, along with those who were committed to remaining in the city (Gale, 1987). On the other hand, the late 1970s saw surges of reinvestment in the city, and an influx of a more affluent, educated, and Whiter populace. In the 1970s, in centrally located neighborhoods like Mount Pleasant, Dupont Circle, Adams Morgan, and Capitol Hill, housing prices were going up, and homes were being renovated (Gale, 1976, 1977; Henig, 1982). Houses that had been turned into boarding houses for rent to poor people were being converted back to single-family homes, for sale to relatively wealthy families (Zeitz, 1979). Evictions in the city were increasing on a massive scale, in part because building owners saw the profits to be made in converting rental apartment buildings to condominiums. By 1978, gentrification and displacement filled the news, was on the lips of all the politicians running for office, and was increasingly recognized as a problem that needed to be tackled head-on, through tenant organizing and city policy (Gately, 1978; Huron, 2014; N.a., 1978; Wells, 2013).

It was in this context that Washington Innercity Self Help, or WISH, came into being. In the mid-1970s, Christian Communities Committed to Change (CCCC), a group of 10 DC Catholic parishes, was working to provide services to the city's low-income elderly. When those involved with CCCC realized that what was needed to create change was not services but self-advocacy among the poor, they reached out to other churches to start something new (WISH Housing Development Program (Revised—January 1987), 1987–1994). Ultimately, a group of about 40 DC churches worked together to found WISH in 1978 (Articles of Incorporation of Washington Innercity Self Help, Inc., 1978–1982; W.I.S.H. Washington Innercity Self Help 10th Anniversary 8th Community Congress, 1988). WISH's original geographic focus was the north central section of Washington, DC, including the neighborhoods of Columbia Heights, Shaw, and Dupont Circle East: neighborhoods that were just at the edge of the revitalization activity (WISH Housing Development Program (Revised—January 1987), 1987–1994). WISH was founded with just three staff members; over the course of its first 10 years of existence, the number of staff members ranged from just one to four (W.I.S.H. Washington Innercity Self Help 10th Anniversary 8th Community Congress, 1988). The staff's role was to facilitate poor people's ability to take collective action to solve their own problems. WISH's power was in its membership, which was made up mostly of low- and moderate-income African American and Latino residents of its target areas. In an internal document, the organization summed up its mission neatly: "W.I.S.H. views its role as a vehicle to bring poor people together so that they can collectively determine their problems and collectively achieve the solution" (Community Economic Development—Washington Innercity Self Help (W.I.S.H.), n.d.).

The organization strived for democratic control from below. To that end, it held an annual congress to elect new board members, report on accomplishments from the past year, and pass resolutions for the upcoming year. Its first annual congress was held one Saturday in the spring of 1980, in the Sacred Heart School, which was affiliated with the Shrine of the Sacred Heart Church, one of the 40 founding churches.[1] The membership considered 27 separate resolutions at the day-long meeting, which taken together highlight the breadth of the group's work. Sixteen of the resolutions dealt directly with housing concerns, seven resolutions addressed issues of concern to the elderly, one resolution dealt with harassment of Latinos by DC police and the federal Immigration and Naturalization Service (INS), one addressed the need for jobs for youth, and another dealt with the need for credit unions as an antidote to the lack of financing available in poor neighborhoods. Most of the resolutions were translated in the written program into Spanish, highlighting WISH's concern for including Latino residents, just as the wave of Central American refugees who would pour into the city over the course of the 1980s was beginning to swell. Here, too, we see the beginnings of WISH's interest in cooperative housing. A resolution on "Tenant Management and Ownership" states that "large numbers of tenants are thinking seriously of buying their apartment buildings," and that WISH resolved to provide organizing assistance to tenants' associations that wished to purchase their homes.[2]

An examination of the resolutions passed by the WISH membership at its annual congresses gives a sense of how the concerns of the WISH membership evolved over the 1980s. Although the membership was concerned with a wide range of issues, from public transportation access to public education, it increasingly focused on questions of affordable housing and displacement.[3] Displacement had been a major concern from the very beginning. A few years after its founding, WISH explained its focus on displacement this way:

> One of the most dangerous and threatening issues to face our target area and all of Washington, D.C. is the displacement of Blacks, Latinos, and poor Whites. Indeed, that is the issue that brought the Sponsoring Committee [of churches] together in the first place and is the issue that holds new emerging leadership together now. Our area is made more vulnerable by the fact that most of our people are renters rather than homeowners. . . . Politicians, news reporters, developers, and ordinary citizens see the massive possible turnover of our city both racially and economically.[4]

WISH fought displacement by working to enable low-income tenants' access to safe, affordable housing in their neighborhoods. Examination of just a single year of WISH's work reveals an astonishing array of accomplishments in terms of supporting low-income tenants. Its achievements in one year, 1982, included the following: it stopped nine illegal condominium conversion attempts; helped pass a new city law, which required an owner/developer to get the agreement of at least 51% of tenants to convert a rental building to condominiums, and also guaranteed lifetime tenancy for senior tenants; stopped more than 300 evictions; won $300,000 for tenants who had been illegally overcharged rents; created or helped develop 100 tenants' associations; won 70 agreements by landlords to make repairs, including major repairs in 60 of the buildings (these were large buildings, with 30–450 units each); demanded that landlords of the 10 worst buildings identified by the WISH Slumlord Coalition be prosecuted unless repairs were made (in the end, three of the landlords were prosecuted, four brought their buildings up to code, and three of the buildings were repaired by the city); helped write and pass a new rent control law for the city; won an agreement to rehab 3500 14th Street, NW, a building of more than 250 units, without evicting tenants; helped 29 WISH members become qualified to purchase one of 53 newly rehabilitated units in Columbia Heights; helped get emergency heat for several hundred people over the winter; through the WISH Senior Housing Coalition, won air conditioning in four of the buildings in which it organized, and security systems in all 14 buildings in which it organized; and through the WISH Homecare Coalition, won $400,000 in additional funds from the City Council for home aid services for elderly and handicapped people. Finally, as of 1982, WISH was working with the Metropolitan Washington Planning and Housing Association and the Southern Columbia Heights Tenants Union to help seven tenants' associations buy their buildings and convert them to limited-equity housing cooperatives.[5] Clearly, WISH's work ranged over a wide variety of housing issues. But over the course of the 1980s, WISH became increasingly interested in tenant cooperative ownership as a way to stabilize communities and empower residents.

Wish and Cooperative Housing: Building Collective Economic and Political Power

The United States has a rich history of Black cooperative economics. Jessica Gordon Nembhard theorizes cooperative activity as a way for African Americans to gain collective political and economic power. She discusses the long history of Black cooperative movement in the United States, and emphasizes the important role cooperative economics has played in African American thinking and organizing. "Almost all African American leaders and major thinkers, from the most conservative to the most radical," she writes, "have at some point promoted cooperative economic development as a strategy for African American well-being and liberation" (Gordon Nembhard, 2014, p. 213). Co-op members, Gordon Nembhard finds, receive economic benefits, but they also, through direct involvement in the collective self-governance of the co-op, learn skills of participatory democracy that can help them in other areas of life. WISH's philosophy of the development of housing cooperatives fits within Gordon Nembhard's framework. The housing cooperative, WISH believed, addressed two needs: the desperate need for housing affordability, and the need for neighborhood-scale participation and democracy. As WISH's executive director, Paul Battle, wrote in 1990, "Our focus on co-ops is intended to create a network of organized low and moderate income homeowners, able to constructively participate in neighborhood affairs. They will become building blocks of an empowered community."[6] The housing co-op, that is, was not just about the material need for housing. It was about building a more empowered populace.

While WISH began assisting tenants and other community-organizing groups with cooperative housing development as early as 1982, the first housing co-op for which the organization could really claim primary credit was on Chapin Street NW, in the Columbia Heights neighborhood. The building's tenants contacted WISH in early 1986, looking for help. A year earlier, their building had been sold out from beneath them, in violation of the city law that required landlords to give tenants the opportunity to purchase their buildings should they choose to sell. The tenants knew their rights had been violated, and they wanted to stay in their homes. But the building was in sorry shape. As a reporter from the Washington, DC *Afro-American* described, it "had a troubled history of blight and neglect under the ownership of various landlords."[7] By 1986, only 5 of the building's 26 units were occupied—the terrible conditions in the building and the violence of the block had driven most other tenants out—and only two tenants were active in the struggle to keep the building.[8]

Those two tenants were Deborah Bruce and Blanca Villalobos.[9] Bruce spoke only English, and Villalobos only Spanish—but they were united in their desire to keep their building. With WISH's help, Bruce and Villalobos created a tenants' association, naming it Tenants Right to Fight.[10] And they started searching for funds to buy the building themselves. With WISH's assistance, they organized a "Candidates' Tour" of their building on the evening of Wednesday, September 3, 1986—a week before the primary elections for mayor and City Council (Brisbane, 1986).[11] The purpose was to bring attention to the building and raise political support for the tenants' fight to keep their homes. At this event, Deborah Bruce, who had become president of Tenants Right to Fight, emphasized that their work was part of a broader struggle for affordable housing. As she told the *Afro-American*, "We intend to renovate the building to keep housing costs much lower so that the people of our neighborhood will not be displaced."[12]

After putting together the funds to buy the building—which they did through convincing banks that they were a good credit risk, securing financing from the city, and holding their own fundraisers, like a disco they organized one month—the tenants were finally able to purchase the building as a limited-equity co-op in June 1987. They named it the Chapin Ciara Cooperative, and moved out temporarily so that renovations could begin.[13] While the building once had 26 one-bedroom units, after renovations it had 11 two- and three-bedroom units, which, WISH noted, were more suitable for families.[14] About a year later, with renovations completed, WISH worked with the co-op to organize a grand opening celebration and building tour. WISH distributed a brochure for the grand opening, illustrated with a drawing of the building, and the words, "Reclaim Housing for the Community."[15] This housing, indeed, had been successfully reclaimed from unscrupulous landlords, and was now under the control of its residents—and, importantly, served as an affordable housing resource for others looking for housing. WISH helped Chapin Ciara recruit new members, distributing a brochure, *Welcome to Home Ownership at 1447 Chapin St. NW*, to explain cooperative ownership to prospective members.[16]

The creation of the Chapin Ciara Cooperative was a triumph for the tenants and for WISH. The co-op was soon to gain international attention. In the fall of 1989, the Chapin Ciara Cooperative was selected by the UN Centre for Human Settlements, also known as UN Habitat, as a Citation Award winner. As the director of Habitat's New York office wrote to Paul Battle, "The award is being given in recognition of WISH's work in the provision of shelter to the poorer segments of the population through an innovative approach that could be replicable internationally."[17] WISH was invited to the UN headquarters in New York on October 1, 1989, World Habitat Day, to receive the award. Deborah Bruce, the co-op president, traveled to New York on WISH's behalf to receive the award (that same year, Bruce had been elected the president of WISH's board).[18] Years later, Battle recalled, "When Deborah Bruce went to the U.N., I was the proudest person in the world."[19] With the encouragement from the receipt of this award, WISH began thinking about how it could, in fact, replicate its work internationally.

WISH had already been making international connections. People working on issues of social justice around the world regularly visited the US capital; WISH's location in DC made its office a convenient stop for these folks, who often wanted to hear about local organizing in a city well known for its inequality and racial segregation. In the late 1980s and early 1990s, various relationships with people connected to South Africa in particular began to coalesce. Early on, members of the South African National Civic Organisation, or SANCO, a group that represented local civic associations throughout South Africa, visited DC and attended a WISH membership meeting. The meeting reminded the SANCO representatives of the organizing work they were doing in Johannesburg—and so a connection was born.[20] Another connection was made through a graduate student named Patrick Bond, who was studying at Johns Hopkins University's School for Advanced International Studies in Washington, DC in the late 1980s. Bond had been working with the DC Student Coalition Against Apartheid and Racism, or DC SCAAR, on pressuring Johns Hopkins to divest from South Africa, an issue being tackled on university campuses across the United States in the 1980s.[21] Through his research on divestment, Bond had amassed information on the investment practices of local banks, and he used that information to assist WISH with its anti-redlining campaign in DC.[22] One of the reasons WISH members could not get loans to purchase their homes was because banks were not lending in neighborhoods considered risky. Although the federal Community Reinvestment Act had been passed in 1977, redlining was still a problem in the city, so WISH organized against it with the help of many, including Bond. In 1981, the WISH membership had passed a resolution targeting Riggs Bank, then the city's premier local bank (motto: "The most important bank in the most important city in the world"), to pressure it to invest in poor neighborhoods. "Riggs Bank," the resolution begins, "has a very poor record of reinvesting in our community despite the fact that communities like ours built the bank, at the same time Riggs provided interest free loans to antidemocratic and racist regimes like South Africa and Chile."[23] The lines connecting flows of capital from a DC neighborhood to a nation across the ocean were being drawn.

Other South Africans were building personal connections with WISH. Cas Coovadia, a tenant activist from Johannesburg, visited DC in the fall of 1991 and spoke at a WISH quarterly membership meeting about the tenants' struggle in South Africa.[24] Coovadia worked with a civic association called Actstop, which had initially formed to fight evictions in central Johannesburg during apartheid, and continued to do anti-eviction work after apartheid's demise.[25] Odette Geldenhuys, a lawyer at the Legal Resources Center in Johannesburg, traveled to DC during this time, and visited a number of WISH housing co-ops with Paul Battle. She was inspired by WISH's work, and, upon her return to South Africa, spoke glowingly of WISH to her colleagues working for housing justice.[26]

Interest in cooperative economics had been growing in South Africa throughout the 1980s. A group called Cooperative Planning and Education, known as COPE, was founded in 1988 to help set up cooperatives in South Africa.[27] Although COPE initially focused on worker co-ops and community businesses, by 1991 it had decided to focus its efforts specifically on housing cooperatives. The reason for this shift in focus, COPE reported in its October 1991 newsletter, was the terrible housing crisis in South Africa, and the many requests for housing assistance it had received. "We will be working mainly in informal settlements where the need for housing is greatest," they wrote, "and inner city situations where residents need control over their accommodation to prevent them being exploited by landlords."[28] As Patrick Bond wrote later of that time in South Africa, "[T]he most obvious terrain of conflict during the early 1990s was housing" (2000, p. 222).

Housing in South Africa: From the "Grey" Years to the Seven Buildings Project

In his novel *Welcome to Our Hillbrow*, Phaswane Mpe describes the central Johannesburg Hillbrow neighborhood in the early 1990s: the violence of daily life, the devastating impact of AIDS, the crumbling and overcrowded housing, the tensions between native South Africans and recent immigrants from other parts of the continent, the constant busy movement of the streets (Mpe, 2001). Hillbrow, by the early 1990s, was infamous. But it was only relatively recently that Blacks had even been allowed to live in central city neighborhoods like Hillbrow. The structure of apartheid, formally instituted when the Afrikaner-dominated National

Party came to power in 1948, was relentlessly spatial. The 1950 Group Areas Act required people of different races to live separately, and city centers were zoned for Whites. The 1954 Natives Resettlement Act provided for the removal of Blacks from areas that had been designated White, like central cities and close-in suburbs. Under this act, Black-owned land was expropriated, and Blacks were resettled either in the townships on the periphery of cities, or to further distant homelands. The 1955 Natives (Urban Areas) Amendment Act worked to further remove concentrations of Blacks living in central city apartments. About 10,000 people were removed from Johannesburg alone under this law, many of them servants. Most were relocated to the township of Soweto, southwest of the city of Johannesburg (Christopher, 1994). The city of Johannesburg was for Whites.

But during the 1980s, people of color started filtering into central Johannesburg. The financial center of Johannesburg had moved from the central business district out to Sandton, a gated and highly fortified suburb, and many Whites moved out as well during this time (Ngwane, 2003). This posed a problem for landlords: their White tenants were fleeing the city, but they were not allowed to rent to Blacks. At the same time, the townships were experiencing a housing shortage, and many non-Whites desperately needed housing (Cull, n.d.). Many landlords simply ignored the law, renting to non-White tenants (Joburg Metro Council, 2006). Residential areas in which the races mixed became known as "grey" areas (Cull, n.d.). The illegal nature of Black occupancy of White cities meant that White landlords could charge exorbitant rents while neglecting the buildings, as Black tenants had no legal recourse. Low-income tenants desperately wanted to stay in the city, in large part because the central location made access to work much easier. "More than anything else," COPE reported in 1992, "inner city residents want *security of tenure*—not to have to worry about being kicked out by landlords at any time."[29]

It was in the context of the illegality of Black occupancy and ownership within urban areas that a group of mostly Black Johannesburg tenants got together, in the late 1980s, to try to wrest control of their buildings from their landlord. These tenants lived in seven different buildings scattered across three different central Johannesburg neighborhoods: Hillbrow, Joubert Park, and Berea. Together, these seven buildings comprised 446 units (Cull, n.d.). The seven buildings were all owned by a single landlord, David Gorfil. Gorfil had purchased the buildings in the early 1980s, and had done little to maintain them over the years.[30] As a local newspaper reported at the time, "Tenants say the buildings are in a sorry state and the most basic infrastructure has gone to ruin: lifts do not work, the plumbing needs to be completely overhauled, all the buildings need to be rewired and most of the foyers and garages rebuilt."[31] The tenants had been working with their local civic association, Actstop, which helped them organize a rent boycott in protest over exorbitant rents. But in 1991, Gorfil issued the tenants in all seven buildings a notice to vacate. Threatened with losing their homes, the tenants approached the

Johannesburg Legal Resources Center for assistance (Cull, n.d.). COPE provided training and organizing assistance to the tenants. An organization of progressive city planners, activists, and academics, Planact, helped with the financing of the purchase. Tenant purchase of buildings was a bold move, something that had never been done in South Africa before. As Paul Battle emphasized in an interview with *Organizing* magazine, "[T]he effort to buy the buildings is unique—the tenants would become the first Black owners of an apartment building in South Africa."[32] The effort of these tenants became known as the Seven Buildings Project (the seven buildings involved were Argyle Court, Branksome Towers, Coniston Court, Manhattan Court, Margate Court, Protea Court, and Stanhope Mansions (Cull, n.d.)). In the spring of 1992, the Seven Buildings tenants asked WISH for help in realizing their dream of cooperative ownership.

WISH Goes to Johannesburg, Johannesburg Comes to WISH

For WISH, working in South Africa in the early 1990s felt like both a moral imperative and an incredible opportunity. Nelson Mandela had been released from prison in 1990, but would not be elected president until 1994; this period of time was, for South Africa, rich with potential but also rife with uncertainty. As WISH described in its 1993 annual report:

> WISH came to work in South Africa as an extension of our local commu-
> nity development work, because the same problems and needs for empow-
> erment and community control are present in urban South Africa and
> urban America. Feeling a sense of both moral commitment and excitement
> over the significant new property-ownership possibilities for African ten-
> ants, plus a chance to start "people-to-people" links at the grassroots level,
> WISH decided to devote the time of three staff members to travel and work
> in Johannesburg for 2 to 4 weeks each, April–July 1992.[33]

Executive Director Paul Battle was the first person from WISH to make the trip. In April 1992, he was formally invited by COPE to work as a consultant on the Seven Buildings Project, and he was paid for 80 hours of work over the course of his month-long visit.[34] While in Johannesburg, he stayed with Pressage Nyoni, a tenant organizer on the project, who lived in Argyle Court, one of the seven buildings, in the Hillbrow neighborhood. The similarities between the situation of tenants in inner-city Johannesburg and inner-city DC were clear to Battle and to the South Africans with whom he worked. As COPE wrote in a 1992 article about Battle's first visit:

> Putting the people first is the slogan on the t-shirts of WISH, Washing-
> ton Innercity Self Help. People living in the inner city of Washington, DC,

capital city of the United States, face the same problems as inner city residents of Johannesburg. As in Johannesburg, there are many low income families living in rented apartments (flats), struggling against bad living conditions, lack of maintenance, high rents and evictions. As in Johannesburg, some tenants have taken action around these problems.[35]

In this article, Battle is asked how the situation in Johannesburg compared with DC. He responds, "The people in buildings here and in Washington are very similar. They need the same motivation and have the same doubts."[36]

Two months after Paul Battle's initial trip to South Africa, two other WISH staffers, Martha Davis and Linda Leaks, traveled to the country to continue the work Battle had begun. Davis, who stayed for two weeks, worked to explain to local banks and the Johannesburg City Council how WISH was working with DC banks and local government agencies to finance tenant purchase and cooperative conversion. Leaks, who stayed for a month, worked with tenant organizers, and shared WISH's strategies for organizing tenants in DC. Seven Buildings Project tenants took Linda's experiences seriously; on her advice, for instance, they decided to hire a tenant organizer for each one of the seven buildings.[37] Highly detailed reports from the trip indicate that Davis and Leaks were constantly in meetings, day and night. It was a deeply moving trip for them both. One of the things that stood out in Davis' mind the most from that trip was the singing. Tenants held enormous meetings in the parking garage below one of their buildings, and they opened and closed every meeting with song. Their voices ricocheted off the concrete surfaces, and left her in tears.[38] In a letter addressed to the "7 Buildings Comrades," written shortly after Davis and Leaks returned to Washington, DC, Davis thanked the tenants for their "great hospitality," and recounted some of her impressions of their visit:

> I particularly remember our trip to Soweto, to the soccer game with Kaizer Chiefs, the after-meeting dinners at Manhattan and Margate, the 10 pm. training session in Pressage's flat (the latest training I have ever done in my life!), Kippie's, the farewell party, and the incredible singing at each of your meetings. If I come back, I'm going to bring a bigger tape recorder to record your singing for everyone in Washington to hear.[39]

She signs off, "Again, thanks for all your love and support on my visit. VIVA the 7-Buildings/WISH partnership!"[40]

The WISH–South Africa exchange continued after the initial visits by Battle, Davis, and Leaks. In late 1992, WISH was visited by Monty Narsoo of COPE.[41] While Narsoo was in DC, Leaks organized a reception for him at the 919 L Street Co-op, where she lived, where he discussed cooperative housing and tenant organizing with co-op members.[42] A few months later, in February 1993, WISH helped representatives from the Standard Bank of South Africa and United States Agency for International Development (US AID) to meet with Riggs Bank to learn about how Riggs was engaging in community reinvestment in DC.[43] Just a few weeks after this visit, an agreement was signed for the Seven Buildings Project tenants to purchase their buildings, although the sale was contingent on the tenants' ability to secure financing (Cull, n.d.). Despite the steady efforts of WISH and the South African organizations assisting the tenants, this financing was still unsecured.

In the fall of 1993, a delegation of five from WISH traveled to Johannesburg for 20 days, again at the invitation of COPE and the Seven Buildings tenants. The delegation included Andrew Williams (who was the first vice president of WISH's board, and also the president of his housing co-op, the Eastside Manor Cooperative, which WISH had helped organize), Deborah Bruce (who at that point was an at-large member of WISH's board and still president of Chapin Ciara Cooperative), Paul Battle, Dorothy Kemp (the executive director of Neighborhood Housing Services), and Karen Kollias (of NationsBank). The purpose of the visit was for Williams and Bruce to share their experiences, first as tenants involved in cooperative purchase, and later as co-op leaders; and for Kemp and Kollias to discuss the role of private and public sectors in supporting the development of housing co-ops.[44] In addition, Battle spoke at a housing conference in Durban, South Africa, the theme of which was, "Housing in the Inner City: Making it Happen."[45] Williams and Bruce's role was in part to bolster the confidence of the Johannesburg tenants. WISH described their work in a report filed later that year:

> 7 Buildings tenants, including leaders appeared to be growing tired. Some are beginning to question if they will ever buy the buildings. The buildings are deteriorating, and the owner is demanding an increase in rents. Some of the tenants have lost jobs, so despair has begun to set in. In order to assist tenants in working through this difficult period, Deborah Bruce and Andrew Williams, shared their experiences, which in many ways parallels that of the 7 Buildings tenants.[46]

The visits back and forth continued. In September 1993, a group of bankers and civic leaders from Johannesburg, including a tenant leader of the Seven Buildings Project, met with WISH members and staff in DC. In November of that year, two South African bankers visited WISH to discuss cooperative loans. In January 1994, 15 South African leaders from Capetown met with WISH staff to discuss organizing, development, and training. Also in January 1994, Cynthia Rakale, a South African graduate student at Howard University, joined the WISH staff to produce the WISH newsletter; her role was also to attend various meetings, including tenant and cooperative meetings.[47] In April 1994, "old friends from Actstop" visited WISH to discuss "organizing and development."[48] The next month—May 1994—Nelson Mandela was elected as president of South Africa, inaugurating a new era of democracy.

That fall, US AID awarded a grant to the Maryland-based Cooperative Housing Foundation to develop a framework for cooperative housing in South Africa. "The purpose of the project," the foundation explained, "is to assist the new government in South Africa to diversify the housing delivery system so as to better to meet the housing needs of low and moderate income households and to assist in the empowerment of citizenry through a democratically-based housing delivery mechanism."[49] CHF's partner organizations on the grant were WISH and SANCO, the South African National Civic Organisation. A five-person delegation, including two representatives from CHF, one from SANCO, and Paul Battle, undertook a 10-day "reconnaissance mission," during which they traveled throughout South Africa to promote the development of cooperative housing.[50] While WISH was still in touch with the tenants of the Seven Buildings Project, by this point it was working at a national scale to help influence South Africa's housing policy.

In March 1996, the tenants of the Seven Buildings Project finally received the financing necessary to purchase their buildings, in the form of a 6 million rand subsidy from the Gauteng Department of Housing (the city of Johannesburg is within Gauteng Province). This was the first time a housing project in South Africa received an institutional housing subsidy (Cull, n.d.). The Seven Buildings Project was, as one expert on post-apartheid Johannesburg puts it, the "most celebrated" of the social housing programs initiated by the Johannesburg city government in 1996 (Murray, 2008, p. 142). But by this time, WISH had decided to return its focus to its local work in Washington, DC. As Paul Battle explained later, "I became uncomfortable with it, because I felt we were spending too much time away from D.C."[51] WISH had done what it could in South Africa, and the Seven Buildings tenants had successfully purchased their homes. A time of intensive back-and-forth work across the two cities had come to a close.

Constructing Countertopographies of the City

The housing activists of Johannesburg and Washington, DC were together constructing a countertopography of the city. A topography, as geographer Cindi Katz notes, is a map of a landscape built by contour lines: lines connecting the same points of elevation across space. A topographic map provides a detailed understanding of the contours of a particular place. A countertopography, as Katz theorizes it, is a way to understand how like processes shape different places across the globe. She describes how countertopographies can be constructed:

> Contour lines are lines of constant elevation, connecting places at precisely the same altitude to reveal a terrain's three-dimensional shape. I want to

imagine a politics that maintains the distinctness of place while recognizing that it is connected analytically to other places along contour lines that represent not elevation but particular relations to a process. . . . This offers a multifaceted way of theorizing the connectedness of vastly different places made artifactually discrete by virtue of history and geography but which also reproduce themselves differently amidst the common political-economic and socio-cultural processes they experience. . . . The larger intent is to produce countertopographies that link different places analytically and thereby enhance struggles in the name of common interests.

(Katz, 2001, pp. 1229–1230)

Activists in Washington, DC and Johannesburg were building connections across place, tracing contour lines from Washington, DC to Johannesburg and back again. They saw similar processes at work: first housing segregation, and later redlining, had kept Blacks from owning housing in central neighborhoods in both cities. The legacy of a lack of democracy, while far more profound in South Africa than in Washington, DC, was another line traced. South African tenants were inspired by the work of WISH housing co-op leaders like Deborah Bruce and Andrew Williams, and by organizers like Linda Leaks, herself a co-op member. And the WISH activists were profoundly moved by the struggles of the South African tenants—sometimes to tears. The relationships built through their ongoing exchanges seemed to, as Katz describes, enhance struggles to secure affordable, democratically controlled housing in both cities. In both places, tenants and activists had a vision of a city that would be a good home for poor people.

But what this countertopography reveals over the long term is the difficulty of creating and maintaining affordable housing in the context of capitalist real estate markets, from the east coast of the United States to the tip of southern Africa. Although the Seven Buildings Project had received a grant from the Gauteng Department of Housing to purchase its homes, it had to take out a loan to finance the substantial repairs the buildings needed after decades of neglect by their old landlord. Some co-op members resisted making payments on this loan; many believed that the repairs were insufficient in relation to the amount they were required to repay (Cull, n.d.). By 2002, five of the seven buildings had gone into default on their loans (Murray, 2008). As of the summer of 2013, only two of the buildings were still owned by their occupants. The other five had reverted to rental status, although at least one was considered an affordable rental.[52] Not all the WISH co-ops have remained affordable housing resources for low-income people, either. As of 2014, of the 10 co-ops WISH had developed by the time of their initial visits to South Africa, 2 had failed and 2 had converted to a market-rate condominium structure, thus rendering them unavailable to other low-income people who need affordable housing. Chapin Ciara Cooperative, WISH's very first limited-equity cooperative, was one of the co-ops that ultimately converted to a condominium ownership structure, still under the leadership of Deborah Bruce. In the fall of 2013, one of its units sold for $479,000 (N.a., 2013)—a typical market-rate price for a condominium in the Columbia Heights neighborhood. The challenge, as a scholar of Johannesburg succinctly describes it, lies in "the difficulties of reconciling the goals of maintaining and upgrading inner-city housing stock with the cost-recovery principles that govern the capitalist marketplace" (Murray, 2008, p. 142). What is true for Johannesburg is true for Washington, DC.

The original idea of the WISH–South Africa exchange might have been to see connections and share experiences between tenants and organizers in these two cities. The personal connections built among people across continents were profound, and in some cases life-changing. But in the end, one of the things this countertopography shows is how hard it is to create and maintain affordable housing controlled by its residents in the context of capitalist real estate markets, no matter where you are on the globe. After what was widely regarded as the failure of the Seven Buildings Project, the Johannesburg City Council moved away from supporting cooperative housing, and toward subsidizing rental housing, which was easier for the state to control. After 25 years of work, WISH folded in 2003, although another organization, Empower DC, arose to take its place, and continues to work on questions of displacement in the city. In DC, as of 2015, tenants' associations are still able to purchase their homes and transform them into limited-equity cooperatives. It is not impossible, in the midst of the capitalist cityscape, to create housing that is both affordable and democratically controlled by its members. But ultimately, the struggle for this housing is a matter of collective political will.

Conclusion

Twenty years after his first trip to South Africa, Paul Battle mused, "Did we do any good, or did we just create some trips for ourselves?"[53] WISH certainly did some good: it built connections and enabled people to see similar situations of racism, economics, and housing crisis in cities on two different continents. Although only two of the Seven Buildings Project buildings remain tenant-owned, and although cooperative housing never took off as a framework for affordable housing provision in the new South Africa, this work was still important. People like Odette Geldenhuys, Pressage Nyoni, and many others involved in the Seven Buildings Project went on to do other important work in affordable housing and legal aid in South Africa.[54]

Today, gentrification is coming to Johannesburg. As in Washington, DC, inner-city neighborhoods are becoming hip, and tenants are fighting to remain in place as rents rise. The struggle for equality in the midst of growth—the theme of this book—bedevils cities around the world. It might behoove activists working for housing justice to follow in WISH's footsteps, building exchanges and drawing lines to connect the experiences of poor people living in different cities across continents. Everywhere, people continue to experiment with new forms of struggle. Through building countertopographies, we may yet construct new ways of staking a claim to urban life.

Acknowledgments

Thanks to Paul Battle, Patrick Bond, Martha Davis, Odette Geldenhuys, and Linda Leaks for speaking to me about the work of WISH and the Seven Buildings Project. Thanks also to Derek Gray, archivist at the Washingtoniana collection of the Martin Luther King Jr. Memorial Library, in Washington, DC, for providing access to the WISH papers. Thanks to the Antipode Foundation for funding my travel to the 4th annual Institute for the Geographies of Justice, which took place in South Africa in 2013. Finally, special thanks to Pressage Nyoni for taking the time to drive me around Johannesburg and telling me his story of the Seven Buildings Project.

Notes

1 1st Annual Congress of W.I.S.H. WISH Papers Series 5, Box 22, Washingtoniana Division, Martin Luther King Jr. Memorial Library, Washington, DC. Folder 22/1: 1st Annual Community Congress (1980); W.I.S.H. Washington Innercity Self Help 10th Anniversary 8th Community Congress. WISH Papers Series 5, Box 22, Washingtoniana Division, Martin Luther King Jr. Memorial Library, Washington, DC. Folder 22/8: 8th Annual Community Congress (1988).

2 1st Annual Congress of W.I.S.H. WISH Papers Series 5, Box 22, Washingtoniana Division, Martin Luther King Jr. Memorial Library, Washington, DC. Folder 22/1: 1st Annual Community Congress (1980). Quote p. 9.

3 WISH 2nd Annual Community Congress. WISH Papers Series 5, Box 22, Washingtoniana Division, Martin Luther King Jr. Memorial Library, Washington, DC. Folder 22/2: 2nd Annual Community Congress (1981); Washington Innercity Self Help 7th Annual Congress; Resolutions. WISH Papers Series 5, Box 22, Washingtoniana Division, Martin Luther King Jr. Memorial Library, Washington, DC. Folder 22/7: 7th Annual Community Congress (1986); W.I.S.H. Washington Innercity Self Help 10th Anniversary 8th Community Congress. WISH Papers Series 5, Box 22, Washingtoniana Division, Martin Luther King Jr. Memorial Library, Washington, DC. Folder 22/8: 8th Annual Community Congress (1988).

4 Washington Innercity Self Help: Proposal: Aetna Life and Casualty. WISH Papers Series 9, Box 38, Washingtoniana Division, Martin Luther King Jr. Memorial Library, Washington, DC. Folder 38/24: Fundraising/Grants (1982–1991). Quote pp. 6–7.

5 Ibid.

6 Proposal from Washington Innercity Self Help (WISH) to Local Initiatives Support Corporation (LISC), March 13, 1990. WISH Papers Series 9, Box 38, Washingtoniana Division, Martin Luther King Jr. Memorial Library, Washington, DC. Folder 38/24: Fundraising/Grants (1982–1991). Quote p. 8.

7 City officials, candidates to tour Chapin St. Apartments. *Washington Afro-American*, September 2, 1986. WISH Papers Series 1, Box 5, Washingtoniana Division, Martin Luther King Jr. Memorial Library, Washington, DC. Folder 5/57: Chapin Ciara Cooperative/ Tenants Right to Fight, Inc.— 1447 Chapin Street NW (1986–1989).

8 Letter from Sara Case, WISH, to Sister Kate McDonnell, Housing Counseling Services, April 2, 1986. WISH Papers Series 1, Box 5, Washingtoniana Division, Martin Luther King Jr. Memorial Library, Washington, DC. Folder 5/57: Chapin Ciara Cooperative/ Tenants Right to Fight, Inc.— 1447 Chapin Street NW (1986–1989); Department of Housing and Community Development Loan Application. WISH Papers Series 1, Box 5, Washingtoniana Division, Martin Luther King Jr. Memorial Library, Washington, DC. Folder 5/57: Chapin Ciara Cooperative/Tenants Right to Fight, Inc.— 1447 Chapin Street NW (1986–1989); Reclaim Housing for the Community: Chapin Ciara Cooperative, July 15, 1988. WISH Papers Series 1, Box 5, Washingtoniana Division, Martin Luther King Jr. Memorial Library, Washington, DC. Folder 5/57: Chapin Ciara Cooperative/Tenants Right to Fight, Inc.— 1447 Chapin Street NW (1986–1989).

9 Letter from Sara Case, WISH, to Sister Kate McDonnell.

10 Bylaws of Tenants Right to Fight, Inc. WISH Papers Series 1, Box 5, Washingtoniana Division, Martin Luther King Jr. Memorial Library, Washington, DC. Folder 5/57: Chapin Ciara Cooperative/Tenants Right to Fight, Inc.— 1447 Chapin Street NW (1986–1989).

11 Candidates' tour of 1447 Chapin Street, NW. WISH Papers Series 1, Box 5, Washingtoniana Division, Martin Luther King Jr. Memorial Library, Washington, DC. Folder 5/57: Chapin Ciara Cooperative/Tenants Right to Fight, Inc.— 1447 Chapin Street NW (1986–1989).

12 City officials, candidates to tour Chapin St. Apartments.

13 Barras, Jonetta Rose, Caught in the squeeze: Tenants fight for affordable housing. *Washington Afro-American*, January 31, 1987; Letter from Sara Case to Geraldine Marshall, July 7, 1987. WISH Papers Series 1, Box 5, Washingtoniana Division, Martin Luther King Jr. Memorial Library, Washington, DC. Folder 5/57: Chapin Ciara Cooperative/ Tenants Right to Fight, Inc.— 1447 Chapin Street NW (1986–1989).

14 Reclaim housing for the community: Chapin Ciara Cooperative, July 15, 1988. WISH Papers Series 1, Box 5, Washingtoniana Division, Martin Luther King Jr. Memorial Library, Washington, DC. Folder 5/57: Chapin Ciara Cooperative/Tenants Right to Fight, Inc.— 1447 Chapin Street NW (1986–1989).

15 Ibid.

16 *Welcome to Home Ownership at 1447 Chapin St. NW.* WISH Papers Series 1, Box 5, Washingtoniana Division, Martin Luther King Jr. Memorial Library, Washington, DC. Folder 5/59: Chapin Ciara Cooperative—1447 Chapin Street NW—Photos and Brochures (n.d.).

17 Letter from Agwu U. Okali, UN Habitat New York Office, to Paul Battle, WISH, September 21, 1989. WISH Papers Series 1, Box 5, Washingtoniana Division, Martin Luther King Jr. Memorial Library, Washington, DC. Folder 5/57: Chapin Ciara Cooperative/Tenants Right to Fight, Inc.— 1447 Chapin Street NW (1986–1989).

18 Hello, WISH. *W.I.S.H. Highlights*, 1(1), August 1989. WISH Papers Series 5, Box 24, Washingtoniana Division, Martin Luther King Jr. Memorial Library, Washington, DC. Folder 24/21: WISH Highlights Newsletter (1989–1993).

19 Phone interview with Paul Battle, April 27, 2013.

20 Ibid.

21 See statement by Patrick Bond in *United States Student Movement Against Apartheid—Hearings at the United Nations Headquarters, New York, June 27, 1986*. African Activist Archive, Michigan State University. Accessible online at africanactivist.msu.edu.

22 Phone interview with Paul Battle, July 8, 2014.

23 WISH 2nd Annual Community Congress. WISH Papers Series 5, Box 22, Washingtoniana Division, Martin Luther King Jr. Memorial Library, Washington, DC. Folder 22/2: 2nd Annual Community Congress (1981). Quote p. 15.

24 Quarterly Meeting Flyer. WISH Papers Series 9, Box 40, Washingtoniana Division, Martin Luther King Jr. Memorial Library, Washington, DC. Folder 40/42: Quarterly Membership Meetings (1991–2003).

25 COPE Funding Proposal and Budget, March 1992 to February 1994. WISH Papers Series 2, Box 16, Washingtoniana Division, Martin Luther King Jr. Memorial Library, Washington, DC. Folder 16/22: South Africa Project—COPE Publications (n.d., 1993–1994).

26 Interview with Odette Geldenhuys, May 28, 2013, Durban, South Africa.

27 What is a Cooperative? A COPE publication. WISH Papers Series 2, Box 16, Washingtoniana Division, Martin Luther King Jr. Memorial Library, Washington, DC. Folder 16/22: South Africa Project—COPE Publications (n.d., 1993–1994).

28 *Co-op Voice: Newsletter of Cooperative Planning and Education (COPE)*, 3, October 1991. WISH Papers Series 2, Box 16, Washingtoniana Division, Martin Luther King Jr. Memorial Library, Washington, DC. Folder 16/23: South Africa Project—COPE and NEWHCO Newsletters (1991–1992). Quote p. 1.

29 *Co-op Voice: Newsletter of Cooperative Planning and Education (COPE)*, 6, November 1992. WISH Papers Series 2, Box 16, Washingtoniana Division, Martin Luther King Jr. Memorial Library, Washington, DC. Folder 16/23: South Africa Project—COPE and NEWHCO Newsletters (1991–1992). Quote p. 6, emphasis in original.

30 Notes, Linda Leaks. WISH Papers Series 2, Box 16a, Washingtoniana Division, Martin Luther King Jr. Memorial Library, Washington, DC. Folder 16a/30: South Africa Project—WISH Visit—Misc. (1992).

31 Haffajee, Ferial. Novel plan for low-cost city housing. *The Weekly Mail*, April 24–29, 1992. WISH Papers Series 2, Box 16, Washingtoniana Division, Martin Luther King Jr. Memorial Library, Washington, DC. Folder 16/26: South Africa Project—South Africa newspaper clippings (1989–1997).

32 Vanover, John. New tactics in Johannesburg. *Organizing*, Fall 1992. WISH Papers Series 2, Box 16a, Washingtoniana Division, Martin Luther King Jr. Memorial Library, Washington, DC. Folder 16a/29: South Africa Project—WISH Visit (1992) [2]. Quote p. 43.

33 WISH: Celebrating our 15th anniversary: 1993 annual report. WISH Papers Series 5, Box 23, Washingtoniana Division, Martin Luther King Jr. Memorial Library, Washington, DC. Folder 23/19: Annual Reports (1987–1994). Quote p. 24.

34 Invoice, July 30, 1992. WISH Papers Series 2, Box 15, Washingtoniana Division, Martin Luther King Jr. Memorial Library, Washington, DC. Folder 15/19: South Africa Project (n.d., 1991–1992).

35 It's not just WISHing! *Co-op Voice: Newsletter of Cooperative Planning and Education (COPE)*, 5, June 1992. WISH Papers Series 2, Box 16, Washingtoniana Division, Martin Luther King Jr. Memorial Library, Washington, DC. Folder 16/23: South Africa Project—COPE and NEWHCO Newsletters (1991–1992). Quote p. 4.

36 Ibid. Quote p. 5.
37 WISH Link. *Co-op Voice, Newsletter of Cooperative Planning and Education (COPE)*, 6, November 1992. WISH Papers Series 2, Box 15, Washingtoniana Division, Martin Luther King Jr. Memorial Library, Washington, DC. Folder 15/19: South Africa Project (n.d., 1991–1992).
38 Interview with Martha Davis, May 19, 2013, Washington, DC.
39 Letter to 7 Buildings Comrades, from Martha Davis (unsigned), August 17, 1992. WISH Papers Series 2, Box 16a, Washingtoniana Division, Martin Luther King Jr. Memorial Library, Washington, DC. Folder 16a/29: South Africa Project—WISH Visit (1992) [2].
40 Ibid.
41 W.I.S.H. reviews the year 1992. *W.I.S.H. Highlights*, Winter 1993. WISH Papers Series 5, Box 24, Washingtoniana Division, Martin Luther King Jr. Memorial Library, Washington, DC. Folder 24/21: WISH Highlights Newsletter (1989–1993).
42 Linda Leaks Staff Report, January 25, 1993. WISH Papers Series 9, Box 36, Washingtoniana Division, Martin Luther King Jr. Memorial Library, Washington, DC. Folder 36/7: Board/Staff (1993).
43 WISH: Celebrating our 15th anniversary: 1993 annual report.
44 Letter from Robert Richards, PACT, to Paul Battle, WISH, September 16, 1993. WISH Papers Series 2, Box 16, Washingtoniana Division, Martin Luther King Jr. Memorial Library, Washington, DC. Folder 16/20: South Africa Project (1993).
45 The New Housing Company Conference Programme. WISH Papers Series 2, Box 16, Washingtoniana Division, Martin Luther King Jr. Memorial Library, Washington, DC. Folder 16/20: South Africa Project (1993).
46 Report to PACT on South Africa trip. WISH Papers Series 2, Box 16, Washingtoniana Division, Martin Luther King Jr. Memorial Library, Washington, DC. Folder 16/20: South Africa Project (1993). Quote p. 4.
47 Staff column, *W.I.S.H. Chronicle*, Winter 1994. WISH Papers Series 5, Box 24, Washingtoniana Division, Martin Luther King Jr. Memorial Library, Washington, DC. Folder 24/20: WISH Chronicle Newsletter (1994–2000). Quote p. 11.
48 WISH: Putting the people first: 1994 annual report. WISH Papers Series 5, Box 23, Washingtoniana Division, Martin Luther King Jr. Memorial Library, Washington, DC. Folder 23/19: Annual Reports (1987–1994). Quotes p. 36.
49 Cooperative housing as an alternative delivery mechanism for low and moderate income South Africans: Implementation plan: Phase 2. WISH Papers Series 2, Box 16, Washingtoniana Division, Martin Luther King Jr. Memorial Library, Washington, DC. Folder 16/21: South Africa Project (1994). Quote p. 1.
50 Ibid.
51 Phone interview with Paul Battle, April 27, 2013.
52 Interview with Pressage Nyoni, June 6, 2013, Johannesburg, South Africa.
53 Phone interview with Paul Battle, April 27, 2013.
54 Interview with Odette Geldenhuys, May 28, 2013, Durban, South Africa.

References

Articles of Incorporation of Washington Innercity Self Help, Inc. (1978–1982). WISH Papers Series 9, Box 36, Washingtoniana Division, Martin Luther King Jr. Memorial Library, Washington, DC: Folder 36/3: Articles of Incorporation (1978–1982).

Bond, P. (2000). *Cities of gold, townships of coal: Essays on South Africa's new urban crisis.* Asmara, Eritrea: Africa World Press.

Brisbane, A.S. (1986, September 10). Barry gains landslide in district, *The Washington Post.*

Christopher, A.J. (1994). *The Atlas of apartheid.* New York, NY: Routledge.

Community Economic Development—Washington Innercity Self Help (W.I.S.H.). (n.d.). WISH Papers Series 9, Box 40, Washingtoniana Division, Martin Luther King Jr. Memorial Library, Washington, DC: Folder 40/52: WISH History and Structure (n.d.).

Cull, T. (n.d.). The Seven Buildings Project: The rise and fall of social housing in the Johannesburg inner city? Unpublished paper.

Fauntroy, M.K. (2003). *Home rule or house rule? Congress and the erosion of local governance in the District of Columbia.* New York, NY: University Press of America.

Fauntroy, W.E. (1986). A report to the citizens of the District of Columbia. Washington, DC: US House of Representatives.

Gale, D.E. (1976). The back-to-the-city movement—or is it? A survey of recent homebuyers in the Mount Pleasant neighborhood of Washington, D.C. Washington, DC: Department of Urban and Regional Planning, George Washington University.

Gale, D.E. (1977). The back-to-the-city movement revisited: A survey of recent homebuyers in the Capitol Hill neighborhood of Washington, D.C. Washington, DC: Department of Urban and Regional Planning, George Washington University.

Gale, D.E. (1987). *Washington, D.C.: Inner-city revitalization and minority suburbanization.* Philadelphia, PA: Temple University Press.

Gately, B. (1978, December 21). Tenant rebellion fueled by increases in rent, evictions. *The Washington Post.*

Gordon Nembhard, J. (2014). *Collective courage: A history of African American cooperative economic thought and practice.* University Park, PA: Pennsylvania State University Press.

Henig, J.R. (1982). Gentrification in Adams Morgan: Political and commercial consequences of neighborhood change. *G. W. Washington Studies.* Washington, DC: Center for Washington Area Studies, George Washington University.

Huron, A. (2014). Creating a commons in the capital: The emergence of limited-equity housing cooperatives in Washington, DC. *Washington History, 26*(2), 56–67.

Jaffe, H.S., & Sherwood, T. (1994). *Dream city: Race, power, and the decline of Washington, DC.* New York, NY: Simon & Schuster.

Joburg Metro Council. (2006). *Joburg! The passion behind a city.* Johannesburg, South Africa: Affinity Publishing.

Katz, C. (2001). On the grounds of globalization: A topography for feminist political engagement. *Signs: Journal of Women in Culture and Society, 26*(4), 1213–1234.

Mpe, P. (2001). *Welcome to our Hillbrow.* Pietermaritzburg, South Africa: University of Natal Press.

Murray, M.J. (2008). *Taming the disorderly city: The spatial landscape of Johannesburg after apartheid.* Ithaca, NY: Cornell University Press.

N.a. (1978, September 7). At-large council race has bids from 11 candidates. *The Washington Post.*

N.a. (2013, October 31). D.C. home sales. *The Washington Post.*

Ngwane, T.I. (2003). Sparks in the township. *New Left Review, 22,* 37–56.

Soul Side. (1989). Bass. On *Bass/103.* Washington, DC: Dischord Records.

Wells, K. (2013). *A decent place to stay: Housing crises, failed laws, and property conflicts in Washington, DC* (Doctoral dissertation, Syracuse University).

WISH Housing Development Program (Revised—January 1987). (1987–1994). WISH Papers Series 5, Box 23, Washingtoniana Division, Martin Luther King Jr. Memorial Library, Washington, DC: Folder 23/19: Annual Reports (1987–1994).

W.I.S.H. Washington Innercity Self Help 10th Anniversary 8th Community Congress. (1988). WISH Papers Series 5, Box 22, Washingtoniana Division, Martin Luther King Jr. Memorial Library, Washington, DC: Folder 22/8: 8th Annual Community Congress (1988).

Zeitz, E. (1979). *Private urban renewal: A different residential trend*. Lexington, MA: Lexington Books.

6

"WE ARE HEADED FOR SOME BAD TROUBLE"

Gentrification and Displacement in Washington, DC, 1920–2014

Chris Myers Asch and George Derek Musgrove

The city was changing at a breakneck speed. After decades of White flight, young professionals were moving back to Washington, DC, anxious for a taste of the city life their parents had left a generation before. To meet the demand, developers converted scores of dilapidated apartment buildings into condominiums, while contractors and individual homebuyers purchased, gutted, and restored house after house in poor, run-down areas of the old L'Enfant city. As higher-income people moved in, housing prices skyrocketed, attracting even more speculators, investors, and homebuyers eager to capitalize on the boom.

While some business owners and city tax collectors celebrated the return of young professionals, others viewed them with dread. The frenzy of real estate speculation that the newcomers set in motion displaced thousands of poor renters and sent them scrambling for affordable housing. So great was the level of displacement that *The Washington Post*'s real estate columnist fretted that the rapid movement of young professionals into the center city was forcing the urban poor and the suburban middle class into a disruptive game of "musical chairs" (Von Eckardt, 1979).

To contemporary residents of Washington, DC, these scenes seem all too familiar after a well-publicized, 15-year burst of development and displacement that has fundamentally changed the physical, demographic, and political terrain of the capital city. Yet these stories describe Washington, DC in 1979, not 2015. The process of gentrification that the city has experienced in the early 21st century goes back much further than current news coverage and popular lore make it seem. Indeed, far from being a new or unprecedented phenomenon, the surge of development and displacement in the early 21st century is in fact the fourth wave of "private revitalization" or "gentrification" to wash over the city in the past century.[1] Earlier waves engulfed Georgetown in the 1920s through the 1950s; Capitol Hill, Foggy Bottom, and Kalorama in the 1940s and 1950s; and Capitol Hill, Hill East, Logan Circle, Dupont Circle, Mount Pleasant, Adams Morgan, and LeDroit Park in the 1970s and 1980s. The contemporary wave, which dates to the late 1990s, has covered nearly all of the old city and beyond, reaching as far north as Petworth and as far east as historic Anacostia. Slowed but not stopped by the economic crisis of 2007–2008, it continues to spread further into formerly low-income parts of Washington, DC (Shin, 2012).

In the past 40 years, historians, geographers, linguists, and anthropologists have produced a rich body of research on gentrification in the city, typically focusing on a single wave or neighborhood (Berry Sherwood, 1978; Gale, 1982, 1987; Henig, 1982; Huron, 2012, 2014; Hyra, forthcoming; Jones, 2010; Lesko, Babb, & Gibbs, 1991; Logan, 2015; Modan, 2007; Paige & Reuss, 1983; Prince, 2014; Ruble, 2012; Smith 1974; Turner, 1998; Wells, 2013; Williams, 1988; Zeitz, 1979). This chapter synthesizes that research, traces the connections between the different waves, and makes the case that gentrification has had a pronounced impact on race relations and city politics, with battles over changing neighborhoods shaping residents' reactions to successive waves.

Although each of the four waves emerged from its own particular historical context, they nonetheless had similar causes. Fundamental to all but one was the expansion of the federal government and its ancillary industries, which attracted young, well-educated professionals to the city. These new residents were typically (but never exclusively) young, White, and childless. Although solidly middle class, they generally were not wealthy, and for economic, and often aesthetic and social, reasons they sought relatively cheaper housing in economically marginalized neighborhoods. Frequently aided by public policies designed to encourage development, their efforts created or expanded pockets of affluence in poor and working-class communities, making them attractive to others of their class and social group. Once these areas became fashionable, additional young professionals and developers flooded in, attracted both by the cachet that these neighborhoods now offered, and the new amenities and investment possibilities made available by their presence.

The new residents displaced renters both physically (by purchasing houses and apartments formerly occupied by renters) and through market pressure (by increasing property values, thereby moving landlords to raise rents). They exerted a similar pressure on the much smaller number of poor and working-class homeowners in these neighborhoods who faced increased tax bills and cultural alienation from their new neighbors. Despite improved services and rising property values, most older residents viewed gentrification as a threat and turned to the federal or city government to mitigate its effects. Until the advent of home rule, their pleas were ignored. In the 1970s, however, the newly minted City Council responded by passing some of the most ambitious anti-displacement legislation in the country, which, although it did not stop the third wave, served as a breaker behind which some of the poor could find safe harbor. In the early 21st century, when the fourth wave rolled across the city, some of the poor were again able to use these laws to steel themselves against the rough surf. The sheer size and power of the fourth wave, however, topped these barriers, swept the poor into the eastern wards and Prince George's County, Maryland, and ended the Black majority that had defined city life for half a century.

The First Wave: Georgetown

When housing advocate and journalist John Ihlder moved to Washington, DC in 1920, housing was scarce and prices were high. Mobilization for the Great War had swelled the city's population to more than 437,000—down from the wartime high of 526,000 in 1918, but still substantially more than the 350,000 who lived in the city at the start of hostilities. A Cornell graduate with a young family, Ihlder sought safe and respectable housing, preferably within walking distance of his office at the Chamber of Commerce just north of Lafayette Park. With most of the affordable downtown housing consisting of rooming houses, outdated apartment buildings, alley dwellings, and properties in African American or mixed-race neighborhoods, he had few viable options. There was, however, the charming but unfashionable neighborhood of Georgetown. In the 1910s, a number of well-bred federal workers, most from the Smithsonian and the State Department, had moved to the area. They were drawn to the beautiful federal-style mansions, quaint row houses, and small-town feel of the old port city. In small but significant numbers they began purchasing and revitalizing homes in the north and east of the neighborhood. Ihlder joined their ranks in 1920 when he bought a three-story brick row house at 2811 O Street, NW (Gale, 1982). Although they could not have predicted it at the time, Ihlder and his neighbors had set in motion a chain of events that would make Georgetown one of the most exclusive neighborhoods in the city and set the template for "private revitalization" for the next six decades.

Founded in the mid-18th century to warehouse tobacco gathered from the surrounding plantations, Georgetown was the oldest community in the District of Columbia. On the heights above the Potomac, the town's elite built beautiful colonial and neoclassical-style mansions that gave the town an air of gentility that was well regarded in adjoining Washington City. In the mid-19th century, Georgetown expanded to handle the traffic of the Chesapeake and Ohio Canal, and light industry came to replace tobacco processing. Workers packed into narrow row houses or boarding houses near the Canal, while middle- and upper-class families purchased spacious federal-style townhouses further up the hill. Population pressures from nearby Washington City brought a burst of alley dwelling construction during the Civil War, as well as dozens of new Victorian-style row houses in the undeveloped Northeast section near Rock Creek, in the late century.

Although dynamic in its first 150 years, by the early 20th century George-town had stagnated. In the first two decades of the new century, the canal faded into irrelevance and local manufacturers lost market share to national competitors. Georgetown's diverse housing stock, once the envy of Washington City, began to show its age, and certain areas of the neighborhood became run down. Younger residents moved away and, outside of an increase during the citywide housing crisis of the Great War, the neighborhood steadily lost population (Gale, 1982).

While forgotten by many in the neighborhoods across Rock Creek, George-town was nonetheless home to a number of diverse and vibrant communities. As historians Kathleen Lesko, Valerie Babb, and C. R. Gibbs have observed, the neighborhood hosted a rich "mosaic" of class and racial groups, from the shabby aristocracy who clung to their outdated mansions atop the hill to the poor Irish and Black workers of the alleys and rooming houses below (Gale, 1982; Lesko, Babb, & Gibbs, 1991).

In this environment, few residents thought much about the handful of young professionals such as Ihlder who purchased and fixed up old houses. They had been moving to the neighborhood for more than a decade with little noticeable impact on the larger community. In 1924, however, the newcomers coalesced into a distinct interest group and began to exert a disproportionate influence on the whole. That year they joined with older elites from the (White) Georgetown Citizens Association to oppose developers' plans to construct modern apartment buildings in the east of the neighborhood near Rock Creek. As the head of the association's Home Owners Committee, Ihlder succeeded in securing zoning restrictions that limited new construction and, the association hoped, maintained the small town feel of the neighborhood. The spectacle of their beautifully restored homes drew the attention of the local press, who, by late decade, began to refer to a "revitalization movement" in central Georgetown (Gale, 1982; Howick Fant, 1982). In 1930, these revitalization advocates allowed the public into their 18th-century mansions and restored federal-style row houses as part of a "house tour" sponsored by St. John's Church. Within a few short years, their efforts altered the perception of Georgetown among many White Washingtonians. Previously dismissed as a crumbling, working-class backwater, by mid-decade the neighborhood was described as "quaint," "genteel," even "fashionable" (Gale, 1982).

The change in Georgetown's popular image coincided with an enormous growth in the federal workforce under Franklin Delano Roosevelt's New Deal, and the two together spurred significant change in the neighborhood. Between 1933 and 1935, FDR called for, and Congress created, an alphabet soup of federal agencies that hired legions of lawyers, clerks, statisticians, and other white-collar workers at the breathtaking rate of 10,000 per year (Gale, 1987). Georgetown attracted a disproportionate share of these newcomers, along with a significant number of journalists and members of Congress. The area even gained a bohemian flavor from the many artists who flocked around First Lady Eleanor Roosevelt. As their numbers increased and the society pages focused on their dinner parties and salons, restoration began to take on a momentum of its own, simultaneously transforming the public perception of the neighborhood and drawing in greater and greater numbers of young professionals (Gale, 1982).

The rapid movement of young professionals into this predominantly working-class neighborhood created uncharacteristic concentrations of wealth and poverty, Black and White, living side by side, as the rest of the city was growing more segregated. Since the 1890s Washington, DC real estate agents, developers, and lenders had labored to create a segregated housing market. Agents steered buyers to different neighborhoods based on race, White developers used covenants to create racial exclusivity, and lenders denied African Americans credit in the legitimate housing market independent of their ability to pay. The Supreme Court gave their activities official sanction in 1926 when it upheld the use of racial covenants among White property owners in *Corrigan v. Buckley*. In 1934, the Federal Housing Administration (FHA) lent executive support to these policies by creating instructions for lenders that required them to designate any non-White or racially mixed neighborhood as "high risk." In the ensuing decades, these FHA guidelines funneled millions of dollars to the White neighborhoods outside of the L'Enfant city and the suburbs beyond. Almost no federally subsidized loans went to Black and mixed-race neighborhoods. By the 1930s, these policies had created a thoroughly class- and race-segregated housing market in the areas outside of the old L'Enfant city (Green, 1976; Jackson, 1980).

Revitalization advocates helped bring these trends to Georgetown. Many new residents associated working-class people and all Black residents with "blight" and applauded any developments that led to their removal. Writing in the *Georgetown News* in 1936, real estate agent Joseph Wise noted that "many excellent people have come over here and taken over small and inferior dwellings, some of which have been inhabited by colored people, and have made them into very acceptable residences. This is a distinct improvement to Georgetown" (Gale, 1982, p. 191).

Unsurprisingly, revitalization led to displacement. Between 1940 and 1960, the number of units occupied by Black renters, the most vulnerable of the neighborhood's working class, dropped from 20% to 3% of the population. In an era before renters' rights, Black Georgetown resident and retired police officer Everett Payne explained the startling simplicity with which this process took place: "see, they'd come in, y'see. And, um, y'see when the people owned it . . . (if) you was rentin', you had to move" (Gale, 1982, pp. 209 and 188).

Some Black residents attempted to fight displacement by purchasing their homes, only to be denied credit by local banks. But homeownership was no bar to displacement. Although Georgetown's small number of Black homeowners remained constant from 1940 to 1950, it too began a steep decline as the community began to ossify. With most of the renters gone, Black schools were drained of students, churches of parishioners, and businesses of customers. With little to keep them in the old neighborhood, and real estate agents offering them significant sums for their homes, these homeowners too moved away (Gale, 1982; Lesko, Babb, & Gibbs, 1991).

By the 1940s, Georgetown revitalization advocates began applying the new concept of "historic preservation" to guide their efforts. Previously, they had not been particularly interested in restoring houses; individual homeowners had simply remodeled their homes in whatever style they preferred. In the 1930s, however, many developed a taste for Georgetown history, consuming book after book on the subject (Gale, 1982). In the following decade, they joined the national push to preserve historic sites that would result in the creation of the National Trust for Historic Preservation in 1949. Working under the assumption that "the majority of residents in Georgetown lived there because of its esthetic qualities, especially the character of the area, created by examples of colonial and Federal architecture," the (all-White) Progressive Citizens Association of Georgetown drew up the Old Georgetown Act, federal legislation designating the entire neighborhood above M Street as a historic area. The bill would have required that all of the facades of houses in the area be maintained in their current form and that any new buildings be submitted to a panel of architects to ensure that they matched the historic character of the neighborhood (*The Washington Post*, 1957).

The congressional hearings on the Old Georgetown Act gave Black residents their first governmental forum for voicing their concerns about displacement. Testifying on behalf of Georgetown's Black community were Rev. J.D. Foy, pastor of Mt. Zion United Methodist Church, and Mrs. Gertrude T. Waters, a schoolteacher. Both voiced their concerns that the historic designation would only accelerate the process of displacement, already well advanced. The bill's supporters countered that the rise of home prices was a race-neutral market force (conveniently ignoring the discriminatory real estate market that had enveloped the city) and claimed that no extralegal coercive practices were being used to displace Black residents. Because no overt racial coercion could be proved, they continued, the bill should be passed. The congressmen, already disinclined to pay much heed to these Black residents, and many of who had colleagues and staff who lived in Georgetown, overwhelmingly agreed (Gale, 1982).

By 1960, what was being called "restoration" had so changed Georgetown that few who knew the neighborhood in the 1920s could recognize it. Between M Street and the Potomac River, much of the old industrial area remained intact, although business had slowed to a crawl. Along the M Street commercial strip, however, working-class-oriented wholesalers, hardware stores, and beauty shops had given way to antique shops and cafés catering to a wealthier clientele. Tucked along the residential streets to the north were the homes of 767 members of the press, 57 congressmen, and scores of their social and economic peers. Although a few working-class families and blue-collar businesses remained, they clearly were relics of a bygone era. Perhaps no event better symbolized this transformation than President-elect John Kennedy's departure for his inauguration from his townhouse at 3307 N Street in January 1961. In 30 short years, Georgetown had been transformed from a neglected working-class community into one of the most expensive and prestigious areas in the city (Gale, 1982; Herken, 2014).

The Georgetown experience is critical for understanding gentrification in Washington, DC. Well through the 1980s, city residents, Black and White, rich and poor, viewed Georgetown as the preeminent symbol of private restoration and the creation of a race- and class-exclusive neighborhood.[2] They diverged, however, in their interpretation of how that process occurred and to whose benefit. As Lesko, Babb, and Gibbs note, in the 1930s and 1940s, as "poorer families began to vie with restorationists for existing property, two parallel Georgetown histories emerged. One is a written record . . . [of] non-racial gentrification by property owners motivated primarily by preserving value of their investments. The other is an oral story told quietly by current and former Black Georgetowners who remember being forced out intentionally by developers and restorers" (1991, p. 89).

The Second Wave: Becoming a National Leader in "Inner City Revitalization"

By the early 1950s, Benjamin Burch must have seen the writing on the wall. A builder specializing in renovating older homes, he had made good money in Georgetown during the late 1940s. But the supply of inexpensive older properties was beginning to dry up in the fast-changing neighborhood. Scanning the city for a new community where he could buy cheaply, he fixed on Foggy Bottom, an old industrial area southeast of Georgetown where alley houses abounded and African American renters predominated. Amateur developers had attempted to flip properties in the northeastern section of the neighborhood as early as the late 1930s, but their efforts had not precipitated a revitalization movement. Young professionals, it appeared, were wary of investing in an industrial slum where most of their neighbors would be poor and working-class African Americans for the foreseeable future. In the early 1950s, however, Burch undoubtedly believed that things would be different. Most of the massive gas storage tanks that had dominated the area near the waterfront were now gone, and developers were considering building apartments in their stead (Berry Sherwood, 1978). Additionally, the Georgetown restoration movement had reached a point where prices were moving beyond many young professionals' means to pay. If Burch could supply an alternative in Foggy Bottom, the neighborhood might just take off.

In 1952, Burch purchased four houses at 2218–24 Virginia Avenue and another at 2423 I Street and began restoring them with the financial backing of the Woodward and Norris real estate firm. He advertised the houses to young professionals then shopping in Georgetown, and they sold quickly (*Evening Star*, 1952a, 1952b). Over the course of the next eight years, he restored 20 more neighborhood houses. A number of developers and flippers rushed to copy Burch's example. Georgetown residents Jonas and Jean Robitscher purchased and remodeled 26 alley houses in Snow's Court, not far from Burch's I Street property. Eleanor Dulles, sister to Secretary of State John Foster Dulles, bought several properties in the adjoining Green's Court. After three years of frenzied construction, these developers and amateur flippers had renovated about 150 buildings, more than a quarter of the neighborhood stock (Beveridge, 1955). Young professionals rushed to snap up the new properties, and Foggy Bottom, along with Capitol Hill and Kalorama, emerged as one of the swells of second-wave private restoration in Washington, DC.

Like the first wave, second-wave restoration was generated by the postwar demand for "in town" housing by young, white-collar federal workers, many of whom arrived during World War II and stayed to lend their talents to the emerging Cold War. African Americans, swept up in the Second Great Migration, also journeyed to the city in large numbers during this period. Together these transplants increased the District's population from 663,000 in 1940 to roughly 900,000 at the height of the war emergency in 1943 before settling at 802,000 in 1950, a level unmatched since (US Census, 1941, 1951, 1996).

They entered a thoroughly segregated housing market. Hemmed in by the invisible walls erected by lenders, real estate agents, and White homeowners, Black migrants packed into a center-city "black belt" that looped in a giant arc from Foggy Bottom in the west around downtown to the southwest. By expanding at the edges, the black belt came to encompass much of the area below Florida Avenue and between Rock Creek and the Anacostia River by the early 1950s, raising fears of "blight" among White residents, city leaders, and the editorial board of *The Washington Post* (Roberts, 1952). Most White newcomers, on the other hand, moved to Georgetown, the (segregated) neighborhoods that ringed the center city, or the growing suburbs of Prince George's, Montgomery, and Arlington Counties. Following the Supreme Court's 1948 decision in *Hurd v. Hodge* invalidating restrictive covenants, and its 1954 decision in *Bolling v. Sharpe* striking down the city's segregated schools, many White residents fled the city altogether for the still (de facto) segregated suburbs (Clement, 2004; Gillette, 2006; Green, 1969; Johnson, 1963; Modan, 2006). Yet some desired the urban experience that many young professionals had made for themselves in Georgetown, and they propelled the second wave.

Long before Burch and his backers began revitalizing properties in Foggy Bottom, a small group of young professionals had created a restoration beachhead across town in Capitol Hill. As early as 1941, they bought and restored houses in the blocks immediately behind the Capitol, and soon after began holding yard-cleaning and house-painting contests. By 1951, there were enough "reclaimed" houses in Capitol Hill for St. Peter's Catholic Church to host a house tour. Four years later, and with support from the (all-White) Capitol Hill Southeast Citizens Association and the (all-White) Stanton Park Citizens Association, revitalization advocates formed the Capitol Hill Restoration Society to "emulate the work of the property owners of Georgetown" (Muller, 2015).

The *Evening Star* became an early champion of the Capitol Hill restorationists and lauded their efforts to reclaim the neighborhood from "deterioration and blight." The newspaper even provided direct help at times. In the early 1950s, several young White professionals purchased houses on Terrace Court, an alley occupied by poor African American renters one half block east of the Supreme Court building. The new owners were denied remodeling permits by the city government, which had deemed the properties blighted and slated them for demolition under the Alley Dwelling Act. After a series of editorials appeared in the *Star* urging the commissioners to reconsider the designation, however, the city granted an exemption. Soon the properties had been restored and were selling for nine times their initial purchase price. The Black renters, of course, were gone (revitalizers secured similar exemptions for alley houses in Georgetown and Foggy Bottom around the same time (Gale, 1982). By 1960, the Capitol Hill Restoration Society proudly proclaimed that its members had renovated 1,000 properties in the area between the Capitol and 8th Street, SE (Gale, 1987; Lewis, 1960c; Logan, 2015; Prothro Williams, 2003).

Second-wave revitalizers were a diverse lot. Restorationists inspired by the Georgetown model predominated in Capitol Hill; developers determined to cash in on the demand for Georgetown properties set the tone in Foggy Bottom. Despite their dissimilarities, both of these groups displaced poor renters, a majority of whom were African Americans. By 1955, for instance, Foggy Bottom developers had created a crazy quilt of class and racial groups reminiscent of 1930s Georgetown. "Some [new residents] are in groups of six or seven remodeled homes," reported the *Evening Star*. "Others are hemmed in by still remaining slums. Nearly all are within a stone's throw of slum houses occupied by low income families, most of whom are colored" (Beveridge, 1955). But through the determined efforts of developers and new residents, the northeastern sections of the neighborhood transitioned quickly. When the *Star* returned in 1960, it was elated to report that the "unbelievably miserable slums almost wholly occupied by poverty ridden Negro families" that had characterized the neighborhood "have been erased." In their stead stood "the restoration neighborhood," a "showplace" where "land values have pyramided [houses on Snow's Court which had sold for $800 when developers first entered the neighborhood, for instance, were now worth between $12 and $42,000], and the surrounding area has become one of the most talked about in the city for desirable apartments and institutional buildings." Over the course of the following decade, large development projects including the Kennedy Center, the Watergate, and the expansion of George Washington University Hospital displaced much of the remaining Black population (Berry Sherwood, 1978; Diner, 1990; Lewis, 1960b).

The only neighborhood where second-wave revitalization did not lead to displacement of the poor was Kalorama Triangle, although only because the area had no poor residents to begin with. Kalorama was not blighted prior to the onset of restoration so much as unfashionable and outdated. The *Evening Star* identified "earlier-type kitchens and bathrooms and a lack of brightness and well kept maintenance" as the main threats to neighborhood stability. Most older residents were high-ranking government officials or socialites, and new residents were established professionals. In 1959, these groups created the Kalorama Triangle Restoration Society (KTRS) to coordinate the ambitious project of renovating all of the properties in the area within four years. Members got off to an impressive start, having begun work on 40 of the neighborhood's 286 units within only a few months. Demonstrating that "private" restoration is never exclusively so, KTRS paired its members' efforts with a successful campaign for city investment in public works. The city responded quickly, repaving all of the streets and sidewalks, and installing additional public lighting in the entire 40-acre neighborhood. One can only suspect that Chair of the District Board of Commissioners Robert McLaughlin, a Kalorama resident, played some role in this development (Lewis, 1960a).

Thanks to the revitalization efforts of private citizens' groups and developers, by 1960 the *Star* was able to boast that Washington, DC "lead[s] the country in the extent of tasteful private restoration of in-town residential neighborhoods."[3] Comparing private restoration to the government-driven "urban renewal" programs that had eviscerated large sections of the old city, the paper held up the former as a more democratic and efficient means for remaking the country's crumbling cities (Berry Sherwood, 1978; Lewis, 1960a).

Such an argument was lost on Black Washingtonians, caught as they were in the rip current created by private revitalization and urban renewal. As private restoration efforts displaced Black residents by the hundreds, urban renewal displaced them by the thousands. In 1954, just two years after Burch purchased his Foggy Bottom properties, the federal government demolished nearly the entire Southwest neighborhood, displacing 23,000 residents, three quarters of whom were African American (City leaders created similar plans for Foggy Bottom, only to abandon them when restorationists made the case that because of their efforts and presence the neighborhood could no longer be considered "blighted" (Berry Sherwood, 1978). When the *Star* printed its 1960 series celebrating DC as the national leader in private restoration, federal planners were seeking to plow highways through much of the center city, a project that had the potential to displace more than 30,000 more people (Gillette, 2006).

During the 1960s, displacement emerged as a key front in the local civil rights struggle, groups like the (all-Black) Federation of Civic Associations, the Student Nonviolent Coordinating Committee, Congress of Racial Equality, Southern Christian Leadership Conference, and the Black United Front weighing in on the matter. Although primarily focused on urban renewal in the 1950s and 1960s, in the 1970s many of these activists would turn their attention to the displacement precipitated by third-wave gentrification (Gillette, 2006).

The Third Wave: Displacing the Poor in the Black Power Era

In April 1976, Joseph Lewis Jr. received a 30-day eviction notice from his new landlord, Centre Properties of Bethesda, MD. So did 26 of his neighbors on the 1700 block of Seaton Street, NW, a narrow, one-block lane of plain, two- and three-story row houses at the foot of the Adams Morgan neighborhood. The previous month, Centre had purchased nine of the block's dingy, renter-occupied row houses at between $11,500 and $20,000 apiece. It intended to capitalize on the growing demand for condominiums and townhouses by renovating the buildings and reselling them for between $55,000 and $65,000. For that to happen, it needed the renters out.

But Lewis and the other renters did not want to leave. Seaton Street was no paradise—its houses were so outdated that in 1965 the National Capital Planning Commission had considered a "Seaton Place Project" that would have leveled all of the buildings and relocated its 130 families to public housing. Few repairs had been made in the interim, and soon after Centre purchased the properties city inspectors found 959 violations spread among the street's 44 houses (Ritchie, 1976; *The Washington Post*, 1965). Yet the renters were deeply attached to their apartments. Many had lived on the block for decades, built dense and nurturing social networks, engaged in neighborhood activism, and viewed their flats as "homes." Nonetheless, a majority of the renters believed that they did not have the time or the resources to fight Centre, so they opted to move. Nine families, however, including Lewis and his family, chose to fight the eviction order. In the early 1970s, they had watched a growing wave of what residents were now calling "gentrification" roll across large portions of the old city, and they were determined not to be swept away.[4] Lewis, who emerged as a leader of the Seaton Street tenants, articulated their sense of outrage: "People are doing this all over—shoving people out. People buy your place, send you a notice and tell you you have to go, and you know nothing about it . . . that isn't right" (Bowman, 1977). While Centre set to work on the empty houses, Lewis and his remaining neighbors secured a lawyer. For more than a year, the Seaton Street tenants fought to remain in their homes, inspiring a citywide "renters' revolt" and helping housing advocates and their allies on the Council pass some of the strongest anti-displacement legislation in the country. The third wave, however, would roll on, largely undiminished.

In the 1970s and early 1980s, a third wave of gentrification swept across Washington, DC. Enticed by rock-bottom housing prices and revitalizers' success in the first- and second-wave neighborhoods, developers, speculators, and amateur flippers snapped up houses and apartment buildings in Logan Circle, Adams Morgan, Mount Pleasant, Columbia Heights, Capitol Hill, Hill East, DuPont Circle, and LeDroit Park. Young professionals followed fast on their heels, propelled by a nationwide "back to the city" trend rooted in a countercultural critique of the suburbs (Logan, 2015; Henig 1982; McBee, 1978).

With White residents leaving the city at a rate of several hundred per month in the early 1970s, one might suspect that there would be plenty of room for the newcomers without having to displace anyone. But years of speculation, discriminatory lending practices, and segregation (not to mention the 1968 riots, the heroin epidemic, and a spike in crime) had left huge sections of the center city nearly uninhabitable and many poor African Americans and Latinos scrambling for decent places to live (Wells, 2013). Developers and affluent newcomers exacerbated the crisis by displacing thousands of renters in the city's poorest neighborhoods. Because many third-wave developers focused on converting old apartment buildings or tracts of townhouses into condominiums, displacement occurred in large and alarming chunks. Within just a few months in 1973, for instance, tenants in 11 Adams Morgan apartment buildings and an entire block of Capitol Hill rooming houses were evicted (Huron, 2014; Lippman, 1974).[5]

Animated by the Great Society and the Black Power movement, local activists mobilized to fight this newest wave of displacement. In the early 1970s, the Adams Morgan Organization (1971), a neighborhood-based tenants' rights group, and the City-Wide Housing Coalition (1973), an umbrella organization that connected tenant activists across neighborhoods, joined the Capitol East Community Organization, which had been fighting displacement in Capitol Hill since the second wave, in a determined fight to keep tenants in their homes (Huron, 2014; Logan, 2015; Shriver, 1982).

In the past, advocates for displaced renters found few friends in government. But with the advent of Home Rule in 1974, tenants and tenants' rights activists could leverage the might of the newly created city government in their struggle with their landlords, and that government was staffed with liberals and civil rights activists uniquely attuned to their concerns. Two such activists were Ward 1 City Councilman David Clarke and Ward 6 Councilwoman Nadine Winter. A White graduate of Howard Law School and former counsel to the Southern Christian Leadership Conference, Clarke valued the economic and racial diversity of his ward and spent the first decade of his Council career working to maintain it. Winter had been a leading social services activist since arriving in the city in 1947. She was the founder and first executive director of Hospitality House, a social services and advocacy organization in Northeast DC, and a founding member of the National Welfare Rights Organization (Powell & Williams, 1997; *Washington*

Afro American, 2011). Coming as they did from the respective centers of gentrification and anti-displacement organizing in the city's west (Adams Morgan) and east (Capitol Hill), Clarke and Winter made anti-displacement legislation a priority, and their colleagues on the Council obliged. As one of its first acts during the Home Rule era, the Council passed the DC Rent Control Act, which placed a cap on rent increases and required that tenants be offered first right to purchase their unit if a building was slated for condominium conversion. The following year, the Council passed the Condominium Act, which set difficult-to-reach benchmarks for developers who sought to convert apartments to condominiums (Huron, 2012; Newton Jones, 1974).

Fresh off of these victories, Clarke and Winter introduced the Real Property Transfer Excise Tax, essentially an anti-flipping penalty imposed on developers who bought and quickly resold property. The first of its kind in the country, it threatened to end the most profitable form of speculation in the city. Stimulated to action by the proposal, powerful real estate and development interests formed the Washington Residential Development Corporation (WRDC) to block the anti-flipping bill. The WRDC lobbied council members generated opposition among business leaders and residents of the gentrifying neighborhoods, and succeeded in bottling up the bill in committee (Wells, 2013).

Stymied before the Council, residents facing displacement turned to the courts. When the Seaton Street renters received eviction notices in April 1976, they contacted the Adams Morgan Organization, which secured pro bono legal help from Johnny Barnes, an attorney and aide to Delegate Walter Fauntroy (D-DC). Barnes filed a class action lawsuit under section 301 of the DC Rent Control Act, but the renters faced an uphill battle. Their first obstacle was legal: section 301 stated that renters must be given first right to purchase their unit if a building is slated for condominium conversion, but it did not clearly apply to single-family homes. The Seaton Street renters also faced an economic hurdle: they had to prove that they had enough money to afford the homes. Most of the tenants were working-class folk who lived check to check. Some were on public assistance. None of them had the money to guarantee loans on the homes (Barnes, 2012). An October 1976 fundraiser held by AMO founder Marie Nahiklan had raised just $300, not even enough for a down payment on one house. In the months that followed, however, the pace of displacement increased and public opinion swung behind the Seaton Street tenants. When the AMO sponsored another fundraiser for the tenants in April 1977, it drew citywide support, with Councilmembers Clarke, Marion Barry, Douglass Moore, Hilda Mason, Chairman Sterling Tucker, and a significant number of Black, White, and Latino neighborhood residents attending. The event earned positive mention from *Washington Post* columnist William Raspberry, and the AMO raised nearly $20,000. Facing an increasing tide of public disapprobation and political pressure, Centre Properties agreed to sell to the tenants just days before the case went to trial (Gately, 1978; Raspberry, 1977; Swanston, 1976).

The Seaton Street renters' victory came just before the crest of the third wave. In the first 10 months of 1978, residents of 2,542 rental units were ordered to move because the buildings in which they lived were being "sold, demolished, or substantially rehabilitated, converted to personal use, or being 'discontinued.'" A 1979 study found that approximately 25,000 apartments, or 12% of the city's units, had been or were in the process of being converted to condominiums. In Adams Morgan, Mount Pleasant, and Capitol Hill, home prices jumped by almost 100% over 1975 levels, slightly less than double the city average, and far beyond the reach of most of the Black and Latino residents who called these neighborhoods home (Camp, 1979; Gately, 1978; Huron, 2012).

Inspired by the Seaton Street protest and threatened by the accelerated pace of displacement, renters staged a number of raucous and disruptive protests that grew into a citywide tenant revolt. In March 1978, the residents of the apartment at 2632 Adams Mill Road in Adams Morgan lit bonfires in front of their building to protest a lack of heat and hot water. Soon after, their neighbors at 2611, 2627, and 2633 Adams Mill Road secured a rollback of rent increases implemented by their landlord, H and M Enterprises, after city inspectors verified their claims of housing code violations and a decrease in services. At 2129 Florida Avenue, tenants forced their building's new owner, who hoped to convert the property into condos, to pay $3,000 "settlement costs" to all of the residents being displaced and to allow two elderly residents to remain in their apartments at their current rents for the rest of their lives. And in March 1979, the Adams Morgan Advisory Neighborhood Commission (ANC) hired three tenants' rights groups to organize renters in 150 of the neighborhood's 280 apartment buildings. Chairwoman Ann Hargrove was not coy about the ANC's aims: "A lot of buildings are being sold and converted. The hope is we can help tenants buy them." Protests had become so commonplace and tenants' organizations so numerous, that *The Washington Post* dubbed 1978 the "year of the renter's revolt" (Gately, 1978, 1979).

Coming as it did during an election year, the renters' revolt forced the Council to revisit Clarke and Winter's reform legislation. In March 1978, the Council passed an emergency bill placing a moratorium on condo conversions. Despite developer opposition, the Council repeatedly renewed the 90-day period for the statute. Also that year, the Council passed the Real Property Transfer Excise Tax. And in 1980, the Council passed the Rental Housing Conversion and Sale Act, giving tenants first right to purchase their building when it was put up for sale. This legislation institutionalized the formula the Seaton Street tenants first argued for three years before. To facilitate tenant purchases of their homes, the city began providing a multitude of financial incentives to low-income residents, including tax breaks, subsidized loans, and grants (Cenziper, 2012; Wells, 2013).

Although some of these laws were honored in the breach and others were allowed to lapse in the 1980s, tenants and tenant activists were nonetheless able to use them to slow displacement in a few choice neighborhoods.[6] By 1980, at least eight tenant groups had bought their buildings and many others had brokered reduced purchase prices for tenants in buildings undergoing condo conversion. In 1984, a relieved Council Chairman Clarke noted that the "controls we superimposed" had led to the "stabilization of rents [and] stabilization of condo values ... [W]e were able to protect the current residents" (Borth & Grams, 1984; Camp, 1979; Huron, 2012).

Yet the tenants' victory was a hollow one. Activists had not so much stopped displacement as slowed it down, and only in certain neighborhoods (Levey, 1981). This was painfully evident on Seaton Street itself. Nine years after the renters' revolt, few of its Black residents remained beyond the nine families who had purchased their houses in 1978. Joseph Lewis Jr. was one of them. The home he had purchased for $18,500 was now worth $100,000—a boon for his family, but far out of the reach of the city's poor. Surveying the scene in 1986, *The Washington Post* reported, "Seaton St. has been transformed from a home for low-income families to a burgeoning spot for real estate speculation." And it was not the exception. "The only apparent difference between Seaton Street and other similar blocks in Adams Morgan" the paper continued, "is that gentrification has occurred faster elsewhere."[7]

Although activists could not stop gentrification, the crack epidemic and subsequent spike in crime did. In 1988, drug-related violence made Washington, DC the murder capital of the United States. The violence was concentrated in the city's poor, Black, and Latino center-city neighborhoods, which included or abutted the gentrifying areas of Capitol Hill, Logan Circle, LeDroit Park, Adams Morgan, and Columbia Heights. By the end of the decade, landlords were lowering the rent to retain rattled young professionals, and sellers watched as prices dropped and sales decreased. Jason Muir, a young White magazine editor who rented an apartment at 13th and Pennsylvania, SE, had a remarkable but nonetheless representative experience. He demanded and received three reductions in rent in only 18 months during the early 1990s after burglars cleaned out his apartment, a hit-and-run driver mangled a truck he had parked in front of the building, and a neighbor's girlfriend was abducted and later found dead. Historian David Levering Lewis, a resident of Capitol Hill since the 1960s, found himself on the owners' side of this trend. In 1993, following a robbery in his front yard that left him with several stitches in his chin, Lewis decided to sell. The house sat on the market for more than a year with only one inquiry before he gave up (Allen, 1994).

By the late 1980s and early 1990s, Washington, DC's gentrifying, old city neighborhoods were a study in contrasts and estrangement. "Stalled gentrification," as anthropologist Brett Williams (1988) aptly named it, had created a unique mix of poverty and affluence, Black and White, blight and opulence unseen since 1930s Georgetown and mid-1950s Foggy Bottom. In Stanton Park, an area of Capitol Hill near Union Station, *The Washington Post* observed a "neighborhood [that] varies almost block by block. Some streets are lined with elegantly refurbished row houses and office buildings; others with ramshackle houses, boarded stores and weedy lots" (Pianin, 1987). The residents reflected the landscape, with Black residents and White residents occupying mirror opposite economic profiles. In 1994, 37% of the city's White population made $75,000 or more compared to 7% of Black residents. Conversely, 49% of the Black population made less than $30,000 as opposed to 20% of White residents (Boo, 1994). Class and racial differences created social distance, and neighbors seldom came into meaningful contact. The middle-class children in the gentrifying neighborhoods attended elite private schools or used the out-of-boundary system to access the good public schools west of Rock Creek Park, while their poor neighbors attended some of the worst public schools in the country (Barras, 2011). White adults worked for the federal government, private small businesses, law firms, and nonprofits; Black adults worked for the city, at service jobs in the lower rungs of the federal bureaucracy, or not at all. There were, of course, a few notable instances of cross-racial cooperation in the gentrifying neighborhoods, including the successful fight to save Eastern Market in Capitol Hill (Simpson, 1987). But these were the exception, not the rule. Darren Reeves, a 22-year-old African American resident of Southwest, summed up the situation in a 1994 comment to the *Post*: "That's the way it works between blacks and whites in this city. We physically live in the same place, but on the real side, we don't. They step away from us and we're just as quickly stepping away from them" (Boo, 1994; Gale, 1987, p. 176).

The Fourth Wave: The End of the Black Majority

Danetta Tucker was on break from her job at the newly opened Giant supermarket in Columbia Heights when she saw the crowd. There, before a gaggle of reporters and campaign aides, Council Chairwoman Linda Cropp was announcing her 2006 bid for mayor. Cropp staked her campaign on the economic development that had brought the city back from the depths of bankruptcy and was then drawing businesses and high-income residents into poor and working-class neighborhoods like Columbia Heights. Cropp could claim a direct hand in the revitalization of the area. Since 1999, she and other city officials had worked with developers and businesses to remake the neighborhood's decaying commercial strip near the intersection of 14th Street and Park Road, NW. Using the newly opened subway stop as leverage, they attracted millions of dollars in investment and created hundreds of jobs, including the one that Tucker had secured at Giant.

Yet Tucker challenged Cropp's claims by yelling: "Don't forget about me. . . . What about my children? We got no place to live." Tucker made only $7.60 an hour, leaving her slightly less than $500 for rent each month—and by 2006 the average price of a two-bedroom apartment in the center city had risen to more than $1,300. Service workers like Tucker—who was fortunate enough to live in a subsidized unit owned by an affordable housing program, but whose lease was about to run out—were being priced out of the neighborhood. Before the cameras, Cropp did all of the right things. She listened intently as Tucker told her story, hugged her when the desperation of her situation caused her to break down and cry, and gave her the name of a staffer to contact. Cropp was undoubtedly sincere, but in the coming months her staff was unresponsive when Tucker needed help. When facing the effects of gentrification, Tucker was on her own (Currie, 2006).

The interaction between Cropp and Tucker was symbolic of the larger relationship between city leaders and their working-class and poor constituents in the years between the late 1990s and 2014. As a fourth wave of gentrification, swelled in no small part by the efforts of elected officials such as Cropp and Mayor Anthony Williams, washed over the city, poor residents faced displacement. When they appealed to their elected representatives for assistance, those officials sympathized, even made an effort to help, but ultimately failed to provide them with the resources they needed to remain in their neighborhoods. As city leaders and old residents struggled to come to terms with the changes overtaking them, the fourth wave fundamentally reshaped huge swaths of the city, in some areas working a transformation reminiscent of that which had engulfed Georgetown five decades before.

With the spread of the crack epidemic, Washington, DC's emergence as the murder capital of the United States, and the financial crisis of 1994–1995, elected officials shifted their emphasis in housing policy from protecting the poor to beckoning middle-class residents and businesses back to the city. In January 2003, Mayor Williams famously announced a plan to attract 100,000 new residents in 10 years. *The Washington Post* mocked what then seemed like a laughably ambitious goal, but Williams plunged ahead. He encouraged the Department of Housing to seize abandoned buildings and sell them to developers; auctioned city-owned properties, including old schools and private homes that had been seized for taxes; worked with Metro to spur development around transit centers; pushed the Small Business Administration to find ways to revitalize the city's neighborhood commercial strips; and begged federal lawmakers to transfer huge parcels such as St. Elizabeths, Walter Reed, and the Navy Yard to the city so that it could build entirely new communities (Brookings Institution, 2003; Timberg, 2003; *The Washington Post*, 2003). Although less ambitious than Williams, city leaders had implemented similar plans in the past with only marginal success. Mayor Marion Barry had built city offices on H Street and U Street in the 1980s to spur development in the old riot corridors. In his last term, Barry brokered a deal whereby a newly built basketball stadium (the MCI Center) would serve as the anchor for a revitalized Chinatown and F Street commercial corridor (Mansfield, 1985; *The Washington Post*, 1987; Woodlee, 1995). But these earlier plans had never focused so heavily on *neighborhood* development, and, more importantly, they did not coincide with the housing boom of the early 2000s.[8]

The DC housing boom was the product of several national developments that disproportionately affected the metropolitan area. First, with the ebbing of the crack epidemic, violent crime dropped in cities nationwide. The change in Washington, DC was dramatic. Murders dropped from a high of 482 in 1991 to 242 in 2000; by 2012, the number had fallen below 100, the lowest total since the 1950s (Metropolitan Police Department, 2015; Suro, 1997). The drop in crime coincided with a Washington, DC wealth boom stimulated by the expansion of lobbying in the 1990s and early 2000s, and the growth of the defense, intelligence, and information technology industries after the terrorist attacks of September 11, 2001. Between 2000 and 2010, corporations almost doubled the amount they spent on lobbying federal lawmakers, from $100 million to $180 million. Defense spending more than doubled during this period as well, rising from slightly less than $300 billion in 2001 to well over $700 billion in 2011. All of this money drew a legion of young tech workers, lobbyists, office staffers, military bureaucrats, lawyers, and contractors into the Washington, DC region (Gowen, 2011; Kotkin, 2012; Mathews, 2012; Plumer, 2013).

Driven by a "new urbanism" that eschewed the energy-wasting car culture of the suburbs for compact, diverse, walkable, urban communities, a significant portion of these new workers poured into the old L'Enfant city, where they expanded on the old centers of stalled, third-wave gentrification in Capitol Hill, Logan Circle, Adams Morgan, Columbia Heights, LeDroit Park, and Shaw.[9] The city government's emphasis on revitalizing neighborhood commercial corridors and locating new development around public transportation hubs only encouraged the migration (Wilgoren, 2003).

Although the "new urbanism" made the cities newly attractive, the promise of massive profits in the housing boom was the primary driver of fourth-wave gentrification. With interest rates at record lows and banks loosening credit requirements, buyers and investors flooded into the market and prices spiraled in response to the demand (NPR, 2008). Realtor Diana Hart recalled that in the first years of the new millennium, "open houses had a circus-like atmosphere—wall-to-wall people, potential buyers describing properties to their spouses on their cell phones as they walked through. It became like the most crowded cocktail party you can imagine." Others, like David Hawkins, recalled that potential buyers approached home sales like a competition, paying whatever it took to "win" a property. "There was almost no fear on the part of the buyers of overpaying for a house," he observed, "because they figured it would be worth more later." The market became so fevered and buyers so sure that prices would continue to rise that some bought properties sight unseen. In 2005, a group of Massachusetts amateur investors purchased a house at 513 Florida Avenue, NW based on an Internet picture. This relatively common practice only warranted notice because, once inside, the owners discovered the mummified remains of the previous owner, an elderly African American man who had died in the bathtub five years before.

Because of practices like these, in the five years between 2002 and 2007, the price of a house in Washington, DC rose by an average of 75%, and often far more in the most desirable neighborhoods (Fleury et al., 2010; Schwartzman, 2005).

With prices rising so quickly, developers and buyers soon ventured beyond the old third-wave neighborhoods to areas outside of the L'Enfant city. By 2002, buyers were snapping up old crack houses in Trinidad and ripping tin sunshades and green AstroTurf off of porches in Old City. Longtime residents were shocked to see young, Black professionals, and even some Whites, cramming into open houses in the East of the [Anacostia] River neighborhoods of Congress Heights, Deanwood, and historic Anacostia (This was, for many East of the River residents, a shocking development. During the 2004 filming of a documentary about Marion Barry, Anacostia community activist Sandra Seegars interrupted an interview when she saw some White people walking nearby. "Oh, white people!" she exclaimed, chuckling to herself. "White people on my street? I don't believe it" (Flor, 2009)).

Even the housing crisis of 2007–2008 did not stop the inexorable advance of new residents. Although prices dropped slightly after the bust, few DC neighborhoods saw them dip below 2004 levels. And by 2012, when homeowners across the country were still struggling with underwater mortgages and abandoned properties, Washington, DC's housing prices again began to rise (Urban Institute, 2014). Meanwhile, young professionals continued to pour into town—nearly 30,000 of them between 2009 and 2011 and an average of 1,000 per month thereafter. Entrepreneurs worked feverishly to capitalize on this demographic, opening a dizzying array of bars, restaurants, and gyms catering to young, white-collar workers with plenty of disposable income. Developers too, shifted their focus to these young people, accelerating the pace of high-end apartment and condo construction (Chang et al., 2013; DePillis, 2014; LaFrance, 2014; Stein, 2014; Swarns, 2013).

All of this activity fundamentally transformed the city's housing market. Between 2000 and 2010, the number of apartments that rented for more than $1,500 tripled, rising from 12,400 to 45,000. Houses followed a similar pattern, with the number of homes valued at $500,000 or more doubling. This was not simply a product of new construction. Rather, many of these high-cost apartments and houses were being carved out of the city's low-cost inventory. Across the same decade, the number of low-rent units dropped by half, plummeting from 70,600 to 34,500. Likewise, the number of low-value homes dropped from 63,645 in 2000 to 17,640 in 2010 (Reed, 2012).

Some longtime residents profited from the changes sweeping over their neighborhoods. "Almost all of the families from my block cashed out," recalled Tania Jackson, an African American who grew up in Columbia Heights. "People were getting offered a ridiculous amount of money for their houses" (Fleury et al., 2010). But the majority of residents in many gentrifying neighborhoods were renters on low or fixed incomes. The incomes of poor and working-class residents remained flat during the early 21st century, and unemployment reached Depression-era levels in the East of the River wards following the 2007–2008 economic crisis. As housing prices skyrocketed, low-income residents felt increasing financial pressure to leave the city (Hendry, Tatian, & MacDonald, 2014; Orr & Rivlin, 2011).

City officials struggled both to maintain and to build new subsidized housing as homebuyers and developers gobbled up low-cost units in the private market. In 2005, Mayor Anthony Williams proposed the New Communities Initiative, a robust city commitment to creating new housing for the poor and working class. The Initiative's concept was not new; like the federal Hope VI program, begun in 1998, it would focus on areas of concentrated poverty, build mixed-income neighborhoods in their stead, and use the profits from the high- and middle-income units to subsidize those for lower-income residents. Although it was a far cry from the urban renewal of the past, Hope VI had its problems. Residents were displaced during construction and many did not return once the projects were complete. Some sites also experienced a net loss of low-income units. New Communities was designed to be different. City planners emphasized community input, adopted a "build first" policy that obligated the city to produce new units before demolishing old ones, and created a plan for comprehensive social services that would renew the neighborhood's "human capital" along with the infrastructure (Anderson, 2014).

The first designated site for the Initiative was the massive neighborhood of subsidized housing bounded by North Capitol Street, New York Avenue, K Street, and New Jersey Avenue, NW, what city planners called Northwest One. Just 10 blocks from the Capitol, Northwest One was to be the Initiative's showplace, a demonstration that the city had figured out how to revitalize a poor community in a gentrifying city without displacing residents. Excited by the Initiative's promises and desperate to answer the pleas of the 52,000 people who had applied for housing assistance in 2006, members of the Council pushed the District Housing Authority to create additional sites in Barry Farms in Anacostia, Lincoln Heights / Richardson Dwellings in Deanwood, and Park Morton just off of Georgia Avenue in Northwest (Anderson, 2014; Currie, 2006).

Eight years after Williams' announcement, however, Northwest One had been stalled by bureaucratic incompetence, voluminous red tape, and private developers' failure to take on low-income housing projects during the recession. Although several hundred low-cost housing units on the site had been demolished, only a handful of affordable units had been built in their stead. Most former residents were scattered throughout the far eastern wards and Prince George's County, and, after eight years of broken promises and interminable delays, many did not even want to come back. A 2014 study of New Communities commissioned by Mayor Vincent Gray's administration found similar problems at the other sites

(Anderson, 2014; Quadel Consulting and Training, 2014; Samuels, 2013). While the city government struggled with New Communities, the housing crisis worsened. By 2013, the affordable housing wait list had grown to more than 70,000 names. Bowing to the reality that it would never be able to clear the list, the city stopped accepting applications (Dvorak, 2013).

Poor DC residents did not wait for the city to find a workable solution to the affordable housing crisis. They utilized what legislative remedies remained from the late 1970s and early 1980s to brace themselves against the wave of wealth washing over the city. As prices began to rise at the turn of the century, low-income residents demanded that the city strengthen rent control guidelines and organized to purchase their buildings. In 2006, they succeeded in getting the Council to pass a series of strengthening amendments to the city's rent control law (Chan, 2000; Kass, 2006; Urban Institute, 2014). The legislation had a broad impact, capping the percentage that landlords could increase the rent each year at about 4%, and covering a majority of the city's rental properties.[10] Renters also pushed back against displacement by engaging in a new round of cooperative organizing. But as during the third wave, this latter approach to securing housing for low-income residents required enormous outlays of time and money, as well as a little luck. Only a handful of tenants' groups, representing a few hundred renters, succeeded in purchasing their buildings (Blount Danois, 2005).

As the fourth wave of gentrification swept across the city, Washington, DC became younger, richer, and Whiter. Well-to-do professionals, most of whom were White, continued to move in, while the poor, most of whom were Black, moved out. In 2011, the city lost the Black majority that had defined "Chocolate City" since 1957 (Kochhar, Fry, & Taylor, 2011; Tavernise, 2011).

Conclusion: "We Are Headed for Some Bad Trouble"

Louise Thomas embodied many of the changes that Washington, DC experienced during a century of gentrification. When she was a teenager shortly after World War II, Thomas and her family were forced out of their Georgetown apartment by the city government, which deemed the structure blighted. But rather than bulldoze the building as it had claimed it would, the city let it stand, and a developer fixed it up and sold it to a White family. After leaving Georgetown, Thomas' family landed in the burgeoning Black community of Columbia Heights, where she lived for the next 60 years. In that time, she watched the third wave roll through the center city, only to crash on the rough shores of the crack epidemic. By the late 1990s, when the crisis began to ebb, she was living in a 28-unit apartment building at 1418 W Street, NW, where her landlord racked up reams of housing code violations and the city did little to address resident complaints. In 2000, the city finally took action. Rather than pressure the landlord to fix the problems, however, housing inspectors condemned the building and demanded that the residents evacuate. Instead, they sued the city for discrimination. The city, in turn, sued the landlords—the first such lawsuit against a slumlord in the city's history—and eventually secured a settlement stipulating that the owners fix up the building, sell it to the residents for one dollar, and refrain from owning rental property in the District in the future.

No sooner had Thomas and her neighbors become homeowners than fourth-wave developers began soliciting them to sell the building. It was a heady experience. People who had never had two pennies to rub together were being offered upward of $100,000 per household. In 2003, Thomas found herself on the losing side of a tenant vote to sell the building. She was now back to renting in a neighborhood where prices were fast moving beyond her means to pay. In 2005, at the crest of the fourth wave, a reporter for *The Crisis* magazine asked Thomas what she thought of the changes enveloping her neighborhood. "Everything is being built for people who have money," Thomas observed. "I was living in Georgetown when all the change happened, and you see Georgetown now. We [in Columbia Heights] are headed for some bad trouble" (Blount Danois, 2005).

In the years after Thomas gave that interview, the strip of 14th Street between Thomas Circle and Clifton Terrace became the epicenter of high-end condo and apartment construction in the city. By 2014, developers had built or were in the process of building apartments and condos on *every single block*. Each of these developments created ground-floor space for trendy bars and high-end restaurants, transforming the streetscape and the nightlife. Where once prostitutes had strolled the dimly lit sidewalks of 14th Street near the intersection of Rhode Island Avenue, there was a Whole Foods and rows of loft apartments. The abandoned old dry cleaner at the corner of 14th and Q had become a pricey French restaurant with an impenetrable wait list. And in Thomas' old W Street building, two-bedroom condos were selling for around $500,000 (DePillis, 2014; Stein, 2015).

To most of the young professionals who prowled the new bars and restaurants, sunned themselves on condominium rooftop decks, and sculpted their bodies in high-end yoga and Crossfit studios, all this activity was not "bad trouble"; it was rebirth. Too young, or unwilling, to remember the local and federal policies and real estate practices that had historically underdeveloped their new neighborhood and impoverished the people they were displacing, they believed that the area had been destroyed by "poverty" or "the riots" and that they were the first ones to give it new life in more than a generation.[11] But as Thomas well knew, the story was far more complicated. Across the span of her lifetime, real estate agents, developers, lenders, landlords, and new residents had taken advantage of historical, state-sanctioned underdevelopment of Black communities to make money off of her homes. Only the determined struggles of residents, aided at times by the city government, had allowed people like her to stay in place. Most of her old neighbors, however, had been swept away.

Notes

1 The authors thank Katie Wells for her insightful comments on this chapter.
Real estate speculation and development have been Washington, DC's second largest industry since George Washington selected the sight for the nation's capital in 1790. Eager to attract settlers to the sparely inhabited plantation country, Washington planned to raise money for the building of the federal facilities through a real estate speculation scheme that would make modern house flippers blush. Although his plan collapsed, throughout the antebellum period local boosters worked feverishly to develop the city lest Congress heed the periodic calls to move the nation's capital to a more developed and central location. As the city expanded in the decades after the Civil War, land speculators and developers pushed working class residents out of the West End and Kalorama to make way for massive mansions, sumptuous apartment buildings, and beautifully manicured parks. By the early 20th century, much of the land in the old L'Enfant city had been occupied, and developers and residents alike turned their attention to restoring older homes that had fallen into disrepair. This latter form of private real estate development is the focus of this study. See Green, C. (1976) *Washington: A History of the Capital, 1800–1950*, Princeton: Princeton University Press. Gillette, H. (2006) *Between Justice and Beauty: Race, Planning, and the Failure of Urban Policy in Washington, D.C.*, Philadelphia: University of Pennsylvania Press.

2 In 1982, as gentrification transformed the Adams Morgan neighborhood, George Washington University students asked residents what the area would look like in twenty years. Twenty three percent of respondents made reference to Georgetown unsolicited. Henig, Gentrification in Adams Morgan, 18. Speaking to a reporter in 1987, Victoria Bernardo, a White occupational therapist who had moved to the Stanton Park area of Capitol Hill, expressed her desire that her new neighborhood follow the Georgetown model, but not to its logical conclusion: "The Hill is evolving into a really pleasant neighborhood," she stated. "Of course we don't want it to be overdone. We don't want it like Georgetown" (Pianin, 1987). See also Smith, Captive Capital, 73.

3 In the late 1960s, private revitalizers remained active in the aforementioned second-wave neighborhoods. They also expanded their footprint to include Dupont Circle (Logan, 2015; *The New York Times*, 1969; Wells, 2013).

4 *The Washington Post*, which had emerged as the city's paper of note, first used the term "gentrification" in 1973 in an article about revitalization in London, the city where the term was coined in 1964 (Edgerton, 1973). The *Post* first used the term to refer to the process in Washington, DC in 1977 (Pierce, 1977).

5 The gentrification of the 1970s and early 1980s was not only much larger and more rapid than in times past, it involved different players. No longer did displacement entail the removal of a multiracial working class by an exclusively White professional class. As desegregation of the city housing market became a reality, displacement entailed the removal of poor Blacks and Hispanics by a multiracial—although still predominantly White—professional class. One of the most active real estate speculators in Logan Circle during the early 1970s, for instance, was Emmanuel Dickey, an African American who flipped scores of properties, including 12 on the one-block-long Kingman Place just north of the circle. Dickey was just as ruthless as his White counterparts. Ignoring their poverty and the discriminatory lending practices that had blocked their access to credit, Dickey disparaged the African American renters

he displaced, stating: "All those black people who got pushed out are so stupid. All they had to do to own those homes was to ask [to buy them]. The people who owned those houses were looking to get rid of them." Tenants threatened by displacement were fully aware of the change. In 1977, Adams Morgan tenant activist Willette McNeil stated "They [developers and real estate agents] want the blacks out so the high class blacks and the whites can come in. They don't want people who have nothing." This change did not, however, have a pronounced impact on the general tenor of gentrification and displacement. The vast majority of new residents remained young, White professionals and the vast majority of those displaced were poor people of color (Bowman, 1977; Williams, 1979).

6 Although it did an admirable job of trying to keep residents in their homes, the city did a miserable job of creating new, affordable housing units. See "Going round in (Logan) Circles," *The Washington Post*, February 3, 1979.

7 With little hint of irony, former AMO leader Frank Smith, who had since been elected to the City Council from Ward 1, argued that the rise in home prices on Seaton Street was a positive development. "I think that the people who bought there have seen a tremendous increase in the value of their properties, and you can't knock that. . . . This is a free country" (Precious, 1986). Smith was not alone; *The Washington Post* seemed to have forgotten the Seaton Street renters as well. Although it published the article just cited in 1986, a more common Seaton Street topic for the *Post* was the private garden two young professionals had created in the empty lot next to their house (P.D.R., 1990; Rogers, 1983).

8 Not all of these programs focused on business districts. At Councilman Frank Smith's urging, beginning in 1988 the city held an annual lottery for homes it had seized for taxes. The lottery provided low- and moderate-income residents the opportunity to gain title to a home for as little as $250, and help securing a low-interest rate mortgage (Mariano, 1993).

9 Suleiman Osman, in his exploration of gentrification in Brooklyn, argues that the new urbanism is not new but stretches back to the 1960s and 1970s (Osman, 2012). Logan sees a similar embrace of what could be called the new urbanism in Capitol Hill in the late 1960s and early 1970s (2015). We agree, but believe that the new urbanism of the 1990s was nonetheless *new* to a younger generation which embraced it after the decline of the crack and crime epidemics made a return to the cities (and specifically to the poorer parts of cities) thinkable for many young people for the first time in their lives.

10 Although rent control helped tens of thousands of residents stay in their homes despite rapidly increasing prices, the law had a number of exceptions to ensure landlords a minimum annual profit and allow them to set new rents once rent-controlled tenants moved out. As the fourth wave increased demand across the city, landlords used these exemptions to dramatically raise rents or push residents out. Others took to brokering voluntary agreements with renters whereby they were given generous buyouts and their former units converted to market rate (Wiener, 2014).

11 One new resident / journalist even blamed the economic devastation of the entire city, including the downtown, where no rioting had taken place, on the riots (Franke-Ruta, 2012). In 2013, one particularly obnoxious new resident took to social media to blame the neighborhood's problems on "black criminals who live and loiter on my street" and to cheer their displacement through gentrification (Stein, 2015).

References

Allen, C. (1994, March 13). Hill in a handbasket. *The Washington Post.*

Anderson, M. (2014, October 31). House broken: How DC's plan to save low-income housing went wrong. *City Paper.*

Barnes, J. (2012, October 4). Interview with George Derek Musgrove. Washington, DC.

Barras, J. (2011, August 26). Neighborhood schooled. *City Paper.*

Berry Sherwood, S. (1978). *Foggy Bottom, 1800–1975: A study in the uses of a neighborhood.* Washington, DC: George Washington University.

Beveridge, G. (1955, October 23). City's Foggy Bottom seen test ground for urban renewal. *Evening Star.*

Blount Danois, E. (2005, May/June). Standing their ground. *The Crisis, 112*(3).

Boo, K. (1994, October 21). Washington: Divided, even where the races meet. *The Washington Post.*

Borth, J., & Grams, M. (1984, June 4). Revitalization puts community at crossroad of change. *The Washington Post.*

Bowman, L. (1977, February 15). Poor again feel pressure from developers. *The Washington Post.*

Brookings Institution (2003). *Neighborhood 10: Ten strategies for a stronger Washington.* Washington, DC: Brookings Institution.

Camp, P. (1979, November 19). The battling tenants. *The Washington Post.*

Cenziper, D. (2012, January 15). In D.C. loan program, mortgage defaults abound. *The Washington Post.*

Chan, S. (2000, October 12). Tenants decry study urging end to D.C. rent control. *The Washington Post.*

Chang, E., Tucker, N., Goldstein, J., Yates, Y., & Davis, M. (2013, October 18). March of the millennials. *The Washington Post.*

Clement, B. (2004). Pushback: The white community's dissent from "Bolling." *Washington History, 16*(2) (Fall/Winter, 2004/2005), 86–109.

Currie, T. (2006, December 17). A long way home. *Washington Post Magazine.*

DePillis, L. (2014, August 19). Why it's so hard to find a cheap apartment in Washington, D.C. *The Washington Post.*

Diner, S. (1990). Washington, the black majority: Race and politics in the nation's capital. In R. Bernard (Ed.), *Snowbelt cities: Metropolitan politics in the Northwest and Midwest since WWII.* Bloomington, IN: Indiana University Press.

Dvorak, P. (2013, April 11). In D.C., a public-housing waiting list with no end. *The Washington Post.*

Edgerton, J. (1973, March 25). Londoners vs. developers. *The Washington Post.*

Evening Star (1952a, September 27). Houses for sale – N.W.

Evening Star (1952b, October 2). Houses for sale – N.W.

Fleury, M., Kashino, M., Leaman, E., Wills, D., Mullins, L., & Wills, E. (2010, April). Tales from the boom and bust. *Washingtonian Magazine.*

Flor, D. (2009). *The nine lives of Marion Barry.* HBO.

Franke-Ruta, G. (2012, August 10). The politics of the urban comeback: Gentrification and culture in D.C. *The Atlantic.*

Gale, D. (1982). Restoration in Georgetown, Washington, D.C., 1915 to 1965 (Unpublished doctoral dissertation, George Washington University).

Gale, D. (1987). *Washington D.C.: Inner city revitalization and minority suburbanization.* Philadelphia, PA: Temple University Press.

Gately, B. (1978, December 21). Tenant revolt fueled by increases in rent, evictions. *The Washington Post.*

Gately, B. (1979, March 29). Tenants groups to organize residents of Adams-Morgan. *The Washington Post.*

Gillette, H. (2006). *Between justice and beauty: Race, planning, and the failure of urban policy in Washington, D.C.* Philadelphia: University of Pennsylvania Press.

Green, C. (1969). *The secret city: A history of race relations in the nation's capital.* Princeton, NJ: Princeton University Press.

Green, C. (1976). *Washington: A history of the capital, 1800–1950.* Princeton, NJ: Princeton University Press.

Gowen, A. (2011, August 15). D.C. enclaves reap rewards of contracting boom as federal dollars fuel wealth. *The Washington Post.*

Hendry, L., Tatian, P., & MacDonald, G. (2014). *Housing security in the Washington region.* Washington, DC: Urban Institute.

Henig, J. (1982). *Gentrification in Adams Morgan: Political and commercial consequences of neighborhood change.* Washington, DC: Center for Washington Area Studies, George Washington University.

Herken, G. (2014). *The Georgetown set: Friends and rivals in Cold War Washington.* New York, NY: Alfred Knopf.

Howick Fant, B. G. (1982). Slum reclamation and housing reform in the nation's capital, 1890–1940 (Unpublished doctoral dissertation, George Washington University).

Huron, A. (2012). The work of the urban commons: Limited-equity cooperatives in Washington, D.C. (Unpublished doctoral dissertation, City University of New York).

Huron, A. (2014). Creating a commons in the capital: The emergence of limited equity cooperatives in Washington, DC. *Washington History, 26*(2) (Fall).

Hyra, D. (forthcoming). *Making the gilded ghetto: Race, class and politics in the cappuccino city.* Chicago, IL: The University of Chicago Press.

Jackson, K. (1980). Federal subsidy and the suburban dream: The first quarter-century of government intervention in the housing market. *Records of the Columbia Historical Society, Washington, D.C., 50,* 421–451.

Johnson, H. (1963). *Dusk at the mountain.* New York, NY: Doubleday.

Jones, W. (2010). Banished: Housing policy in the District of Columbia and the struggle of working families. In R. Walters & T.-M. Travis (Eds.), *Democratic destiny and the District of Columbia: Federal politics and public policy.* Lanham, MD: Lexington Books.

Kass, B. (2006, August 12). New law keeps rent control strong in the district. *The Washington Post.*

Kochhar, R., Fry, R., & Taylor, P. (2011). *Wealth gaps rise to record highs between whites, blacks, Hispanics.* Washington, DC: Pew Research Center.

Kotkin, J. (2012, March 19). The expanding wealth of Washington. *Forbes.*

LaFrance, A. (2014, April 18). New apartment buildings are geared for millennials. *The Washington Post.*

Lesko, K., Babb, V., & Gibbs, C. R. (1991). *Black Georgetown remembered: A history of its black community from the founding of the "Town of George" in 1751 to the present day.* Washington, DC: Georgetown University Press.

Levey, B. (1981, January 8). Our town: Friendly but in flux. *The Washington Post.*

Lewis, R. (1960a, August 27). Washington's restoration areas: I. Kalorama Triangle. *Evening Star.*

Lewis, R. (1960b, October 22). Washington's restoration areas: II. Foggy Bottom. *Evening Star.*

Lewis, R. (1960c, November 19). Washington's restoration areas: III. Capitol Hill. *Evening Star.*

Lippman, T. (1974, March 24). Adams-Morgan house prices soaring: Row house prices soaring in Adams-Morgan boom. *The Washington Post.*

Logan, C. (2015, January). Mrs. McCain's parlor: House and garden tours and the inner-city restoration trend in Washington, D.C. *Journal of Urban History, 39*(5).

Mansfield, V. (1985, May 30). H Street rebuilding sparked. *The Washington Post.*

Mariano, A. (1993, August 13). A winning way to own a home in D.C. *The Washington Post.*

Mathews, D. (2012, September 25). Is the government making Washington rich? (In charts, of course). *The Washington Post.*

McBee, S. (1978, September 4). Is there a national back-to-the-city trend? Probably not. *The Washington Post.*

Metropolitan Police Department. (2015). District crime at a glance. http://mpdc.dc.gov/page/district-crime-data-glance.

Modan, G. (2007). *Turf wars: Discourse, diversity and the politics of place.* New York, NY: Wiley-Blackwell.

Muller, J. (2015, January). Celebrating 60 years of preservation. *Hill Rag.*

Newton Jones, L. (1974, August 2). District mayor signs rent control measure. *The Washington Post.*

NPR (2008, May 9). The giant pool of money. *This American Life.* National Public Radio.

Orr, B., & Rivlin, A. (2011). Affordable housing in the district: Where are we now? Washington, DC: Brookings Institution, Metropolitan Policy Institute.

Osman, S. (2012). *The invention of brownstone Brooklyn: Gentrification and the search for authenticity in postwar New York.* New York, NY: Oxford University Press.

Paige, J., & Reuss, M. (1983). Safe, decent, and affordable: Citizen struggles to improve housing in the District of Columbia. In S. Diner & H. Young (Eds.), *Housing Washington's people: Public policy in retrospect.* Washington, DC: University of the District of Columbia.

P.D.R. (1990, August 2). Hiemstra and Hill: Reclamation experts. *The Washington Post.*

Pierce, N. (1977, July 30). Will "saved" cities mean suburban slums? *The Washington Post.*

Pianin, E. (1987, November 7). Stanton Park enjoys rising homes prices. *The Washington Post.*

Plumer, B. (2013, January 7). America's staggering defense budget, in charts. *The Washington Post.*

Powell, M., & Williams, V. (1997, March 29). D.C. Council Chairman David A. Clarke dies. *The Washington Post.*

Precious, T. (1986, December 6). Gentrification comes to Seaton Street. *The Washington Post.*

Prince, S. (2014). *African Americans and gentrification in Washington, D.C.: Race, class and social justice in the nation's capital.* Burlington, VT: Ashgate.

Prothro Williams, K. (2003). *Capitol Hill Historic District.* Washington, DC: DC Historic Preservation Office.

Quadel Consulting and Training LLC. (2014). Policy advisor's recommendations on the District of Columbia's new communities initiative. Accessed at http://dcnewcommunities.org/wp-content/uploads/2014/09/Policy-Advisors-Recommendations-on-the-NCI-Program.pdf.

Raspberry, W. (1977, April 13). Team effort on Seaton Place. *The Washington Post.*

Reed, J. (2012). Disappearing act: Affordable housing in D.C. is vanishing amid sharply rising housing costs. Washington, DC: Center on Budget and Policy Priorities.

Ritchie, J. (1976, May 20). City charges 959 housing violations. *The Washington Post.*

Roberts, C. (1952, January 27). Progress or decay: Washington must choose! *The Washington Post.*

Rogers, P. (1983, August 18). Seaton Street's garden. *The Washington Post.*

Ruble, B. (2012). *U Street: A biography.* Baltimore, MD: Johns Hopkins University Press.

Samuels, R. (2013, July 7). In District, affordable housing plan hasn't delivered. *The Washington Post.*

Schwartzman, P. (2005, October 16). The forgotten neighbor on Florida Ave. *The Washington Post.*

Shin, A. (2012, December 20). D.C. house inspires 168 bids in red hot real estate market. *The Washington Post.*

Shriver, J. (1982, July 21). Ward 1 race splits an old alliance. *The Washington Post.*

Simpson, A. (1987, September 17). Eastern market gets a new boost. *The Washington Post.*

Smith, Sam, (1974). Captive Capital: Colonial Life in Modern Washington. Bloomington: Indiana University Press, 65–110.

Stein, P. (2014, October 3). Gym nauseum: Does D.C.'s new wealth explain the boutique-fitness boom? *City Paper.*

Stein, P. (2015, February 9). The complicated history of a D.C. block smeared by Rep. Schock's former adviser. *The Washington Post.*

Suro, R. (1997, December 31). Drop in murder rate accelerates in cities: District, P.G. County among leaders in trend. *The Washington Post.*

Swanston, W. (1976, October 7). A neighborly party to aid the Seaton Street Fund, *The Washington Post.*

Swarns, R. (2013, January 18). A trendy turn in Obama's town. *The New York Times.*

Tatian, P., & Lei, S. (2014). *Washington, D.C.: Our changing city.* Washington, DC: Urban Institute.

Tavernise, S. (2011, July 17). A population changes, uneasily. *The New York Times.*

The New York Times. (1969, October 5). Near Washington's Dupont Circle, Victorian houses are in fashion again.

The Washington Post. (1957, February 15). Old Georgetown act.

The Washington Post. (1965, May 2). Seaton Place project eyed by NCPC.

The Washington Post. (1987, April 18). Better times at 14th and U.

The Washington Post. (2003, January 4). Mr. Mayor, try a really big magnet.

Timberg, C. (2003, January 3). Williams makes a promising start: Despite D.C.'s fiscal straits, mayor pledges improvements. *The Washington Post.*

Turner, M. (1998). Moderating market pressures for Washington, D.C. rental housing. In W. D. Keating, M. Teitz, & A. Skaburskis (Eds.), *Rent control: Regulation and the rental housing market.* New Brunswick, NJ: Center for Urban and Policy Research.

US Census of Population and Housing, 1940. (1941). Washington, DC: Government Printing Office.

US Census of Population and Housing, 1950. (1951). Washington, DC: Government Printing Office.

US Bureau of the Census. (1996). *Intercensal Estimates of the Total Resident Population of States: 1940 to 1949.* Washington, DC: Government Printing Office.

Von Eckardt, W. (1979, February 3). Going round in (Logan) Circles. *The Washington Post.*

Von Eckardt, W. (1979, December 15). The eclipse of utopia. *The Washington Post.*

Washington Afro American (2011, August 21). Councilwoman Nadine Winter, champion of the poor dies at 87.

Wells, K. (2013). A decent place to stay: Housing crises, failed laws, and property conflicts in Washington, D.C. (Unpublished doctoral dissertation, Syracuse University).

Wiener, A. (2014, December 12). Losing control. *City Paper.*

Wilgoren, D. (2003, July 10). At core of city, old-timers, recent arrivals seek a new balance. *The Washington Post.*

Williams, B. (1988). *Upscaling downtown: Stalled gentrification in Washington, D.C.* Ithaca, NY: Cornell University Press.

Williams, J. (1979, September 11). Gambles in "no man's land" have paid off for investors. *The Washington Post.*

Woodlee, Y. (1995, October 23). Arena deal seen as "coup" for Barry administration. *The Washington Post.*

Zeitz, E. (1979). *Private urban renewal: A different residential trend.* Lexington, MA: Lexington Books.

PART II

Contemporary Urban and Economic Policy

PART II

Contemporary Urban and
Economic Policy

7

SITUATING ENTREPRENEURIAL PLACE MAKING IN DC

Business Improvement Districts and Urban (Re)Development in Washington, DC

Susanna F. Schaller

Introduction

The "livable city" moniker has come to encapsulate a vision of city life that will attract a class of potential urbanites seen as key to maintaining and bolstering the tax bases of fiscally strapped city governments (Florida, 2002; Kearns & Philo, 1993). Harnessing the competitive advantage—street-level neighborhood life, cultural and ethnic diversity, and a broad choice of entertainment venues and businesses—requires cleaning up commercial spaces and marketing images free of deterioration (Florida, 2002; Holcomb, 1993; Kearns & Philo, 1993). Since the 1970s, business improvement districts (BIDs) have become a preferred tool to refashion central-city urban districts to appeal to consumers, new businesses, and higher-income residents.

BIDs are also used to recruit key interest groups, namely property owners, to invest their resources in the areas where they are located. Through a self-managed assessment of local, mostly commercial but also residential, properties (Hoyt & Gopal-Agge, 2007), BIDs ensure a stable, institutionalized source of funding for targeted reinvestment. Both scholars (see Grossman, 2010) and policy advocates (Houston, 1997) promote BIDs as a grassroots governance solution, yet the imperative to serve the aims of those who ostensibly pay for the assessment is built into their governance structure. Therefore, property owners are from the outset viewed as the rightful decision makers (Briffault, 1999; Christopherson, 1994; Justin & Goldsmith, 2006; Mallet, 1994). Consequently, the BID governance model raises important questions about who gets to participate in the revitalization and urban design planning processes (McFarlane, 1999). This question is particularly fraught in the DC context, given the histories of exclusion and incorporation that have created a starkly divided and segregated and now an increasingly hip yet exclusionary city (Hyra, 2015; Prince, 2014; Schaller, 2007).

This chapter examines the context in which BIDs won approval as a possible governance mechanism in Washington, DC in the mid-1990s and delves into the micro-politics of a neighborhood BID establishment process in Adams Morgan, at the time one of the most ethnically and economically diverse neighborhoods in the District. It will highlight how the implantation of BIDs, which are regularly framed as an innovative and progressive policy tool, was far from uncontroversial in a city marked by political, spatial, and economic inequities. Thus, this chapter also hones in on the discourses deployed to legitimize BIDs in DC.

Washington, DC, at once the monumental city and crucible of power, has also been profoundly marked by the social inequalities that characterize US society. It has been and continues to be a divided city and histories of racial fears, economic marginalization, and discrimination are inextricably implicated in the production of the city's urban landscape and refracted in the micro-politics of neighborhood life (Gillette, 2006; Hyra, 2015; Prince, 2014; Schaller, 2007). Even as DC has undergone a widely celebrated urban renaissance, it has been and continues to be a divided city. Situating the BID establishment process in DC's history foregrounds how these governance districts grew out of and draw on those principles, urban planning discourses, policies, and practices implicated in producing DC's fractured urban landscape in the first place; thus, they should be viewed with a critical eye (Christopherson, 1994; Mallet, 1994; McFarlane, 1999; Schaller, 2007; Schaller & Modan, 2005). This is not to say that DC, as a city, has not benefited from the planning interventions spearheaded by BIDs and the city agencies with which they work. To the contrary, downtown has been re-envisioned as a 24/7 neighborhood, large tracts of land that had lain fallow since the 1968 riots have been redeveloped, crime has dropped precipitously (not only in DC), and DC boasts some of the "hottest" urban neighborhoods in the country. The aim to create a lively mixed-used downtown district and to improve the cleanliness, safety, aesthetics, and infrastructure remains laudable. At the same time, the underlying governance model has devolved planning for and management of urban areas to BIDs, restructuring actors' ability to influence and shape urban redevelopment planning.

What Exactly Are BIDs?[1]

The literature offers multiple definitions of BIDs (Morçöl, Hoyt, Meek, & Zimmermann, 2008). In the United States, the legal predecessors of BIDs are special purpose governments (Caruso & Weber, 2006; Foster, 1996; Justice & Goldsmith, 2006; Morçöl, 2006). As such, they are enabled through local or state legislation, which prescribes their district boundaries, organizational form, and programmatic functions. BIDs are usually established as nonprofit organizations, although other forms exist; some states, for example, create BIDs as municipal authorities, others as charitable organizations (Morçöl, 2006, p. 2). To establish individual districts, BID organizers have to petition local stakeholders to either voice their approval (affirmative petition) or voice their opposition (negative petition) to the BID; usually stakeholders are defined as commercial properties. In some municipalities, commercial tenants are given a voice in the process.[2]

BIDs have increasingly expanded their programmatic scope. Although they are to provide "supplementary activities," such as street cleaning, security, and streetscape design (Houstoun, 1997; Mallet, 1994; Mitchell, 1999), the larger BIDs also actively engage in planning the restructuring of local urban economies. So on one hand, they may purchase new street furniture, hang banners, provide holiday lights and signage to create a place identity and to steer and welcome visitors to the district; on the other hand, BIDs also coordinate urban redevelopment planning with the city and take on larger capital improvement projects, such as redesigning public spaces and urban parks. In some cities, as in DC, they even hire off-duty police officers to provide extra security. BID managers may also advocate for city ordinances establishing loitering laws and regulating the activities of street vendors (Mitchell, 2003).

Proponents hail BIDs as effective public-private partnerships that enable local governments to efficiently catalyze and coordinate economic revitalization through property-based revenue collection (Justice & Goldsmith, 2006; Schaller & Modan, 2005). The funds raised through a special mandatory assessment on commercial properties are reinvested in the district. In some cases—this is a recent development—multiunit residential properties are also assessed. Delinquent owners face a lien on their property. Hence, BIDs are assured a relatively secure budget. The fees are variably calculated; generally, they are based on formulas taking into account the square footage and/or assessed value of the individual commercial properties within the BID district.

This fundraising mechanism distinguishes BIDs, and particularly neighborhood-based BIDs, from other economic development and place-making agents, such as community development corporations (CDC) or Main Street organizations. Unhampered by funding conditionality, BIDs enjoy a level of financial sustainability that may allow them a degree of autonomy not enjoyed by these other nonprofit agencies, thereby increasing their decision-making discretion as well as their ability to adhere to their board's mission and goals (cf. Schaller, 2007).

The membership of the board of directors of BIDs is defined by the specific enabling legislation, which also determines whether directors are elected or appointed (Morçöl, 2006). Nonetheless, voting power on the board of directors is generally weighted by property ownership and the assessed value of property. Most boards, depending on the class of BID, include representation of government officials, merchants, and community and cultural institutions, as well as residents; collectively these usually add up to form a minority share on the board

(Briffault, 1999; Mallet, 1994). The reasoning behind this distribution of representation goes back to the broadening legal definition of special districts, which encompasses the formation of BIDs (Justice & Goldsmith, 2006). Special district funds, by their legal definition, must be used to accrue benefits to those who pay; therefore, restricting representation to those stakeholders is viewed as reasonable and equitable (Justice & Goldsmith, 2006).

The mission of BIDs is to focus narrowly on the revitalization of a particular micro-jurisdiction within the city. They restructure the urban landscape into discrete marketplaces where property owners and business owners purchase the safety and cleaning services they want. They also manage the creation and branding of the district. Focused on creating consumption spaces, BIDs consequently create an artificial boundary between the residential space of everyday life and the presumed commercial space of consumption (Davila, 2004; McCann, 1999; Schaller & Modan, 2005). This division of neighborhood space is complicated in predominately residential areas, which are also important sites of social, political, and cultural interaction (Modan, 2007; Schaller & Modan, 2005).

Entrepreneurial city strategies have necessarily been pushed down to the neighborhood or district level (Brenner, 2004, p. 473). The entrepreneurial city then self-consciously relies on entrepreneurial local "communities" that can and are willing to spearhead their own revitalization and economic development because they are given the leeway to formulate local solutions to specific, place-based problems. As part of a public-private partnership to facilitate targeted reinvestment in a specific geographic area, BIDs are especially well suited to the task (Grossman, 2010). However, discourses used to legitimate some of these new governance arrangements anticipate critiques of privatization and can be confounding; they conjoin language associated with local political activism, notions of community-based development, and the marketization of place (Cummings, 2002). The multilayered policy discourse surrounding BIDs, then, interlaces notions of localism, choice, and self-help with grassroots, empowerment, and collaboration and offers policy entrepreneurs legitimating arguments that help to counter critiques. Examining the BID enabling process in DC and the establishment of a particular BID in Adams Morgan provides insights into how neoliberalization processes and entrepreneurial governance strategies become embedded in neighborhoods through the articulation of locally based interests with a wider redevelopment and governance discourse.

A Methodological Note

This work is based on a multilevel case study design. I employed the extended case method (Burawoy, 1991) to examine the BID establishment process that unfolded in one of the most ethnically and economically diverse areas in Washington, DC (Schaller, 2007). I wanted to understand the local-level interest alignments that supported and/or hampered the formation of BIDs in DC in the context of larger postindustrial economic and political processes shaping Washington, DC. I engaged with this issue first as an economic development professional in the organization charged with organizing a model neighborhood BID (1999–2000) and then deliberately as a researcher (2005–2007). I spoke with key city officials and DC Downtown BID executives and coordinated and conducted mapping workshops and interviews with diverse neighborhood stakeholders, including economic development professionals, Advisory Neighborhood Commission (ANC) officials, residents, and merchants in Adams Morgan.

Washington, DC came to the BID movement fairly late compared to other cities. Yet it fully embraced BIDs in the mid-1990s to redevelop the city's core and, at the time of the study, was exploring ways to create a model for neighborhood-based BIDs (NBIDs) as well. Given that Adams Morgan, one of two adjacent neighborhoods designated as the site for this model, was at the time recognized as the most ethnically and economically diverse area in a starkly segregated city, it presented a key case to examine how BIDs might be grafted onto such a complex political, social, and economic environment.

Situating BIDs in DC's Planning and Governance Trajectory

While most visitors to the US capital in the 1990s expected the monumentality of Washington, DC, the Federal City, they were little prepared for DC (the District of Columbia), a city of neighborhoods marked by contradictions in wealth and even by abject poverty. DC, like so many US urban centers, has struggled with outmigration, and its neighborhoods, particularly "minority" neighborhoods, have been subjected to disinvestment and neglect. By the 1990s, DC had notoriously been labeled the murder capital of the United States. But planning efforts intended to break through this image of tying "urban" and "inner city" to "crime and grime" (Modan, 2007). These initiatives focused on reclaiming an urban living image that evoked alternate associations: exciting, convenient, culturally textured, and, above all, safe. While the first imperative in DC was to ensure "clean and safe," a simultaneous planning discourse recalled the city's historical legacy and the vision enshrined in L'Enfant's plan and the McMillan Plan of 1901. It sought to institutionalize governance arrangements that could spearhead redevelopment and revitalization activities to accomplish the rebranding and restructuring of the city. To this end, planners, policy makers, and city advocates rejuvenated notions from the progressive era and City Beautiful. From this perspective, private "bourgeois civic engagement" remained the only feasible solution to stem the steady decline of crisis-prone cities such as DC (see Monti, 1999). BIDs conform to this notion of enlightened privatism (Grossman, 2010).

A few highlights of DC's planning history as they relate to BIDs as a policy tool, however, should raise questions about a governance mechanism that is based on and that privileges property ownership in planning for urban revitalization in US cities (Mallet, 1994). By the time BIDs arrived in DC, this place-based strategy was being drawn over a palimpsest of territorial histories (Harvey, 2005) that had created a highly inequitable city. Underlying neighborhood geographies told, and continue to tell, the stories of restrictive covenants, enforced by politically connected all-White neighborhood associations, as well as redlining, which first drew resources into White neighborhoods to enhance and secure property values and then facilitated systematic disinvestment (Gotham, 2000; Manning, 1998). DC's space also holds within it the root shock (Fullilove, 2005) of urban renewal that razed entire neighborhoods and tore apart social networks (Gillette, 2006). The city's inequitable space embodies unfinished coalition building (McGovern, 1998), the struggle for home rule, the 1968 riots, and international immigration in response to US policies in Latin America (Manning, 1998), as well as the 1991 Latino uprisings in Mount Pleasant that highlighted the particular grievances of a population fairly new to the city, seeking recognition and voice (Modan, 2007).

On April 4, 1968, DC burned, and the event scarred the city's urban space for decades. In DC, large tracts of downtown as well as the surrounding neighborhoods lay smoldering. The 1960s riots (1964–1968) that shook cities across the country resulted from a confluence of factors, including macroeconomic restructuring, federal urban policy, and systematic racial regulation. One of the outcomes on the governance side, however, was the reinstatement of home rule five years after the riots. DC residents could finally elect their municipal government, and DC, dubbed "Chocolate City," was a metaphorical utopia where black folks' majority status was translated into an assertion of self-consciousness, self-determination and self-confidence" (Carrol, 1998). Still, middle-class flight was further eviscerating the city's population and its tax base. At the same time, DC was unable to tax commuter income as well as a large proportion of property within DC.

In the two decades from 1950 to 1970, the population as well as the geographic area of the Metropolitan Statistical Area (MSA) tripled (Manning, 1998, p. 336). As a result, the city's position in the region declined significantly, both in terms of population numbers and in terms of the changing landscape of jobs (O'Cleireacain, 1997). By 1990, 64% of jobs within the MSA were located outside of the District of Columbia (Manning, 1998, p. 343) and more than two-thirds of the jobs within the city were held by non-District residents (Manning, 1998; Shapiro & Bowers, 2003).

Fiscal Crisis, Entrepreneurial Governance, and the Emergence of BIDs

By 1995, the city had plunged into fiscal crisis and the Financial Control Board took over the management of the city. The Control Board instituted painful measures to balance the budget, while at the same time investing resources in professionalizing DC government agencies, upgrading technology, and creating oversight agencies. It also undertook measures to plan the city's comeback. Additionally, a consensus emerged among planners, government officials, research institutes, and citizen advocates that DC's future hinged on its ability to attract residents, retail, and business. To do this, DC had to create a dynamic downtown neighborhood (adding a residential component) as well as conserve its historically protected human scale and its aesthetically remarkable and architecturally significant residential neighborhoods. BIDs were conceived as one effective tool to manage the restructuring of city spaces, such as downtown, and to create the accompanying image campaign necessary to attract and hold investment.[3] In this way, governance networks to institutionalize the partnership between the private sector and government agencies became formalized.

The regime shift also facilitated the establishment of BIDs, creating a key governance mechanism to both raise funds for and manage ambitious redevelopment projects. Under the leadership of Chief Financial Officer Anthony Williams (subsequently Mayor Anthony Williams), the city focused on strategies to increase efficiency and competition through the implementation of public-private partnerships. Additionally, the expansion of the municipal agencies engaged in comprehensive planning for the city represented a potentially positive step; it signaled that the city would move beyond downtown redevelopment to incorporate neighborhoods in the planning process.[4]

BID-enabling legislation had faltered twice, failing to move through the City Council in both 1989 and 1992. But "[by 1995] we were in such bad shape . . . things were so bad that there was a lot of pressure to try anything."[5] The city needed to find entrepreneurial ways to leverage its resources. With the rewriting of legislation, political maneuvering, negotiation, and finally a move from the taxation-writing committee to the economic development committee, the legislation went before the City Council for a vote—this time it passed.

The process for incorporating BIDs in DC is a more inclusive one than in other cities. In DC, BIDs are incorporated as nonprofit agencies. Their approval process per legislation requires submission of a business plan; an affirmative petition from at least 25% of property owners, from owners holding at least 51% of the assessed value, and from 51% of merchants; as well as formal mayoral approval after a public hearing. As originally passed, legislation in DC required the participation of commercial *tenants* (merchants), not just property owners.

Nevertheless, the establishment of BIDs in DC, as indicated by the political process, was a controversial endeavor. Elected officials on the DC Council, as well as administration executives, while in theory favoring BIDs, questioned key aspects of the BID model. One government official summed it up: "we wanted to think about what constitutes a 'majority' when imposing a mandatory assessment" and to think about "the role of government." BIDs raised the question of how much control over its own development the city might have to relinquish. Other officials cited their continued unease with BIDs as being related to the potential negative impact on small businesses, particularly "mom and pop" stores, already under financial stress. It is not surprising, then, that the BID concept also faced strident opposition from residents, small merchants, the vending community, and homeless advocates; these activists' concerns were not without foundation and had found allies on the City Council (Wolf, 2006). By 1996, however, political opportunity structures (Tarrow, 1996) favored BID advocates; the governance of the city had been largely delegated to the Control Board, and the DC Council membership had changed. From the vantage of the Downtown BID executives, council members more pragmatic in their outlook had gained seats.

Enticing the Creative Class

The vision of a newly created Interactive Downtown Task Force (IDTF) became more closely aligned with that of the preservationist movement in 1995. The IDTF developed a plan for downtown that focused on creating the kind of shopping, cultural, and entertainment as well as residential district that would attract people back to DC's downtown and create a 24/7 urban environment. Under the auspices of the Control Board and at the behest of the IDTF, Congress gave the DC Council the authority to delegate economic development powers to "an approved District instrumentality."[6] These powers included the ability to enable Tax Increment Financing (TIF) districts, through which the city could issue taxable and tax-exempt bonds (Maszac, Gross, & Porter, 1996).[7] The TIF districts' oversight, accordingly, could be devolved to private organizations, such as the sales-tax TIF, which was placed under the management of the Downtown DC BID, for example. These tools enabled DC to subsidize and attract investment by private-sector developers and real property owners, who in turn were given direct fundraising and management powers to implement their vision of place. The establishment of BIDs facilitated the governance of place-based, economic development in targeted areas in the city.

A 2003 study commissioned for the Office of Planning concluded that the District received a limited fiscal boost from additional job creation. Therefore, one avenue of revenue growth, as argued by professional planners and economists, was to increase the population, and with it the pool of taxable income (Shapiro & Bowers, 2003, p. 17). This finding coincided with the recommendations advanced by the Brookings Institution in 1998. The goal articulated by this report was to increase the District's population by 100,000 residents by the year 2010. And, as a comment by one of DC's planning officials in 1999 indicated, these should be households making at least $100,000 annually.[8] One of the key strategies to capture new residents, Shapiro and Bower assert in the report, is to "complement and extend Washington's tourist and city beautiful" amenities to redefine its common perception as a "home of bureaucrats and poor people" (2003, p. 18).

In DC, BIDs were and still are not only about place making; they also provide leadership and coordinate planning for the city's future development. In 2006, one of the executives of both the Downtown BID and Mount Vernon Triangle BID described the work of BIDs as follows:

> Some things we can't do, we provide leadership on them. [For example,] the downtown is zoned for residential since 1991 but it's not happening. Why? Well we've got to bring them now but how do we bring them now? Maybe if we had a slight tax-abatement for people to take a little bit of the risk out, they'd do it. So let's try that. We sort of solved that problem by providing the leadership. Likewise on retail. . . . So Eisenhower does the highways, people moving out to the suburbs, cheap land out there, no one is charging for the gas bill. . . . So how do we put together the leadership for TIF (tax increment financing) for downtown? We have to play more of an active role.

In large areas of the city, redevelopment then is coordinated through a network of actors, including city agencies (Department of Transportation, Deputy Mayor's Office of Economic Development and Planning, and Office of Planning being the main agencies), nonprofit agencies formed to aggressively market the city (Washington, DC Economic Partnership, Washington, DC Convention and Tourism Corporation and Cultural Tourism DC), and the Downtown DC BID, whose main members are the commercial property owners and developers.[9]

Through the BID structure, DC's government effectively allows the private sector to mitigate its risk by relinquishing management of place-making and redevelopment areas to BID organizations. And the evolving geography of BIDs in DC suggests a contiguous area particularly in target areas, such as the downtown, central city, and mid-city planning areas, which are to be managed by these entities. Pro-growth coalitions and cooperation with the private sector, particularly with the land-based business community, represent a leitmotif in the history of Washington, DC's development. For instance, the language of the "old" urban renewal plans (Hyra, 2012), which had already echoed City Beautiful tenets, presages the vision for DC that guided the planning initiatives in the late 1990s and 2000s and reverberates through the plans seeking to promote and legitimize BIDs as a governance tool for the District. The 1959 Redevelopment Land Agency (RLA) report asserts: "Here is an opportunity for persons to live who prefer the amenities of . . . a highly convenient and attractive location to a long commuter's journey to a larger suburb" (cited in Gillette, 2006, p. 163). The Washington Board of Trade, the Committee of 100 (created in 1923 as an association of private citizens, including prominent businessmen who adhered to the principles of the City Beautiful movement), and the Federation of Citizens Association lent active support to this redevelopment vision (Gillette, 2006, pp. 124, 59).

Spearheaded by many of the same or related organizations, BIDs represent another incarnation of this planning trajectory, and the initiatives and accomplishments are impressive. The geography of BIDs incorporates areas with large-scale redevelopment projects, such as the Verizon Center, which underwrote the enabling of the Downtown BID in 1997, the Mount Vernon Triangle mixed-use development, and the Anacostia Waterfront development.

Re-imaging campaigns, such as the one encountered on the Downtown DC BID Web site in early 2007, portray a "Downtown DC launched on a meteoric ascent to world class prominence, diversity and excitement." On the same page, the Downtown BID[10] declared:

> Downtown is now DC's hottest new residential neighborhood, dining destination and the cultural and entertainment center of the region. Here you'll find busy streets, bustling stores, happening restaurants and bars, new condos, movie theaters, museums, galleries.

The main focus of these representations was on the aesthetics of places, buildings, and architecture as well as on consumer and cultural activities. It was not on the working-class people laboring behind the scenes to maintain the space, nor on those who currently lived in adjoining neighborhoods. Rather, the marketing materials sent to me and posted on the Web sites of the various organizations involved in marketing DC's regeneration (when they include pictures of people rather than architecture) portrayed professional, clean-cut-looking individuals of indeterminate ethnicity engaged in consumer activities, such as sitting at outdoor cafés, going shopping, or reclining in a grandiose hotel lobby.

> Place matters. It matters if we are going to grow the private sector. It matters if we are going to attract and retain residents in the city. We must have real places—vibrant and welcoming places—where businesses can take root, where the Industry Networks can thrive, and where people can live and work and raise their families with dignity and opportunity. To succeed in promoting neighborhood commercial districts, merchants need to be organized to provide cleanliness, safety, and a pleasing environment for shoppers, workers, visitors, and residents. The new Business Improvement Districts—Downtown DC, Golden Triangle, and now Georgetown—point the way to a new model of accomplishing this important task.[11]

The 1998 Citizens Plan, quoted here, advances a vision that runs through the literature on place making. And, generally, it presents a positive vignette of urban life. The question is how we arrive at this end place. Because of concentrated property ownership in the central business district, it was fairly easy for downtown property owners to create the BID after overcoming the first, onerous hurdle of passing the enabling legislation. Interestingly, the plan, in apparent accordance with the DC enabling statute, cites BIDs as a model through which to organize merchants in support of these aims as well.

The next section turns briefly to the specificity of the processes that created the Adams Morgan Partnership BID. The case is interesting because the community development corporation (CDC) spearheading what was to be an Adams Morgan/Mount Pleasant BID wanted to buck the trend and build the BID with the active support of merchants. On the neighborhood level in an ethnically and economically diverse district, the BID establishment process proved more complex and worth examining. The fragmentation and the diversity of property ownership, the predominance of residential properties, and the presence of vocal and locally rooted merchant and residential interests presented a dense and multi-faceted micro-political context.[12]

The Adams Morgan Partnership BID: The Micro-politics of Place Making

The Adams Morgan Partnership BID was not established until 2006 and then only after a long, arduous process. The idea for a neighborhood BID for Adams Morgan emerged as early as 1996 and initially included the adjacent Mount Pleasant neighborhood. Adams Morgan, which is known as the former heart of the "Latino Barrio," and Mount Pleasant, which had the highest concentration of Latinos in the city in the late 1990s, have been held up as models for integrated living (Cadaval, 1998; Henig, 1982). The Adams Morgan name, a symbol of unity among Black and White parents organizing to integrate their segregated elementary schools in the late 1950s and early 1960s, embodies this ideal of "Diversity with Unity," albeit not without tension (Henig, 1982).

The Adams Morgan neighborhood has two main commercial corridors, Columbia Road and 18th Street, which counted 330 businesses in the late 1990s. Columbia Road was perceived as a mixture of Latino stores and chains catering to the local market, and the 18th Street corridor was seen as the heart of the neighborhood's famous or infamous nightlife. During my research, complex cleavages of the commercial corridors became apparent. Conversations with local officials, merchants, residents, and ANC officials delineated differences between merchants identified as newcomers and old-timers, Latino (immigrant) and non-Latino (nonimmigrant), as well as businesses catering to daytime versus nighttime clienteles. These differences shaped how people talked about and perceived the NBID establishment process.

The BID idea did not originate from within the neighborhoods, but was conceived as a political project by the area's council member and initially met with opposition from local property and business owners as well as resident activists.[13] However, as the District faced mounting fiscal crises in the mid-1990s, community development corporations (CDC) also came under pressure to diversify their funding and to implement commercial development projects and programs focusing on income generation. The CDC in the Adams Morgan/Mount Pleasant area, which had been created out of the aftermath of the 1991 Latino uprising,[14] accordingly reorganized its programmatic focus in 1997 to build a strong business department. And, with the active support of and funding from the District's Department of Housing and Community Development (DHCD), the CDC began to spearhead the possible development of a neighborhood BID.

At the time, the establishment of an NBID in Adams Morgan and Mount Pleasant seemed to build naturally on the organization's revitalization work. The CDC already managed a public grant for commercial façade improvements in Mount Pleasant and the Department of Housing and Community Development, which provided community development block grant funding, and was interested in seeing the CDC expand its revitalization efforts through the further incorporation of the private sector. Additionally, the Mount Pleasant and Adams Morgan business associations with which the CDC worked were already functioning as a voluntary NBID in that they organized supplemental street cleaning and spearheaded beautification projects and community festivals (see Schaller & Modan, 2005). The CDCs proposal to formalize an NBID then rested on the argument that it would distribute the financial and time burden of these voluntary efforts more evenly across all businesses, eliminating free riding by less engaged business owners.

Besides innovative financing, which included funds leveraged from the municipal government, the proposal coincided with the fairly traditional BID schema, following the same enabling legislation as the downtown BIDs in Washington, DC. As the regulations read, a majority of the members on the BID board must be property owners. Furthermore, voting could be structured to reflect the proportion of funds property owners contribute to the organization, creating a hierarchy of voice. In accordance with these regulations, the CDC's design of the NBID restricted participation to business owners and property owners; residents were not incorporated as stakeholders with a decision-making voice.

Democracy at Work: Defining Stakeholders

The proposal immediately ignited controversies first inside the CDC and then in the wider community. Interestingly enough, the NBID plan sparked heated discussions among the CDC staff. The CDC's mission was to promote sustainable economic communities through business, housing, and human resource development in low- and moderate-income neighborhoods with significant Latino populations (www.cdsc.org/grantees). The main cleavages can be traced to very different theoretical (ideological) positions held by different staff members; some gave primacy to economic development and programmatically separated housing from commercial corridor revitalization and small business development. Others emphasized that the CDC had to politically address the dynamic interaction between economic revitalization, the real estate market, and narrowing housing opportunities for low-income residents. While the latter conceived of the commercial corridor as a social, political, and economic space, the former defined the commercial corridor as the exclusive domain of business.

Several staff members questioned the NBID model (Schaller and Modan, 2005) and whether its development would further or contradict the CDC's founding ethos to empower low- and moderate-income Latinos in the area. Underlying this question was a concern that a "revitalization" focused on place rather than people might empty neighborhoods of the CDC's supposed beneficiaries by catalyzing or supporting gentrification processes, thereby reducing it to economic and physical planning, stripping it of any progressive redistributive aims. Specifically, the discussions also focused on the impact an NBID might have on vulnerable, particularly immigrant-owned, small businesses on the corridors. In spite of these concerns, the CDC moved forward with the project with the intention of empowering merchants in the process.

In the recollection of the staff person who ran the BID project at the time, the CDC held four to five meetings with merchants (attended by 4–15 merchants) at the organization's offices. When presented with the structure of the BID and the assessment formulas, as well as the reality that the legislation allowed property owners to pass the assessment through to their tenants, in the words of the staff person, "the BID fizzled." The increasingly negative assessment of the BID concept, particularly by Latino merchants and vendors who were organizing into a separate business association, contributed to the CDC's decision to lay aside the BID project. The Mount Pleasant Business Association, which at the time represented the majority of the largely immigrant merchants on its neighborhood's commercial corridor, also withdrew its support, and the center of gravity shifted to Adams Morgan. However, this did not end the controversies.

The Adams Morgan Business and Professional Association (AMBPA) assumed responsibility for the planning for the BID. The leadership who took over the subsequent organizing effort was characterized as "relatively new merchants on 18th Street." In the assessment of a Downtown BID executive, "the BID in Adams Morgan was going nowhere until whoever the guy that owns [a café and bar for young professionals] . . . became the leader and said, 'I think this is a good idea.'" The new business leadership, however, was perceived as not inclusionary enough and insensitive to the opinions and concerns of the merchants who had been in the neighborhood for a longer time, before the beginning of gentrification. Several local people I interviewed expressed the belief that the interests of old-time merchants, specifically the small, immigrant-owned stores in the neighborhood, selling products such as "Quinceañera dresses, baptism paraphernalia, or soccer shirts," were not sufficiently addressed during the process. There is a sense that this category of merchants, "independent immigrant stores," was not "legitimately courted by the original campaign for the BID."[15] A former city official involved in the process reiterated this sentiment. Like the ANC commissioner, he suggested that some of the merchants felt the process was not "legitimate." He characterized the divide as an old-timer versus newcomer dynamic. "I think a lot of the actual business owners don't really have a say. It becomes the newcomer business owners, the landlords and then a third entity of people who I view as having this power play."

Disregarding this opposition, AMBPA officials went ahead to form the Adams Morgan Partnership, the nonprofit organization that was to become the BID governance structure in 2004. In order to be able to submit the application that would begin the legislative process to legally register the partnership as a BID under DC law, the partnership still had to gather support petitions from property owners and commercial tenants. By early 2004, the partnership had only managed to gather 11% of the necessary 25% of property owners and 15% of the necessary 51% of assessed value and was facing opposition from tenants. Complicating the process was the fragmented ownership pattern in Adams Morgan and the high proportion of absentee landlords. A final power struggle emerged within the AMBPA with the election of a new board of directors. Behind the scenes, one property owner, who was holding out the last 2% needed to reach the threshold so the partnership could submit the application and petitions to the city for review, was lobbying to have certain people placed on the board. The compromise resulted in a shared chairmanship on the Adams Morgan Partnership Board of Directors.[16]

In 2005, the DC government committed the necessary funds to hire a full-time, salaried person to manage the petition process and achieve the threshold of votes required from the property owners. In June, the partnership submitted the application, which was introduced on an emergency basis. Given the difficulty the partnership had faced in organizing the requisite votes from commercial tenants, the NBID had received an exemption for the requirement to secure approval from merchants, and the amendment legally registering the BID was passed in August.

Advocacy literature and scholarly works, rooted in public choice theory, portray BIDs as a return to localized control over resource allocation, thereby enhancing local democracy (see Grossman, 2010; Houston, 1997; Levy, 2001). "I mean to me this is democracy at a lower level," one BID executive noted during a 2006 interview: "you are giving the money back. You are letting the people spend money to influence [planning and development]."[17] In the words of another executive that same summer, BIDs were "about bringing the business community folks together, the building owners together to form something that works to address their issues."

Remarkably, however, even when strong BID proponents and BID practitioners were asked about specific processes, in this case the one establishing the Adams Morgan Partnership BID, a contradiction emerged. On one hand, when talking generally about BIDs, one Downtown BID executive claimed that BID processes were about "bringing folks together." On the other hand, in reference specifically to Adams Morgan, this same executive, later on in the conversation, conceded the following:

> So I knew there was no way to organize a BID [in Adams Morgan] because two things: because one was the way the legislation was written required 51% of the tenants to agree. It took them over 6 years—even without doing the requirement—to dig up the 51% of the assessed value and 25% of owners; it took them that long; it took them, what, almost 10 years.[18]

It follows that really the most expedient way, and really the only way, to ensure the BID establishment process is to narrow the field of participants. By 2007, reality reflected this trend. All BIDs in DC had received exemption from the merchant approval provision.

In the post discussions of the BID in 2006, the sense that the BID was implemented as a project conceived and wanted by only a few seemed to linger. There was also a sense that the neighborhood was on an inexorable path of change that small stores, who continued to rely on the immigrant and local markets, might not survive. The following quote from an ANC commissioner illustrates what some see as the consequences of BIDs, which by design are meant to stabilize and support gentrification processes:

> I see a lot of the business, who really headed up the BID, as being relative newcomers. And that's a tough one if you have a relative newcomer have this idea, which by itself is not controversial and should be beneficial to all businesses, but I think that for a lot of longer-term businesses . . . for Valdemar Travel, you know somebody who has been at that corner 18th and Columbia and who was synonymous with Adams Morgan to have somebody come in and say, "Well, we need to do this and this to run our businesses correctly." I think they felt this was an awful bit of sort of White intrusion telling us how we should manage our neighborhood and do our thing. And, slowly, one by one, businesses that have been here 30 or 40 years have all been picked off. And when they leave it's not a new entrepreneur that takes their place. It's a chain that takes their place or an expansion of an existing business that takes their place.[19]

Today, the Adams Morgan BID, approved in 2005, covers the two commercial corridors in official Adams Morgan, and works in tandem with the citywide revitalization initiative to promote Adams Morgan as a diverse and exciting destination location.

Conclusions

BIDs, by carving out a fixed jurisdictional district, set neighborhood boundaries. In this manner, they demarcate and create a set of local constituents. At the same time, the work of BIDs is to increase local economic activity; therefore, the work of traditional BIDs is to create both a "clean and safe" environment and a marketable image in order to attract people willing to invest and spend their money in the district. Ironically, these processes may undermine precisely the vibrancy and diversity that made these places so interesting in the first place.

The formation of a neighborhood BID and the remaking of its commercial corridor into a primarily economic and consumer-oriented space may circumscribe the definition of who constitutes the local community. As noted, Adams Morgan is famous for its organizational density; it is also infamous for the vociferous community arguments that have at times consumed neighborhood life (Henig, 1982). During the concluding phases of the BID establishment process, confrontations were seen as power struggles among leaders within different sub-communities, businesses, and organizations serving them. The interests that aligned were, however, not simply conditioned by their tenure status in the neighborhood, tenants versus owners, but by a combination of structural and ideological factors. As such, neighborhood merchants, largely but not exclusively immigrant merchants, who had invested in the neighborhood during its era of decline, felt increasingly threatened by the changes on the commercial corridor. As their consumer base shrank, some long-time businesses perceived the BID as an incarnation of the existential threat they faced as gentrification proceeded. Newer, entrepreneurially focused merchants who, on the other hand, were investing in the neighborhood to capture the increasingly affluent local market as well as visitors whom they hoped to attract by marketing Adams Morgan's funky identity, were interested in marketing this atmosphere to increase consumer sales.

Interestingly, the neighborhood ANC, the only elected local governance body, removed itself from the debate. One of the commissioner commented:

> I think we'd like to see many of the ultimate goals of the BID, but as people started to divide and there ended up being these huge fights over if we were to have the BID and what the BID would look like, I think the ANC [argued that] we are not taking a position on that, we are not being taxed for it, we are not the ones who are having to write a check every month or every quarter to the BID.

Yet residents are inextricably linked to life on the commercial corridor. Their perceptions and experiences of the neighborhood's commercial corridor spaces form individual identities and condition people's daily routines, habits, and ability to stay. With gentrification and historic districting processes, specifically highlighted in the Williams administration's comprehensive plan, the identities of Adams Morgan's sub-neighborhoods, Kalorama Heights, Washington Heights, and Lanier Heights, have become more prominently marketed. This marks a reassertion of neighborhood identities predating desegregation and threatens to supersede the progressive history and identity embodied in the name Adams Morgan, which for many still reverberates with complex meanings associated with the important historic struggles for racial equity, neighborhood organizing against urban renewal, and the formation of a Latino space in DC. As a Latino tenant remarked:

> Actually where we live, they want to call the neighborhood Washington Heights. They don't want to be from Adams Morgan because of the diversity. Historic Washington Heights or Kalorama Heights, they don't want to be with Adams Morgan.

The conflict over the establishment of a BID in Adams Morgan exemplifies this struggle over who eventually has a say in the future development of a neighborhood (Schaller and Modan, 2005). While the BID's stated goal was to "enhance the image of the neighborhood as a destination for visitors" in the eyes of many residents and longtime merchants the BID's focus on marketing the neighborhood to outsiders failed to adequately capture the layer of meanings embedded in the word *diversity*. It is inextricably entwined with the neighborhood's history and the daily life of residents and merchants. Diversity in this view means a complex social fabric made up of people, businesses, and places, shaped by the interactions they sustain with one another (Schaller and Modan, 2005). This sense of diversity is experienced as under threat or already gone.

Urban scholar Monti proffers: "There is nothing new about business men dunning each other so that they can improve the area where their shops are located. This has been going on for over 200 years in the United States . . . latter day 'business improvement districts' reassert the legitimacy of bourgeois values in parts of cities which seem to have forgotten them" (1999, pp. 13–14).

In this line of argument, BIDs hark back to the Progressive Era when self-interested yet enlightened private-sector engagement and investment were seen to serve the collectivity. What stands out in this viewpoint is that strategies to "revitalize" urban areas need only focus on reestablishing civility through the physical redesign of urban space to banish the social disorder caused by bad behavior. Left out of the analysis is an examination of the underlying structural causes and the historical regulation of social relations that led to urban disinvestment, poverty, and neighborhood decline. This excursion through DC's Downtown and Adams Morgan BIDs served to illustrate the ways a focus on the economic function of space conjoined with an acceptance of a local governance mechanism that privileges property owners and circumscribes urban belonging.

Notes

1 Much of this section comes from my doctoral work (Schaller, 2007), and sections were presented as part of a conference paper written with Gabriella Modan for the 2011 RC21 conference held in Amsterdam.

2 In some states, such as New Jersey, municipalities can authorize BIDs without a petition.

3 The Economic Resurgence of Washington, DC: Citizens Plan for Prosperity in the 21st Century, November 1998.
4 This strategy was outlined in Mayor Williams' draft comprehensive plan released in July 2006.
5 Interview: Deputy Executive Director, Economic Development at the Downtown DC BID, July 2006.
6 District of Columbia Bond Financing Improvements Act of 1997.
7 The IDTF chair, Herb Miller, is a major developer in DC and a close ally of the Barry administration since 1982. His corporation's investments in the downtown Gallery Place project, often cited as the anchoring project for the downtown revival, was subsidized through TIF. As such, it is difficult to separate private benefit from public good. See James Jones, "Miller time." Loose lips, *Washington City Paper*, May 5, 2006, accessed www.washingtoncitypaper.com/lips/2006/lips0505.html on March 22, 2007.
8 Mount Pleasant ANC Meeting, 1999.
9 See www.wdcep.com/livingindc/index.php, accessed January 2007.
10 These quotes and the images described here come from the Downtown DC BID's website: http://www.downtowndc.org/ The website was accessed in early 2007.
11 The Economic Resurgence of Washington, DC: Citizens Plan for Prosperity in the 21st Century, November 1998.
12 Several informants and government officials, as well as Downtown DC BID executives, noted this as a factor complicating the establishment of BIDs in DC's neighborhoods Coordinator of ReStore DC in the Deputy Mayor's Office for Planning and Economic Development, April 2006. Executive, Downtown BID, July 2006).
13 Interview with deputy executive director of the Downtown DC BID, July 2006.
14 The shooting of a Latino man by a District police officer triggered the riots, followed by a curfew and the occupation of the neighborhood by 1,000 police officers in riot gear (*The Washington Post*, May 8, 1991, p. A01). Commentary among community activists sometimes refers to another riot as the only solution to gentrification.
15 Interview with ANC commissioner, July 2006.
16 Interview with pro bono consultant to the Adams Morgan Partnership, April 2006; interview with Adams Morgan ANC commissioner, July 2006.
17 Interview with Downtown BID, summer 2006.
18 Ibid.
19 Interview with Adams Morgan ANC commissioner, July 2006.

References

Brenner, N. (2004). Urban governance and the production of new state spaces in Western Europe, 1960–2000. *Review of International Political Economy, 11*(3), 447–488.
Briffault, R. (1999). Government of our time: Business improvement districts and urban governance. *Columbia Law Review, 99*(2), 365–477.
Burawoy, M. (Ed.). (1991). *Ethnography unbound: Power and resistance in the modern metropolis.* Berkeley, CA: University of California Press.
Cadaval, O. (1998). *Creating a Latino identity in the nation's capital: The Latino Festival.* New York: Garland Publications.
Carroll, K. (1998, February 1). The meaning of funk. Special to *The Washington Post.*
Caruso, G., & Weber, R. (2006). Getting the max for the tax: An examination of BID performance measures. *International Journal of Public Administration, 29*(1–3), 187–219.

Christopherson, S. (1994). The fortress city, privatized spaces, consumer citizenship. In A. Amin (Ed.), *Post-Fordism reader* (pp. 409–427). Cambridge, MA: Blackwell.

Cummings, S. (2002). Community economic development as progressive politics: Toward a grassroots movement for economic justice. UCLA School of Law, UCLA Public Law Series, Paper 601 (http://repositories.cdlib/uclalaw/plltwps/6–01).

Davila, A. (2004). *Barrio dreams*. Berkeley, CA: University of California Press.

Florida, R. (2002). *The rise of the creative class and how it is transforming work, leisure, community and every day life*. New York, NY: Basic Books.

Foster. K. (1996). Specialization in government the uneven use of special districts in metropolitan areas. *Urban Affairs Review, 31*(3), 283–313.

Fullilove, M. T. (2005). *Root shock: How tearing up city neighborhoods hurts America, and what we can do about it*. New York, NY: Random House: One World Book.

Gillette, H. (2006). *Between justice and beauty: Race, planning, and the failure of urban policy and Washington, DC*. Baltimore, MD: Johns Hopkins University Press.

Gotham, K. F. (2000). Urban space, restrictive covenants and the origins of racial residential segregation in a US city, 1900–1950. *International Journal of Urban and Regional Research, 24*(3), 616–633.

Grossman, S. A. (2010). Reconceptualizing the public management and performance of business improvement districts. *Public Performance & Management Review, 33*(3), 361–394.

Harvey, D. (2005). *A brief history of Neoliberalism*. New York, NY: Oxford University Press.

Henig, J. (1982). *Gentrification in Adams Morgan: Political and commercial consequences of neighborhood change*. Washington, DC: GW Washington Studies.

Holcomb, B. (1993). Revisioning place: De- and re- constructing the image of the industrial city. In G. Kearns & C. Philo (Eds.), *Selling places: The city as cultural capital, past and present* (pp. 133–144). Oxford, UK: Pergamon Press.

Houston, L. (1997). *BIDs: Business improvement districts*. Washington, DC: Urban Land Institute and International Downtown Association.

Hoyt, L., & Gopal-Agge, D. (2007). The business improvement model: A balanced review of contemporary debates. *Geographic Compass, 1*(4), 946–958.

Hyra, D. (2012). Conceptualizing the new urban renewal: Comparing the past to the present. *Urban Affairs Review, 48*(4), 498–527.

Hyra, D. (2015). The back-to-the-city movement: Neighbourhood redevelopment and processes of political and cultural displacement. *Urban Studies, 52*(10), 1753–1773.

Justice, J. B., & Goldsmith, R. S. (2006). Private governments or public policy tools? The law and public policy of New Jersey's special improvement districts. *International Journal of Public Administration, 29*(1–3), 107–136.

Kearns, G., & Philo, C. (1993). *Selling places: The city as cultural capital, past and present*. Oxford, UK: Pergamon Press.

Levy, P. R. (2001). Making downtown competitive. *Journal of American Planning Association, 4*, 16–19.

Mallet, W. (1994). Managing the postindustrial city: Business improvement districts in the United States. *Area, 26*(3), 276–287.

Manning, R. D. (1998). Multicultural Washington, DC: The changing social and economic landscape of a post-industrial metropolis. *Ethnic and Racial Studies, 21*(2), 329–353.

Maszak, P., Gross, N. and Porter, S. (1996). Stirrings of hope for downtown D.C. business initiatives, tax breaks, and regulatory reform bring promise of new development. *Legal Times*, October 20.

McCann, E. J. (1999). Race, protest, and public space: Contextualizing Lefebvre in the US city. *Antipode, 31*(2), 163–184.

McFarlane, A. (1999). Race, space and place: The geography of economic development. *San Diego Law Review, 36*, 295–354.

McGovern, S. J. (1998). *The politics of downtown development: Dynamic political cultures in San Francisco and Washington, DC.* Lexington, KY: The University Press of Kentucky.

Mitchell, D. (2003). *The right to the city: Social justice and the fight for public space.* New York: The Guilford Press.

Mitchell, J. (1999). Business improvement districts and innovative service delivery. Grant report for The Pricewaterhouse Coopers Endowment for Government. www.businessofgovernment.org/pdfs/Mitchell.pdf (accessed October 2000).

Modan, G. (2007). *Turf wars: Discourse, diversity, and the politics of place.* Malden, MA: Blackwell Publishers.

Monti, D. (1999). *The American city: A social and cultural history.* Malden, MA; Oxford, UK: Blackwell Publishers.

Morçöl, G. (2006). Business improvement districts: A new organizational form in metropolitan governance. *International Journal of Public Administration, 29*(1–3): 1–4.

Morçöl, G., Hoyt, L., Meek, J. W., & Zimmermann, U. eds. 2008. *Business improvement districts: Research, theories, and controversies.* Boca Raton, FL: Auerbach Publications.

O'Cleireacain, C. (1997). *The orphaned capital: Adopting the right revenues for the District of Columbia.* Washington, DC: Brookings Institution Press.

Prince, S. (2014). *African Americans and gentrification in Washington, D.C.: Race, class and social justice in the nation's capital.* Burlington, VT: Ashgate Publishing Company.

Schaller, S. (2007). *Bidding on urbanity with business improvement districts: Re-Making urban places in Washington, DC.* (Doctoral Dissertation). Ithaca: Cornell University.

Schaller, S., & Modan, G. (2005). Contesting public space and citizenship: Implications for neighborhood business improvement districts. *Journal of Planning Education and Research, 24*(4), 394–407.

Shapiro, J., & Bowers, K. (2003). Washington, DC; Economic Policy Papers. Prepared for the District of Columbia office of Planning by Phillips, Preiss Shapiro Associates.

Tarrow, S. 1994. *Power in movement: Social Movement and contentious politics.* Cambridge: Cambridge University Press.

Wolf, J. F. (2006). Urban governance and business improvement districts: The Washington, DC BIDs. *International Journal of Public Administration, 29*(1–3), 53–75.

8

BUDGET GROWTH, SPENDING, AND INEQUALITY IN DC, 2002–2013

Natwar M. Gandhi, James Spaulding, and Gordon McDonald

Introduction

The District of Columbia's budget growth has mirrored its population and its economic development increase since the late 1990s. A decades-long population decline reached its nadir in 1998, a time when the District was under the authority of the Financial Control Board imposed by Congress. In the 15 years since, the District's population has grown by more than 14%, and government operating budget expenditures have more than doubled in nominal terms, growing by 42% in real terms. On a per capita basis, real expenditures have grown, but after peaking in 2008, they fell during the Great Recession and as of 2013 have not yet returned to their 2008 level. During the growth period (1998–2008), signs of unequal growth are evident as income inequality has expanded and poverty levels remain high for particular racial and ethnic groups.

This chapter examines operating and capital budget expenditure growth in the District since 2002 and relates that growth to population changes and the broader economic conditions the District experienced over time. More than half of the District's operating budget is spent on human support service and education functions and, when public safety is included, the proportion exceeds two-thirds. District expenditures on core functions such as public safety and public works have grown at fairly steady rates over the 2002–2013 period. Spending in such areas as economic development and capital (from current-year operating budget revenues) has varied more, increasing when revenues increased, but feeling the brunt of decreases when revenues tightened.

Capital budget expenditures have grown considerably, especially since the mid-2000s with the start of a new school modernization program. Facilities such as libraries and recreation centers have also drawn increasing capital funding. In addition to its spending on improvements to streets and highways, the District's capital contribution to the Washington Area Metropolitan Transit Authority more than doubled between 2007 and 2013.

Spending on infrastructure could reinforce the District's growth, if new residents are attracted by modern facilities and better transportation options. But as the District has grown, income distribution data suggest an increasing disparity between high- and low-income residents over this time period. Budget decisions will always involve a balance between the present-day needs of the current population and the vision of the city's future.

A Brief History

The District government is unique in that it performs the functions of many levels of government in one budget. It operates a motor vehicles department and a Medicaid office, like a state; a library system and a department of health, like a county; and a police department and a department of public works, like a city. It is also a school district, and it funds a network of charter schools as well.

The District entered a period of financial crisis in the 1990s, as it ran budgetary deficits and had its bond ratings downgraded to junk-bond levels. In response, Congress created the Financial Responsibility and Management Assistance Authority (commonly referred to as the Control Board) in 1995. The Control Board had ultimate authority over the District's budget (i.e., approving it before it was sent to Congress, until the District managed four consecutive surpluses). In February 2001, when the financial audit for fiscal year 2000 was completed, the fourth consecutive surplus was certified. Beginning with the 2002 budget, the mayor and Council reassumed full budget decision-making authority.[1]

During the Control Board's time, a major change took place in the financial relationship between the District and the federal government. The federal government historically provided a special payment to the District to compensate it for some of the costs of the federal presence as well as the state-like functions it performed. This payment increased over time to a level of $660 million in 1996 and 1997. The 1997 National Capital Revitalization and Self-Government Improvement Act (the Revitalization Act) eliminated this federal payment—phasing it down to $190 million in 1998 and ending altogether in 1999. In exchange, it also made the following changes to relieve the District of some of its spending on state-like functions. First, the federal government took over the District's costs for its courts and prison system. Additionally, the federal share of the District's Medicaid costs was increased from 50% to 70%, reducing the District's share to 30%. Finally, the federal government assumed all unfunded pension liabilities through 1997 for District employees, so that the District was responsible for pension costs for its employees only for service from 1998 forward.

The District experienced a revenue slowdown in 2002–2003, after the 9/11 terror attacks of 2001. Revenues then quickly picked up and growth continued into 2008, until the Great Recession took effect and revenues began to decline. In response, the District used a portion of its fund balance—that is, the cumulative budgetary surpluses it had built over time—to supplement revenues and ensure that operations would not be affected so severely. However, expenditures still decreased noticeably in 2009 and 2010. The 2009 American Recovery and Reinvestment Act (ARRA) helped the District maintain certain services during the Great Recession—for example, by increasing federal dollars to support the District's Medicaid program (as it did for all states).

During the 2000s, the District's population grew, reversing a long decline in population that had started in the 1950s. To some extent, population growth began in the 1990s, taking the Census Bureau by surprise. Based on intermediate estimates between 1990 and 2000, early projections for the 2000 population were around 520,000, but the actual 2000 census showed 572,079—about 10% more than expected. The population stayed near that level through about 2007, but growth between 2007 and 2013 was rapid, as the District added more than 1,000 net new residents per month during this period. A greater population typically means more revenue for the District government, and it also means more demands for government services requiring spending. Thus, to some extent, the positive relationship between population and budget growth was to be expected.

With the 1997 Revitalization Act helping make the District's revenues and expenditures more predictable, a growing population and economy, and with sound financial management after the Control Board's departure, the District's finances are on very solid footing. Wall Street rating agencies have taken notice, as the District's bond ratings have been upgraded from junk-bond levels of single-B and double-B in the mid-1990s to double-A levels today. This improved bond rating is critical as it allows the District to borrow funds with favorable interest rates.

Methodology

The starting point for this chapter's analysis is 2002, the year the District reassumed full control of its budget. It represents a relatively low point for District expenditures, in that growth from 2000–2002 was relatively slow compared to prior or more recent periods. However, comparability of the data becomes more problematic the farther back in time one goes.

The analysis includes expenditures in the District's General Fund operating budget and the General Capital Improvements Fund. These are the primary operating and capital budgets, respectively, for revenue sources within the District's control. Federal funds are generally not included in the analysis, as the focus is on how the District has allocated its own resources.

The presented data is for actual expenditures rather than budget because of the changes that occur to the budget as each year proceeds. The mayor proposes an operating and capital budget in advance of each fiscal year, the Council makes changes and adopts the budget, and the District sends it to Congress for approval.[2] The approved budget is a plan for spending during the upcoming year, as developed before the year starts. However, if revenues increase or decrease during the course of the year, the budget might be increased or cut to match the revenues. In addition, budget authority is moved between agencies each year, depending in part on changing needs and priorities, and furthermore, each year ends with some budget unspent. Thus, the analysis in this chapter uses actual expenditures each year to estimate where priorities finally settled and what services were delivered that year.

Because of the multiple levels of government functions the District government performs, its expenditures are difficult to compare to other cities or to states. District revenues are also unique because its major revenue sources combine property taxes (typically a local-level tax) with sales and income taxes (typically state-level taxes). Revenues are constrained in unusual ways: Congress prohibits the District from imposing a commuter tax; a building height limitation means that property taxes are limited per square foot of building footprint in the city; and an unusually large share of the commercial District is occupied by federal buildings or other buildings out of the District's taxing reach (Gillette, 1995).

Expenditure Growth

District budget expenditures have grown over the 2002–2013 period along with its revenues. In certain budget areas, expenditures have grown fairly steadily, regardless of economic conditions. Other areas fluctuate more with the overall level of revenues. Operating budget growth has mirrored the economy in the region, growing and contracting as revenues did the same. Capital budget expenditures have likewise grown and contracted, but because of time lags inherent in capital projects, the peaks and valleys have come at different times and the effect has been almost counter-cyclical.

Operating budget expenditures include those funded by the District's major revenue sources—income, property, and sales taxes—as well as other smaller taxes and nontax revenue. They pay for the government's day-to-day operations, such as salaries for teachers, police officers, and sanitation workers. Additionally, they cover the local share of benefit payments in programs such as Medicaid and Temporary Assistance for Needy Families (TANF), contracts to perform government functions in areas such as corrections and information technology, and most other functions of government.

Capital budget expenditures include spending on long-term infrastructure and other needs, such as new or reconstructed schools, libraries, and recreation centers; certain economic development projects; and improvements to roads and highways. The bulk of capital expenditures is financed by the proceeds of long-term bonds the District issues in support of approved projects, although other financing mechanisms have become increasingly important. The mayor and Council adopt a capital budget to be sent to Congress each year, as with the operating budget, but there are two differences. One, the capital budget is part of a six-year capital improvements plan (CIP), so the budget each year is actually an update of the previous year's CIP. Two, capital budget authority does not expire at the end of each year, so spending on a project might actually occur in years following the year the budget is provided to the project.

Operating and capital budget spending thus show different patterns over time, although to some extent the areas of emphasis for each—especially in education—overlap. The following sections detail the District's operating and capital budget expenditures between 2002 and 2013.

Overall Operating Budget Expenditure Totals

General Fund expenditures increased steadily from 2002 through 2008, then declined in 2009 and 2010 during the Great Recession. Growth resumed in 2011 and surpassed the 2008 peak in 2013 (see Table 8.1).[3] On average, expenditures grew by 5.5% per year over the entire period. On a real-dollar basis, however, by 2013 expenditures had not yet re-attained their 2008 peak level, and after accounting for the District's population growth, per capita real expenditures remain below 2006–2009 levels.

TABLE 8.1 District General Fund expenditures: nominal, real, and real per-capita

Year	Expenditures ($ millions)	Price Index (2013 = 100)	Real Expenditures ($ millions)	Population Estimate	Real Per-Capita Expenditures ($)
2002	3,629	73.5	4,936	573,158	8,612
2003	3,813	76.2	5,007	568,502	8,807
2004	3,988	77.6	5,139	567,754	9,052
2005	4,397	80.6	5,454	567,136	9,617
2006	5,264	83.3	6,318	570,681	11,071
2007	5,506	86.7	6,351	574,404	11,057
2008	6,273	90.7	6,913	580,236	11,915
2009	6,048	91.1	6,640	592,228	11,212
2010	5,674	93.1	6,092	605,125	10,068
2011	5,851	96.0	6,097	619,624	9,840
2012	6,142	98.6	6,228	633,427	9,832
2013	6,562	100.0	6,562	646,449	10,150

Sources: The Price Index is from Bureau of Labor Statistics CPI-All Urban Consumers, Washington-Baltimore, DC-MD-VA-WV, All Items. Population estimates are from the Bureau of the Census.

TABLE 8.2 District expenditure growth rates

	Expenditures ($ millions)	Annual Average Growth Rate	Real Per-Capita Expenditures ($)	Annual Average Growth Rate
2002	3,629		8,612	
2008	6,273		11,915	
2010	5,674		10,068	
2013	6,562		10,150	
2002–2008 period		9.5%		5.6%
2008–2010 period		-4.9%		-8.1%
2010–2013 period		5.0%		0.3%
Overall, 2002–2013		5.5%		1.5%

During the 2002–2008 period, expenditures grew at nearly a 10% annual rate. This growth occurred while the District's population remained relatively constant, so in real per capita terms, expenditure growth was relatively rapid (see Table 8.2). The decline in spending in 2009–2010 occurred as the population had begun its upswing, so this decline was even sharper when seen in real per capita terms.

Operating Budget Expenditures by Function

The simplest way to view expenditures by function is to look at *appropriation titles*—that is, each cluster of agencies in the District's appropriations act, through which the District receives its appropriation authority from Congress. Each year, more than 65% of the District's expenditures are in agencies in three appropriation titles: *Human Support Services* (e.g., Department of Health Care Financing, Department of Human Services, Child and Family Services Agency); *Public Education System* (e.g., DC Public Schools and Public Charter Schools, the subsidy to the University of the District of Columbia); and *Public Safety and Justice* (e.g., Metropolitan Police Department, Fire and Emergency Medical Services, Department of Corrections). A growing share of spending has been devoted to the *Financing and Other* title, which includes the District's debt service payments. The remaining expenditures are spread across agencies in three other appropriation titles. Growth by appropriation title is shown in Figure 8.1.

Looking more deeply within appropriation title, or function, reveals where District spending has increased since 2002, as well as which areas expanded when revenues increased and scaled back when revenues declined.

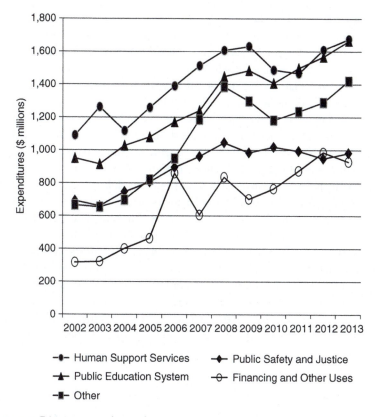

FIGURE 8.1 District expenditures by appropriation title (functional area).

Health Care, Including Medicaid

Medicaid, the federal-state program providing health care to the low-income population, represents one of the District's major cost areas. The federal government and states share the cost of the Medicaid program, and each state has a different Federal Medical Assistance Percentage (FMAP), or cost-sharing percentage. These percentages are usually based on state per capita income, and they range from 50%, for states with high per capita income like Connecticut and Maryland, to more than 74% for Mississippi. The District's per capita income is high when compared to states, and it would qualify for only a 50% federal percentage based on the FMAP formula. But the Revitalization Act took the District out of the formula and set its FMAP at 70%, in recognition of its high poverty rate even in a high per capita income jurisdiction. This means that the District spends only 30 cents of each dollar spent on Medicaid—the federal government pays the other 70 cents.[4]

Health care and Medicaid expenditures grew at an average annual rate of 6.4%, faster than overall expenditure growth during the 2002–2013 period. Medicaid was once budgeted in the Department of Health (DOH), but a separate Department of Health Care Finance (DHCF) was established in 2009 to manage Medicaid and the financial components of other health-related programs. The measure here is expenditures in the two agencies combined.

As one component of the 2009 ARRA, state FMAPs were enhanced to provide states with much-needed fiscal relief. In the District's case, the FMAP was increased from 70% to as high as 79.29%.[5] Figure 8.2 shows District expenditures actually made from local funds in DOH and DHCF, and it shows a second data series that includes the enhanced federal Medicaid dollars for 2009–2011. For these agencies, like many other District agencies, actual local-source expenditures were lower in 2009 and 2010 compared to 2008. This is because the District paid only 21 cents on the dollar of total Medicaid expenditures, rather than the usual 30 cents. But Medicaid spending in total could continue to increase because of the additional federal funds. The data series including the enhanced FMAP shows what would have been had District expenditures remained at 30% of the total, and these figures are more representative of services provided than the actual expenditure figures. The gap between the two lines represent District dollars that were freed up to use for other purposes without affecting total Medicaid spending.

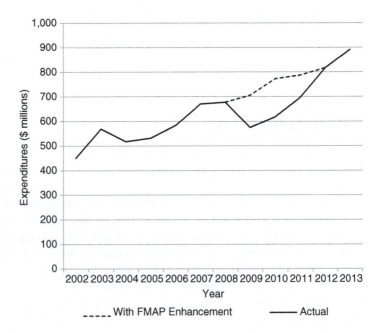

FIGURE 8.2 District expenditures on health care and Medicaid, without and with enhanced FMAP.

Human Services

The other major component of the Human Support Services appropriation title is a set of agencies revolving around the Department of Human Services (DHS). These include the Department of Behavioral Health (DBH) and the Child and Family Services Agency (CFSA). Both of these agencies were once part of DHS, were put under receivership in the late 1990s, and were established as separate agencies as they emerged from receivership. They also include the Department of Youth Rehabilitation Services (part of DHS until 2006) and the Department of Disability Services (part of DHS until 2008). Although these agencies make up a large part of the District's budget, their expenditures have grown more slowly than overall expenditures. In particular, after CFSA expenditures more than doubled between 2004 and 2008, and DBH expenditures went up by more than 50% between 2004 and 2009, expenditures at both agencies have declined in recent years.

Primary Education

Primary education expenditures have grown at about the same rate as overall District expenditures. Primary education includes DC Public Schools (DCPS), DC Public Charter Schools (DCPCS), the Office of the State Superintendent of Education, and several agencies that split out from the DCPS budget during the time period. Within this area, spending on DCPCS increased six-fold between 2002 and 2013, reflecting rapid enrollment growth in charter schools as well as an inflation factor that is part of the funding formula for both DCPS and DCPCS. Expenditure changes for DCPS are harder to track consistently because of the change in the agency budget structure over the period, but it is clear they have increased more slowly, as DCPS enrollment declined through 2010 before increasing slightly over the past three years.

As with the FMAP enhancement, additional federal funds related to ARRA helped the District maintain education spending during 2009–2011, allowing the District to reduce spending of its own dollars while maintaining services. However, these enhanced federal dollar amounts going to education were smaller than what was provided for Medicaid. Within the District's overall expenditure decrease between 2008 and 2010, local source spending in primary education decreased by a relatively small amount.

District officials have recognized that improving primary and secondary education is crucial to the District's continued growth, especially if young families are to be attracted to move into the city and stay in the city as their children reach school age. As will be discussed later in this chapter, the District has spent a great deal of its capital improvement dollars on schools' infrastructure, but increased spending on schools in the operating budget can also be seen as a result of this emphasis.

Public Safety

Public safety expenditures, measured by expenditures by the Metropolitan Police Department, the Fire and Emergency Medical Services Department, and the Department of Corrections, grew slowly and steadily over the 2002–2013 period. These expenditures have grown relatively slowly and have decreased as a share of total expenditures, declining from more than 15% of the total in 2002–2004 to 12.4% in 2012 and 12.1% in 2013. Along with primary education, public safety showed a very small reduction in spending in the 2008–2010 period, perhaps indicating it is a core function that needed to be maintained when other budgets were being reduced more in the face of the revenue decline.

Economic Development (Including Housing and Employment Services)

Expenditures on economic development have been one of the major variable portions of the District's overall expenditures, increasing through 2008 and then falling by nearly 50% between 2008 and 2010. The rebound in 2013 is due to a large investment in the Housing Production Trust Fund by city government. This additional investment for affordable housing was repeated in 2014. Expenditures in this area are a small portion of the District's total, so relatively small dollar changes have a greater percentage impact on their share of the total.

Debt Service, Pay-as-You-Go Capital, Pensions, and Other Post-employment Benefits

Debt service expenditures have increased faster than overall expenditure growth, reflecting a renewed commitment to the District's capital program since the mid-2000s. This expenditure increase has occurred over a period of time with relatively low interest rates in the economy in general. The District has taken advantage of these low interest rates in its new borrowing and in refinancing much of its outstanding debt at lower rates. Furthermore, the District's improving bond ratings mean it can borrow at a lower interest rate than the days its bond ratings were in the double-B or single-A range. Even if it had spent a constant level on debt service, the District could have borrowed somewhat more than in past years (and committed more to the capital program) because of all of these factors. But the fact that debt service expenditures have increased means that borrowing has increased by even greater amounts. Pay-as-you-go (Paygo) capital expenditures have also grown, further reflecting the commitment to the capital program.

The District has fully funded its defined benefit pension plans and has made substantial progress toward full funding of its retiree health care commitments, often referred to as "other post-employment benefits" (OPEB). It is thus better off than many jurisdictions that are struggling to maintain adequate funding for their plans. Several factors have contributed to this result. For example, the District's defined benefit plans cover only police officers, firefighters, and teachers. Other employees hired after 1987 are in a defined contribution plan, for which the District makes annual contributions but has no future liability (pre-1987 hires are in the federal Civil Service Retirement System (CSRS)). Also, in the Revitalization Act of 1997, the federal government assumed the accrued unfunded liability related to the police/firefighter, teacher, and CSRS plans. The District is responsible for funding pension benefits related to years of service after 1997. Additionally, around the time OPEB liabilities first became an issue, the District ended 2005 with a large surplus. The District used $138 million of this surplus to make a down payment toward reducing this liability in 2006. There has been a strong commitment to fully meet the pension liabilities, and the District budgets and spends sufficient amounts each year to maintain full funding of its pensions and continues to reduce its OPEB liability.

Operating Budget Expenditures by Function

Budget structures change and new agencies are created from year to year, but this analysis groups the District's operating agencies consistently when making comparisons across time. The agencies detailed earlier in this chapter are a small number relative to the more than 100 agencies in the operating budget, but they account for more than 75% of expenditures each year. Their expenditure growth is summarized in Tables 8.3 and 8.4.

Capital Budget Expenditures

This section details the District's capital expenditure growth from 2002 through 2013. The District made large capital investments in recent years and this investment sets the framework for future economic growth. Capital spending has increased from less than $500 million per year in FYs 2004–2005 to more than $940 million per year in FYs 2008–2013, a more rapid growth rate than operating budget expenditures over that period. While capital spending surged in 2008, along with operating budget expenditures, capital spending remained high in 2009 and actually peaked in 2010 as operating budget expenditures fell. Although not necessarily planned as counter-cyclical activity, spending on capital projects might seem to serve that function, as spending sometimes lags behind the associated financing decisions. It appears that large Paygo transfers in 2006 and 2008, as well as increased borrowing during a time of operating budget growth, paid off in capital expenditures that peaked a few years later. In many years, the District spent more on highway and street construction than any other type of capital, and

TABLE 8.3 Summary, expenditures by function

	2002		2008		2010		2013	
	Dollars ($million)	Percent of Total	Dollars ($million)	Percent of Total	Dollars ($million)	Percent of Total	Dollars ($million)	Percent of Total
Health and Medicaid	449	12.4%	677	10.8%	617	10.9%	890	13.6%
Human Services	542	14.9%	797	12.7%	706	12.4%	676	10.3%
Primary Education	849	23.4%	1,296	20.7%	1,270	22.4%	1,549	23.6%
Public Safety	550	15.2%	825	13.2%	804	14.2%	796	12.1%
Economic Development	59	1.6%	332	5.3%	171	3.0%	246	3.8%
Debt Service, Paygo, Pensions, and OPEB	355	9.8%	907	14.5%	689	12.1%	831	12.7%
Subtotal	2,804	77.3%	4,834	77.1%	4,257	75.0%	4,988	76.0%
All Other	825	22.7%	1,439	22.9%	1,417	25.0%	1,573	24.0%
Total	3,629	100.0%	6,273	100.0%	5,674	100.0%	6,562	100.0%

TABLE 8.4 Growth rates, expenditures by function

	Average Annual Growth Rates			Overall Annual Average, 2002–2013
	Growth, 2002–2008	Growth, 2008–2010	Growth, 2010–2013	
Health and Medicaid	7.1%	-4.5%	13.0%	6.4%
Human Services	6.6%	-5.9%	-1.4%	2.0%
Primary Education	7.3%	-1.0%	6.8%	5.6%
Public Safety	7.0%	-1.3%	-0.3%	3.4%
Economic Development	33.3%	-28.3%	12.9%	13.8%
Debt Service, Paygo, Pensions, and OPEB	16.9%	-12.9%	6.5%	8.0%
Subtotal	9.5%	-6.2%	5.4%	5.4%
All Other	9.7%	-0.7%	3.5%	6.0%
Total	9.5%	-4.9%	5.0%	5.5%

these projects have specific sources of funding, both federal and local. However, the biggest increase in capital spending between 2002 and 2013 was in school construction.

The Capital Program

The capital budget gets less attention than the operating budget. It is much smaller, with expenditures in the range of $450 million to $1,050 million per year rather than the $5 billion to $7 billion of the operating budget.[6] In addition, because the capital budget is financed primarily with bonds (borrowed funds), taxpayers may not see the link to their tax dollars as directly as with the operating budget. But a vibrant capital program can set the stage for future economic growth as infrastructure is built or rebuilt and as new facilities allow the District to provide better services to taxpayers.

Capital spending is typically financed by issuing bonds to investors, with a promise to repay principal and interest over a 20- to 30-year period. Capital projects are initiated to build long-lasting assets—a school, a library, a new computer system, or an economic development project. Because these assets will benefit taxpayers over a long period, it is appropriate to pay for them over a long period, through debt service payments in future year operating budgets. The District uses General Obligation bonds and income-tax-secured revenue bonds to finance its general capital program, and it has also issued a variety of specific revenue-backed bonds and certificates of participation for certain projects.[7]

Capital projects can also be financed through direct payments from the operating budget. Paygo capital simply means using operating budget dollars—raised through taxes or other operating budget revenue sources—for capital projects. Technically, the Paygo dollars are transferred from the General Fund to the Capital Fund, then they are spent from the Capital Fund on the capital project. Paying "as you go" is distinguished from paying over time, by borrowing through bonds and repaying principal and interest. Both types of capital spending have operating budget impacts: Paygo spending counts as an operating budget expenditure in the year the dollars are transferred, while operating budget debt service expenditures are budgeted each year to repay borrowed dollars for the 20- to 30-year life of the bond.

Finally, capital spending on transportation projects has other financing sources. The federal Highway Trust Fund accounts for nearly all federal funds that support the District's capital projects. The District matches the federal funds by dedicating the local motor fuel tax, as the federal program requires. Additionally, the District has dedicated a variety of local funding sources to transportation, most consistently the rights-of-way fees paid by utilities that use the District's streets to lay gas, power, or phone lines.

Capital Borrowing and Spending in the District: By Agency

The District's capital spending lagged during the 1990s. When budgets are tight, capital spending may seem relatively easier to postpone than operating budget spending. In the District's case, the descent of its credit rating to junk bond status in 1995 made it extremely hard to issue bonds, and the US Treasury had to step in to ensure the District had access to capital markets.[8]

Capital borrowing and spending accelerated over the 2002–2013 period. From an average of about $425 million per year between 2002 and 2005, borrowing has increased to an average of about $725 million per year between 2010 and 2013. Capital spending has likewise increased, after somewhat of a lag. From all local sources, the District has spent an average of nearly $1 billion per year from 2008 through 2013, compared to an average of about $500 million per year in 2004–2006.

The most visible expansion of capital spending has been the school construction program. In the FY 2006 budget, the District added $150 million of new funding for DCPS, in addition to the usual annual allotment, which had been in the range of $150 million to $175 million in recent years. In succeeding years, budgets and eventually spending continued to increase. Between 2004 and 2007, spending on school construction never exceeded $150 million per year, but each year since 2008, it has exceeded $250 million.

After schools, the next largest shares of capital spending are for road construction and other transportation projects. Road construction spending is managed by the District Department of Transportation (DDOT), and the District also makes a large capital contribution to the Washington Metropolitan Area Transit Authority (WMATA). Between them, DCPS, DDOT, and WMATA have generally accounted for more than half of all capital spending from local sources each year since 2008 (see Figure 8.3).

Spending by some of the other major capital agencies is shown in Figure 8.4. This includes spending on projects for the Office of the Chief Technology Officer, which averaged nearly $100 million per year in 2002–2007 but has fallen off sharply since; increased spending on libraries and recreation centers in 2009–2011; and spending by the Deputy Mayor for Planning and Economic Development, which has varied over the period, similar to the variations in this agency's operating budget expenditures. Additionally, the Department of General Services' spending peaked in 2010–2011 with the purchase of a building at 225 Virginia Avenue SE, construction of a government center building at Minnesota Avenue and Benning Road, and construction of the Consolidated Forensics Lab.

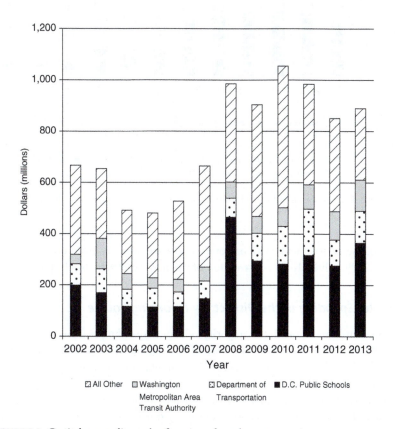

FIGURE 8.3 Capital expenditures by function, three largest agencies.

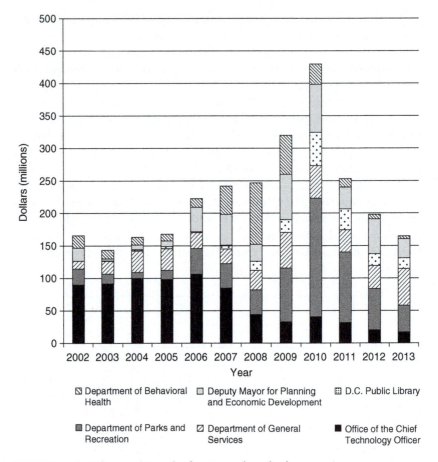

FIGURE 8.4 Capital expenditures by function, selected other agencies.

Finally, the Department of Behavioral Health spent nearly $200 million during 2007–2009, primarily on construction of the new St. Elizabeths Hospital.

Capital Spending in the District: By Financing Source

As previously mentioned, the majority of capital spending is financed by bonds the District issues each year. But one of the big increases in operating budget spending in the mid-2000s, as revenues expanded, was in Paygo transfers to the capital budget.

Historically, the District has borrowed primarily by issuing General Obligation bonds, which it has a legal obligation to repay from any source available. Starting in 2009, the District has issued income tax-secured revenue bonds, for which it pledges income tax revenue to repay. Income tax receipts during the year go first to a trustee account. Once enough revenue has accumulated to make that year's debt service payments (plus any required reserve amounts), the remainder of the revenues flow through to the General Fund to support other operating budget expenditures. Because the coverage rate, that is, the amount of income tax revenue collected each year compared to the amount needed to make the debt service payments, is so high, bonds backed by income tax revenue receive a higher rating than General Obligation bonds. Thus, the interest rate the District pays is lower. The District has also issued other types of debt such as certificates of participation (COPs), revenue bonds, and Grant Anticipation Revenue Vehicle (GARVEE) bonds.

Overall, borrowing has increased greatly in recent years. The District has benefited from low interest rates, both because of low interest rates in the economy as a whole and because of improvements in its bond rating. The increase in borrowing has resulted in increased debt service expenditures in the operating budget, even with the low interest rates the District has enjoyed.

Part of the increase in capital financing has come from Paygo capital spending, which allows capital spending to take place without increasing the District's borrowing and thus, its debt service. Paygo capital transfers increased markedly in FY 2006 in the operating budget, and remained high in 2007 and 2008. Over several years, the District allocated year-end surpluses to Paygo capital in the succeeding year. Because the surpluses were not guaranteed to repeat, this was, in effect, a one-time use of one-time revenues. Additionally, the District made a commitment to spend $100 million of the operating budget on capital, through Paygo transfers, for school construction, starting in FY 2008. It reversed that decision two years later, but it kept school construction funding at the levels it would have been at by borrowing more instead. While transfers from the operating budget were at their highest in 2006, the associated capital spending from Paygo peaked in 2008 and 2009.

Figures 8.5 and 8.6 show capital expenditures by source of funding. Figure 8.5 shows bond-funded expenditures compared to those from all other sources, and Figure 8.6 provides details on expenditures from the other sources.

Growth and Income Inequality in the District

The District's population grew steadily from about 2005 onward, a period leading up to and continuing through the Great Recession. To some extent, the District, and the metropolitan region, did not fare as poorly during the recession as many other parts of the country, and the District's revenues have recovered sufficiently to allow expenditure growth in the years following the recession. But income inequality remains a concern and may have grown during this period, and the District's poverty rate has not decreased appreciably since the end of the recession.

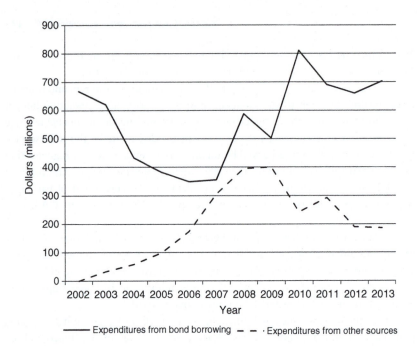

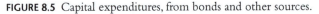

FIGURE 8.5 Capital expenditures, from bonds and other sources.

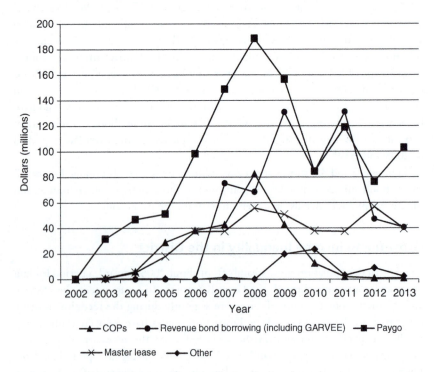

FIGURE 8.6 Capital expenditures, details on other financing sources.

Income inequality can be measured by the Gini coefficient, which ranges from 0 to 1. A value of 0 for a given population means that all incomes are equal. So the bottom 20% of the income distribution has 20% of total income, and the top 1% has only 1% of total income. A value of 1 is the other extreme—one person has all income, and everyone else has no income.

Based on analysis of District income tax data, the Gini coefficient for the District's population increased from 0.595 in 2002 to 0.656 in 2006 just before the Great Recession, indicating an increase in inequality. It fell during the recession to 0.605 in 2009, and rose again to 0.627 in 2012 as recovery continued.[9]

There is a clear cyclical component to this measure. The decline in real estate values and capital gains income during the recession greatly reduced incomes at the top of the income distribution, appearing to reduce income inequality—even though those in lower strata of the distribution were suffering as well. But the measure did not decline in 2009 to as low a value as in 2002, the end of the prior recession, which was somewhat milder. It remains to be seen whether the resumption of the increase in inequality continues through the next business cycle.

Related to the figures on income distribution, the District's poverty rate has remained persistently high. It fell from about 19% in 2004–2005 to just more than 16% in 2006, then increased again during the recession, as is to be expected. But after peaking at 19.2% in 2010, it has remained near 19% in 2011–2013. The recovery has not spread throughout the District's population in such a way as to reduce the poverty rate. Additionally, the poverty rate is particularly high for certain racial and ethnic groups. In 2012, the poverty rate for African Americans and Hispanics was 26% and 22%, respectively, while for Whites it was 7%. Increasing inequality and a still-high poverty rate will continue to challenge those making budget decisions in the near future.

Conclusion

The increase in overall operating budget expenditures since the end of the Control Board period appears rapid, but it has been smaller in real per capita terms and has actually declined slightly in those terms since 2006. Population growth has been swift since 2008, and the operating budget should be expected to grow in certain areas to keep up with population. Further analysis could be undertaken to examine spending by population subgroup—for example, spending on schools as the school-age population declines or grows, or spending on antipoverty programs as the poverty rate increases or decreases and whether the programs actually lift some of the population out of poverty.

When revenues declined during the Great Recession, the District maintained spending in public safety, education, and Medicaid (the latter thanks to federal assistance), and made reductions in areas that were less a part of core municipal government functions, such as economic development and Paygo capital. The federal assistance for Medicaid meant that local-source Medicaid expenditures decreased, representing a substantial portion of the measured decrease in local expenditures.

Capital budget expenditures represent a significant, but often overlooked, portion of the District's spending. Some of the District's capital expenditures represent a portion of its economic development agenda, but other forms of economic development are off-budget and not captured in this analysis. A low interest rate environment, improvements in the District's bond ratings, and a commitment to Paygo capital all enabled expansion in the capital program over this time period.

As reflected in both its operating and its capital budget expenditures, the District government's budget has grown as the city itself has grown. However, increasing revenues and budgets have not masked persistent poverty and the widening inequality of income in the city. The recent emphasis on school construction could be a step toward an eventual diminishing of income inequality, if it can be matched by improved educational outcomes for students. Affordable housing issues have come to the fore, and the District has made additions to the budget for the Housing Production Trust Fund in response. Spending in these areas, as well as in health care, could lead to increasing opportunities for more and more of the District's residents.

Notes

1 The District ended the year with deficits in 1994, 1995, and 1996 and ended with surpluses from 1997 through 2013.
2 As one aspect of the unique relationship between the District and the federal government, Congress approves the District's budget as part of the congressional appropriations process.
3 All operating budget expenditure figures in this chapter are based on a modified data series of General Fund expenditures. These data match the budget-basis expenditures in the District's Comprehensive Annual Financial Report (CAFR) each year, table A-5, with certain exceptions made to maintain comparability across years. A full comparison of these data to CAFR data and further details are available from the authors on request. All years in this chapter refer to District fiscal years, and all dollars are nominal except where noted.
4 Administrative costs and certain other expenditures have different federal/District splits.
5 The FMAP was subject to adjustment each quarter from mid-2009 to mid-2011. See www.gpo.gov/fdsys/pkg/FR-2010–10–29/pdf/2010–27412.pdf for notice of the District's 79.29% rate.
6 As with the operating budget data, the capital data here are for local-source expenditures only. Federal funds for capital consist mostly of Highway Trust Fund grants for the District Department of Transportation.
7 Revenue-backed bond examples include bonds for New Communities, which are new or replacement construction for neighborhoods with a high concentration of public housing, backed by revenues dedicated to the Housing Production Trust Fund on an

annual basis; and bonds backed by a Payment-in Lieu-of Taxes associated with development in the neighborhood of the federal Department of Transportation. Note that expenditures on the baseball stadium and on projects financed through Tax Increment Financing are excluded from the data in this chapter.

8 The District's credit rating has rebounded to the AA- / AA- / Aa2 level for its General Obligation bonds and to AAA / AA+ / Aa1 level for its Income-Tax-Revenue Backed bonds, as of December 2014, in ratings by Standard and Poor's, Fitch Ratings, and Moody's Investor Service, respectively.

9 Details can be found on the Web page for the District's chief financial officer by searching for "CFO income inequality October 2014."

Reference

Gillette, H. (1995). *Between justice & beauty: Race, planning, and the failure of urban policy in Washington, D.C.* Baltimore, MD: Johns Hopkins University Press.

9

BICYCLING IN THE WASHINGTON, DC REGION

Trends in Ridership and Policies Since 1990

Ralph Buehler and John Stowe

Introduction[1]

Governments of large US cities have the goal to encourage more bicycling to alleviate peak-hour congestion on roadways and public transport, reduce CO_2 emissions, improve local air pollution, combat oil dependence, and enable health-enhancing physical activity as part of the daily travel routine (Banister, 2005; Buehler, Pucher, Merom, & Bauman, 2011; Heinen, Van Wee, & Maat, 2010). This chapter documents and compares cycling policies and trends in the Washington, DC area. It focuses on the time period since the late 1990s when the District of Columbia's population and economy increased strongly.

This chapter's goal is to provide a better understanding of variability and determinants of cycling in the DC metropolitan region. The biking data presented in this chapter originate from the Metropolitan Washington Council of Government (MWCOG) Household Travel Survey, the US Census Bureau, and information obtained directly from local bicycling experts. During the past 20 years, cycling levels and cyclist safety have been increasing in the Washington, DC region. Since the late 1990s, all jurisdictions have greatly expanded their on-street bicycle lanes and implemented other innovative programs. Washington, DC, Alexandria City, and Arlington County have implemented more bike-friendly policies and have been at the forefront of experimenting with innovative measures. In spite of the progress, many challenges remain for cycling. Area cyclists are predominantly male, between 25 and 65 years old, White, and from higher-income groups. Cycling appears to be spatially concentrated in neighborhoods of the urban core jurisdictions that experienced strong population growth. The remainder of this chapter provides an in-depth comparison of trends and differences in bicycle planning, bicycle infrastructure, and programs across jurisdictions in the DC region.

Trends in Cycling in the Washington, DC Region

The Study Area: The Washington, DC Region

Table 9.1 provides an overview of socioeconomic and spatial characteristics of the urban core and inner suburban jurisdictions of the Washington, DC region (MWCOG, 2009). The socioeconomic characteristics, such as income and race, associated with biking rates are presented. Median household incomes in the region are higher than the US national average of $53,000 (USDOC, 2014). Even Washington, DC—the least wealthy jurisdiction in this study—had a median household income 21% higher than the national average. Higher household incomes in the Washington, DC area are partially offset by 40% higher costs of living compared to the national average for urban areas (USDOC, 2014). Municipal averages hide large income discrepancies within jurisdictions. For example, in Washington, DC, median household income east of the Anacostia River was only $34,966 in 2008–2012—well below the national median (USDOC, 2014). Table 9.1 also shows that DC-area jurisdictions have higher shares of minority populations than the national average of 26%. Washington, DC and Prince George's County are African American–majority jurisdictions at 51% and 64%, respectively.

Table 9.1 also lists population density, share of households without cars, percentage of university and college students in the population, and Metrorail stations per inhabitant for each jurisdiction, because these variables are significant correlates of bicycling and bike commuting (Heinen et al., 2010; Krizek, Forsyth, & Baum, 2009). Higher population density serves as a proxy for shorter distances between trip origins and destinations. Washington, DC, Arlington, and Alexandria have three to four times greater population densities than suburban Fairfax, Montgomery, and Prince George's Counties.

University students have been found to cycle more than the adult population as a whole. Students account for 8% to 12% of the population in Washington, DC jurisdictions. Individuals in households without automobiles are also more likely to cycle. Causation may run both ways because individuals who prefer cycling may decide not to own an automobile. The share of carless households in Washington, DC, 37%, is eight times greater than in Fairfax County, where only 4% of households are carless. In the other jurisdictions, roughly 10% of households are carless. The high share of households without cars in Washington, DC may be partially explained by the accessibility the Metrorail and bus systems provide (APTA, 2014). Moreover, in parts of the District with high poverty rates, many households may not be able to afford the cost of owning and operating an automobile.

Trends and Geographic Variability in Cycling Levels and Trip Purpose

Over the past 20 years, cycling levels have been increasing in the Washington, DC area (see Table 9.2) (MWCOG, 2010; TPB, 2006, 2010a; USDOC, 1980–2000,

TABLE 9.1 Sociodemographic and spatial characteristics of Washington, DC and adjacent jurisdictions, 2008–2012.

Jurisdiction	Population	Land Area (Square Miles)	Population per Square Mile	Percent of University Students	Percent of Car-Free Households	Percent White	Household Median Income	Metrorail Stops per 100,000 Inhabitants
Washington, DC	605,759	61	9930	12%	37%	40%	$64,267	6.6
Arlington	209,077	26	8041	9%	12%	71%	$102,459	5.3
Alexandria	140,337	15	9356	9%	10%	64%	$83,996	2.1
Fairfax	1,083,770	395	2744	8%	4%	64%	$109,383	0.6
Montgomery	974,824	495	1969	8%	8%	58%	$96,985	1.1
Prince George's	865,443	485	1784	10%	9%	22%	$73,568	1.7

Sources: MWCOG, 2009; USDOC, 2014

2014). Between 1994 and 2008, the bike share of all trips increased in all jurisdictions except Fairfax County (MWCOG, 2010; TPB, 2010b). In both 1994 and 2008, Washington, DC had the highest share of trips by bike among all jurisdictions in the area—followed by Alexandria. In addition to the MWCOG survey results for 1994 and 2008, the US Census Bureau tracks the regular mode of transportation for commuters for each jurisdiction (see Table 9.2). Between 1990 and 2008–2012 (averaged), the number of regular daily bike commuters increased almost threefold in the region—from 6,086 to 16,980 (USDOC, 2014). The number of regular daily bike commuters increased fourfold in the District of Columbia and more than twofold in Alexandria City, Arlington County, and Montgomery County. In spite of the strong increases in the number of bike commuters, in 2008–2012 cyclists accounted for a small share of overall commuters: 3.2% in Washington, DC, 1.2% in Arlington County, 1.0% in Alexandria, and 0.5% or less in the other jurisdictions.

Local counts of bicyclists on bridges and trails also support the apparent increase in cycling levels over the past 20 years. For example, counts of commuters show an increase in cyclists entering downtown Washington, DC from 800 daily cyclists in 1986 to 3,310 in 2013 (DDOT, 2011–2014; TPB, 2006, 2010a). Another count shows a more than twofold increase in peak-hour cyclists entering the urban core of Washington, DC and Alexandria between 1999 and 2013 (TPB, 2010a, 2014). Local travel surveys and counts, however, cannot be interpreted as representative of the population. Also, results are often incomparable over time and across jurisdictions.

The analysis so far hides the variability in cycling levels within the six jurisdictions. The sample size of the MWCOG regional travel survey is not large enough to disaggregate results for all trip purposes. Even though small sample sizes for bike commuting on the census tract level cast some doubt on the reliability of Census Bureau data, the data can serve as a proxy for the regional variability in cycling (see Figure 9.1). Bike commute levels are highest in census tracts inside the Capital Beltway (Interstate 495). Census tracts in College Park, Rockville, and Bethesda have the highest cycling commute levels of the Maryland suburbs. Old Town Alexandria and Arlington County's Crystal City and Rosslyn-Ballston Corridor have the highest bike commute shares for northern Virginia. Within Washington, DC, cycling commute shares are highest in the Capitol Hill, Columbia Heights, Adams Morgan, Mount Pleasant, Palisades, and U Street neighborhoods. Even in the most bicycle-oriented census tracts, bike commuting rarely accounts for more than 5% of regular commuters.

In general, bike commute levels are lower in areas farther from the regional core, in hilly terrain, and in census tracts including or adjacent to light manufacturing, cemeteries, airports, interstate highways, or large bodies of water. In the Washington, DC region, as in many other US regions, many low-income and residentially segregated neighborhoods are within close proximity to those types

TABLE 9.2 Trend in bicycling levels for all trips and among regular commuters in Washington, DC and adjacent jurisdictions, 1990 to 2008–2012.

	Bicycle Share of all Trips (%)		Number of Regular Daily Bicycle Commuters		Bicycle Share of Regular Commuters (%)	
	1994	2008	1990	2008–2012	1990	2008–2012
Washington, DC	1.3	1.5	2,292	9,347	0.8	3.2
Alexandria City	0.6	1.1	359	864	0.5	1.0
Arlington County	0.5	0.8	661	1,621	0.6	1.2
Fairfax County	0.5	0.3	967	1,453	0.2	0.3
Montgomery County	0.4	0.6	916	2,350	0.2	0.5
Prince George's County	0.2	0.4	891	1,344	0.2	0.3

Sources: MWCOG, 2010; USDOC, 2010, 2014

of land uses. Within the urban core, cycling levels are lowest east of the Anacostia River, northeast of the District, between the Rosslyn-Ballston Corridor and I-395 in Arlington, and along the western part of Alexandria adjacent to I-395.

The results presented later in this chapter disaggregating the MWCOG data by socioeconomic and demographic groups suffer from small sample size (only 100 cyclists reporting 418 bike trips for the entire MWCOG sample), but are presented using 99% confidence intervals estimated using the small sample available. The data should only be interpreted as rough indicators for differences in actual cycling levels between population subgroups.

In the Washington, DC region, disparities exist among cyclists by gender, age, income, and race. In 2008/2009, cycling in the Washington, DC region seems slightly less male dominated than in other urbanized areas in the United States: 27–39% of bike trips in the Washington, DC area were by women compared to 25% nationally. The age of cyclists also differs. Nationally, almost 50% of bike trips are made by individuals between 5 and 24 years old. In Washington, DC, the majority of bike trips (64–75%) were made by 25- to 65-year-olds. Cyclists in Washington, DC seem wealthier than the national average. The wealthiest 25% of the population makes 35% to 47% of bike trips in Washington, DC compared to 26% of bike trips nationally. Last, cycling in the Washington, DC region seems to be dominated by Whites, who accounted for 84% to 92% of all bike trips in 2008 (vs. 77% nationally). African Americans only accounted for 3% to 9% of bike trips recorded in the MWCOG survey (vs. 11% nationally), despite accounting for a higher share of the regional population than the national average.

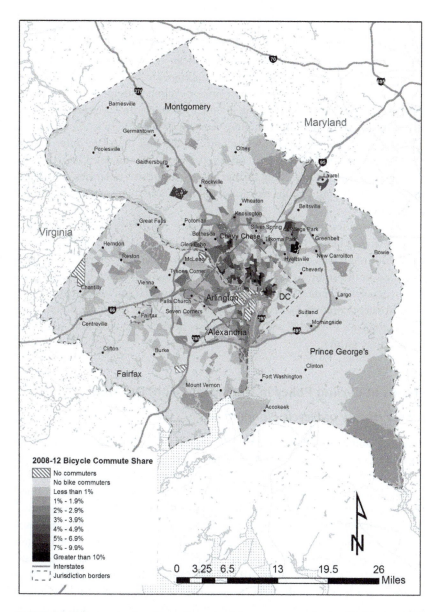

FIGURE 9.1 Variation in the share of regular bike commuters in the Washington, DC region, 2008–2012.

Source: USDOC, 2014; map created by J. Stowe

Overall, MWCOG data suggest that Whites cycle at much higher rates than African Americans in the Washington, DC region. This aligns with low bike commute levels in predominantly African American census tracts east of the Anacostia River. However, these findings are based on small samples. National-level data for all trips suggest similar cycling rates for both Whites and African Americans. By contrast, the 2008–2012 American Community Survey (ACS) data suggest that bike commute rates for Whites are twice as high as for African Americans, but very low for both groups and therefore differentiated by only 0.3 percentage points (0.6% vs. 0.3% of commuters). Unfortunately, the available data do not allow further investigation of similarities and differences of racial/ethnic groups by socioeconomic status, demographic factors, or geography.

An exploratory study by American University researchers (Bratman & Jadhav, 2014) analyzed barriers to cycling among 260 DC residents in Wards 7 and 8, where the residential population is 95% African American. Barriers to cycling identified in this study were similar to barriers commonly cited for the population in general, including trip distance, lack of separate facilities like lanes or paths, physical safety, comfort, theft, or travel speed. One of the key study findings was that respondents in Wards 7 and 8 had a higher desire for owning a car than other racial/ethnic groups.

Trends in Cycling Policy in the Washington, DC Area

A Brief History of Bicycle Planning

Modern planning for bicycling in the Washington, DC region started in the 1970s, progressed very slowly in the 1980s, experienced a hiatus in the 1990s, and saw a revival since the early 2000s. In 1972, the Washington Area Bicycle Association (WABA), the region's largest pro-bicycling lobbying organization, was formed (Hanson & Young, 2008; WABA, 2010–2014). During the 1970s, local jurisdictions and the regional planning board published their initial bicycle plans in subsequent years: Alexandria City and Arlington County in 1974; Washington, DC and Montgomery County in 1978; and the regional Transportation Planning Board (TPB) in 1977 (Bike Arlington, 2011; City of Alexandria, 2011a; DDOT, 2005, 2010–2014; Fairfax County, 2011; Montgomery County, 2008; Prince George's County, 2011; TPB, 2010a). Bicycle plans of the 1970s were often limited to specific corridors or were part of other planning documents, such as comprehensive plans or transportation master plans. Bicycle plans typically called for the construction of on-street and off-street bikeways. Prince George's County's 1975 plan was an exception because it focused on the construction of a shared-use trail network only.

There were only a few new pro-bike initiatives in the 1980s, such as the inclusion of bicycling in Arlington County's transportation master plan and the introduction of Alexandria's bicycle map. Similarly, the implementation of most of the initial plans from the 1970s was slow and mainly limited to the construction of off-street bike trails and paths or signage for bike routes without any dedicated infrastructure for cyclists. Progress in building bike lanes was very slow in Washington, DC—in spite of WABA's strong lobbying efforts and the City Council's vote to increase pay for DC's bike coordinator and to hire two assistant bike coordinators.

In the 1990s, interest in bicycle planning reemerged at regional and local levels. Bicycling became part of the TPB's regional long-range transportation plan in 1991 and the TPB published its regional vision for bicycling in 1998 (TPB, 2001, 2006). Arlington County updated its transportation master plan with an expanded bicycling section in 1994 (Hanson & Young, 2008). Alexandria established a bicycle study committee in 1992 and published a bicycle transportation and multiuse trail master plan in 1998. Montgomery County adopted its Countywide Park Trails plan in 1998 and Prince George's County created a bicycle trails advisory group in 1998. Washington, DC, however, did not have a dedicated bike planner during the decade. The position had been abandoned in 1991 as part of citywide cost-cutting measures—even though the federal government had paid 85% of the bike coordinator's salary.

Building on the progress of the 1990s, bicycle planning experienced a renaissance in the 2000s. The TPB published its regional bicycle priorities plan in 2001 and authored and updated its regional bicycle plan in 2006 and 2010. Following WABA's lobbying and Mayor Anthony Williams' buy-in to promoting bicycling, Washington, DC hired a full-time bicycle planner in 2001 and released its bicycle master plan in 2005—including new off-street trails, a proposed network of 50 miles of bike lanes, more bike parking, and the mention of a possible bike-sharing system. The District's decision to hire a bike coordinator and promote cycling was partly motivated by increased federal funding for cycling made available through federal transport legislation and a federal mandate that all US states hire bike coordinators. Across the Potomac in Virginia, Arlington included bicycling in the goals and policies section of its 2007 transportation master plan. Alexandria hired its first bicycle planner in 2004, adopted a bicycle mobility plan in 2008, and updated its bicycle map in 2009. Montgomery and Prince George's Counties adopted bicycle master plans in 2005 and 2009, respectively. Fairfax County adopted a comprehensive bicycle initiative in 2006 and published a county bicycle map in 2009. As of 2010, all jurisdictions, MWCOG, and WMATA have staff dedicated to bicycle planning (TPB, 2010a).

Off-Street Paths and Shared-Use Trails

Between the 1970s and 2000, most jurisdictions focused on building off-street trails and shared-use paths—often in collaboration with the National Park Service

(NPS, 1990). In 2010, there were 490 miles of trails and shared-use paths connecting the entire region (TPB, 2010a). Trails in the DC region are typically shared between cyclists and other non-motorized users and are either paved or made of compacted gravel. The late 1970s saw the opening of several trails such as the Rock Creek Park trail in Washington, DC and regional trails, such as the Chesapeake and Ohio (C&O) towpath between Washington, DC and Cumberland, MD (1971), the Mount Vernon Trail connecting Arlington, Washington, DC, Alexandria, and Fairfax County (1973), and the Washington, DC and Old Dominion (W&OD) trail connecting Arlington County, Fairfax County, and Loudon County, VA (1974) (NPS, 1990).

Today, roughly 190 miles of the regional shared-use trail network are entirely separated from roadways, often following old railway lines or canals, such as the W&OD trail or the Capital Crescent Trail between Georgetown in Washington, DC and Silver Spring in Montgomery County (NPS, 1990; TPB, 2010a). About 300 miles of trails run adjacent to roadways. For example, Arlington County's Custis Trail, which opened in 1982 and connects to both the Mount Vernon and W&OD trails, mainly follows the Interstate 66 corridor (Hanson & Young, 2008).

Compared to the 1970s and 1980s, construction of regional trails has slowed since the year 2000, but new stretches of regional trails continue to be built (TPB, 2010a). For example, the City of Rockville in Montgomery County built 20 miles of trails between 1998 and 2005 (City of Rockville, 2011a). Similarly, between 2000 and 2010, Washington, DC added 10 miles of trails to increase total trail mileage to 66 miles (ABW, 2014; DDOT, 2010–2014). While bike commuting on trails has been increasing, the majority of shared-use paths are most heavily used on weekends for recreation. For example, counts by the National Park Service indicate that 75% of bike trips on the Mount Vernon Trail are for recreation and only 25% are for transportation (NPS, 2011).

The region has also made progress in widening sidewalks and including bicycle and pedestrian facilities on new bridges to provide important connections for cyclists. For example, the rebuilt Woodrow Wilson Bridge crossing the Potomac River between Alexandria City and Prince George's County includes an improved shared-use bike path providing a safe connection for cyclists between the Mount Vernon Trail in Virginia and connecting routes in Maryland (TPB, 2010a). There are also shared-use sidewalks (some separated from traffic) on all but one of the bridges crossing the Potomac and Anacostia Rivers (DDOT, 2010–2014). Nevertheless, while the region has improved a number of important bridge connections, many shared-use paths on bridges remain narrow, crowded, and insufficiently separated from car traffic. This is especially the case for the older bridges crossing the Anacostia River.

On-Street Bike Lanes and Innovative Bike Infrastructure

In contrast to the expansion of trails, few bike lanes had been built by the late 1990s. For example, Arlington County had only 3 miles of bike lanes in 1995

(Bike Arlington, 2011; TPB, 2010a). In 2001, Washington, DC had only 3.2 miles of bike lanes, even though the city's 1978 plan had called for 17 miles of on-street lanes—which had not been built (DDOT, 2010–2014). Since then local jurisdictions have significantly expanded their supply of on-road bike lanes. Table 9.3 compares the supply of on-street bikeways and paved off-street trails for the year 2013. Bike lane supply ranged from 74 miles in Montgomery County and 66 miles in Washington, DC to only 5 miles in Prince George's County. Montgomery County had 278 miles of paved off-street trails compared to only 21 miles in Alexandria.

The comparison of total miles of bike paths and lanes hides variability in geographic size and jurisdiction population. Adjusting for land area, the core jurisdictions have the greatest supply of bike lanes and paths (see column 5 in Table 9.3). Alexandria, Arlington, and Washington, DC have been building bike lanes at a much faster rate than surrounding jurisdictions. For example, bike lane supply in Washington, DC increased 22-fold from 3.2 miles in 2001 to 66 miles in 2013. Similarly, bike lane supply in Arlington increased more than tenfold from 3.2 miles in 1995 to 34 miles in 2013. Many of the bike lanes were installed on roadways that previously had extra wide car travel lanes or parking lanes with excess width. One example of this was 15th Street, NW in Washington, DC, which had relatively low car traffic volumes. Moreover, local jurisdictions typically "installed" on-street bike facilities during regular repaving of roadways, thus greatly reducing the cost of building bikeways—often as low as the extra cost of restriping the roadway.

The core jurisdictions have also led the region in experimenting with innovative bicycle infrastructure measures. For example, Washington, DC has installed bike boxes at several intersections since 2010. Bike boxes give bicycles an advanced

TABLE 9.3 Supply of bike lanes and paved off-street paths and trails, 2013 (measured as centerline miles). Source: Data collected directly from bicycle planners in each jurisdiction.

Jurisdiction	On-Street Lanes, incl. Cycletracks (miles)	Paved Off-Street Trails (miles)	Total Lanes and Trails (miles)	Total Lanes and Trails per Land Area (miles / sq. miles)	Total Lanes and Trails per population (miles / 100,000 residents)
Washington, DC	66	62	124	2.02	21
Arlington County	34	50	83	3.21	39
Alexandria City	9	21	30	1.99	21
Fairfax County	25	200	225	0.57	21
Montgomery County	74	278	352	0.71	36
Prince George's County	5	85	91	0.19	11

stop line in front of automobiles, increase cyclist visibility for motorists, facilitate cyclist-turning movements, and allow cyclists to pass by traffic congestion and avoid tailpipe emissions. In 2013, Arlington began construction of two bike boulevards—traffic-calmed residential streets prioritizing bike travel—to provide safe alternative routes parallel to Columbia Pike, a major thoroughfare in the area (Arlington County, 2014).

Washington, DC also installed the region's first bicycle-activated traffic light at the intersection of 16th Street, NW, U Street, NW, and New Hampshire Avenue, NW. Moreover, Washington, DC was the first city in the region to install contra-flow bicycle lanes. The lanes run along 15th Street, NW, New Hampshire Avenue, NW, and G and I Streets, NE, restricting car traffic to one direction but allowing cyclists to ride in either direction (DDOT, 2014b). Washington, DC also built bidirectional bike lanes in the median on the portion of Pennsylvania Avenue, NW that runs between the US Capitol and the White House. Special striping on the roadway provides a 10-inch buffer between cyclists and car traffic. There are also protected cycletracks on South Dakota Avenue, NW, 15th Street, NW, 1st Street, NE, L Street, NW, and M Street, NW in Washington, DC. In contrast to buffered bike lanes, cycletracks provide additional vertical physical barriers to protect cyclists from car traffic. These physical barriers have typically been flexible plastic bollards, but in early 2014, concrete curbs were installed for the 1st Street, NE cycletrack and a short section of the M Street NW cycletrack (DDOT, 2010–2014).

Most area jurisdictions have marked road surfaces on several streets with "sharrows"—featuring two chevrons and a drawing of a bicyclist—reminding car drivers to share the road with cyclists. All jurisdictions have expanded their network of signed bike routes. These bike routes sometimes overlap with bike lanes and paths, but typically guide cyclists on "sharrowed" roads and streets with low car traffic volumes. In 2014, Washington, DC had 98 miles of signed bike routes. Bike route signs and "sharrows" do not require extra space on roadways and are easier to implement than separate bike paths and lanes that require dedicated space for cyclists. However, signed routes do not separate cyclists from car traffic and thus may discourage more risk-averse groups from cycling. This is especially relevant and may be particularly problematic given the region's relatively rare use of traffic-calming measures.

Indeed, in other North American cities, such as Vancouver and Portland, traffic calming is an integral part of the bike network (City of Portland, 2010; City of Vancouver, 2010; Pucher & Buehler, 2008; Pucher, Buehler, & Seinen, 2011). Traffic calming combines low speed limits with physical alterations of the road surface designed to slow or divert car traffic. Measures include speed bumps, humps, chicanes, median islands, raised crosswalks, curb extensions, street closures, and special pavement. Low speed limits and limited car traffic allow cyclists and motorists to share the road. Traffic-calmed neighborhood streets can often provide crucial connections between otherwise disjointed bike paths or lanes.

Spatial Distribution of Bikeways

Figure 9.2 compares the spatial distribution of the construction of new bike lanes in Washington, DC between the early 2000s and 2012. The map shows that in the past decade, the District Department of Transportation (DDOT) focused its new bikeways in or near the city's central business district (CBD), which stretches from 23rd Street, NW to 2nd Street, NE and D Street, SW/SE to Massachusetts Avenue, NW (DDOT, 2014a). Neighborhoods with the greatest increase in bikeways include Capitol Hill, Columbia Heights, Shaw, and Logan Circle. These neighborhoods already had some of the city's highest cycling levels in the early 2000s, and as the network of bike lanes has expanded in these neighborhoods, cycling commute levels have increased as well. Causation may run both ways, however. High levels of cycling in the early 2000s may have increased demand for bike lanes in these neighborhoods. More bike lanes in turn likely encouraged more commuters to ride their bicycles. As of summer 2014, the draft of DDOT's Multimodal Long Range Transportation Plan announced an ambitious goal to build bike lanes and cycle tracks throughout the city reaching neighborhoods farther from downtown—including Georgetown and east of the Anacostia River (DDOT, 2014a).

DDOT's spatial strategy for developing the city's bike network appears to begin with connecting the CBD with neighborhoods in bikeable distance. With continued expansion, the bike network will eventually reach neighborhoods farther away from the main employment center. In the meantime, bike commuters from those outlying neighborhoods will likely pass through the bike facilities already built closer to the CBD. However, the construction of bicycle lanes in neighborhoods close to the CBD has not been uncontroversial. In neighborhoods close to the CBD, public opinion associates bike lanes and cyclists with redevelopment, rising property values, and economic pressure on poorer and mainly African American households. Indeed, in the 2000s, neighborhoods like Capitol Hill, Columbia Heights, Shaw, and Logan Circle experienced gentrification and redevelopment with an influx of many young White professionals who seem more likely to ride bicycles (Urban Institute, 2015). Additionally, critics point to the relative lack of bike lanes in the more distant neighborhoods, especially east of the Anacostia River, as evidence of the District government's neglect of predominately African American neighborhoods.

There has not been much research into the connection of cycling levels, bikeways, redevelopment, property values, and displacement. A handful of peer-reviewed academic publications, relying on qualitative research methods such as ethnographies and interviews, investigate the connection of gentrification with cycling and bike infrastructure in US cities—including Washington, DC (Gibson, 2013; Hoffmann & Lugo, 2014; Hyra, 2015). They report that communities and developers both perceive cycling and bikeways as connected with redevelopment, property values, and displacement. However, no study has empirically linked cycling and gentrification using quantitative data on cycling levels, bikeway supply, and indicators of gentrification.

Indeed, some of the fastest changing neighborhoods in Washington, DC have been among the areas that saw a significant increase in bikeway supply and cycling levels. However, quantitative data suggests that bikeways and cyclists are unlikely to be the root cause of gentrification in those neighborhoods. The low prevalence of cycling in the city's population and among newcomers suggests that cyclists are a minority among both old and new residents. A study presented to the National Neighborhood Indicators Partnership (Dann, 2014) analyzed the likelihood for newcomers who moved into one of the largest 70 US cities in the past year to commute by bicycle using 2007–2011 ACS PUMS data. The study found that in the 70 largest US cities, 1.7% of newcomers cycled to work, compared to 0.9% of existing residents. For Washington, DC, the study extrapolates a 3.1% bike commuter share for newcomers in 2007–2011, compared to 2.5% for existing residents. However, the difference between existing residents and newcomers is not statistically significant at the 90% level (Dann, 2014). In any case, this indicates that 97% of newcomers did not cycle to work. This is also reflected in census tract commute data: in almost all census tracts in DC, more than 95% of commuters do not regularly cycle to work. The low prevalence of cycle commuting among newcomers suggests that neither cyclists nor the bikeway supply could be a primary cause of redevelopment, increasing property values, or displacement in areas close to Washington, DC's CBD.

A review of the literature yielded no rigorous academic peer-reviewed study empirically demonstrating a positive quantitative relationship between on-street bike lanes and property values adjacent to the lanes after controlling for other factors known to determine property values. In fact, a hedonic pricing study from Minneapolis found *lower* property values for homes closer to on-street bike lanes (Krizek, 2006). Several studies found a positive relationship between the presence of off-street bicycle paths—typically in parks or along rivers—and property values of adjacent homes (Krizek, 2006; Lindsey & Nguyen, 2004). Thus, most existing research does not support the idea that restriping the roadway surface to accommodate cyclists could be the root cause for the spikes in property values seen in some neighborhoods in Washington, DC over the past 20 years. However, an Internet search of nonacademic popular press news outlets reveals a large number of realtor companies and homeowners claiming that bike lanes boost property values and business sales. It may be that bicycling and bikeway supply are correlated with gentrifying neighborhoods and increasing property values through distance to the CBD. New residents moving into DC may be choosing lower-income, minority neighborhoods close to the city center, that are most conducive to short trips by bicycle.

Rededicating roadway lanes and parking space from use for cars to bikeways has also been controversial. During the 20th century, the automobile gained full reign over streets in the United States—removing trolley tracks and most cyclists from roadways as well as relegating pedestrians to sidewalks and dedicated crosswalks (Norton, 2008). Additionally, most American drivers are used to parking their cars along streets, often for free (Shoup, 2005). Installing new bicycle infrastructure requires space on roadways previously dedicated to the automobile. DDOT initially installed bikeways along roadways where car traffic counts indicated unused roadway capacity. But growing the bikeway network has meant reducing car travel or parking lanes, sometimes leading to political resistance. For example, construction of the M Street cycletrack was delayed by a dispute over on-street parking outside the prominent, historically Black Metropolitan African Methodist Episcopal Church (DeBonis, 2013). The church objected to the removal of on-street car parking because of the cycletrack's physical barrier intended to protect cyclists from car traffic. This barrier would have limited on-street car parking during church services. As a compromise, DDOT installed an unprotected bike lane on that city block, preserving on-street car parking spaces for the church. Similar conflicts about space can be found in cities throughout the country and the Washington, DC region, such as along Alexandria City's King Street, where wealthy—mainly White—residents opposed bike lanes because of a loss of free on-street car parking (Sullivan, 2014).

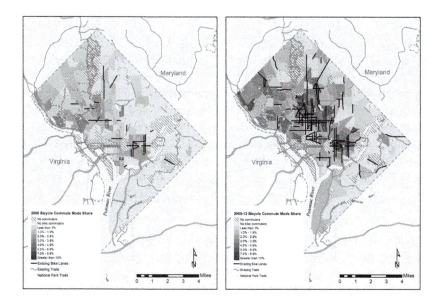

FIGURE 9.2 Supply of bike lanes and paths and cycling commute levels in Washington, DC, early 2000–2003 (left) and 2008–2012 (right).

Source: USDOC, 1980–2000, 2014; map created by John Stowe

Bike-Transit Integration, Bike Sharing, and Bike Parking in Buildings

Integrating bicycles with public transportation may be mutually beneficial for both modes (Brons, Givoni, & Rietvield, 2009; Martens, 2007). Bike parking at transit stops and dedicated space for bikes on trains and buses can enlarge the catchment area of public transport beyond typical walking distances. Cyclists can ride their bikes to and from transit stops and make longer trips than would be otherwise possible just by bike. Public transport also provides an alternative when regular cyclists experience inclement weather or mechanical failure. Daily Metrorail access trips by bike during the morning peak increased from 965 in 2002 to 2,384 in 2012, although the bike share of access trips remained low at 1% in 2012 (WMATA, 2010–2012). The busiest stations in the region for bike access were Union Station in Washington, DC, Hyattsville in Maryland, and Alexandria Transit Company, Pentagon City and East Falls Church in Virginia (NVTC, 2011). Statistics about bikes on buses were only available from Metrobus. Of the roughly 400,000 daily passenger trips on Metrobus, approximately 650 (0.2%) were made by passengers with bicycles (WMATA, 2010–2012).

With the exception of the Prince George's County bus system, all buses had front-mounted bike racks with space for up to two bicycles in 2013 (Alexandria Transit Company, 2013; WABA, 2010). Transit systems do not charge for transporting bikes on bus racks. Cyclists can also bring their bikes on Metrorail for free, but only four bicycles are allowed per car and only outside of peak commute hours (weekdays from 7–10 a.m. and 4–7 p.m.). All Metrorail stations are equipped with elevators and cyclists are required to use elevators because bikes are not allowed on escalators (WABA, 2010). Maryland's MARC commuter rail, serving the northern suburbs, does not allow any full-size bikes on its weekday commuter trains. VRE, Virginia's regional rail system, allows bicycles on midday trains, but bans bikes from morning inbound and afternoon outbound trains. MARC, VRE, and Metro allow folding bicycles on their trains at all times (WABA, 2010).

There are about 1,900 bike rack spaces and 1,300 bike lockers available at transit stations and park-and-ride lots in the Washington, DC region (NVTC, 2011; WABA, 2010; WMATA, 2010–2012). Spaces in bike racks are available on a first-come, first-serve basis and are free of charge. Lockers protect bicycles from weather and theft and can be rented on a yearly basis.

In 2009, Washington, DC's first full-service bike station opened next to Union Station. The bike station provides indoor, secure parking spaces for 140 bikes. Cyclists can park their bikes for $1 per day, $12 per month, or $96 per year (NVTC, 2011; WABA, 2010). The station also offers bike repair, bike lockers, and changing rooms, but does not provide showers. Station staff are present from 7 a.m. to 7 p.m. on weekdays and from 9 a.m. to 5 p.m. on weekends, and bike station members can access the station with a key card at any time (DDOT, 2010).

Bike Sharing

Washington, DC was the first area in North America to experiment with third-generation bike-sharing systems—consisting of bicycles, docking stations, and computerized kiosks for self-service bike rental with credit or debit cards (CaBi, 2014; DeMaio, 2009; Shaheen, Guzman, & Zhang, 2010). In 2008, Smart-Bike opened a small pilot project with 120 bikes and 10 kiosks in Washington, DC (SmartBike DC, 2010). In September 2010, SmartBike was replaced with Capital Bikeshare (CaBi). CaBi was the first regional bike-sharing system in North America. It is jointly operated by Arlington County, Alexandria, Montgomery County, and Washington, DC. CaBi is considerably larger than SmartBike, with 2,600 bikes and 334 stations in 2014.

CaBi has been expanding steadily since its launch in 2010. The initial phase of 100 stations was installed by February 2011. Washington, DC announced plans that fall to add 32 new stations in 2011 and 50 in 2012, as well as plans to expand some high-volume stations (CaBi, 2014). Arlington began expanding in 2011 as well, and both Washington, DC and Arlington have continued to fill in their networks. Alexandria joined in September 2012 with 8 stations and expanded to 16 stations in 2014, and Montgomery County joined in May 2013 with 45 stations in place by early 2014 (CaBi, 2014; City of Alexandria, 2011b; City of Rockville, 2011b). The bankruptcy of Bixi, CaBi's equipment supplier, delayed further expansion for several months in 2014, including infill stations in existing jurisdictions and the planned addition of College Park, MD (Lazo, 2014), but expansion eventually resumed.

Funding for Washington, DC's share of CaBi ($6 million) came from federal Congestion Mitigation and Air Quality (CMAQ) funds and a 20% local match. Arlington County's funds ($835,000) originated from the Virginia Department of Transportation and other local monies (DDOT, 2010–2014). Similar to Washington, DC, the City of Alexandria used CMAQ funds to pay for the installation of CaBi (City of Alexandria, 2011b). Montgomery County was able to obtain Job Access Reverse Commute (JARC) funds from the Federal Transit Administration (City of Rockville, 2011b). Because of JARC requirements, the county distributes free CaBi memberships to qualifying low-income residents.

CaBi's 17,000 members made more than 1 million trips in the first year of operation, between September 2010 and September 2011 (CaBi, 2014). By its third anniversary in 2013, CaBi had more than 23,000 members and 5 million trips; the system had reached 6 million trips by February 2014. The greatest challenge for the system is balancing bicycles between stations during the morning and afternoon commutes. In the morning, demand for bikes is highest in residential neighborhoods, while demand for bike parking is greatest in downtown locations. Commuter movements from residential neighborhoods to workplaces downtown in the morning result in empty kiosks without bikes in residential neighborhoods and full kiosks without available bike parking spaces in down-town. Bicycle theft and vandalism have been minimal. The system sees about seven cases of vandalism and one missing bike every month; about two-thirds of missing bikes are later recovered. Bike theft may be minimal because the design of CaBi bikes is unique and bikes are built with special parts that cannot be used on other bikes and need special tools to be disassembled (CaBi, 2014).

In the District of Columbia, the highest density of CaBi stations is in the downtown area in Wards 2, 6, and 1 with 5.4, 3.5, and 1.7 docking stations per 10,000 residents. The more outlying wards 4, 8, 3, and 7 have a lower density of CaBi stations (0.5, 0.6, 0.9, and 1.0 stations per 10,000 residents). This distribution of CaBi stations is in line with the main usage of CaBi either for short trips or commute trips to work.

There have been no statistical representative surveys based on a random sam-ple of CaBi members. Analysis of a (nonrepresentative) sample of respondents to CaBi's 2011 member survey shows that the majority were male (55%), car owners (52%), White (81%), and younger than 34 years old (66%) (CaBi, 2012). Thus, compared to statistics of typical cyclists in the area presented earlier in this chapter, CaBi members were younger, less likely to own a car, and more likely female. However, both CaBi member survey respondents and area cyclists were predominately White (>80%). African Americans accounted for only 3.0–9.0% of area cyclists and 3.5% of respondents to the 2011 CaBi membership survey.

Bike Parking in Buildings and Public Spaces

Parking for bicycles at trip origins and destinations is as important for cyclists as car parking is for drivers. Ordinances in all jurisdictions require some form of bicycle parking—typically depending on office space or retail floor area, number of units in residential buildings, or number of car parking spaces provided. Arling-ton County and Montgomery County additionally require showers and chang-ing facilities for bicyclists in buildings larger than 50,000 and 100,000 square feet, respectively (MWCOG, 2011). Washington, DC mandates bicycle parking in off-street car parking garages (DDOT, 2010–2014). Prince George's County's bike parking requirements are limited to special transit-oriented developments in the county. In Fairfax County, commercial developments may be required to provide bike parking and showers when requesting a variance or special-use permit.

Area jurisdictions do not systematically track the number of bike parking spaces. Washington, DC estimates that in 2011, about two-thirds of car parking garages in the city provided bike parking (DDOT, 2010–2014). Arlington County estimates that 4,000 to 6,000 secure bike parking spaces have been built since requiring bike parking in 1990 (Bike Arlington, 2011). Some data is available on the number of bike racks supplied in public spaces, such as on sidewalks or in public squares. Between 2002 and 2009, Washington, DC installed 1,162 bike racks. Arlington County provides 600 public short-term bicycle racks, including a covered bike parking shelter at the Shirlington Transit Center. Arlington plans to install 50–70 new bicycle racks per year. Alexandria has been installing about 100 new bicycle parking spaces each year, including a number of on-street "bike corrals" that convert a car parking space into dedicated bike parking surrounded by bollards (City of Alexandria, 2011a). Washington, DC, Arlington, Alexandria, and Montgomery County have bicycle rack request programs that allows businesses and citizens to request bike rack installation. DDOT pays for bicycle racks if employers cover the cost of installation.

Promotion, Incentives, Advocacy, and Education

There are many bike promotion events and educational programs in the Washington, DC region. Some programs are provided regionally while others are local initiatives. The following briefly summarizes several key efforts to increase cycling and improve its safety for all groups. The programs generally promote cycling and safety for all groups, such as Safe Routes to School. In addition, this section highlights a few programs targeted specifically at increasing cycling among minorities (WABA, 2010–2014).

Cyclist Education

Similar to other regions in North America, the Washington, DC region offers bike education courses for adults and children. The Washington Area Bicyclist Association's (WABA) Confident City Cycling course provides a refresher in riding skills for interested adults. Arlington also offers classes for adults in Spanish. Together with local and state governments WABA also provides cycling courses for children. Washington, DC's week-long Street Smarts for Kids program offers cycling classes that focus on cycling safety for children in grades 3 through 5. DDOT estimates that in 2009 and 2010 an average of 4,000 children participated in youth bicycle education courses (Alliance for Biking and Walking, 2010).

Rockville was the first city in Maryland to develop and implement a comprehensive K-5 grade pedestrian and bicycle safety education program for children. In 2011, Fairfax County's first Braddock Bike Day safety event provided cycling education and bike rodeos for 75 participants. Moreover, in collaboration with WABA, local jurisdictions participate in the federally funded Safe Route to Schools (SRTS) program—offering financial and planning support for schools that wish to improve safety for walking and cycling to school. In the summer of 2013, the Virginia DOT hired Toole Design Group as a consultant to run its SRTS Program, resulting in coordinators being hired in Arlington and Fairfax for the first time, and continued funding in Alexandria, which already had a coordinator. However, recent changes under the latest federal transportation bill, MAP-21, have weakened SRTS funding, putting some of these programs at risk.

Bike Promotion

All jurisdictions participate in the national Bike to Work day. Between 2002 and 2013, the number of participating cyclists in the six jurisdictions increased sevenfold from 2,035 in 2002 to 14,673 in 2013 (WABA, 2010–2014, 2011). There are other annual bike ride events, such as Bike DC; the annual 50 States and 13 Colonies Ride; and the Vasa Ride in March organized by WABA and the Swedish Embassy. More frequent bike events include the City Bikes Ladies rides on Sundays, organized by City Bikes, and Critical Mass rides on the first Friday of every month. "Kidical Mass" is also spreading across the region, with casual family bike rides regularly held in Washington, DC, Arlington, and most recently Alexandria and Rockville. There are also regular bike clinics and co-ops in many jurisdictions—such as Phoenix Bikes in Arlington, VéloCity in Alexandria, and the Bike House in Washington, DC. These organizations hold community events and other educational opportunities for youth as well as adults to learn about bicycling and bicycle repair. Bike clinics and co-ops also provide a venue for cyclists to interact and share experiences, such as BicycleSpace, a new bicycle shop, which organizes group rides and other events for cyclists. Additionally, in 2013, Washington, DC became one of about 10 cities across the country selected to host a Tour de Fat festival, organized by New Belgium Brewery to benefit local bicycle nonprofits. The ArtCrank traveling bicycle poster show came to the region for the first time in 2014 as well.

WABA's Bicycle Ambassadors attend public events and engage in one-on-one consultation about cycling and cyclist safety. The City of Alexandria, WABA, and the National Park Service also partnered to sponsor a similar ambassador program to promote non-automobile travel in Alexandria. At some large events, such as the Cherry Blossom festival in Washington, DC in the spring, WABA volunteers provide valet parking for bikes. There is no charge for cyclists, but event organizers pay a fee to WABA. When using the bike valet parking, cyclists leave their bikes at a guarded WABA stand, receive a uniquely numbered claim ticket for their bicycle, and later reclaim their bikes using their ticket.

In 2010, WABA launched its East of the River program in Wards 7 and 8 to better serve neighborhoods it perceived as "historically disconnected from the infrastructure and community needed to support biking" (WABA, 2014). The program seeks to improve biking infrastructure, especially bridge crossings, provide bicycle education classes, and ensure bicycling is accommodated in future developments. Additionally, Black Women Bike DC launched in 2011 with a mission to "build community and interest in biking among Black women in the District through education, advocacy, and recreation" (Black Women Bike, 2014).

The organization holds bike rides every third Saturday of the month—in varying locations. Moreover, the group offers workshops and guides on cycling, such as a "bike buying guide" or "cycling in winter" or "how to cycle safely" workshops (Black Women Bike, 2014).

Information and Incentives for Cyclists

All jurisdictions provide bicycle maps in print and online. Arlington distributes 60,000 maps per year (Bike Arlington, 2013). Maryland and Virginia also provide statewide maps of facilities for bicyclists. Google Maps and Ride the City provide online bicycle trip planning tools that allow cyclists to find the best route between trip origins and destinations. Ride the City allows cyclists to distinguish between the safest route, following bike lanes and paths as closely as possible, and the most direct route for those cyclists who are comfortable cycling in traffic. Cyclists can also access Google Maps and Ride the City on their smartphones while en route. Several other apps provide additional features for cyclists. Spotcycle reports the availability of CaBi bikes and docks nearby; RideScout provides directions for making a trip by biking, transit, driving, taxi, and CaBi, sorting by time and cost; and Nimbler DC provides trip routing using a combination of transit and CaBi or a personal bike.

The MWCOG offers a guaranteed-ride-home program for workers who commute to work by bike, transit, or on foot at least two days per week (MWCOG, 2011). Once signed up, the program guarantees up to four free rides home per year in case of emergency. The program intends to remove the uncertainty and increase flexibility for non-automobile commuters. The MWCOG's Commuter Connections program also provides detailed information about bike commuting for individuals and employers. Information for employers comprises local initiatives, as well as federal programs, such as the pretax parking cash-out and the $20 bicycle transportation fringe benefit. In the 2012–2013 school year, Commuter Connections launched SchoolPool (Commuter Connections, 2014), a spinoff of its ride-matching program, helping to connect families wishing to bike, walk, or carpool to school.

In 2011, the Fairfax County Department of Transportation offered a Bike Benefit Match Program to employers who provided the $20 federal bicycle transportation fringe benefit (Fairfax County, 2011). For qualified employers, the county matched 50% of the total amount in fringe benefits. Employers could use matching funds to purchase bike racks, lockers, or marketing materials. Arlington County offers an innovative incentive for its employees to cycle to work (Bike Arlington, 2011). County employees who cycle for at least half of their commutes receive $35 per month. Moreover, Arlington's car-free-diet program offers online resources for commuters to compare differences in costs as well as emissions between commuting by car and bike. Individuals can also make an online pledge to drive less and cycle more.

Advisory Committees

Washington, DC has a Bicycle Advisory Council that meets bimonthly and is appointed by the DC City Council to advise the District government on bicycling issues. Arlington County has a bicycle advisory committee that meets once a month and is appointed by the county manager to focus attention and resources on bicycling. Alexandria has a bicycle and pedestrian advisory committee that is a voluntary forum for citizen input in bicycle planning and programming and meets on a monthly basis. Additionally, Fairfax Advocates for Better Bicycling works with Fairfax County staff on projects such as the Bicycle Master Plan, bicycle safety and police outreach, and Safe Routes to School programs. Montgomery Bicycle Advocates work to support Montgomery County efforts to improve facilities and programs for bicyclists. Prince George's County has a Bicycle and Trails Advisory Group that is chaired and organized by the Transportation Planning Section of the Planning Department and meets quarterly to facilitate discussion between local implementing agencies and citizens interested in bicycle and pedestrian issues. Finally, MWCOG has a bicycle and pedestrian subcommittee that provides advice and assistance to the Technical Committee, evaluates the Regional Bicycle and Pedestrian Plan, advises long-range transportation planning, oversees the regional Street Smart Pedestrian and Bicycle Safety Campaign, and facilitates technology transfer and information sharing across jurisdictions and state programs.

Legal Advocacy

In addition to direct outreach to individuals and campaigns for improved infrastructure, local advocates have also argued for changes to laws concerning bicyclists. While many of these are directly related to safety, such as safe passing distances, others address aspects of law enforcement and the legal system that have had disproportionate or discriminatory outcomes. The most contentious of these involved Washington, DC's mandatory bicycle registration law, with years of complaints culminating in an investigation by the Police Complaints Board, which found that the law had been "used as a retaliatory and pretextual search tool against [minorities and] other unpopular groups" (Police Complaints Board, 2005). The registration law was repealed in 2008. More recently, WABA has pushed for changes to the legal structure governing recovery of damages from accidents: Washington, DC, Maryland, and Virginia are some of the last American jurisdictions to apply the "contributory negligence" standard. WABA argues that, combined with routine misapplication of bicycle laws by investigating officers, this legal environment creates an impossibly high bar against recovery for injured cyclists, especially those without the resources to hire an attorney (Billing, 2014). DC Council Members introduced bills proposing changes to Washington, DC's contributory negligence law in 2014 and 2015.

Summary and Policy Recommendations

Between 1990 and 2008–2012, bicycling has increased in the Washington, DC region. The number of regular bike commuters nearly tripled during this time period. In spite of the increase, in 2008–2012, cycling accounted for only 0.6% of commutes in the Washington, DC region. In 2008–2012, the urban core jurisdictions of Washington, DC (3.2%), Arlington (1.2%), and Alexandria (1.0%) had higher cycling levels than the region and suburban areas. However, even within the urban core, cycling was spatially concentrated in certain neighborhoods, such as Capitol Hill, Adams Morgan, and Mount Pleasant in Washington, DC, and the Rosslyn-Ballston Corridor and Old Town Alexandria in Virginia. In only a few bicycle-oriented neighborhoods in Washington, DC did bicycling account for more than 5% of regular commuters.

Modern bike planning in the Washington, DC region has its roots in the 1970s with plans to build on-street bike lanes and off-street bike paths. The region's initial focus had been on building off-street, shared-use paths. In 2014, 490 miles of shared-use paths connected the entire region. Until the late 1990s, bike infrastructure supply was mostly limited to shared-use, off-street bike paths and very few on-street bike lanes had been built. Since the late 1990s, all jurisdictions have expanded their networks of on-street bike lanes and signed bike routes. Washington, DC, Arlington, and Alexandria have expanded their networks of on-street lanes more aggressively than suburban Montgomery, Fairfax, and Prince George's Counties. Washington, DC has also been the regional leader in experimenting with innovative bicycle infrastructure, such as traffic lights for cyclists, bike boxes, contra-flow bike lanes, cycletracks, and a state-of-the-art bike parking station at Union Station. Together with Arlington County, Washington, DC launched the nation's first regional bike-sharing program.

In spite of this progress, many challenges remain for cycling. For example, data suggest that area cyclists are still predominantly male, between 25 and 65 years old, White, and from higher-income groups. Programs tailored to specific groups could help increase cycling for everyone in Washington, DC. Some efforts are already under way. All jurisdictions are extending their network of bicycle facilities, which will make cycling more convenient and less stressful, and will extend cycling's appeal to more risk-averse groups. Even though the supply of bike lanes has increased significantly over the past decade, the bike network remains fragmented and often requires cyclists to ride in roads with heavy car traffic. Further expansion of the bike lane network will require narrowing or removing travel lanes or parking from cars, which will be less politically acceptable than many of the easier measures implemented so far. Moreover, area-wide traffic calming of residential neighborhood streets should be part of this package to enable cyclists to share roads with slow-traveling cars. Cities like Portland, Seattle, and Vancouver have created bike boulevards—traffic-calmed residential streets that prioritize cycling over car travel.

More research is needed into the racial/ethnic discrepancy in cycling levels and the potential connection of bikeways, increasing property values, and neighborhood change in Washington, DC. Existing data on the breakdown of cyclists in Washington, DC by various demographic groups suffer from small sample sizes, but suggest significantly lower cycling levels among African Americans. At the national level, the National Household Travel Survey suggests no difference in cycling rates—1.0% of trips—among both African Americans and Whites, while the US Census Bureau reports a 0.3 percentage point difference in bike commute rates between African Americans and Whites (0.3% vs. 0.6%). Some scholars, realtors, and public commentators connect bicycling and bikeways to the displacement of poorer, mainly African American residents in inner-city neighborhoods. However, existing data point to such a small prevalence of cycling among both newcomers and long-time residents in inner-city neighborhoods that it is unlikely cycling or cycling infrastructure is a significant cause of displacement. Moreover, quantitative peer-reviewed studies do not confirm a relationship between bike lanes and property values—when controlling for other variables. A more likely explanation is that bicycling and bikeway supply are correlated with changing neighborhoods and increasing property values through distance to the CBD. New residents moving into DC choose neighborhoods close to the city center, and these neighborhoods are within bicycling distance from the CBD. However, more research and better data are needed to answer this question.

Note

1 The authors would like to thank the Virginia Tech Institute for Society, Culture and Environment for supporting this research. This research builds on a two-year research project funded by the US Department of Transportation, Research and Innovative Technology Administration (RITA) via the Mid Atlantic University Transportation Center "Determinants of Cycling in the Washington, DC Region." Some of the content was published in the journal *World Transport Policy and Practice* (WTPP) in 2012 and is used here with permission of the WTPP editor. Virginia Tech graduate assistants Andrea Hamre and Kyle Lukacs contributed information and data and provided review comments on earlier drafts.

References

Alliance for Biking and Walking (ABW). (2010). *Bicycling and walking in the United States: 2010 benchmarking report.* Washington, DC: Alliance for Biking and Walking.
Alliance for Biking and Walking (ABW). (2014). *2012 bicycling and walking benchmarking report.* Washington, DC: Alliance for Biking and Walking.

Alexandria Transit Company, (2013). Bike-N-Roll on all Dash buses. Retrieved from www.dashbus.com/news/newsDisplay.aspx?id=69754.

American Public Transport Association (APTA). (2014). *Transportation factbook 2013.* Washington, DC: American Public Transport Association.

Arlington County. (2014). *The Columbia Pike Corridor.* Arlington County. Retrieved from http://projects.arlingtonva.us/projects/columbia-pike/.

Banister, D. (2005). *Unsustainable transport: City transport in the new century.* London, UK; New York, NY: Routledge.

Bike Arlington. (2011). *Bicycling in Arlington.* Arlington, VA: Arlington County.

Bike Arlington. (2013). *2013 Arlington bicycle program DES DOT staff work program update.* Arlington County, VA: Arlington County.

Billing, G. (2014). 10 questions about contributory negligence, answered. Retrieved January 30, 2014, from www.waba.org/blog/2014/09/10-questions-about-contributory-negligence-answered/.

Black Women Bike. (2014). *Black Women Bike DC vision & mission.* Washington, DC: Black Women Bike.

Bratman, E., & Jadhav, A. (2014). How low income commuters view cycling. Retrieved August 19, 2014, from www.citylab.com/commute/2014/07/how-low-income-commuters-view-cycling/374390/.

Brons, M., Givoni, M., & Rietvield, P. (2009). Access to railway stations and its potential in increasing rail use. *Transportation Research A, 43*, 136–149.

Buehler, R., Pucher, R., Merom, D., & Bauman, A. (2011). Active travel in Germany and the USA: Contributions of daily walking and cycling to physical activity. *American Journal of Preventive Medicine, 40*(9), 241–250.

CaBi. (2012). *Capital Bikeshare 2011 member survey.* Washington, DC: District Department of Transportation and LDA Consulting.

CaBi. (2014). *Capital Bikeshare in Washington DC.* Washington, DC: Alta Bicycle Share.

City of Alexandria. (2011a). *Cycling in Alexandria.* Alexandria, VA: City of Alexandria Transportation Planning.

City of Alexandria. (2011b). *Minutes of council meeting, October 11, 2011.* Alexandria, VA: City of Alexandria, City Council.

City of Portland. (2010). *Portland bicycle plan for 2030.* Portland, OR: City of Portland.

City of Rockville. (2011a). *Bike planning.* Rockville, MD: City of Rockville.

City of Rockville. (2011b). *Rockville to participate in bike sharing program.* Rockville, MD: City of Rockville.

City of Vancouver. (2010). *Cycling.* Vancouver, BC: City of Vancouver Engineering Services.

Commuter Connections. (2014). *Welcome to SchoolPool Matching.* Washington, DC: Metropolitan Washington Council of Governments.

Dann, R. (2014). Factors associated with the bicycle commute use of newcomers: An analysis of the 70 largest U.S. cities. Retrieved August 20, 2014, from www.neighborhoodindicators.org/sites/default/files/publications/dann.pdf.

DeBonis, M. (2013, August 15). How a downtown bike lane has become a political headache. *The Washington Post.*

DeMaio, P. (2009). Bike-sharing: History, impacts, models of provision, and future. *Journal of Public Transportation, 14*(4), 41–56.

District Department of Transportation (DDOT). (2005). *DC bicycle master plan.* Washington, DC: District Department of Transportation.

District Department of Transportation (DDOT). (2010). *Bicycling in Washington, D.C.* Washington, DC: District Department of Transportation.

District Department of Transportation (DDOT). (2010–2014). *Bicycle program.* Washington, DC: District Department of Transportation.

District Department of Transportation (DDOT). (2011–2014). *DC bicycle count statistics.* Washington, DC: District Department of Transportation.

District Department of Transportation (DDOT) (Cartographer). (2014a). DC Central Business District. Retrieved from http://ddot.dc.gov/sites/default/files/dc/sites/ddot/publication/attachments/dc_central_business_district_bikes_0.pdf.

District Department of Transportation (DDOT). (2014a). *The District of Columbia's multimodal long-range transportation plan. Bicycle element.* Washington, DC: District of Columbia Retrieved from www.wemovedc.org/resources/DraftPlan/B-Bicycle_Element.pdf.

District Department of Transportation (DDOT). (2014b). *G and I Streets proposed bike lanes.* Washington, DC: District of Columbia. Retrieved from http://ddot.dc.gov/sites/default/files/dc/sites/ddot/publication/attachments/G%20%26%20I%20NE%20fact%20sheet_Apr2014.pdf.

Fairfax County. (2011). *Countywide bicycle master plan.* Fairfax, VA: Fairfax County Department of Transportation.

Gibson, T.A. (2013). The rise and fall of Adrian Fenty, mayor-triathlete: Cycling, gentrification and class politics in Washington DC. *Leisure Studies.* Online only www.tandfonline.com/doi/pdf/10.1080/02614367.2013.855940.

Hanson, R., & Young, G. (2008). Active living and biking: Tracing the evolution of a biking system in Arlington, Virginia. *Journal of Health Politics and Law, 33*(3), 387–406.

Heinen, E., Van Wee, B., & Maat, K. (2010). Bicycle use for commuting: A literature review. *Transport Reviews, 30*(1), 105–132.

Hoffmann, M.L., & Lugo, A.E. (2014). Who is world class? Transportation justice and bicycle policy. *Urbanities, 4*(1), 45–61.

Hyra, D. (2015). The back-to-the-city movement: Neighbourhood redevelopment and processes of political and cultural displacement. *Urban Studies, 52*(10), 1753–1773.

Krizek, K.J. (2006). Two approaches to valuing dome of bicycle facilities' presumed benefits. *Journal of the American Planning Association, 72*(3), 309–320.

Krizek, K.J., Forsyth, A., & Baum, L. (2009). *Walking and cycling international literature review.* Melbourne, Australia: Victoria Department of Transport.

Lazo, L. (2014, April 12). Capital Bikeshare expansion hindered by bankruptcy of Montreal-based bike vendor. *The Washington Post.*

Lindsey, G., & Nguyen, D.B.L. (2004). Use of greenway trails in Indiana. *Journal of Urban Planning and Development-Asce, 130*(4), 213–217.

Martens, K. (2007). Promoting bike and ride: The Dutch experience. *Transportation Research Part A, 41*, 326–338.

Metropolitan Washington Council of Governments (MWCOG). (2009). *Regional mobility & accessibility study.* Washington, DC: Metropolitan Washington Council of Governments.

Metropolitan Washington Council of Governments (MWCOG). (2010). *2007–2008 regional household travel survey.* Washington, DC: Metropolitan Washington Council of Governments.

Metropolitan Washington Council of Governments (MWCOG). (2011). *Commuter connections.* Washington, DC: Metropolitan Washington Council of Governments, Commuter Connections.

Montgomery County. (2008). *Master plan of bikeways.* Silver Spring, MD: Montgomery County Planning Board.

National Park Service (NPS). (1990). *Paved recreational trails of the national capital region.* Washington, DC: National Park Service.

National Park Service (NPS). (2011). *Trail count factsheet.* Washington, DC: National Park Service.

Northern Virginia Transportation Commission (NVTC). (2011). *A guide to bicycle and transit connections in northern Virginia.* Arlington, VA: Northern Virginia Transportation Commission.

Norton, P.D. (2008). *Fighting traffic: The dawn of the motor age in the American city.* Cambridge, MA: The MIT Press.

Police Complaints Board. (2005). Pretextual stops of bicyclists (p. 36, footnote 37). Washington, DC: Office of Police Complaints.

Prince George's County. (2011). *Bicycle and trails planning.* Marlboro, MD: Prince George's County Planning Department.

Pucher, J., & Buehler, R. (2008). Making cycling irresistible: Lessons from the Netherlands, Denmark, and Germany. *Transport Reviews, 28*(1), 495–528.

Pucher, J., Buehler, R., & Seinen, M. (2011). Bicycling renaissance in North America? An update and re-assessment of cycling trends and policies. *Transportation Research A, 45*(8), 451–475.

Shaheen, S., Guzman, S., & Zhang, H. (2010). *Bikesharing in Europe, the Americas, and Asia: Past, present, and future.* Paper presented at the 89th Annual Meeting of the Transportation Research Board, Washington, DC.

Shoup, D. (2005). *The high cost of free parking.* Chicago, IL: APA Planners Press.

SmartBike DC. (2010). *Program information.* Washington, DC: SmartBike DC.

Street Smart. (2014). Street smart. http://bestreetsmart.net/about.php.

Sullivan, N. (2014, January 22). King Street bike lanes bother residents who will lose street parking along busy route. *The Washington Post.* Retrieved from www.washingtonpost.com/local/king-street-bike-lanes-bother-residents-who-will-lose-street-parking-along-busy-route/2014/01/21/c374b620–7fa5–11e3–9556–4a4bf7bcbd84_story.html.

Transportation Planning Board (TPB). (2001). *Greenways and circulation systems.* Washington, DC: Transportation Planning Board, MWCOG.

Transportation Planning Board (TPB). (2006). *Bicycle and pedestrian plan for the capital region.* Washington, DC: Transportation Planning Board, MWCOG.

Transportation Planning Board (TPB). (2010a). *Bicycle and pedestrian plan for the national capital region.* Washington, DC: Transportation Planning Board, MWCOG.

Transportation Planning Board (TPB). (2010b). *Changes in daily travel patterns.* Washington, DC: Transportation Planning Board, MWCOG.

Transportation Planning Board (TPB). (2014). *2013 Central employment core cordon count of vehicular and passenger volumes.* Washington, DC: Metropolitan Washington Council of Governments. Retrieved from www.mwcog.org/uploads/committee-documents/k11ZXV5e20140127094130.pdf.

Urban Institute. (2015). Washington, DC: *Our changing city.* Retrieved January 8, 2015 from http://datatools.urban.org/features/OurChangingCity/.

US Department of Commerce (USDOC). (1980–2000). *United States census.* Washington, DC: US Census Bureau.

US Department of Commerce (USDOC). (2010). *American fact finder: 1990 decennial census, journey to work.* Washington, DC: US Census Bureau.

US Department of Commerce (USDOC). (2014). *American community survey 2008–2012.* Washington, DC: US Department of Commerce.

Washington Area Bicyclist Association (WABA). (2010). Bikes on transit. Washington, DC: Washington Area Bicyclist Association.

Washington Area Bicyclist Association (WABA). (2010–2014). *Washington Area Bicyclist Association.* Washington, DC: Washington Area Bicyclist Association.

Washington Area Bicyclist Association (WABA). (2011). *Bike to work day.* Washington, DC: Washington Area Bicyclist Association.

Washington Area Bicyclist Association (WABA). (2014). *East of the River program.* Washington, DC: Washington Area Bicyclist Association.

Washington Metropolitan Area Transit Authority (WMATA). (2010–2012). Bike and ride. Washington, DC: Washington Metropolitan Area Transit Authority.

10

ANCHORING A FEDERAL AGENCY IN A WASHINGTON, DC COMMUNITY

The Department of Homeland Security and St. Elizabeths

Margaret Cowell and Heike Mayer

Introduction

The neighborhood that surrounds the District of Columbia's St. Elizabeths hospital campus is one of the most disenfranchised areas within the largely thriving Washington, DC region. Compared to the regional averages, residents in this neighborhood experience higher rates of unemployment and lower educational attainment and household incomes. Largely untouched by the recent economic growth that so much of the region has seen in recent years, the St. Elizabeths neighborhood and Ward 8 in which it is located have seen very few employment opportunities and scarce amenities. Soon, however, their fortunes may be changing; the former hospital campus at St. Elizabeths is being repurposed to become the headquarters of the Department of Homeland Security (DHS), one of the fastest growing organizations within the federal government. This new anchor institution will have far-reaching effects beyond the walls of the approximately 150 acres it will occupy. Economic development and strategic planning efforts being put into place today will determine, in part, the extent to which these effects are positive. Drawing from a larger study of the innovation cluster potential in Ward 8 (DC Office of Planning, 2012), this chapter includes an exploration of the DHS economy in Ward 8 and the broader region, as well as a discussion of how local and federal leaders envision this anchor institution in the community, and an overview of the potential challenges and pitfalls associated with locating a federal agency in a disenfranchised community.

Anchor Institutions

Many communities have strong and sometimes complex relationships with a single corporation, factory, public-sector outpost, educational institution, military base, or some other important entity. These types of institutions, often called anchor institutions, are "large organizations, typically educational, medical or cultural, that are deeply rooted in their local geographies and that play an integral role in the local economy" (Initiative for a Competitive Inner City, 2010, p. 1).

Anchor institutions are often considered direct and indirect "magnets for economic development" (Ehlenz et al., 2014, p. 1). The revenue that anchor institutions produce as a community's largest employer (Harkavy & Zuckerman, 1999), from their landholdings (Appleseed Inc., 2003), and by their procurement of goods and services from the local community (Alperovitz, Howard, & Dubb, 2009) are the direct benefits that communities sometimes experience. The attraction of knowledge workers and their families (Fulbright-Anderson, Auspos, & Anderson, 2001), workforce development programs (Nelson & Wolf-Powers, 2010), and the purchase of goods and services in the surrounding area by both residents and non-residents (Yates, 2009) are indirect benefits that sometimes also occur.

Depending on the scale of the anchor institution and the host community, the indirect and direct benefits can help a neighborhood, community, or region through the combined effects of import substitution, drawing resources in from outside of the region, and educating and training a local workforce (Initiative for a Competitive Inner City, 2010). There is no typical relationship between an anchor institution and its host community; many anchor institutions locate in areas where profits can be maximized or advantages leveraged, while others prioritize historical legacies and traditions, perceived neighborhood need, or cultural amenities when making decisions about where to locate (Webster & Karlstrom, 2009). A unique local or natural history may tether a museum to a certain locality, just as a recreational resort anchor may be tied to the natural features of an important mountain or lake.

Anchor institutions are sometimes key stakeholders in the revitalization of abandoned, neglected, or underutilized suburban neighborhoods (Hahn, Coonerty, & Peaslee, 2003). Recent challenges related to economic restructuring, foreclosures, disinvestment, and suburban outmigration have left many communities looking to anchor institutions for stabilization or support (McKee, 2010). Some anchor institutions have been recognized for their revitalization efforts in host communities or for their development of symbiotic relationships (Appleseed Inc., 2003; DeVol, Koepp, Wong, & Bedroussian, 2003; Work Foundation, 2010). Altruism, however, is not usually the primary motivation for anchor institution investment; many anchor institutions invest because their own institution benefits directly and indirectly from the investments that they make in their host communities. Such investments may help them to better compete for employees, clients, partners, and other resources. The Initiative for a Competitive Inner City has noted that an anchor institution's "ability to attract the best resources hinges not only on their own health but also on the health of their surrounding communities" (2010, p. 1).

While such investment may result in positive economic outcomes for the host community, it may also mean that the fates of both community and anchor become inextricably intertwined. If the anchor falters or struggles, such reliance can expose vulnerabilities for a community that has put all of its eggs in one proverbial basket. An overly specialized economic base is just one of the ways that reliance on anchor institutions can put a host community at risk. While the partnership between a community and its anchor institution is often positive—with the anchor acting as an impetus for economic development and community revitalization (Cisneros, 1995; Initiative for a Competitive Inner City, 2010)—this relationship can sometimes be fraught with inequities or exploitative practices (McKee, 2010). The physical and social changes that accompany an anchor institution's investment within a community can sometimes engender conflict within the host community (Fulbright-Anderson et al., 2001). This may particularly be the case when the interests of nearby residents, who sometimes live in disenfranchised communities experiencing prolonged economic or social distress, collide with anchor institution revitalization efforts (Cromwell, Giloth, & Schachtel, 2005; Lowe, 2008). In the District, where the federal government frequently acts as an anchor and often experiments with federal policy initiatives, such conflicts are fairly common (Gillette, 2006).

Existing research has focused largely on individual anchor institutions and their revitalization efforts in general (CEOs for Cities, 2007). However, comparatively less is known about how anchor institutions and historically disenfranchised communities can succeed together. Scholars in the economic and community development fields, including this particular research project, are beginning to investigate the unique opportunities associated with anchor institution development in a disenfranchised community. In this chapter, we ask what we can learn from the St. Elizabeths case with an eye toward understanding how local and federal leaders may better incorporate the community in the development process. First, we begin with an introduction to the St. Elizabeths case.

The St. Elizabeths Opportunity

The year 2010 marked the beginning of a multiyear, multibillion-dollar effort to consolidate the majority of the Department of Homeland Security's Washington, DC-area operations into one campus in the District of Columbia. Located within the Southeast quadrant of the District, the St. Elizabeths campus overlooks both the Potomac and Anacostia Rivers (see Figure 10.1). Naturally cut off from most of the District by the Anacostia River, St. Elizabeths' neighborhood, and Ward 8 in which it sits, is one of the most impoverished sections in the metropolitan region. The campus itself, which once housed the first federal psychiatric hospital in the United States, includes dozens of historic buildings, many in disrepair. St. Elizabeths' campus is intersected by Martin Luther King Jr. Boulevard, resulting in two campuses:

the West Campus (182 acres), which is owned by the federal government, and the East Campus (118 acres), which is owned by District government. Current plans call for DHS facilities to occupy the majority of the West Campus and a series of commercial, education, residential, and civic developments on the East Campus.

District government and DHS have numerous goals for this consolidation effort. For DHS, the most important goal is to become more efficient by stream-lining its operations and reducing the number of occupied buildings, which presently total 70 buildings in 46 locations across the region. In a 2010 speech to the House Committee on Appropriations, former DHS Undersecretary for Management Elaine Duke testified that "extreme dispersion imposes significant inefficiencies in our daily operations that can be magnified considerably at the most important moments" (DHS, 2010b). In addition to decreasing vulnerabili-ties, DHS's consolidation goals include increasing efficiencies, improving com-munication, and contributing to an emerging "One DHS" culture that optimizes department-wide prevention, response, and recovery capabilities.

For District leaders, an important goal related to the St. Elizabeths redevelop-ment is the adaptive reuse of a former hospital facility and its vast pastoral-like spaces. That many of the buildings on both the East and West Campuses have been

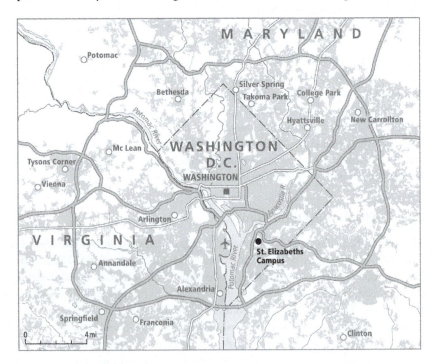

FIGURE 10.1 St. Elizabeths Campus Location.

Cartography: Alexander Hermann

neglected over the past few decades will pose a significant challenge. Although many buildings have been mothballed for preservation purposes, some have been woefully neglected and are slated for demolition. Because of financial and legal problems in recent decades, the National Trust for Historic Preservation listed the campus as one of America's 11 Most Endangered Places in 2002. Despite these significant challenges, District and DHS leaders have supported plans to adaptively reuse as much of the original campus as possible, realizing that the opportunity to redevelop such a large plot of land and such a wealth of historic structures does not come often in a city as developed as Washington, DC. As former Mayor Vincent Gray has often noted, this St. Elizabeths redevelopment is a "once-in-a-lifetime opportunity" for the District of Columbia (O'Connell, 2012).

A broader goal, which is the foundation of this research study, is to capitalize on DHS's development as an anchor institution on the West Campus in order to create an innovation hub on the East Campus. Alongside District leaders, neighborhood stakeholders, and regional decision makers, we led an effort to develop an innovation strategy that promotes entrepreneurship, workforce development, and education in order to increase opportunities for the Ward 8 community and for the region as a whole. Early on we realized that one of the biggest hurdles would be the existing disconnect between the DHS economy and the community economy of Southeast DC. In addition to the physical separation caused by the Anacostia River, other challenges include a median income in Wards 7 and 8 ($32,898)[1] that is less than 60% of the District's median income ($56,519) and an unemployment rate of 18.3% as compared to 9.2% for the District as a whole. Transcending these sociodemographic disparities will be a difficult task and is further complicated by the physical barriers that DHS requires for a high-security facility in a dense urban area. Nevertheless, District government and DHS remain steadfast in their efforts to ensure that this emerging development links residents and local businesses to opportunities at St. Elizabeths.

Research Design

In an effort to translate goals into actionable policy and planning efforts, we completed a multiyear study in 2012 to develop an innovation strategy for the St. Elizabeths campus and surrounding neighborhood. In so doing, we utilized data from the federal government, including the Federal Procurement Data System, and our own qualitative collection methods to better understand the DHS economy and its relationship with Ward 8, the District, and the Washington, DC metropolitan region. Our local analysis is based on DHS documents, public documents, news reports, detailed interviews with DHS officials, focus group responses, and stakeholder engagement meetings. The data used for this analysis were gathered from the Federal Procurement Data System (FPDS) Web site (www.fpds.gov/fpd-sng_cms/) during January 2011. Contracting data for all federal agencies is stored in a free but password-protected area of the Web site. FPDS is the repository of all federal contracting data for contracts in excess of $25,000.

Our qualitative collection efforts included interviews with approximately 10 DHS leaders from various departments, including Science Technology, Private Sector, University Engagement, Office of Policy, and Office of Employment Services. These interviews followed a standard set of questions intended to elicit open-ended responses. Interviews ranged from approximately 60 minutes to 90 minutes each. We also conducted three focus groups, which included approximately 90 leaders from the public and private sectors, including officials and leaders working in the fields of education, innovative technologies, and federal government contracting. The focus groups also followed a standard protocol intended to elicit open-ended responses from participants and lasted approximately two hours each. Representatives from key regional organizations, including private-sector contractors, venture capitalists, university researchers, and development corporations were included in these discussions.

Concurrently, six stakeholder engagement meetings were held with local representatives working within Ward 8 in the areas of education, small business development, and workforce development. These meetings each lasted approximately two hours and followed a predetermined set of questions designed to obtain feedback and recommendations on early research and planning efforts. Participants included local business owners, social service providers, educational service providers, school principals, workforce training programs, and local government officials. Later we present the key findings of our analysis and then discuss how our findings might better inform the planning and implementation process for an innovation hub at St. Elizabeths.

Findings

With nearly 220,000 employees across the country, DHS represents a small but growing portion of the US workforce. In 2010, nearly 12% (26,965) of those employees lived and worked in the Washington, DC metropolitan area, primarily in the areas of management, program analysis, and administration (see Table 10.1). The Washington, DC region also attracts a large number of private-sector homeland security–related jobs because the region is home to both DHS headquarters and many of its directorates (Mayer & Cowell, 2014). Like many capital cities and knowledge hubs, the Washington, DC region has high concentrations of professional and technical services, administrative services, and education services firms and workers. Our research identified certain subsectors—including computer programming and related services, security services, and universities and colleges—as not only strong within the region but also receiving significant amounts of DHS contract activity, suggesting several potential niches for area firms to serve DHS needs. Tables 10.2 and 10.3 highlight the potential overlap between DC's industry sector specialization, and the types of industry sectors to which DHS often issues contracts. Table 10.2 lists the top 15 industry sectors by the value of DHS contracts with firms in these sectors. Table 10.3 lists the top 15 industry sectors in Washington, DC based on the value of their location quotient, a measure of industry concentration.

The District of Columbia captures a significant portion of DHS's contracts annually, nearly $15.5 billion between 2005 and 2010. Within the District, however, contracting amounts vary greatly by geography. In 2010, Ward 8 homeland security contractors performed work in the amount of only $754,606, less than 1% of total homeland security procurement activity in the District of Columbia (see Table 10.4). Thus, contracting activity in Ward 8 is very low and does not represent a large share of total procurement activity in the District. However, contracting activity in Ward 8 increased annually by about 22.9% between 2005 and 2010, indicating a potentially dynamic economic process. The contracting work that does occur in

TABLE 10.1 Top 25 job titles for DHS national capital region employees, as of April 2010

Series	Job Title	Total
343	Management and program analysis	4,227
301	Miscellaneous administration and program	3,638
1801	General inspection, investigation, enforcement, and compliance series	2,469
1811	Criminal investigating	1,996
2210	Information technology management	1,642
1802	Compliance inspection and support	1,471
83	Police	1,433
340	Program management	878
1102	Contracting	811
80	Security administration	808
905	General attorney	708
303	Miscellaneous clerk and assistant	590
132	Intelligence	585
201	Human resources management	524
1895	Customs and border protection	495
501	Financial administration and program	287
1101	General business and industry	245
1896	Border patrol enforcement series	233
560	Budget analysis	223
801	General engineering	215
510	Accounting	208
391	Telecommunications	201
930	Hearings and appeals	148
326	Office automation clerical and assistance	132

Source: Department of Homeland Security

TABLE 10.2 Top 15 industry subsectors by $ amount of DHS contracts, 2005–2010

1	541 Professional and technical services	$33,605,700,436
2	561 Administrative and support services	$14,670,969,540
3	334 Computer and electronic product manufacturing	$6,249,549,806
4	336 Transportation and equipment manufacturing	$6,018,266,908
5	236 Construction and buildings	$2,103,345,217
6	518 Data processing, hosting, and related services	$1,916,589,885
7	321 Wood product manufacturing	$1,373,645,368
8	517 Telecommunications	$1,124,452,349
9	611 Educational services	$1,075,451,509
10	443 Electronics and appliance stores	$831,424,604
11	333 Machinery manufacturing	$831,352,937
12	315 Apparel manufacturing	$727,828,509
13	562 Waste management and remediation services	$686,273,108
14	423 Merchant wholesalers, durable goods	$643,716,070
15	237 Heavy and civil engineering construction	$630,142,843

Source: Department of Homeland Security (2010a), FPDS Procurement Data

TABLE 10.3 Top 15 industry subsectors in which DC has a location quotient >1, 2010

1	813 Membership associations and organizations	8.99
2	519 Other information services	4.53
3	611 Educational services	3.82
4	515 Broadcasting, except Internet	3.61
5	541 Professional and technical	3.21
6	487 Scenic and sightseeing transportation	2.66
7	711 Performing arts and spectator	2.24
8	712 Museums, historical sites, zoos, and parks	2.1
9	721 Accommodation	2.03
10	511 Publishing industries, except Internet	1.99
11	814 Private households	1.9
12	531 Real estate	1.65
13	561 Administrative and support services	1.44
14	622 Hospitals	1.26
15	812 Personal and laundry services	1.19

Source: Bureau of Labor Statistics, LQ Calculator

Ward 8 has primarily been performed in areas related to high-tech products and services such as electronic computer manufacturing, and Internet, information, and consulting services. Some lower-tech activities such as building construction, security guards, and patrol services also took place in Ward 8 (see Table 10.5).

TABLE 10.4 Homeland security procurement in the District of Columbia, Ward 8, Washington, DC–Arlington–Alexandria MSA and the United States, 2005–2010

	2005	2006	2007	2008	2009	2010	Total	Average annual growth rate, 2005–2010
District of Columbia	$1.2B	$2.3B	$2.4B	$3.5B	$3.3B	$2.7B	$15.5B	14.1%
Ward 8	$218,649	$9,446,304	$2,560,908	$4,399,918	$633,331	$754,606	$18,013,716	22.9%
Rest of Washington, DC–Arlington– Alexandria MSA	$2.8B	$3.1B	$3.2B	$4.8B	$3.9B	$3.8B	$21.5B	5.2%
all other MSAs	$10.6B	$9.2B	$6.5B	$7.3B	$6.5B	$6.2B	$46.3B	-8.6%
DHS $ total	$14.6B	$14.6B	$12.1B	$15.6B	$13.7B	$12.7B	$83.4B	-2.3%

Source: Federal Procurement Data System (FPDS) www.fpds.gov/fpdsng_cms

TABLE 10.5 Detailed information about top 10 vendors in Ward 8

	Vendor name	Total, 2005–2010	Headquarters location	Other important information
1	Datatrac Information Services, Inc.	$8,999,398	Richardson, TX	Acquired by Computer Sciences Corporation in 2007
2	Master Security Company, LLC	$2,791,302	Cockeysville, MD	Provides security solutions
3	Executive Information Systems	$2,265,955	Bethesda, MD	Supports software developers and manufacturing partners' sales and marketing efforts to government customers
4	2PI Solutions, Inc.	$1,985,262	Washington, DC (5335 Wisconsin Avenue NW Suite 440)	IT, shredding and recycling services, construction and facilities maintenance
5	Bradley Technologies, Inc.	$1,922,934	Silver Spring, MD	Security services
6	Anteon Corporation (VA)	$1,243,842	Fairfax, VA	Now part of General Dynamics
7	DTM Corporation	$684,419	Washington, DC (7600 Georgia Ave NW, Suite 316)	Security solutions, facility management and automation resources
8	SRS Technologies	$359,891	Originally in Newport Beach, CA (now Fairfax, VA)	Acquired by ManTech located in Fairfax, VA in 2007; provides information technology, and system engineering and integration services and products
9	Kardex Systems, Inc.	$342,098	Zurich, Switzerland	Storage solutions
10	Grant Thornton LLP	$237,685	Chicago, IL with offices in DC	Auditing, management, consulting, etc.

Source: Federal Procurement Data System (FPDS), www.fpds.gov/fpdsng_cms

Overall, the quantitative data analysis shows that procurement activity in homeland security is not presently concentrated in Ward 8. Although some activity has taken place over the past six years, much of it is likely associated with the preparations and start of the construction activities around the new DHS facility on the St. Elizabeths campus. Of the top 10 vendors performing work in Ward 8, none is located or headquartered in Ward 8. Most of these firms are traditional government contractors, some of which were acquired by large systems integrators such as Computer Sciences Corporation or General Dynamics.

From the qualitative data, we see a slightly more robust description of the homeland security economy in the region; however, the main storyline generally remains the same—while DC and the broader region are expected to see continued gains related to the federal government and the homeland security economy, those gains are not guaranteed for places like Ward 8. Results from the focus groups with homeland security contractors, innovators, and entrepreneurs, as well as homeland security education stakeholders, are presented first. We then discuss the findings from the Ward 8 stakeholder focus groups, which tended to focus more on the specific challenges and opportunities related to the St. Elizabeths development.

The *homeland security contractors group* identified a strong potential for DC-based firms in contracting with government agencies such as DHS. There is also potential in the intersection of financial opportunities with technology companies and academic researchers. DC offers homeland security firms access to government and the ability to influence the national agenda. The area's highly educated labor force, strong public-private connections, and the general quality of life make DC an attractive location for these firms. This focus group identified a major weakness in the obstacles that exist in doing business with DHS; specifically, the constant changes in DHS linkages and vulnerabilities, and differing standards for DHS components. DHS contractors felt that support for innovation has great potential to transform the way the federal government operates, promote entrepreneurship, and strengthen linkages between the private sector and federal government. To that end, contractors suggested several elements for the St. Elizabeths campus: advanced concepts labs and prototyping facilities; a demonstration "marketplace" for DHS products and services; and a conference center at the St. Elizabeths site.

The *homeland security education focus group* yielded insights into the strengths, weaknesses, and opportunities of the homeland security education sector. In general, homeland security education experts noted that Washington, DC has a highly educated and skilled labor force in the area of homeland security. There is strong academic as well as R&D expertise, which also benefits from tight linkages between universities and the homeland security industry. The proximity to policy makers and industry experts in DC helps with setting up partnerships. However, universities have generally lagged in commercializing their technologies. The lengthy and complicated security clearance process is also seen as a barrier to employment in this industry. Large systems integrators have a huge, often unmet, demand for workers with intelligence, analytics, and cybersecurity skills and they are concerned about the availability of qualified candidates. The secondary school system is not prepared for these demands and the education community could be more aware of the needed skill sets. There are great opportunities in aligning university programs with labor demands in the industry, and also to reach into the lower levels of the educational pipeline. Ideas discussed include: setting up a consortia to support cyber research; creating an incubator for researchers; creating internship programs; and establishing a preclearance processing service, programs to connect DC residents to DHS jobs, and co-location of universities to enhance collaboration.

The *innovation and entrepreneurship focus group* highlighted DC's strengths in the intelligence and security field, particularly as it relates to technology/R&D capacity, intelligence infrastructure, access to federal government agencies and decision makers, diverse customer base, good universities, robust venture capital community, and emerging models for technology transfer and commercialization. This group saw as major weaknesses the lack of an entrepreneurial drive and a dearth in translation of opportunities into entrepreneurship. It noted the slowness of federal government, which does not keep up with typical entrepreneurial speed. There is also a lack of experienced serial entrepreneurs and investment capital (particularly angel capital) within the region. Opportunities were seen in efforts to increase commercialization and entrepreneurship. Ideas for the St. Elizabeths campus included: an on-campus incubator (with a broad focus, not just homeland security), a test bed facility, public investment for ventures, partnerships between the Small Business Innovation Research program[2] and the investment community, a showcase facility, research consortium, mentor programs, and efforts to increase collaboration between firms, entrepreneurs, universities, and the investment community.

Within Ward 8, the format of the focus groups shifted slightly to incorporate more immediate suggestions and the questions focused more on the needs and concerns of neighborhood residents. At the *workforce development roundtable*, participants identified a number of key strengths and weaknesses within Ward 8. Participants noted a number of organizations already working on job training and workforce development initiatives within the neighborhood, although the top workforce development service providers in the District and in Ward 8 are struggling to maintain operational funding. Participants noted that clearer communication channels regarding funding opportunities and partnerships with DHS and related agencies are necessary if the community economy is expected to effectively engage in this process. Several potential opportunities were identified, including having private-sector employers involved in structuring the training programs to meet their needs, emphasizing work opportunity tax credits to small businesses in the surrounding area, and developing programs that address workforce development issues from a multigenerational perspective (i.e., children, parents, grandparents).

The *business development stakeholders* similarly identified a number of organizations already at work as one of the main strengths of Ward 8. Along with having lots of land available for redevelopment, stakeholders also noted the strength of the neighborhood's transportation network, including easy access to downtown and I-295, two Metro stations, bus lines, and freight rail opportunities. Numerous loyal small businesses were also identified as potential points of contact for outreach efforts moving forward. Significant challenges were also highlighted; namely, that Ward 8's share of jobs in the homeland security industry is presently low and any federal government contract money going to Ward 8 is likely channeled out of the community because the businesses are not actually based there. Business owners suggested: schools with state-of-the-art facilities to prepare students for forthcoming jobs; increased opportunities for small businesses and restaurants, which may employ less-skilled workers, to subcontract with larger contractors; creation of a minority business development fund; and policies to ensure that small businesses are not driven out when chain stores and larger commercial development happens.

Finally, *education providers* in Ward 8 described a variety of existing and planned programs that correspond with the emerging needs of the homeland security economy and the St. Elizabeths campus. Notable existing programs include Ballou High School's STEM and STAY programs (for adult learners in science and technology), and Urban Alliance's internship program, among others. Like other stakeholders in Ward 8, educational service providers also confront funding shortages and uncertainties, which have made the stability of many programs a difficult challenge. Additional challenges include below-average educational attainment and higher than average dropout and truancy rates. Service providers in the St. Elizabeths area suggested that nontraditional learning programs and educational pathways are necessary for much of the Ward 8 population. Along those lines, and related to the opportunities at St. Elizabeths, stakeholders suggested: development of a homeland security–themed or concept high school; combined studies with on-the-job-training based on Boston's Year Up model; certificate programs for related careers such as emergency telecommunicator/dispatcher, or certified protection officer; and creating opportunities around food services and other essential services on the East Campus.

From the quantitative data as well as the focus groups and Ward-based stakeholder meetings, we discovered a number of potential opportunities for the Ward 8 community related to the redevelopment of the St. Elizabeths campus and the relocation of DHS operations. Along with the identification of these opportunities came careful warnings about potential challenges and pitfalls. The quantitative analysis reminds us that the disconnect between the Ward 8 community economy as it exists today and the homeland security economy within the broader region is a significant challenge and one that should not be underestimated. Leaders from all areas of the economy strongly recommended the development of a strategy that anchors DHS within the community, and in so doing begins to tether Ward 8 to the capital city economy, so that residents begin to reap the gains that much of the rest of the region has experienced in recent years.

"St. Elizabeths East Is Coming Alive"[3]

Since our report was delivered to the DC Office of Planning in December 2012, a number of developments have occurred on the St. Elizabeths campus. The usual roadblocks associated with a multi-jurisdictional planning process of this size have arisen, but a number of key developments have transpired.

Among the most visible developments on the site is the St. Elizabeths East Gateway Pavilion, which opened in October 2013. Located at the heart of the East Campus, the pavilion is a multiuse venue designed to accommodate farmers' markets, casual dining, community meeting space, and a variety of other cultural, commercial, and arts events. Although the activation of the space has been somewhat slow to date, periodic events with retail and restaurants partners suggest that interest is growing.

Although not yet visible, other early wins on the East Campus include the formalized commitments in 2013 from three programmatic anchor tenants: Citelum USA, Microsoft Corporation, and SmartBIM/Treasury Advisory Services. Other recent solicitations have focused on finding a university anchor, an open call to artists, summer events grants, and RFPs for Design-Build renovation of the Chapel, a Gateway DC Café operator, and assorted demonstration projects.

In the summer of 2014, Mayor Gray helped unveil the new R.I.S.E. Demonstration Center, which will "connect the innovation economy, the surrounding communities and residents of Washington, D.C. until the development of a permanent St. Elizabeths East Innovation Hub" (St. Elizabeths East, n.d. b).[4] The demonstration center includes a Digital Inclusion Center, a computer training facility developed in partnership with the Office of the Chief Technology Officer (OCTO) and primarily funded by the DC Office of Planning; demonstration and lecture halls, flexibly designed to facilitate both training programs and demonstrations from anchor tenants; and classroom and conference spaces for job training and placement services.

Infrastructure preparations continue as well, but with some delays. Comprehensive planning efforts in 2012 helped the District secure $113.5 million through 2016 in capital budget dollars. Much of the funds will be used for ongoing efforts to design and build public infrastructure necessary for future on-site developments, including roadways, lighting, streetscapes, demolition of some non-contributing structures, and connecting elements between the campuses and surrounding community. However, the District announced in June 2014 that solicitations tied to the planned infrastructure work would be canceled and that a new Request for Proposals (RFP) would be issued. During the summer of 2014, the District also issued an RFP for Phase I development of the East Campus, seeking proposals for a master developer to develop selected parcels. By late July, the District received five responses to the RFP. Current plans call for a new infrastructure RFP to allow for better coordination between the infrastructure contractor and the new master developer.

The West Campus has also experienced a series of both successes and delays since 2012. The first wave of consolidations occurred in September 2013, when the Coast Guard began moving its headquarters from nearby Buzzard Point to a new energy-efficient location on the West Campus. More recent developments include a June 2014 Request for Qualifications (RFQ) from the General Services Administration to renovate the Center Building, which will become DHS's headquarters. The work is slated to cost between $100 million and $140 million with an expected delivery of July 2017. Although the timeline for DHS consolidation and relocation has been plagued by a myriad of delays, current plans still call for other DHS agencies to move to the campus in the future. However, funding concerns have caused GSA to explore alternative funding strategies, including a complicated swap of other federally owned buildings in exchange for expensive renovation services of buildings on the West Campus.

The developments on the East and West Campuses of the St. Elizabeths area illustrate that there are opportunities surrounding the development of a neighborhood based on anchor institutions such as federal government entities. Other investments in Ward 8 include the potential redevelopment of the Barry Farm neighborhood to the west; the expansion of popular DC bookstore and restaurant Busboys and Poets in Anacostia; and a $300 million soccer stadium at nearby Buzzard Point to be funded by a public-private partnership. While other private investments have been slow to follow, initial public commitment seems vital to the success of the anchor and the surrounding community. In the case of St. Elizabeths, anchor institutions such as DHS still show a long-term commitment that will be crucial to the neighborhood's future vitality.

Conclusion

Anchor institutions can play an important role in their host communities. Although not all anchor–community relationships are mutually beneficial, leaders may increase the likelihood of a positive outcome with careful planning and attentive stewardship. As DHS prepares to consolidate its Washington, DC–area operations on the St. Elizabeths campus, its investment in this neighborhood has the potential to become an important anchor institution for the surrounding Ward 8 neighborhood. Leading up to this consolidation, it will be important to keep in mind a number of challenges and opportunities we have identified. Among the more exciting opportunities are the federal government's investment on the West Campus and the District government's investment on the East Campus. Other opportunities related to education, housing, small business development, and innovative spin-offs have been identified, especially on the East Campus and in areas immediately adjacent to the campus. Significant challenges within the Ward 8 community remain, however, and should also be considered in any development strategy for the St. Elizabeths Campus. Namely, a significant disconnect between the education, employment, and income levels of Ward 8 residents and

DHS employees will likely be a challenge for leaders trying to integrate the DHS development with the local community in any meaningful way.

As our research has found, the homeland security economy represents a significant and growing portion of the federal government's expenditures. DHS, by association, is a powerful and influential player within the broader national economy and within the region. When it consolidates at St. Elizabeths, DHS will have the potential to simultaneously serve as both an anchor for the host community and as a conduit to the broader capital city economy. This dual role is not a given, however; it is a goal that District leaders must strive to achieve and maintain.

Anchor institutions of this scale can help to revitalize underutilized areas, increase employment, and develop university–industry relationships, but it does not happen without careful planning and steadfast governance strategies. District leaders would do well to consider who the players on the St. Elizabeths campus should be, how these players will interact with each other and with the larger regional economy, and, most important, how the surrounding community will relate to, and benefit from, the anchor of the East and West Campuses. To ensure that this opportunity is not missed, District leaders must continue working to align the goals of DHS and the local community, build viable bridges between the two that move beyond the superficial, and sustain this agenda, despite challenges along the way.

Notes

1 St. Elizabeths is located in Ward 8. However, because of data availability, some calculations refer to Wards 7 and 8. Wards 7 and 8 have similar demographics and are the only two wards located east of the Anacostia River.
2 The Small Business Innovation Research (SBIR) program is a highly competitive program that encourages domestic small businesses to engage in federally supported research and development that has the potential for commercialization. Through a competitive awards-based program, SBIR enables small businesses to explore their technological potential and provides the incentive to profit from its commercialization.
3 Quote from St. Elizabeths East, n.d. a.
4 St. Elizabeths East. "RISE-DC." Accessed on August 25, 2014. http://stelizabethseast. com/rise-dc/.

References

Alperovitz, G., Howard, T., & Dubb, S. (2009). Cleveland's worker-owned boom rust-belt to recovery. *Yes*. www.yesmagazine.org/issues/the-new-economy/clevelands-worker-owned-boom.

Appleseed Inc. (2003). Anchor institutions and their role in metropolitan change. White Paper on Penn IUR Initiatives on Anchor Institutions.

Birch, E. (2007). Special report: Anchor institutions. *Next American City*. Summer.

CEOs for Cities. (2007). Leveraging anchor institutions for urban success. White Paper. Retrieved from www.ceosforcities.org/pagefiles/CEOs_LeveragingAnchorInstitutionsforUrbanSuccess_FINAL.pdf.

Cisneros, H. G. (1995). The university and the urban challenge. Washington, DC: US Department of Housing and Urban Development.

Cromwell, P. M., Giloth, R., & Schachtel, M. R. B. (2005). East Baltimore Revitalization Project: Opportunities and challenges in transforming an urban neighborhood. *Journal of Higher Education Outreach and Engagement, 10*(2), 113–126.

Department of Homeland Security. (2010a). Budget-in-Brief: Fiscal Year 2010. Retrieved from http://www.dhs.gov/xlibrary/assets/budget_bib_fy2011.pdf

Department of Homeland Security (DHS). (2010b). Testimony of Elaine Duke before the United States House Committee on Appropriations on DHS Headquarters Consolidation. Retrieved from www.dhs.gov/news/2010/05/19/testimony-elaine-duke-united-states-house-committee-appropriations-dhs-headquarters.

DeVol, R., Koepp, R. Wong, P., & Bedroussian, A. (2003). *The economic contributions of health care to New England.* Santa Monica, CA: Milken Institute.

District of Columbia Office of Planning. (2012). DC innovation strategy for Saint Elizabeths final report.

Ehlenz, M., Birch, E., & Agness, B. (2014). "The Power of Eds and Meds: Urban Universities Investing in Neighborhood Revitalization and Innovation Districts." Penn Institute for Urban Research, Philadelphia, PA: University of Pennsylvania.

Fulbright-Anderson, K., Auspos, P., & Anderson, A. (2001). Community involvement in partnerships with educational institutions, medical centers, and utility companies. Paper prepared for Aspen Institute Roundtable on Comprehensive Community Initiatives. Retrieved from www.aecf.org/KnowledgeCenter/Publications.aspx?pubguid ={D6374635–8A58–484A-AE37–76198A62E1E0}.

Gillette, H. (2006). *Between justice and beauty: Race, planning, and the failure of urban policy in Washington, D.C.* Philadelphia, PA: Penn Press.

Hahn, A., Coonerty, C. and Peaslee, L. (2003). Colleges and universities as economic anchors: Profiles of promising practices. Providence, RI: Campus Compact.

Harkavy, I., & Zuckerman, H. (1999). *Eds and meds: Cities' hidden assets.* Washington, DC: Brookings Institution Center on Urban and Metropolitan Policy.

Initiative for a Competitive Inner City. (2010). Leveraging anchor institutions to grow inner city businesses: A resource for inner city entrepreneurs.

Lowe, J. S. (2008). A participatory planning approach to enhancing a historically black university-community partnership: The case of the e-city initiative. *Planning, Practice, and Research, 23*(4), 549–558.

Mayer, H., & Cowell, M. (2014). Capital cities as knowledge hubs: The economic geography of homeland security contracting. In S. Coventz, B. DeRudder, A. Thierstein, & F. Witlox (Eds.), *Hub cities in the knowledge economy* (pp. 223–246). London, UK: Ashgate.

McKee, G. A. (2010). Health-care policy as urban policy: Hospitals and community development in the postindustrial city. Working Paper. Federal Reserve Bank of San Francisco's Community Development Investment Center.

Nelson, M., & Wolf-Powers, L. (2010). Chains and ladders: Exploring the opportunities for workforce development and poverty reduction in the hospital sector. *Economic Development Quarterly, 24*(1), 33–44.

O'Connell, J. (2012, March 30). St. Elizabeths renovation as security campus faces resistance. *The Washington Post*. Retrieved from www.washingtonpost.com/business/economy/st-elizabeths-renovation-as-security-campus-faces-resistance/2012/03/30/gIQAzqJKlS_story.html.

St. Elizabeths East. (n.d. a) "News and Events." Retrieved from http://stelizabethseast.com/news-and-events/.

St. Elizabeths East. (n.d. b) "RISE-DC." Retrieved from http://stelizabethseast.com/rise-dc/.

US Office of Personnel Management, Fedscope Database Available here: http://www.fedscope.opm.gov/.

Webster, H., & Karlstrom, M. (2009). Why community investment is good for nonprofit anchor institutions: Understanding costs, benefits, and the range of strategic options. Chicago, IL: Chapin Hill at the University of Chicago.

Work Foundation. (2010). Anchoring growth: The role of anchor institutions in the regeneration of UK cities. Retrieved from www.theworkfoundation.com/Reports/270/Anchoring-Growth-The-role-of-Anchor-Institutions-in-the-regeneration-of-UK-cities.

Yates, J. (2009). The Evergreen Cooperative Initiative: Can "anchor institutions" help revitalize declining neighborhoods by buying from local cooperatives? *OWNERS AT WORK XXI*(1). http://www.geo.coop/node/402.

PART III

Development Impacts in District Neighborhoods and Beyond

11

BEYOND GENTRIFICATION

Investment and Abandonment on the Waterfront

Brett Williams

Talking about gentrification focuses attention on neighborhood change: an influx of new, usually wealthier, often younger, often Whiter residents, the appearance of new shops that cater to them, and the displacement of those who have lived there before. Sometimes gentrification evokes quaint and bounded change in a single place. When gentrification seems to be everywhere, some call it *supergentrification*. But does the typical idea of gentrification distract us from what's really going on?

In this chapter I suggest that it does. I have come to believe that gentrification inadequately captures the dialectics of investment and abandonment, development and displacement, accumulation and dispossession that shape urban life and property relations (Harvey, 2010; Marcuse, 1985/1986/2010; Smith, 1979). Surplus capital loves and seeks out real estate. Investment and abandonment are always there. Abandonment welcomes investment and investment can presage abandonment. Change is constant and each contains the seeds of its opposite. Dialectics are nested within dialectics. Uptown booms when Southeast languishes, DC grows fat with defense contracts as Detroit faces bankruptcy, and overdevelopment upstream means ruin down the river. As investment in real estate remakes the waterfront into a more expensive place, residents face dislocation and displacement, over-policing and stigma, transitional investments by large companies in predatory lending, and no job opportunities at all despite the feel of money in the air.

A Few of the Waterfront's Dispossessed

For the past three years, I've been following young people born in the 1990s who are struggling to come of age in DC's low-income waterfront neighborhoods. I follow their struggles to find jobs and housing, to get school-like credentials, and to stay out of jail. Staying out of jail is not as easy as it sounds: most of them have done at least a little time. They all take pride in graduating high school or earning a GED. These credentials, however, mean little to employers, and college is impossible. For-profit schools prey on their hopes and derail them with various online scams. One young woman has thrown hundreds of dollars into a quest for a degree in forensics. Amidst these young people's troubles with finding a place to sleep and ways to get around, passing drug tests and hiding ankle bracelets to search for work, one of the most disturbing things I've learned is how businesses target their struggles and aspirations for profit and suck away the few resources they control.

One day I went with my young friend Annie to buy a car. She works the overnight shift at Checkers, which serves fast food to people coming home from work or a night out. Annie sleeps on the floor at her girlfriend's house because her girlfriend's children sleep in the only bedroom. She walks to work and back, often in the middle of the night, and it was becoming too scary and hard for her. Annie also reasoned that with a car she could escape the boundaries of her neighborhood and find a better job. Meticulously assessing her monthly minimum-wage income in the form of biweekly checks, the salesman calculated that she could use one of those checks for the $400-something used car note and live off the other one. Young people apparently hear their checks assessed this way often, for they like to say, with fragile confidence: "One for the car note and one for me," which is practically delusional. The loan company charged Annie 23% interest on a $15,000 loan for a used car. When her car was totaled two months later, the insurance company reimbursed the loan company for the cost of the car, but the loan company is still pursuing her for the interest she would have paid if she had driven the car and made monthly payments over the whole five years. If she had been someone like me, she could have bought this used car with cash and spent thousands less. Her neighborhood places her in a captive market besieged by lenders, and her credit score (tainted by a long-ago repo) consigns her to usury. Like the mortgage crisis, the explosive growth in car loans for low-income people stems from Wall Street banks and private equity firms that invest in lenders and bundle loans into complex securities sold all over the world.

My friend Tanisha graduated high school, got certified at University of the District of Columbia as a child care worker, makes minimum wage, and supports her mother and long-time boyfriend. Like many young people, she moved as a teenager into a contributory role in the family. Upon barely reaching adulthood, they feel a shift in responsibility toward themselves. Bright and brazen, Tanisha tried to manage a better-paying job in the suburbs. But traveling there on several buses was arduous and frightening. She didn't know the way, there were no public telephones, and she was far away from everyone and everything she knew. She returned to the child care center in her neighborhood and eventually leased a cellphone, her only way to connect to her dispersed family and friends and to listen to music. Like many young people, her cellphone is essential at the same time as it tethers her to high-interest debt. It goes on and off, alerting her constantly about the amount she owes. The smart phones that so delight university students would be invaluable for Tanisha, but as things stand she has not bought a phone but a device that keeps her in debt and trumpets how much she owes. All of the young people I know find their phones vital and struggle to keep them on, but the phones are more often off. I find it maddening to watch them constantly trying to round up money, add minutes, use the minutes up, and start all over again.

Opportunities to profit from poverty blossom in changing neighborhoods, which are riddled with shops offering debt at high interest. These often tawdry shops mask deep connections to Wall Street, where, for example, the national chain Famous Pawn is traded as PWN. At tax time, the young people I know anxiously wait for their refunds, for along with all the informal work they do for income they usually manage to eke out some regularly waged jobs. Tax preparers appropriate a large portion of the anticipated refund and then advance the remainder immediately, in effect making a large secured loan at high interest.

Anthony's life at this point illustrates several themes that are common to these young people. I first met him when he was a lovable 8-year-old, knocking at my door with an offer to walk my dogs. He was always on hand to help out and I often spotted him in the Safeway parking lot hustling shoppers who might need help with their bags. All his life he has hustled to find work mowing, digging, raking leaves, caring for pets, and shoveling snow, opportunities that can sometimes open up when newer and richer residents move in. Unlucky in many ways and sometimes careless, Anthony is blessed with a staunch girlfriend with a job whose mother occasionally allows him to stay over. Most often he sleeps on the floor in an apartment across the hall. He used to borrow my washing machine to launder the shirt he wore every day. None of the young people has a room of their own, and they most often refer not to where they live but to where they stay. Having no real address and an off-again, on-again phone hindered Anthony's search for work, but he pursued it doggedly. To save money he hops the Metro. But then he got a $75 fine for doing so and wore an ankle bracelet like a scarlet letter as he tried to find work.

All of these young people face a job market that's beyond grim: a job that promises more than minimum wage is most often in the far suburbs, and even minimum wage jobs that provide too little to live often require a disqualifying "pee test." A person with such an income has to find ways to supplement it. Anthony isn't much for weed, but he has learned a capitalist lesson about money: that it must be invested, put to work so that it will grow. So when he earns cash for small jobs, he sometimes reinvests in something small to sell, like a splif. He seems to always get caught, and because it's hard for the law to communicate with him he gets in more trouble for missing a court date or failing to pay a fine. I have learned how precarious his life is, how much bad luck he has, how many mistakes he makes, how impossible it is for him to find work (even if he were truly literate), and how hard it is for him to be good. At this writing Anthony has been in jail for more than a year for a collection of minor nonviolent crimes, including missed court dates and failure to pay fines, and he is not unusual. The temptations and the oppression are just too large. Young men walk a precipice as they search for work and try not to deal. I learned how normal and how devastating it is to think about and do time, how stuck and vulnerable they feel, how close to what they call home they stay, and how hard it is not to look at a windfall as seed money that could be invested to make a little more. The difficulties they face may reflect the wave of investment and dispossession cresting along the waterfront, and it is hard not to think about how their lives would be different if that investment had included their need for stable housing and meaningful work.

Reclaiming abandoned waterfronts for economic engines has caught favor in many parts of the world since the success of Baltimore's Inner Harbor in the 1980s (Breen & Rigby, 1994; Sieber, 1991; Wennersten, 2014). When I first explored DC's Anacostia waterfront, I was enchanted by the ways it seemed offbeat, its edginess, if you will. I was concerned about projects to enclose and develop it because that meant exacerbating the problems of overdevelopment and pollution in the watershed. But I also worried those charming offbeat denizens of the waterfront would give way to more sterile landscapes and fake communities. I was thinking in terms of gentrification in seeing them as the indigenous people of the waterfront. Looking at the waterfront over time reveals that investment and abandonment were always there. Periods of investment have infused money and infrastructure, while times of abandonment have allowed the waterfront to recharge and shelter difference. But abandonment also welcomes and harbors investment and developers have warehoused properties along the water for many years, both anticipating investment and making it happen.

Investment and Abandonment Over Time

Before the waterfront had been enclosed and named a waterfront, real indigenous people did live along the shore, fishing, farming, and trading. River life was lush until British fur traders looted beavers (to provide fur hats for English aristocrats) and massacred the indigenous Nacotchank. The tobacco plantations of the new settlers eroded the land and silted up the river, making it impassable. One of the first installations of the new American state was the Washington Navy Yard, which began as a shipbuilding facility and soon turned to munitions making. The massive infusion of infrastructure with toxic discharge carried the seeds of abandonment and those who could afford to moved north, making it appear that the city had turned its back on the water for a long while (Wennersten, 2008; Williams, 2001).

During this time, the government placed many devalued institutions along the water. Right after the Civil War, freed slaves demanded land and were awarded a parcel on the east side of the river from James Barry's 375-acre farm. St. Elizabeths Hospital (an insane asylum at the time) was built next door. On the west side of the river, DC General Hospital and the DC Jail seemed to confirm that this was cheap property for poor people. Barry Farm thrived as a landowning, secure community until World War II, when the Suitland Parkway skewered it for military transport.

After the war, three more commuter highways crossed the Anacostia River to help Marylanders get through the area quickly and military bases gave the water a somewhat grim feel. Then, in the 1950s, wrenching urban renewal pushed many people next to and across the river, mostly into large housing projects, including a refurbished Barry Farm. Urban renewal made many investors' fortunes. Thus, government projects during a time of abandonment both reflected and recreated the low value of the waterfront, making it a good deal for investors in building roads and public housing. Abandonment encouraged investment in its wake.

I first began hanging out seriously along the waterfront because the National Park Service hired me, along with student and community ethnographers, to try to learn if Anacostia Park (stretching for five miles along the river) was meeting the needs of its neighbors (Williams, Ramos, & Brown, 1997). We were amazed at what we learned: this undeveloped park with no amenities was precious to nearby residents, who did many important things there. The west side of the river was home to gay clubs not welcomed elsewhere in the city, including The Edge, where Black, working-class men built runway traditions with spectacular dancing and political parody. Seafarers' Yacht Club was the first African American boating club on the East Coast. Many of its members lacked actual working yachts, but Seafarers gathered there to socialize and run service projects. Down closer to the Navy Yard were stained glass and stone-carving studios, a free community garden called the Garden of Love, and farther west a bustling fish market. I found a memorial to a dead fisherman holding his canvas chair and tackle box and met a man who lived outside, found and repaired bicycles, and gave them away.

On the river's east side, many people visited the undeveloped park to find peace. They also went there to be together: almost every weekend the park bustled with family, class, and church reunions. Go-go, DC's indigenous music, got its start in Anacostia Park, and people still love to reminisce about outdoor concerts there. Along the river people fished to supplement their groceries, although the fish were increasingly compromised. All in all it was an anthropologist's dream: marginalized people doing interesting things to make their lives more meaningful and complete (Williams, 2001).

Then, in 2004, the waterfront's development seemed to begin in earnest with the founding of a public-private corporation to award contracts and approve plans. I began attending meetings organized by developers with glossy, bossy, modular

PowerPoints heralding the new places they were making, purged of messy uses. Residents in attendance often raised the specter of urban renewal, both projects examples of an enduring plan to purge the city of Black people. In 2002, I wrote in despair about the pathologizing of communities along the water's edge in order to dispossess them of their homes and access to public space. "Washington is poised to return from squalor" (Loeb, 1998, B1). "Federal planners see a palette of [other] possibilities: town houses and homes, offices, museums, a waterfront park, more federal agencies, and tourist sites in this desolate wasteland," announced *The Washington Post* (Vogel, 1999). It (the Anacostia River) flows through "blighted, crime-ridden neighborhoods," but the plan is to redevelop those neighborhoods into a "live-work-play jewel that would be a magnet for residents and visitors" (Wilgoren, 2001, p. 19) and a "major destination for aquatic recreation" (Vogel, 1999). I was angry and nostalgic about how condos, retail, and fake fitness communities would replace uses that seemed to me more authentic. This investment in the waterfront excludes people deeply attached to it: those who come to court, picnic, hold family reunions, net herring, or fish. Activist Dianne Dale fumed that "if somebody doesn't stop development on the river in terms of asphalt, concrete, and steel, then the river is going to die."

Developers name and make places. They pathologize and enclose the waterfront as they celebrate and sanitize it; they both decry and incorporate the edginess. The clubs I found so inspiring were simply sitting on cheap land while developers waited for the land's value to rise and found ways to hasten it. After government relocation and debt financing help solidify rising property values, public housing succumbs to mixed use. Rather than improve an old place, planners imagine massive change that will make a whole new one (Lowman, 2009).

I will consider each side of the river in turn, beginning on the western shore. First the government announced a move. In 2000, the US Department of Transportation moved to the waterfront and the government passed the Southeast Federal Center Public-Private Development Act (Fehr & Montgomery, 2000). In 2004, the federal government revealed that the 200-year-old Navy Yard would become a bustling purchasing hub, an administrative superyard with a daily workforce of 11,000 people processing billions of dollars in defense contracts. Businesses with close ties to the Navy began to move nearby along the shore. The City Council announced that it would refurbish a bridge to help people get to work. Between 2000 and 2004, $40 million worth of land was sold along the western side of the river, including many cheap and supposedly vacant lots.

To woo the Nationals baseball team to a riverfront stadium, DC overwhelmed competition with extensive public financing and special debt-financing mechanisms. The city created a $440 million ballpark package financed by 30-year bonds, which would be repaid with proceeds from taxes on tickets and businesses. In 2004, a TIF (Tax Increment Financing) district was set up around the new stadium, anchoring development along the eastern side (Whoriskey, 2004). The city argued that because 80% of baseball fans were from Maryland and Virginia, the stadium would not drain, but rather increase resources to fund DC schools and hospitals. In 2006, the City Council established a DOT PILOT, payments in lieu of taxes, area to help developer JBG finance infrastructure costs for a new waterfront park (Wilgoren, 2001).

After the initial flurry of baseball talk, the prices developers paid for abandoned lots, rundown warehouses, and industrial sites spiked, more land started trading hands, and developers closed almost $220 million in deals between 2004 and 2006 (Hedgpeth, 2006). Talented developer Douglas Jemal began selling his downtown properties: "I want to get some money in my pocket and go to Anacostia. I want to build Baltimore's Inner Harbor there." One fellow DC developer, John Akridge, said of Jemal: "He's invested just in front of the development wave and ridden the values up. Now he's looking to harvest that value." However, public housing was in the way, and, in 2005, the Arthur Capper-Carrollsburg (ACC) homes were emptied and redeveloped as the "Capitol Quarter" (some redevelopment at ACC had been in the works since at least 1998 when DC opened discussions with the marines about taking over). In 2005, big box developer Ronald Cohen paid $51.6 million for a block of gay clubs, a closed soup kitchen, and several repair shops. Already high-density zoning made the land valuable. More change looms for the much-loved Washington fish market, which is to become a "true urban destination, with restaurants, shops, residences, a new hotel, a cultural anchor and a promenade anchored by public plazas and new piers. And abutting the new fish market is planned a gleaming new soccer stadium (Montgomery & Barker, 2004; Nakamura, 2005a, 2005b, 2006; O'Connell & Davis, 2014).

But the mixed-use and fitness destination development is only partly echoed across the water, which is emerging as a militarized place mirroring the Navy Yard and enhancing the bases already there. The Coast Guard has moved into St. Elizabeths Hospital and the neighborhoods surrounding it are poised to become the Homeland Security Regional Innovation Center (see Cowell & Mayer, this volume). This founding contradiction between making the waterfront an urban fitness destination and drowning it in security may anchor for now the dialectic of investment and abandonment. How will the city change with the influx of defense contractors on the western side of the river and the concentration of homeland security on the east?

On the eastern side of the river, federal parkland has saved the river from industrial depredations. Investment has been in the works for a long time because land was cheap and Metro was coming. The administration of Mayor Barry began to bill the stop as a regional economic development center. To lure developers, the city sketched plans for a 125-acre theme park dubbed the Anacostia Cultural Complex with a manmade lagoon, an amphitheater, museums, an aquarium, a restaurant, and a cinema complex. By 2003, Poplar Point, the river's last wetland, was chosen for development. This development was actually stopped by a coalition of determined activists. In 2004, the District's Department of Transportation (DCDOT) began to move to the foot of the 11th Street Bridge and the city moved to persuade private developers to get to work on Howard Road. That summer developers across the country came to check it out. Anticipating waterfront development, speculators bought up inexpensive properties in the Anacostia Historic District, walking away from them when the foreclosure crisis hit the city in 2008.

During all this churning, Barry Farm appeared abandoned and isolated by the highways that bound it (Burchfield, 2009). Community organizers and residents decried "demolition by neglect" as the housing authority stepped up evictions, failed to replace families in empty units, and allowed the buildings to deteriorate. The printed rationale for razing Barry Farm, as well as public statements from developers and the housing authority, are filled with concerns about the poverty of the people. They juxtapose that poverty with the vision of mixed use and their sense of the dire effects of the concentration of poverty. In their vision, poverty is like a tumor that must be extracted. Or maybe it's contagious. Either way, they posit the poor as agents of their own infection and poverty as a malady that can be cured at the neighborhood level by deconcentrating the poor, dispersing them, and importing new residents with more money. Living near people of means will supposedly provide varied role models for poor people and allow them to leverage their new neighbors' resources to find jobs. This strategy assumes that poverty is a neighborhood-level problem so the solutions must lie in the neighborhood. But neighborhoods do not allocate resources or make policy decisions. Larger processes make people poor. The distress at Barry Farm today is better explained by the withdrawal of resources during a time of abandonment.

The problem with the poverty deconcentration solution is that several cities have tried it and it never works. At best, people who are dispersed report that their lives are not much better. They often report that their lives are worse. Their incomes don't grow. Their health grows far worse, even worse than other low-income people. They suffer high rates of arthritis, asthma, diabetes, hypertension, heart disease, and stress, and they miss the support networks that used to help them manage illness (Manjarrez & Popkin, 2007). They miss the people with whom they used to share child care, telephones, and rides. They want to return. Teenagers are often criminalized in new neighborhoods and they experience little change in access to jobs or educational achievement.

Role models are actually quite varied in neighborhoods of concentrated poverty. New residents do not provide inspiration for how to be more middle class or access to their connections. They tend to hunker down and avoid the old residents. Their issues are different and they drift to formal organizations rather than the support systems organized by the poor. They may be very concerned about property values. What deconcentration does best is disappear the poor, making them less visible and derailing their potential political power (Hyra, 2015).

Barry Farm has a legendary past and is one of the few public housing developments left in the whole city and almost the only one with units large enough to house large, complex families (Ture, forthcoming). It seems unfathomable that DC's housing authority would close such a place, in a city where homelessness is epic and shelters and hotels are bursting. The housing authority closed its waiting list in 2013 because it held 70,000 people with an average wait of 39 years. The claim that razing public housing is good for poor people because they won't have to live near other poor people is hollow and insulting, but it helps mask a land grab: it may look like we're kicking you out of your home, but you'll be better off in the end.

The social networks built by people who are poor are broad and deep. People help each other out with child care, they share fish and garden provisions, they help each other get to clinics, dialysis, and other appointments, they check to make sure elderly people survived the night. They help each other meet health emergencies; they share information on job prospects, they share telephones and rides, they give shelter to people in distress. Families and social networks do much of the work our institutions do not.

Efforts to deconcentrate the poor are seriously flawed. Neighborhoods do not cause poverty and people don't catch poverty from each other. All dispersal does is shatter social networks and isolate people in strange surroundings where they may be stigmatized and even criminalized. They do no better economically or educationally and their health deteriorates: research shows troubling spikes in asthma, stress, hypertension, and depression. Dispersal erases the visibility, community, and political potential of public housing residents. Even if they are eventually allowed to return, there is little research showing that mixed-income housing works as planners claim, that it provides role models or connections to opportunity (see, for example, Gans, 2010; Goetz, 2002; Greenbaum, 2008; Greenbaum et al., 2008; Steinberg, 2010).

Often dispossession is accompanied by a racialized discourse devaluing the displaced, for stigmatizing and scapegoating residents helps to ease their removal (Ture, forthcoming). The economic conditions create a situation in which people make choices that sometimes appear to reaffirm that discourse. But much more than discourse is at work in the relationship between finance capital and urban life. This is a particularly harsh period of dispossession because the wealthy already hog too many resources and many people's lives are teetering and churning. With great speed and angst, speculators roar through devalued neighborhoods, offering cash to people with big medical bills, a large car note, or a relative with needs. The institutions of the government respond to people's difficult and unsettled circumstances through punishment and incarceration. Investment rarely takes the old residents' needs seriously; at best, poor neighborhoods host predatory lenders, fast food, and liquor stores. Businesses rarely pay more than the minimum wage and never for 40 hours. Although they may think "one check for rent and the other for me," they often need to go into debt, if just to stay connected. People with a foothold in Section 8 housing or a house with deferred maintenance may have no utilities but are probably deluged with unhoused friends and kin. As the lives of Anthony, Annie, and Tanisha symbolize, when you are in a low-income neighborhood that is churning, it can be very hard to make sound choices.

To look at a broader dialectic, the city's growth has alternated between the river and the hills. The grandparents of these young people were DC's civil rights generation. They integrated schools and neighborhoods and were able to secure newly non-segregated jobs, often in the public sector. Many joined public unions. Some were able to move into the hills: the formerly all-White streetcar suburbs that were transformed with the lifting of restrictive covenants and the *Bolling v. Sharpe* decision that integrated DC schools. Others were displaced into public housing along or east of the river. The residents of uptown neighborhoods fared a little better economically, purchasing row houses, which over time, became like gold to their descendants. Now most of these grandparents live in multigenerational homes, housing their middle-aged children (some of whom were also able to get government jobs) and their grandchildren, who in the current flurry of investment and dispossession find it hard to get a foothold.

Nesting the dialectic of investment and abandonment within urban nature, overdevelopment of the Anacostia watershed has overloaded the lower watershed with so many toxins that the Anacostia Riverkeeper once quipped that the owner of a new million-dollar condo had just purchased a million-dollar view of her own raw sewage. Development of the waterfront took place without regard for the health of the watershed or the river, which would have been better served had investment moved upstream to green the city. The Anacostia River does not need more impervious surfaces around it but rather wetlands to act as speed bumps during floods and to nurture wildlife. It's too late to save most of the waterfront. But with climate catastrophe looming, we need to jettison out-of-control Wall Street–fueled development, hunker down, and pay attention to the vulnerabilities of urban people and urban nature. Thinking dialectically offers hope, for in the throes of change another kind of change is possible.

References

Breen, A., & Rigby, D. (1994). *Waterfronts: Cities reclaim their edge*. New York, NY: McGraw-Hill.

Burchfield, A. (2009, November 18). Barry Farm: A development plan shrouded in uncertainty. *AWOL*, pp. 11–12.

Fehr, S. C., & Montgomery, D. (2000, June 8). Sea change seen on waterfront. *The Washington Post*.

Gans, H. (2010). Concentrated poverty: A critical analysis. *Challenge, 53*(3), 82–96.

Goetz, E. (2002). Forced relocation vs. voluntary mobility: The effects of dispersal programmes on households. *Housing Studies, 17*(1), 107–123.

Greenbaum, S. (2008). Poverty and the willful destruction of social capital: Displacement and dispossession in African American communities. *Rethinking Marxism, 20*(1), 42–54.

Greenbaum, S., Hathaway, W., Rodriguez, C., Spalding, A., & Ward, B. (2008). Deconcentration and social capital: Contradictions of a poverty alleviation policy. *Journal of Poverty, 12*(2), 201–228.

Harvey, D. (2010). *The enigma of capital. And the crises of capitalism.* New York, NY: Oxford University Press.

Hedgpeth, D. (2006, June 26). Anacostia group looks beyond the ballpark. *The Washington Post.*

Hyra, D. (2015). The back-to-the-city movement: Neighborhood redevelopment and processes of political and cultural displacement. *Urban Studies, 52*(10), 1753–1773.

Loeb, V. (1998, March 8). Seeking a better view on the D.C. waterfront. *The Washington Post*, pp. B1, B8.

Lowman, S. (2009, March 26). Picturing the ideal Anacostia waterfront; at monthly public forums, sleek images meet the realities of redevelopment. *The Washington Post.* District 1, p. 10.

Manjarrez, C., & Popkin, S. (2007). *Poor health: Adding insult to injury for Hope VI families.* Washington, DC: The Urban Institute.

Marcuse, P. (1985). Gentrification, abandonment, and displacement: Connections, causes, and police responses in New York City. *Journal of Urban and Contemporary Law, 28,* reprinted in revised form as Abandonment, gentrification and displacement: The linkages in New York City. In N. Smith & P. Williams (Eds.), *Gentrification of the city* (pp. 153–177). Boston, MA: Allen & Unwin, 1986; and in L. Lees, T. Slater, & E. Wyly (Eds.), *The gentrification reader* (pp. 333–348). London: Routledge, 2010.

Montgomery, L., & Barker, K. (2004). DC stadiums seen as one-two economic punch. *The Washington Post*, pp. B1, B5.

Nakamura, D. (2005a, January 1). DC seeks to buy land for "ballpark district." *The Washington Post*, pp. B1, B9.

Nakamura, D. (2005b, October 26). D.C. seizes 16 owners' property for stadium. *The Washington Post*, pp. B1, B4.

Nakamura, D. (2006, June 8). Nats tell D.C. it's too late for underground parking. *The Washington Post*, pp. B1, B4.

O'Connell, J., & Davis, A. (2014). Gray urges council to approve soccer stadium land deals. *The Washington Post*, pp. B1, B3.

Sieber, R. (1991). Waterfront revitalization in postindustrial port cities of North America. *City & Society, 5*(2), 120–136.

Smith, N. (1979). Toward a theory of gentrification. *Journal of the American Planners Association, 45,* 538–548.

Steinberg, S. (2010). The integration debates: Competing futures for American cities. In C. Hartman & G. D. Squires (Eds.), *Competing futures for American cities* (pp. 213–228). New York, NY: Routledge.

Ture, Kalfani (forthcoming) *We are all cried out here in the Farms.* Doctoral Dissertation, Department of Anthropology. Washington, D.C.: American University.

Vogel, Steve (1999) D.C. Navy Yard Poised for Rebirth. *The Washington Post,* June 19: B1, B4.

Wennersten, J. (2014). *The historic waterfront of Washington, D.C.* Charleston, NC: The History Press.

Whoriskey, P. (2004, September 23). Stadium deal is typical for teams; D.C.'s financing plan in line with others. *The Washington Post*, pp. B1, B6.

Wilgoren, D. (2001). SE riverfront vision aims for HUD funds. *The Washington Post*, pp. B1, B7.

Williams, B. (2001). A river runs through us. *American Anthropologist, 103*(2), 409–431.

Williams, B. (2002). Gentrifying water and selling Jim Crow. *Urban Anthropology, 31*(1), 93–121.

Williams, B., Ramos, T., & Brown, J. (1997). *Rapid ethnographic assessment, park users and neighbors, Civil War defenses of Washington and Anacostia Park, District of Columbia, for park management plans*. Washington, DC: Juárez and Associates.

12

AT ESHU'S CROSSROAD[1]

Pan-African Identity in a Changing City

Michelle Coghill Chatman

Washington, DC has been associated with diverse groupings of Black national-ists and pan-Africanists for decades. These communities, bounded by ideology and identity more so than geographic location, usually consisted of small, yet robust, physical places and spaces where people of similar values congregated and organized. Spurred by the Black Power movement of the 1960s and 1970s, these groups and their activities reflected a multiplicity of sometimes overlapping per-spectives and strategies about Black advancement. This included Black nation-alism[2] (both militant and nonmilitant perspectives) and pan-Africanism. Author Algernon Austin distinguishes between what he calls "cultural nationalists," who prioritized promoting racial pride through the adoption of the arts, fashion, and African names, from the "cultural" Black nationalists (some of whom would also later identify as pan-Africanists), who were more concerned about the "political and economic racial structures that affected Black life" (2006, p. 109). For "cul-tural" Black nationalists, power, not performance, was essential. Therefore, politics reached beyond dressing in dashikis and wearing afros. It encompassed nation building and securing independent educational, political, and cultural institutions such as schools, businesses, and political organizations that supported Black libera-tion (Austin, 2006).

This chapter will not delve into the nuances between these groups, although it is worth noting that scholars make distinctions between them. What follows does not constitute a review of pan-Africanist ideology. Rather this discussion explores how the dynamics of gentrification and "revitalization," occurring in predomi-nantly Black neighborhoods, have led to tensions and shifts in the pan-African community and its claims to space. I focus on how African-centered/pan-African businesses, educational institutions, and spiritual organizations have been impacted by changes occurring in their gentrifying neighborhoods, how individuals associated with these institutions have responded to these shifts, and the choices these same institutions have made to sustain themselves.

DC as Pan-African Space

As early as the 1950s, a number of African-centered groups existed in Washington, DC. These groups consisted, or consist, of various individuals and organizations who consider themselves of African descent and thereby connected to an African diaspora. Among these organizations are various West African drumming and dance troupes, including Melvin Deal's African Heritage Drummers and Dancers, Kankouran West African Dance Company, Farafina Kan, Tam Tam Mandingue, Djimo Kouyate, Memory of African Culture (MAC), and Blacknotes, a spoken word and jazz ensemble that combines West African drum rhythms with contemporary R&B to produce a distinctly pan-Africanist message of Black power and liberation. DC's African-centered political and economic groups include the All African People's Revolutionary Party (AAPRP), the African Diaspora Ancestral Commemoration Institute (ADACI), the African Socialist Party (ASP), the Tubman/Toure Chapter of the Universal Negro Improvement Association (UNIA/ACL), the Leadership Council of the Pan-African Nation (LC-PAN), and A.P.P.E.A.L., Inc., a financial literacy and economic empowerment organization founded by the late Lasana K. Mack, a former DC treasurer and highly respected DC pan-Africanist. The United Black Community (UBC); the IKG Cultural Resource Center, founded by Egyptologist Anthony Browder; the Ankobea/Abusia Society; and the African American Holiday Association (AAHA) make up some of the cultural groups associated with pan-Africanism. Numerous African diasporic religious groups have also thrived in DC, including the Yoruba Temple of Spiritual Elevation and Enlightenment, the Temple of Nyame, the Circle of Light/ASI Society, and Spirit Central.

The schools, shrines, and cultural and political organizations that comprise the DC pan-African community are sustained, in part, by the businesses that cater to that particular population. The lower Georgia Avenue business district, between Euclid Street and Columbia Road, what I call the "Pan-African Marketplace," has served as a pan-African business district for more than 30 years, and it has been impacted by recent demographic shifts occurring throughout DC. This area was a booming venue of Black cultural enterprise during the Afrocentric era of the late 1980s and early 1990s. As a student activist at University of the District of Columbia (UDC), and a member of the Pan-African Student Union (PASU), I frequented the area to hear lectures, browse in the bookstores and businesses, and listen to the elders speak of Black consciousness and liberation. I recall with fondness the temperament of the time period and the presence of elder scholars. Fliers that promised the coming of Dr. Asa Hilliard, Dr. Leonard Jeffries, Dr. Frances

Cress Welsing, Dr. Na'im Akbar, Steve Cokley, Dr. Donna Marimba Ani, Omali Yeshitela, and numerous others lined the walls of the various establishments. There was a vibrancy in the air, particularly during warmer months, when Bob Marley's Africa Unite or something by Fela Kuti would blast out of shops as street vendors sold incense, oils, books, and jewelry along Georgia Avenue. Women and men adorned with dreadlocks, naturals, and cornrows, dressed in dashikis, African print skirts, and revolutionary t-shirts with the images of Malcolm X or Marcus Garvey, would gather along the corridor to exalt in their Blackness. The area had a vibe that appealed to the Black nationalist yearnings of my friends and me. "Would-be revolutionaries" who, born in the 1960s, were too young to have our own stories of "The Struggle," and so we lived vicariously through those of our elders.

One of the most prominent businesses along the corridor was undoubtedly the House of Knowledge Complex located at 2849 Georgia Avenue. It was open from the mid-1970s until the early 1990s. The Complex housed several smaller businesses, including a bakery, Hetep Holistic Foods, the Tape Connection, Heal Thyself, and Jewels of Aton. The building was owned by longtime DC activist and entrepreneur Baba Hodari Abdul-Ali, who from 1977 to 1984 owned and operated Liberation Information Distributing Company, a wholesale distributor of books and periodicals about Africa, Black people, and Islam. In 1981, Hodari founded Pyramid Books, whose holdings consisted of material written by Blacks in the diaspora that would not be found in typical bookstores. According to one community member, Deborah "Wala" Bernard, who worked at the bookstore for a while during the 1980s, "Pyramid books was a rich and wonderful place where you could meet cultural people of the day" (Personal communication, June 12, 2012).

By 1990, Pyramid Books had grown to be the first chain of independent Black-owned and Black-oriented bookstores in the United States with locations in Maryland and California.[3] The store's distinct mission was reflected in its external appearance, which featured the bust of a Black Egyptian pharaoh demanding the attention of by passersby. The store hosted author talks, arts events, and various community gatherings. The success of Pyramid Books may have inspired the opening of similar businesses in other parts of DC, such as Sisterspace and Books, Yawa Books, and Karibu Books. Such businesses flourished during the early 1990s, but eventually the increase of online shopping and competition from major book retailers and increased rents, particularly on U Street, where Sisterspace and Books was located, pushed these businesses out and led to the closure of numerous Black-owned bookstores in DC and in other Black communities around the country (Hyra, 2012). Pyramid Books closed its doors in 1996 and Baba Hodari succumbed to cancer in 2011. However, his memory and the vibrancy that his business and others inspired on Georgia Avenue lives on among members of DC's pan-African community.

Blue Nile Herb Store at 2849 Georgia Avenue is one of the few businesses of that era that has managed to keep its doors open. The proprietor, Baba Duku, opened Blue Nile in 1970 as a wholesale distributor of herbal medicines. He began retail operations in 1974, and presently sells more than 300 homeopathic herb mixtures, essential oils, vitamins, candles, and books on vegetarianism and healthy living. Baba Duku and his assistant, Baba Kweku, are a repository of health information and offer consultations on naturopathic remedies for ailments ranging from asthma to arthritis.

Gentrification impacts throughout the city and certainly along Georgia Avenue and in the Shaw neighborhood have begun to alter the look of the "Pan-African Marketplace," and other Pan-African businesses have had to close (Hyra, 2015; Prince, 2014; Ruble, 2010). Seven Powers of Africa, a small shop that sold African clothes, fabrics, jewelry, and religious items, closed in the summer of 2009 because of declined business. An Ethiopian-owned coffee shop now occupies the space that remained vacant for three years after Seven Powers closed. The coffee shop is flanked by a cell phone accessory store and a recently constructed development of condominiums. Other businesses, Everlasting Life and Soul Vegetarian, two vegan restaurants that were operated by the African Hebrew Israelite community, have also closed. Woodlands Vegan Bistro, at 2928 Georgia Avenue, NW, now occupies the space that was once Everlasting Life. The restaurant underwent renovations to modernize its dining area to make it more appealing to patrons. Woodlands' vegan fare has become quite popular among the new White neighbors in the area, and they can often be found frequenting the establishment. Whereas this was once a venue, a space where Blacks convened to commune in safe "Black space," the present venue now has a more diverse clientele. Sankofa Video, Café, and Books,[4] at 2714 Georgia Avenue, which sells progressive films and books made by Africans of the diaspora, has also managed to stay afloat. These African-centered businesses, cultural and arts organizations, and diasporic religious groups illustrate the city's identity and reputation as a pan-African space. For the remainder of this chapter, I focus on education as an important part of pan-Africanist thought and action in DC, a city that is home to some of the oldest African-centered independent schools in the country.

African-Centered/Pan-African Schools

Independent Black schools emerged out of the social and political unrest of the 1960s and 1970s that gave rise to the Black Power movement (Kifano, 1996; Shujaa, 1994). In neighborhoods across America, Blacks asserted their right to determine the educational standards for their children by establishing schools that operated independently of the public school structure. These schools were founded as a means of resisting the Eurocentric educational model that disempowered Black students by teaching them to subscribe to the existing structures and ideologies of White supremacy (Akoto, 1992; Hilliard, 1992; Lomotey, 1992; Sefa Dei, 1994). By establishing their own institutions of learning, Black activists aspired to counter oppression, control their own destinies, and fortify Black youth with the cultural and political knowledge to advance Blacks in the diaspora. These schools, which were autonomous and supported by the Black community through tuition and donations, often advanced a Black nationalist agenda that stressed Black self-determination, African cultural reclamation, and academic excellence. These schools are referred to in the literature as pan-African or African-centered schools because pan-Africanist ideology, the belief that all African people are one, was a centralizing theme for identity formation, school pedagogy, and political and economic mobilization. Grounded in the diasporic history and the culture(s) of African people, these Black-controlled school environments aimed to enable Black students to feel more connected to, represented in, and empowered by the educational process (Shockley & Frederick, 2010). Such schools and supplemental education programs were established in Black communities in Detroit, Michigan; Chicago, Illinois; East Palo Alto, California; Philadelphia, Pennsylvania; and Trenton, New Jersey. However, Washington, DC is the veritable birthplace of the African-centered education movement, as it is home to some of the earliest alternative schools and programs.

Student activist Don Freeman, along with poet Gaston Neal, created one of the earliest schools, the New School for Afro-American Thought, in 1965 (Humanities Council, 2010). The New School was a privately funded cultural and educational center that operated on 14th Street and Florida Avenue, NW for the six years of its existence. A documentary on the history of the school's formation states that it "became a neighborhood nexus for political debates, educational forums, and performances by artists" (Humanities Council, 2010). With its overtly pan-Africanist agenda, the New School stands among the forerunners in African-centered education. Later, three significant institutions in the African-centered educational movement emerged in DC: Ujamaa Shule, Nationhouse/Positive Action Center, and ROOTS Activity Learning Center. All of these institutions have been impacted, in varying ways, by changes brought about by gentrification.

Ujamaa Shule

Ujamaa Shule (Ujamaa), is the oldest full-time, independent, African-centered school in Washington, DC (see Figure 12.1). Ujamaa was founded by Dr. El Sezengakulu Zulu, a former student activist and graduate of Howard University School of Law. The historic institution has provided African-centered education to children in the DC area for nearly 50 years. For many of those years, the school operated from its current location at 1554 8th Street, NW, in the heart of the Shaw community, one of the most rapidly gentrifying areas in the city (Hyra, forthcoming). A considerable amount of commercial development has occurred there in recent years, including the renovation of the historic Northern Market,

FIGURE 12.1 The Ujamaa School. From: Derek Hyra.

or O Street Market. The Market, which was abandoned for decades, now houses a new Giant Foods Store and upscale residential apartments.

Across from the O Street Market, on N Street, many of the low-cost apartments have been replaced by a sleek set of condominiums. A block away from Ujamaa is a vivid and contradictory example of the reality of class inequality in the city. Directly across from the new condominiums on 7th Street sits Bread for the City, a nonprofit organization that provides an array of services, including low-cost medical services at its Zacchaeus Free Clinic. On any given day, a collection of Black men, varying in age from 20 something to 60 something, can be found hanging out in the front of the stores of this village of buildings. They are talking, laughing, and recovering from the previous night's escapades. It is unclear if most or any of them work, or even if it is the same group of men who hang out there each day. They stand outside of the liquor store next to Bread and the Clinic, a veritable *Tally's Corner* (Liebow, 1967) of today. Yet the men's tenure on the corner may be soon coming to an end. In the past year, new urbane shops have opened, including a gourmet coffee shop and a pet store, early indicators that the neighborhood is changing and will not accommodate the likes of 21st-century "loiterers."

The new developments stand in contrast to the slightly aged, three-story, yellow structure that is Ujamaa Shule. Several members of the pan-African community have reported that the school has received complaints from White neighbors about the noise level of the school and appearance of the façade. The school's founder, Baba Zulu, was unwilling to comment for this chapter, as he is extremely protective of Ujamaa. However, a community member and supporter of Ujamaa, Raymond Boku (a pseudonym), offered his thoughts.

> To my knowledge, there haven't been many complaints. They've faced a little pressure, they had to paint the school and move the school buses on the lot because they were considered an eyesore, but that's about it.

Mr. Boku comments on the changes he has seen slowly occur over the past 25 years or so, noting the connections between the violent crack/cocaine epidemic of the 1980s and the subsequent decline of many Black neighborhoods.

> When I grew up in the community, there was a lot of drugs and violence around 7th and P. People got locked up and their houses just sat there. I went away to college in the 80s and came back and those houses had been bought by White people. There was a time when you wouldn't see a White person walking down the street, but now about 85% of the neighborhood is White.

The 40-something-year-old community member went on to share his thoughts on the future of the school. Mr. Boku is concerned about eminent domain, the ability of the state to seize property that has been slated for development, and thinks that Baba Zulu, as the owner of the property, should sell the building or convert it into apartments and lease it to tenants. He estimates that the property is worth millions and would garner a handsome sum that could be used to open several other Ujamaa schools throughout DC. He admits that the school's founder opposes this idea. Mr. Boku's thoughts reflect a genuine concern about the school and the conflicting ideas between members of the pan-African community on how best to respond to some of the challenges gentrification engenders.

Baba Zulu's resistance to selling the property is understandable given that Black property ownership has historically been so tenuous. Persevering through the racist practices of redlining and discriminatory lending has made acquiring property in parts of DC a laudable accomplishment. In addition, selling a property that has been a pillar in the pan-African community for decades may be interpreted as yielding to gentrification and an endorsement of capitalism, a system many Black nationalists repudiate. Yet Mr. Boku remains somewhat optimistic, stating that even the newcomers in the neighborhood recognize the school's contribution. "A lot of children have come through the school. I believe they [Whites] think he is doing something good. If they wanted to come after him, they would." Another community member, Mama Safona (a pseudonym), argues that the school is constantly under scrutiny by the White residents in the neighborhood, who "don't come in calm and peaceful, but who complain and raise hell." This constant assault, she states, is yet "another thing schools like these have to deal with."

NationHouse

NationHouse[5] is another pioneering DC African-centered independent educational institution. The school was founded by four Howard University student activists: Akili Anderson, Kwame Agyei Akoto, Akua Serwaa Akoto, and Kehembe Eichelberger. For 32 years, it occupied a large, brick, corner building at 770 Park Road, NW, in the rapidly gentrifying Petworth neighborhood. The school's red, black, green, and yellow exterior had huge wooden Adinkra[6] symbols affixed to it, signaling to others that it is not a typical house or building. NationHouse opened its doors in 1974, expanding its educational capacity as the founding families and surrounding African-centered community grew. Nationhouse served as not only a school, but as a cultural center for pan-Africanists in DC, a place where people would convene for lectures, community meetings, Kwanzaa programs, fundraisers, Akoms (Akan religious ceremonies), and other nation-building events. Rather unexpectedly, the stately structure at Park Road closed in 2012 and the school relocated to the Deanwood area in the northeastern part of the District.

Baba Agyei, as he is called in the pan-African community, has served as Nationhouse's executive director since its opening. Baba Agyei is from Columbus, Mississippi and received his baccalaureate and master's degrees from Howard University. A trained historian, Baba Agyei recalled some of the changes he saw take place in the area over the past 30 years. He stressed how changes to the neighborhood and redevelopment had severely reshaped the composition of the community.

> Two African [Black] men who owned metalworking shops that did work for the school have closed. [Additionally,] the Black women's business office building closed; the auto repair shop closed, two Black churches in the neighborhood . . . are gone. Well, one changed hands twice, the first time it was sold to a Black congregation, the second time to a Latino congregation.

He asserts that many of these changes were brought on by the increased real estate investment in the neighborhood that followed the construction of the Petworth Metro station on Georgia Avenue, just blocks away from the school's former location on Park Road. After the addition of the subway, other business development increased, which amplified property taxes in the neighborhood.

> Gentrification is happening all over. [Former Mayor Adrian] Fenty encouraged and facilitated its progress. He made the city very attractive to

young White folks, professional folks. Being Chocolate City is no longer fashionable.

Although plans for DC's redevelopment were in place prior to Fenty's tenure as mayor, he and former Mayor Anthony Williams have become the "faces" of gentrification among many in the city. Baba added that many families had started moving to the Northeast quadrant of the city and Prince George's County. The combined effect meant that change was imminent.

> The increase in taxes and inspections and the decrease in enrollment had become financially burdensome. We made the decision as a family to relocate if we were to survive. It was made reluctantly, but we did what we had to do. So we decided to move to be closer to our current population of families located in NE [Northeast DC] and Prince George's County.

Other tensions that affected the school's decision to move were the opening of a police substation on the same block as NationHouse and the repeated inspections the school was being subjected to from the DC Public School Board. Baba shared how he resolved the situation. "At one time we had 4 or 5 inspectors in our office at one time. I told them we don't take public money, so you have to leave. And they did."

NationHouse is now located on 61st and Dix Street, in DC's political Ward 7, an area very different economically and demographically from its previous Park Road location in Ward 4. Yet Baba asserts that changes are happening there as well. Today's NationHouse sits across the street from a public housing development. As the city continues to demolish what remains of these low-income residences, more upscale development will take place. Baba acknowledges the magnitude of this trend that is impacting communities in DC and across the country.

> We don't see it as something we need to fight. You can't fight it. It's inevitable. You just adapt to it and if we have to move again, we'll make that decision as a family.

ROOTS Activity Learning Center

ROOTS Activity Learning Center,[7] established by Dr. Bernida Thomas in 1977, is another independently founded African-centered school with a long and successful history of providing quality African-centered education in Washington, DC. The independent school is comprised of two abutting buildings located at 6222 North Capitol Street, NW. During an interview with ROOTS director

Dr. Thomas, better known as Mama Bernida, she offered her general views on how gentrification has impacted pan-African spaces:

> It's taking away our restaurants, it's taking away our bookstores, it's taking away our cultural centers . . . it's turning those spaces that make us feel comfortable and make us feel a part of humanity, that celebrate us, and it's taking those spaces and turning them into European spaces.

This conversation revealed her belief that spaces of African identity expression enable people to maintain a sense of connection and well-being in a covertly racist, consumerist, and capitalist culture. It allows them space to express religious freedom and cultural values, where they can safely adorn themselves symbolically, ideologically, and materially in their understanding of African culture and identity.

Mama Bernida also discussed the "predatory tone of developers and investors," who see buildings as vehicles to capital rather than the cultural and political institutions they are viewed as by the pan-African community.

BT: Developers are coming in and they're offering very high prices for the property, and of course they know they can do a lot of things to the property, so it's a difficult situation.

MC: So they've approached you?

BT: They've approached everybody!!! EVERYBODY!! You know. But what I know is [that] they can build up five stories on both buildings, they can make billions and that's just not gon' happen. Kamari [her granddaughter] is gonna own this, she's in college. It ain't gon' be about that. Even though the taxes are TREMENDOUS! And personally I have no intention of selling my house that I've been in forever and ever, raised both of my children in.

Mama Bernida also shared the surprising revelation that the first White family enrolled in ROOTS Activity Learning Center this year. I chose to include the full conversation here in an attempt to convey Mama Bernida's shock and surprise.

BT: Well, actually to my total surprise we had our first White client at the private school ... this young White couple with their infant baby about 15 months old and they came to ROOTS with their baby and paid for whole year, I'm like [opens mouth widely in surprise]. I'm like put your jaw back up (laughs). The child is still an infant but we have the best infant/toddler center. We are considered gold status by the DC government so we know why they came.

MC: Do you anticipate that more will come?

BT: I'm like wow! I don't know. That blew me.

MC: Did it shock you because they came or because they paid for the whole year up front?

BT: BOTH!

MC: And they know that you are an African-centered school?

BT: YES! They know. It's clear. You know, you can't tell somebody they can't come the only thing you can do is give them the parent handbook and tell 'em who you are and what you are.

MC: So what happens when five more [White] families come in September?

BT: Exactly. I have no idea. I don't even have a plan.

Mama Bernida reports that, at one time, Blacks would pay their full year's tuition up front, and invest in an African-centered education for their children. Yet few are able to do so today and even fewer, she laments, are supporting independent African-centered schools. She fears the long-term effect this will have on the future of independent schools and subsequently the future of Black people. As she explains,

> If Black people would put their money where their mouth is, we can sustain our African centered schools . . . or one day . . . like they say, we used to have our own banks and our own this and our own that. We'll be saying we used to have African-centered schools that taught our children. I'm saying if Black people don't say, I'm putting my money where my mouth is, it's gonna die out. It's gonna die because Black people sometime feel like they're just entitled to have whatever is free. But freedom is not free.

Mama Bernida expressed concern about today's economic conditions, which have contributed to family instability and a growing homeless population at the school. She notes that many of the children are transient and fail to maintain continuous enrollment. She offered,

> We've had children that will be here but they are not here and they come back but another group has left. It's very transient. It's transient in a way that keeps reducing the enrollment. So for the first 15 years we [ROOTS Charter School] housed 120 kids but last year it was down to 118. This year it's 91. At The Activity Learning Center. . . Baba Kamau, when he was alive, would have 30 children in the 5th–8th grade. And then in Mrs. Jones' class there were 20 children . . . so we'd always have 50 kids that were elementary age. But now it's something like 13 kids. Just 13 kids and they span from 1st grade through 8th grade and that is again because of the fact that parents are not paying to have their children educated.

Baba Agyei shared that two White families had expressed interest in enrolling their children in NationHouse when it was located on Park Road. He explained to these parents that the version of history the school taught, and its overall robust African-centered curriculum, would be contrary to what they had been taught in school. Agreeing with his assessment, the parents did not pursue enrollment any further. This too, demonstrates the different choices that leaders of African-centered institutions have made in how they negotiate changes occurring in their midst. On a related matter, he commented on the school's decreased enrollment, which, for a private institution that does not accept public funding, makes it difficult to sustain itself. Although the school refinanced and renovated its building on Park Road, it did not experience the increased enrollment it expected. According to Baba Agyei, the loan repayments, combined with the rise in property taxes and the declined income from fewer enrolled students simply became too "burdensome" (Personal communication, March 13, 2015). Thus, the school made the emotional and difficult decision to sell the property and relocate its services to another part of the city.

Religious Space

Besides education, another important function that these schools provide is space for other pan-Africanist groups to congregate, particularly religious groups. On Sundays, the cafeteria/multipurpose room at ROOTS Public Charter School is transformed into a worship space for the Temple of Nyame, one of the oldest Akan shrines in DC. During the 1960s, many urban-dwelling Blacks adopted precolonial traditional African religions as an expression of African identity. The Yoruba and Akan religions are perhaps the most widely practiced African diasporic religions in the United States. In her history of the Akan religion in the United States, Nana Asantwee Opokuwaa writes of the ancestral quest of the late Nana Yao Dinizulu I, who journeyed to Ghana in 1965 to learn of his family's origins. It was on that sojourn that Nana Dinizulu was initiated into the religion as an Akan priest. Upon his return to the United States, he began initiating Black men and women into the Akan religion and training them to be servants and worshippers of the Akan deities (Opokuwaa, 2005). Among those early initiates was Nana Kwabena Aboagye Brown from Mount Vernon, New York.

Nana Brown established the African Cultural and Religious Society (A.C.R.S) in 1973. A.C.R.S. was one of the pioneer organizations in the promotion and practice of traditional African culture in the Washington, DC area, In 1978, A.C.R.S. evolved into the Temple of Nyame, an Akan religious shrine based out of the Browns' home, located at 15th and T Streets, SE in the Anacostia neighborhood, another gentrifying area. The services of the Temple include spiritual consultations, medicinal herbal baths, marriage and family counseling, initiations, spiritual rites, and other activities. Each summer, the Temple of Nyame holds a public ceremony in the spacious yard of the Browns' Anacostia home. People from the pan-African community and African religious groups within DC and beyond come together for prayer, drumming, singing, dancing, food, and the worship of Akan and Yoruba deities. Similar ceremonies are held at various points during the year, and the festivities often go into the late night hours. I've attended past ceremonies and often neighbors, mostly men, gather in lawn chairs, just outside the fence, to observe the events as if watching a ball game or a show. Although they never join the service, neither do they complain or disrupt the events. On occasion, the few who remain for the feast at the end of the service are offered plates of food in the spirit of neighborliness. As one of the oldest and most visible Akan shrines in Washington, DC, I sought Nana Brown's perspective on the changes he sees occurring in the city he has called home for more than 40 years. Nana Kwabena comments,

> I see the changes around me, so I know they are coming. We haven't had any problems yet, but we could never practice our religion in another neighborhood. Right now we are insulated here among our people. The gods protect us.

With the growth of its congregation, the Temple had to find alternative space for its weekly worship services. Mama Bernida responded to its need, and in 2014, the Temple of Nyame began holding its lively Sunday religious services at the ROOTS Public Charter School. Although DC is a multicultural city, these groups are still marginalized for their religious practices. The elements of ancestral reverence, deity propitiation, spirit possession, spiritual cleaning and healing, and ritualistic offerings of food continue to be viewed negatively in mainstream society, where Judeo-Christian religion is considered the norm.

ROOTS exists as a safe space for Temple of Nyame worshippers, whereas prayer and singing in Yoruba and Twi, and spirit trance by the deities, may be frowned upon in other spaces. Nana Kwabena agrees that spaces like ROOTS are essential to the sustainability of pan-African religious and community groups who need a place of "their own" to connect with ancestors and gods, and to express themselves in a way meaningful to them as a people. With the increased cost of real estate in DC, ROOTS also gives the Temple of Nyame a space to expand its visibility and outreach, without the financial burden of purchasing additional property.

African-centered educational institutions and organizations are the most impactful and enduring creations of the Black Nationalist/Pan-Africanist movement of the 1960s. The influence of this educational approach is evident in the numerous African-centered supplementary programs, public school models, and other charter schools who attempt to emulate the independent school model (Giddings, 2001; Henry, 1998; Murrell, 1999; Weber, 1993). In DC, several charter schools have been founded with an African-centered aim such as Tree of Life Community Public Carter School, NIA Public Charter School, and KIMA

Academy of Magnificent Achievers. Mama Bernida started the ROOTS Public Charter School in 1999. Of these institutions, only ROOTS PCS and Tree of Life Community PCS are still open.

Conclusion

For pan-Africanists in DC, African-centered schools are more than brick-and-mortar constructions; they are institutions of empowerment, community, and resistance against oppression. They operate as veritable village centers, often used for cultural entertainment, summer programs, African rites of passage, and religious ceremonies. They allow for the expression of religious freedom and cultural identity where individuals can adorn themselves symbolically and materially in the riches of African culture. Where individuals can speak back to hegemony, and strategize their involvement in African liberation efforts. Further, these spaces allow a neighborhood vibrancy and diversity that is often lost when gentrification overtakes a community and erases its history, White washing its physical space.

It is not my intention to portray pan-African institutions as powerless victims here, but to demonstrate how these three institutions have had to make difficult choices to survive in a changing city. Prior to the relocation of NationHouse, these schools were all situated in communities that have and are continuing to experience redevelopment and have had to negotiate the economic and demographic shifts that are germane to this process. Neither is it my intention to vilify all Whites in the city or argue against economic vibrancy. Rather, my goal has been to demonstrate how communities and institutions are also affected by these dynamics and to give voice to what stands to be lost as certain neighborhoods revitalize. Just as Eshu, the Yoruba deity of chance and opportunity, is believed to stand at the crossroads of change, the pan-African community also stands at that juncture, invoking the guidance of the gods, as it faces an uncertain future.

Notes

1 Eshu, the West African Yoruba deity, is believed to be the holy messenger who translates the petitions of humans into the language of Olodumare (God). Yoruba practitioners seek Eshu, the first and last deity (Orisha) invoked in ritual space, to help them make good choices at life's crossroads. Source: Karade, B. I. (1994). *The Handbook of Yoruba Religious Concepts*. Boston, MA: Red Wheel/Weiser.

2 Austin argues that Black nationalism in 20-century America is a term applied to a wide range of phenomena, from "nation building, to ethnic politics to cultural nationalism to public opinion" (2006, p. 22).

3 Information about Pyramid Books and Baba Hodari Abdul-Ali obtained at www. sourcewatch.org/index.php?title=Hodari_Abdul_Ali Accessed June 12, 2012.

4 Sankofa Video, Café, and Books is owned by filmmaker Haile Gerima, most noted for his film, *Sankofa* (1993), which tells the story of Mona, a Black supermodel who is transported through time and finds herself on a plantation during the days of slavery.

5 For more information on NationHouse School, visit www.nationhouse.org.

6 Adinkra is the name given to colorful, hand-painted, hand-embroidered cloth traditionally used for mourning by the Akan people of Ghana and the Ivory Coast (Cote d'Ivoire). Stylistic symbols called Adinkra symbols are printed on these cloths. Traditionally, the cloths and symbols expressed the wearers' feelings and sentiments about the deceased. They are used worldwide today and in popular culture. For more information, visit www.amazon.com/The-Adinkra-dictionary-visual-language/dp/0966153219. One of the most exhaustive pieces written on Adinkra symbology is *The Adinkra Dictionary: A Visual Primer on the Language of Adinkra* by W. Bruce Willis, 1998.

7 For more information on ROOTS Activity Learning Center, visit www.rootsactivitylc.org.

References

Akoto, K. A. (1992). *Nationbuilding: Theory and practice in Afrikan centered education*. Washington, DC: Pan Afrikan World Institute.

Austin, A. (2006). *Race, black nationalism, and Afrocentrism in the twentieth century*. New York, NY: New York University Press.

Giddings, G. J. (2001). Infusion of Afrocentric content into the school curriculum: Toward an effective movement. *Journal of Black Studies, 31*(4), 462–482.

Henry, A. (1998). Invisible and womanish: Black girls negotiating their lives in an African-centered school in the USA. *Race, Ethnicity, and Education, 1*(2): 151–170.

Hilliard, A. G. (1992). Behavioral style, culture, and teaching and learning. *Journal of Negro Education, 61*(3), 370–377.

Hyra, D. (2012). Conceptualizing the new urban renewal: Comparing the past to the present. *Urban Affairs Review, 48*(4): 498–527.

Hyra, D. (2015). The back-to-the-city movement: Neighbourhood redevelopment and processes of political and cultural displacement. *Urban Studies, 52*(10), 1753–1773.

Hyra, D. (forthcoming). *Making the gilded ghetto: Race, class, and politics in the cappuccino city*. Chicago, IL: The University of Chicago Press.

Kifano, S. (1996). Afrocentric education in supplementary schools: Paradigm and practice at the Mary McLeod Bethune Institute. *Journal of Negro Education*, 209–218.

Liebow, E. (1967). *Tally's Corner: A study of Negro streetcorner men*. Boston, MA: Little Brown.

Lomotey, K. (1992). Independent black institutions: African-centered educational models. *The Journal of Negro Education, 61*, 455–462.

Murrell, P. C. (1999). Chartering the village: The making of an African-centered charter school. *Urban Education, 33*(5), 565–583.

Opokuwaa, N. A. K. (2005). *Akan protocol: Remembering the traditions of our ancestors*. Lincoln, NE: Authors' Choice Press.

Prince, S. (2014). *African-Americans and gentrification in Washington, D.C.: Race, class, and social justice in the nation's capital*. Burlington, VT: Ashgate.

Ruble, B. (2010). *Washington's U Street: A biography*. Baltimore, MD/Washington, DC: Johns Hopkins University/Woodrow Wilson.

Sefa Dei, G. J. (1994). Afrocentricity: A cornerstone of pedagogy. *Anthropology & Education Quarterly, 25*(1), 3–28.

Shockley, K., & Frederick, R. (2010). Constructs and dimensions of Afrocentric education. *Journal of Black Studies, 40*(6), 1212–1233.

Shujaa, M. J. (1994). *Too much schooling, too little education: A paradox of black life in white societies.* Trenton, NJ: Africa World Press.

Weber, M. (1993). Immersed in an educational crisis: Alternative programs for African American males. *Stanford Law Review, 45,* 1099–1131.

13

"IT'S COMPLICATED . . . "

Long-Term Residents and Their Relationships to Gentrification in Washington, DC

Kathryn Howell

When the DCUSA complex opened in the Columbia Heights neighborhood of Washington, DC in 2008, District residents had one of their first "big box" retail opportunities anchored by Target. The three-story mall was the centerpiece of a 13-acre mixed-use redevelopment that would have been unheard of outside of downtown DC a decade before. Contrasted against previous large-scale redevelopments in Washington, DC—notably the urban renewal that destroyed African American neighborhoods in Southwest DC in the 1950s and the downtown development of Chinatown beginning in the late 1990s—elected officials, developers, and some new residents considered this development a win-win for neighborhood residents and the District government. Columbia Heights was considered an unsafe place for investment because of high rates of crime, gang violence, and poverty, and the District's investment in the form of discounted land and infrastructure investment would spur massive redevelopment and change for the neighborhood. Residents would benefit from cleaner streets, increased amenities, reductions in crime, and improved city services.

Neighborhood residents—particularly homeowners and White residents—as well as the local community development corporations, city agencies, and elected officials saw the planning process as inclusive of neighborhood goals and needs. The DC Department of Housing and Community Development (DHCD) partnered with the Development Corporation of Columbia Heights (DCCH) to bring together more than 250 residents over a year to develop a neighborhood plan that included guidance for the selection of real estate developers. The design was a multimodal, mixed-use, compact design atop a Metro station, and all residential development required a 20% set-aside of affordable housing (Washington Architectural Foundation, 1997). At the same time, tenant organizers, neighborhood residents, and mission-driven developers used legal protections and funds from DHCD to preserve almost 2,200 units of subsidized and market-affordable housing throughout the neighborhood (Department of Housing and Community Development, 2009).

Although many long-term, low-income residents remained, the rising rents and home values meant that the neighborhood changed from being primarily an affordable, largely low-income, majority African American neighborhood to a more mixed-income neighborhood with a growing share of non-Hispanic White residents (see Figure 13.1). While African Americans continue to represent the largest share of the neighborhood's population (39.8%), the non-Hispanic White population increased by 330% between 2000 and 2010, rising to 26.7% of the neighborhood's population (US Census, 2010). These demographic changes, in combination with the physical redevelopment, were visual indications of the way long-term minority residents' position in the neighborhood would be different moving forward. While 20% of the total housing stock in Columbia Heights continues to house low-income residents of color, the spaces outside their homes changed—as did the power they had to act in the community.

This chapter examines the remarkable history of redevelopment in Columbia Heights, the government, advocate, and resident actors who were part of that redevelopment, and the ways the lives of residents who remained in the neighborhood were affected by the approaches to neighborhood change. This chapter argues that the District of Columbia government, neighborhood groups, housing advocates, and developers instituted some of the best practices in urban planning and housing policy, which sought to deconcentrate poverty and focus on dense, mixed-use, mixed-income, and multimodal transit-oriented development. The neighborhood was recognized by both the Urban Land Institute and the Congress for New Urbanism within two years of opening the "big box" retail at the DC USA project (Baker, 2010; Congress for the New Urbanism, 2009). However, these best practices exposed a tension between neighborhood planning and citywide goals, as well as the conflicting goals within the neighborhood. While the residents who remained retained power in the collective and private spaces of their homes and residential buildings, the dramatic changes in the concentration of poverty and race meant that African American and low-income residents' ability to control public and social spaces in the community was challenged by the neighborhood's changing form. More importantly, a narrative of dysfunction about Columbia Heights from 1968 to 2002 continues to justify changes throughout the neighborhood.

Methods

The data for this chapter come from an ethnographic study (2010–2012) on the effects of change on Columbia Heights' long-term residents. This study included participant and direct observation in public spaces, community meetings, public hearings, meetings of nonprofit housing and community advocates, and District government agency staff. I also interviewed 55 residents, advocates, agency staff members, and elected officials. The project also relied on my experience working as a policy specialist in District government from 2007 to 2009. Finally, I analyzed historical planning and policy documents; newspaper articles, photos, maps, and public testimony.

Planning for Place

Across the United States, increases in residential construction and subsequent demographic changes have resulted in conflicts in urban neighborhoods home to low-income, minority communities throughout the second half of the 20th century. These changes have been rooted in policies that have been in place since the mid-20th century when cities, in partnership with the federal government, sought to counter the flight of jobs and residents to the suburbs—itself encouraged by federal policy—by "modernizing" central city neighborhoods and business districts (Jackson, 2008; Kruse, 2007). Initially justified as slum clearance, in the wake of turn-of-the-century depictions of conditions in the tenements and slums of US cities, these redevelopment projects have typically eschewed public processes and ignored existing community members and institutions to "revitalize" urban centers. These redevelopment efforts have implicitly prioritized the knowledge and political or social goals of planners, policy makers, and engineers over knowledge of the existing community (Jackson, 2008; Stone, 1989).

Urban renewal and highway development projects had a particularly strong impact on many central city ethnic and low-income communities in the middle of the 20th century, in many cases physically dividing neighborhoods, razing buildings, and removing existing residents to make way for future development. The resulting backlash, in the context of the civil rights movements of the late 20th century, engendered a shift in thinking about the nature of low-income neighborhoods, the competence of neighborhood-based groups, and, for a time, a trend toward greater support for community-based development. Community development corporations thrived briefly through direct federal funding that, although short-lived, created the framework for community action over the past 30 years (Rubin, 2000; Twelvetrees, 1989). Despite its problems, urban redevelopment has remained a focal point of federal and local policy throughout the past century (Hyra, 2008; Jackson, 1985).

Current federal housing policy focuses on physically changing historically low-income neighborhoods through direct intervention in programs such as HOPE VI (Goetz, 2013) and through market-based, large-scale developments (Hyra, 2008). Despite its stated concern with providing housing options for low-income residents, policy rarely addresses the existing and resulting social organization and infrastructure of the community. The focus on physical place over social space, or the spaces of interaction, has resulted in fundamental changes in the collective voice, identity, and power of low-income communities (Crenson, 1983; Davis, 1991), the acceptable social norms of behavior within the communities (Freeman, 2006; Venkatesh, 2006), and on the social networks of individual households within these communities (Kleit, 2005).

The causes and nature of neighborhood change have long been debated. The Chicago School of Sociology argued for a system of neighborhood succession whereby neighborhoods naturally transition from "good" to "bad" over time, with good neighborhoods moving to the periphery (Park, 1925/1984). The argument for a natural succession set the stage for a technical, apolitical view of neighborhood change that has influenced policy and practice by normalizing central city decline (Dear, 2002). More recently, after years of decline stemming from failed urban renewal projects, White flight, and long-term disinvestment, cities have begun to frame neighborhood change in terms of the positive effects of poverty deconcentration on low-income households and on crime rates in order to encourage investment by developers and new residents (Newman, 2004). Researchers have framed neighborhood change as emerging from both intentional investment by upper-middle-class residents (Smith, 1979) and from targeted investment by development capital and city governments (Harvey, 1996). Harvey (1996) argues place-focused redevelopment emphasizes the exchange value of neighborhoods over their use value, thus devaluing existing physical and cultural structures.

As neighborhoods change, long-term practices in federal and local housing policy have focused on building and preserving affordable housing—defined in terms of units preserved or created, rather than the existing or resultant communities. This implicitly allows future low-income renters to benefit from the new amenities gentrifiers bring such as improved infrastructure, parks, retail, and services (Freeman, 2006). The focus on individual and unit-based development in federal policy places housing in a vacuum apart from the communities in which it is situated. Mobility programs like Moving to Opportunity (Briggs, Popkin, & Goering, 2010; Goering, 2005) and Gautreaux (Rosenbaum, 2000), as well as place-based programs like HOPE VI (Manzo, Kleit, & Couch, 2008) and tax incentives such as the federal Low-Income Housing Tax Credit (Julian & McCain, 2009) exemplify the idea that housing units placed in neighborhoods with prescribed components such as low poverty or racial concentration are sufficient to address the needs of low-income communities. Programs also increasingly emphasize the importance of urban design, at times arguing that good design can foster inclusion (Cisneros, 2009; Talen, 2002), often ignoring preexisting histories, cultures, and social institutions in those communities (Day, 2003; Kleit, 2005).

In addition to the challenges inherent in these types of redevelopment, symbolic boundaries between groups in changing neighborhoods, particularly between ethnic groups, have been reinforced by the years of social and spatial segregation that have caused "white suburban residents to be not just ignorant of but actually afraid of the city." Further, "they have grown up in isolation, separated from others, and have developed their attitudes and behaviors toward African Americans in the absence of risk and productive interaction. They are nurtured on simplified myths of difference, danger, and hostility" (Goldsmith, 2002, p. 133). The segregation and White flight that concentrated poverty and race in the urban core also concentrated White middle-class households in the suburbs (Kruse, 2007), changing the expectations and social norms of suburban middle-class residents who subsequently have moved to cities in the most recent back-to-the-city movement. These conflicting expectations and urban fear may help to explain why, contrary to research that argued that the proximity of low-income residents to higher-income residents would lead to increased access to social networks, Kleit (2005) and Freeman (2006) both found little evidence that new residents in changing communities were interacting with long-term residents.

Housing activists and scholars have revived the community development frame for affordable housing by focusing on the relationship between housing and justice. Some authors describe this as part of a basic "right to the city" (Mitchell, 2003), "the right to change ourselves by changing the city" (Harvey, 2008b), or as an individual right to decide where to live (Julian & McCain, 2009). Mitchell differentiates between "rights talk," or the discourse of rights, and legal rights. He argues that while discourse has power and can help to justify power, rights talk provides "a set of instructions about the use of power. But they do so by becoming institutionalized—that is, by becoming practices backed up by force," through the creation of a legal right (Mitchell, 2003, p. 27). He further argues that the institutionalization of rights produces space by changing the way power is used and appropriated.

Notably missing from policy and planning discussions is how changing demographics and community norms will affect remaining low-income residents. As balances of power and interests in changing communities shift within neighborhood organizations, public discourse, and city government, new and old residents increasingly conflict, and often, long-term residents can no longer take an active role in their communities (Crenson, 1983; Davis, 1991; Freeman, 2006).

Columbia Heights, 1904–1996

Columbia Heights was the District's first streetcar suburb at the turn of the 20th century. Located up the hill from the downtown areas, Columbia Heights has been a crossroads of race and class. When the neighborhood first developed, it was exclusively White and was proudly "free from the objectionable classes" (Columbia Heights Citizens' Association, 1904). At the heart of the neighborhood, 14th Street, NW grew into a major shopping and entertainment district in Washington,

DC, which was largely segregated until the 1950s. However, it was flanked by Howard University and the Shaw/U Street corridor, an African American community that developed after the Civil War and became a center for Black culture and education (Ruble, 2010).

Columbia Heights itself remained segregated through the use of restrictive covenants until the 1950s. In 1955, a local newspaper reported that the all-White, all-homeowner neighborhood association could not remain solvent because the membership had declined significantly. By 1960, seven years after President Eisenhower desegregated DC schools, the share of African Americans in Columbia Heights exceeded 75%, while citywide, African Americans were only 54% of the population (The Evening Star, 1955).

Throughout the early 1960s, Columbia Heights, like many African American neighborhoods in the District, became largely disinvested by the city and developers and housing quality declined as inspections grew less frequent. African Americans often paid higher rents for lower-quality housing in places like Columbia Heights because they were typically shut out of suburban communities and higher-income White neighborhoods west of Rock Creek Park, resulting in rising frustration in the community (Clement, 2004/2005; Cherkasky, 1996/1997).

By 1968, U Street, DC's "Black Broadway," had also become the center of African American activism. Organizations such as the Poor People's Campaign, the Student Nonviolent Coordinating Committee (SNCC), and the Black United Front were located around 14th and U Streets, NW. On the evening of April 4, 1968, when the news spread to 14th Street that Martin Luther King Jr. had been assassinated, African Americans, led by Stokely Carmichael, who worked with

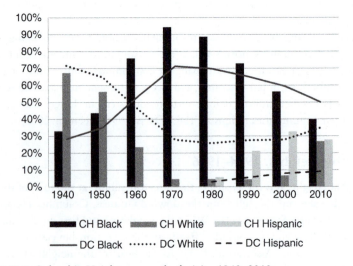

FIGURE 13.1 Columbia Heights race and ethnicity, 1940–2010.

SNCC in DC, marched down 14th Street to request that business owners close their stores out of respect. But soon the crowd was out of hand and rioting and looting began. Over the next 12 days, 14,000 federal troops were called in to restore order and prevent additional rioting near federal buildings, and to avoid the police violence that was defining riots elsewhere (Jaffe & Sherwood, 1994; White et al., 2008). By the end of the riots, half of the property on 14th Street, NW was destroyed and 5,000 permanent jobs were lost, most of which were low-wage, low-skilled jobs (Franklin, 1968; Weil, 1968).

After the riots, Columbia Heights went through several efforts to rebuild with limited success. In the first few years, the federal National Capital Planning Commission (NCPC) through the Redevelopment Land Authority (RLA) developed Urban Renewal Area Plans in the three riot corridors: H Street, NE, 7th Street, NW, and upper 14th Street, NW. However, the RLA was fraught with complaints of slow and poor management of previous processes, and the NCPC was too federally focused. A 1983 report from the University of the District of Columbia argued that organizations planning at the neighborhood level felt that "their plans ... seemed to have been treated as wish-lists by District and federal officials, to be gratified for a time, then dropped" (Paige, 1983, p. 63).

The riots sparked a movement in the neighborhood for community control of redevelopment, businesses, and housing. Jason, a young planner who was responsible for developing the plan, explained that this was the beginning of Black activism in Columbia Heights and recalled that RLA's approach was to allow the community to drive the planning process. Newspapers, and Jason's own experience, illustrated a publicly contentious relationship between the community organizations and RLA as the neighborhood mobilized opposition to the external imposition of an urban renewal plan. Unfortunately, African Americans in Columbia Heights, as elsewhere in riot-torn corridors, did not have access to the capital that would have allowed for community control in the neighborhood. A 1973 plan for the 14th Street Urban Renewal Area stated that the neighborhood "has the typical characteristics of a depressed decayed area—widespread poverty, high rates of transiency and dependency, unemployment and underemployment, vacant and substandard dwelling units, high crime levels particularly narcotics trade, and a burned out half abandoned commercial strip" (Community Services Advisory Committee, 1973, p. 2).

As a result of the lack of private investment, the only redevelopment in Columbia Heights after the riots was through federal programs for low-income housing, creating significant long-term affordability along 14th Street at the center of the neighborhood. However, many parcels of land remained razed and vacant, and the neighborhood continued to decline, resulting in dangerous housing conditions, violence, and gangs, reflecting the hallmarks of socioeconomically segregated neighborhoods. Latinos, moving from Adams Morgan and Mount Pleasant, grew in number in Columbia Heights in the wake of violent civil wars in their home countries, opening businesses and filling rent-controlled apartments in the northern part of Columbia Heights. The neighborhood grew more diverse, such that between 1980 and 2000, the Latino population grew from 5.4% of the neighborhood's population to 32.7%, representing one of the highest concentrations of Latinos in Washington, DC.

Redevelopment and Neighborhood Change

By the 1990s, Columbia Heights had already started to change as new residents who could not afford the nearby Adams Morgan neighborhood or the U Street Corridor moved east and north into Columbia Heights. In 1997, the Development Corporation of Columbia Heights (DCCH), in partnership with the Department of Housing and Community Development (DHCD) and the Washington Architectural Foundation (WAF), convened a two-day charrette for neighborhood residents to discuss the neighborhood's vision for the future of Columbia Heights. Between 250 and 300 residents attended. Organizers highlighted four issues that were unique to the neighborhood and would influence the changes in the community: the opening of a new Metro stop at 14th and Irving Streets in 1999; the significant acreage of city-owned land in the four blocks surrounding the Metro entrance; the interest in the parcels developers had already expressed; and the increases in population and income in the community. The planning process continued for a year after the charrette, and it included community meetings to obtain feedback on the work done by a smaller group of residents, city planners, and architects between meetings.

During the charrette, residents outlined the underlying principles they felt were important for the redevelopment. While the participants were considered representative of the neighborhood's population by White participants and organizers, this perception seems to be based on race only. None of the long-term, low-income, minority renters interviewed for this study participated, or felt included in the planning process. However, the charrette participants came to a consensus on the principles for the physical and social elements of community. Although residents had input about the types of development, the preservation of particular buildings, and the overall goals, what was not in doubt was the fact that the neighborhood would become intensively developed. The new plan was used as "mandatory guidance" in the request for proposals that was released for the parcels in 1998. While the process was considered collaborative by participants and elicited significant consensus, the implementation ran into significant problems as each group focused on different parts of the plan and different mechanisms for implementation.

As the city continued the process of physical planning, residents, tenant organizers, and mission- driven developers worked together to assert the rights of long-term residents to stay in the neighborhood. One of the primary tools used to ensure that residents could remain in their homes was the Tenant Opportunity to Purchase Act (TOPA). Passed in 1980 in response to gentrification pressures in Dupont Circle and Shaw, TOPA gives renters the right of first refusal when their buildings are for sale (96th Congress Testimony of Marion Barry, 1980). Tenants have the option to buy and create a cooperative or condominium ownership structure, or they can assign their rights to another developer who will retain it as rental. The city supports that right for low-income renters by offering rolling funding for acquisition and rehabilitation of multifamily buildings and by funding tenant organizers and technical assistance providers who help tenants through the challenging process of forming and incorporating a tenant association, selecting a developer, applying for funds, and managing redevelopment.

Between 1999 and 2009, 2,174 affordable units were created or preserved in Columbia Heights using District funds, either through TOPA or through traditional housing finance programs like the Low Income Housing Tax Credit or local Housing Production Trust Fund (Department of Housing and Community Development, 2009). In some cases, the units were already subsidized with Section 8 or HUD-insured mortgages, but others were market-affordable or rent-controlled buildings. A DHCD staff member involved in the redevelopment explained that the RLA plan required affordable housing set-asides in exchange for discounts on the sale of city-owned land, but:

> the affordable housing our agency has developed has proceeded parallel but outside the RLA's solicitations. We have saved on a case-by-case basis whole buildings from conversion, and our tenant First Right Purchase program has been instrumental in it. What affordable buildings remain today are almost 100% due to the fact that the District's law TOPA ... has saved whole blocks of buildings that would have otherwise converted to condos—so it's been a life-saver for saving what affordable housing does remain.

The bulk of affordable housing in this case was created as a result of a reactive policy. While 250 units were created through a planning process specifically for Columbia Heights, TOPA projects were not geographically targeted. As a result, projects in Columbia Heights competed with projects throughout the city for limited funds. There was no citywide mechanism for proactively addressing questions of affordable housing preservation in Columbia Heights or other gentrifying neighborhoods. While many households asserted their TOPA rights, a greater number moved because of rising costs, illegal evictions, intimidation, and normal migration. By 2012, nearly 20% of the housing units in the neighborhood were income-restricted through preservation or new construction. However, this number represents an overall loss of affordable housing in a neighborhood that was overwhelmingly affordable through subsidies and market affordability.

The neighborhood continues to change, but the large-scale residential and commercial development that defined the first decade of the 21st century in

Columbia Heights has slowed, and the population of primarily African American and Latino low-income renters has stabilized. The effects of the redevelopment extend beyond the built environment. Between 2000 and 2010, the population of White residents increased 330%, growing from 6.5% of the population to 26.7%, while the African American and Latino populations declined by 25% and 11%, respectively, now representing 39.8% and 27.8% of the neighborhood's population. Meanwhile, incomes have also shifted. Almost 20% of Columbia Heights households earn more than $100,000 per year, compared to only 6% in 2000. The percentage of residents earning less than $35,000 per year shrank from 63% to 38%.

The demographic changes and interviews with residents and planners suggest three primary eras of residents in Columbia Heights: those who moved to the neighborhood before the 1980s, those who arrived between 1980 and the charrette, and those who arrived in the midst of the redevelopment and beyond. Each group has a different perspective on the neighborhood and of the way its position in the neighborhood will be different moving forward, as the demographics and built environment shift. While many low-income, long-term residents have the right to stay in their buildings because of TOPA and can control those spaces against complaints from their new higher-income neighbors, the rules governing public spaces are controlled and ultimately implemented by new residents who have different expectations of public behavior, understandings of safety, and relationships to police power.

The narrative that emerged during the redevelopment framed Columbia Heights as a formerly beautiful shopping district with a theater, streetcar, and beautiful architecture. The riots in 1968, it was felt, were a turning point that destroyed the neighborhood. Until 2002, gang violence and drugs turned the neighborhood into a "war zone." Then the redevelopment changed it again and brought it back to its former glory. Implicitly, this narrative focuses entirely on the built environment and belittles the community and people who lived in Columbia Heights between 1968 and 2002 and built lives. This narrative about the redevelopment has impacted the way the neighborhood and its long-term residents—particularly people of color—are thought about and governed in public spaces.

However, in the midst of the violence in Columbia Heights, many long-term residents still have positive memories and a sense of ownership of the old neighborhood. As Melissa, executive director of a nonprofit that helped organize tenants to purchase their buildings, explained that many long-term residents often debated whether to leave the neighborhood when she first started working in Columbia Heights in the 1980s. Residents struggled to balance affordability, family ties, and safety. She said there was:

> This strong sense of "but this is where my people are from. I don't want to leave, and I'm going to stand my ground." So I think that kind of community of new young folks doesn't realize how bad it really was. But also how

much of a sense of "this is ours. We need to protect it." And so the tenant purchase stuff grew out of that. So when the tenants had an opportunity, we didn't have to say much to rah them up to get them to do bake sales and everything else they needed to do because they too had lived there for generations or years and felt this was theirs even though they didn't own it and may have been living in poor conditions.

Other residents, while also acknowledging the violence, spoke about picnics and barbeques in vacant lots in the neighborhood, sleeping in Meridian Hill/Malcolm X Park[1] on hot summer nights, or having parties in the parks throughout the neighborhood. Some talked about how they felt safer during the 1980s and 1990s because they knew their neighbors and had people who checked up on them in the community. The open spaces, although a space for criminal activity and seen as a sign of the neighborhood's decline, were also adapted as community social spaces. One space at the heart of the neighborhood, now a grocery store, was a large community garden. Pearl, an African American woman who has rented in the same building for 30 years, explained:

> From this building all the way to 14th Street, we had all that. It was a big basketball court. And then had benches out there the kids could sit. And then, right in back of us where there's a senior citizen buildin' was a huge field—went all the way to 14th Street. People planted gardens out there. Yea. It was . . . you know—and it was a beautiful sight to see then too.

Similarly, Columbia Heights and the surrounding neighborhoods have an important history for Latinos who have since moved to other neighborhoods in DC or to Prince George's County, Maryland. David, a Latino who has worked in community services in Columbia Heights and grew up in nearby Mount Pleasant, explained the connections that long-term residents and those who have left the neighborhood have with the local organizations and places in Columbia Heights:

> People walk by CARACEN [Central American Resource Center] all the time, and they're like I remember when I first applied for my citizenship. . . . And to people, it means a lot. I remember like kids—as a matter of fact there's this kid who's actually—he makes like $100,000 now. . . . And I remember he used to come to Latin American Youth Center when I used to volunteer there. And he still comes like no matter—if he's ever in the DC area, he always comes to Latin American Youth Center. But it's like that with everyone . . . you still come back to the place where you call home. And to those people, this place will never change. Even though you drive 'em out. You push 'em out. They still come back and they still feel like they're at home. They're more entitled to that piece of land that's owned by someone

that's new or come from other places—just 'cause they can't afford it doesn't mean that it's not theirs.

Those who lived in the neighborhood viewed the neighborhood's history with a mixture of pragmatism and nostalgia, acknowledging the challenges and sense of community that existed in their chosen community. Unfortunately, the story that is told by developers, newer affluent residents and city government is one of violence, self-destruction, and decline—a Wild West narrative that justified massive and ongoing change to tame, not just the physical, but social spaces in the neighborhood.

Collective Power, Public Spaces

Many residents remained in their neighborhood because of affordable housing preservation, property tax abatements for seniors, and rent control, but Columbia Heights dramatically changed around them—from the growth of a densely built environment to the demographic shift to a Whiter, more affluent population. A less visible change was the way in which new and old residents used, interacted in, and enforced norms in the neighborhood's public spaces. Washington, DC residents have a long history of using parks and open spaces as extensions of their homes that dates back to the days before air conditioning made row houses and apartment buildings bearable in the dense heat and humidity of the Southern summer. On street corners and in public parks, Columbia Heights has a strong history of people just hanging out. While some of these activities have involved illegal behaviors such as drug sales, the pervasive assumption by affluent residents who have arrived since redevelopment is that African American and Latino neighbors who hang out are engaging in illegal or dangerous activities. As the neighborhood has changed, new residents have imposed different expectations on the parks and sidewalks of Columbia Heights to the exclusion of many who have seen those spaces as part of their daily life for decades.

Daily Living

As the neighborhood has changed, the physical presence of minorities has not translated into Elijah Anderson's (2012) "Cosmopolitan Canopy" where no one group sets norms. New residents have that power, which has transcended social class. Ann, a single White woman who has been in the neighborhood 22 years, said that "one of the big challenges is that people don't come home, close the doors and live inside because this is definitely a community where people live outside." The indoor-outdoor tensions have been growing with new residents moving in. She shared a story recently where she had come home tired and focused and did not greet her neighbor Mr. Russell and another friend on the neighboring porch.

They told her about it later, and she described her own behavior as a "breach of etiquette" because Columbia Heights, like many of DC's African American neighborhoods, has a culture of acknowledging people when you pass them, and speaking to neighbors on their porches.

In the spring of 2012, developers presented a redevelopment plan before the ANC regarding the redevelopment of a property that residents had complained about for years as being an eyesore. In the summer, the developers brought the project before the ANC to get support for a variance that would increase the allowable floor-to-area ratio. The project was initially criticized because the design did not match the look and feel of the rest of the street. Taking that into consideration, they returned in the fall of 2012 with a new design, including a low stone wall to match the other properties along busy 13th Street. However, several commissioners soundly criticized the wall. One stated, "Walls invite significant amounts of loitering in this neighborhood" and create issues with hanging out. Another argued "It [the wall] is also an invitation for graffiti" because "any solid surface is a canvas." The developer and architect suggested that they could change the plan if this was not "safe and not sanitary in some ways."

Catharine, an African American professional who grew up and now owns a home in the neighborhood, discussed the hanging out as an important part of the community.

> I think there are a lot of things like that in our neighborhood for different people depending on where you are on the spectrum, and I think the parks are like that too. I'm not somebody who's going to go kick it at 14th and Girard Street [Park], but I like that it exists as something there. I also miss some of the people that I used to see hanging out on the street . . . like I would walk to work every day when I would work . . . and they would give me the weather report for the day or like tell me what was going on in the neighborhood, and I miss that sort of feeling.

For her, those who hung out in public places were part of her community—people who checked on her and made her safe in the neighborhood. They were part of the fabric of Columbia Heights that has largely been lost as spaces are redeveloped. Layers of race and class overwhelm the discussion. On one street where Melissa's organization provided technical assistance to two buildings, she has had constant battles with the high-income homeowners who also live on the street. She explained:

> The townhouses were already being bought up, and what used to be a street where people sat on their porches, sat on their stoops, became a—weed and seed [community policing effort] against our building because too many people hung out outside. So I fought that big time. At that point, it was all

low and moderate income tenants—it was before the condo building came in. And I talked about history, I talked about Washington. I said, "look." They would be complaining—"look at all those kids hangin' out outside." I said, "I see—there's 2 kids riding their bicycle, one's about 9, one's about 11—their mother's sitting on a step smoking a cigarette. Yes, she's talking to a man," and described what I was seeing and was saying, "if this was in Arlington [Virginia] with all White families, we'd say this was a lovely community scene."

Incidents like these made many long-term African American residents talk about how the neighborhood no longer feels like theirs anymore. Catharine shared a story about how her neighbors called the police because two of her young male cousins were waiting for her on the stoop of her mother's row house:

So I went over there and I knocked on the door, and I was like, "I just want to introduce myself, and I want you to know that those two boys belong at our house, and I appreciate the fact that you may have been concerned about something, but two boys sitting on a front stoop—even if they don't belong there—do not constitute anything other than needing some place to sit down." This is not where two or more are gathered drug dealing is going on. Can you give me a break? So it's like that kind of thing makes you think that your neighborhood is not your neighborhood. And that's the way that I've been feeling lately. I feel like I can't—I don't feel the same level of comfort that I felt when I went away to college. I don't feel the same sense of "oh, it's not dangerous." I don't feel the same way of I see my neighborhood as my place, and this is where I belong. I very much feel the sense of there are people here that don't know me and may react negatively to me. I have to modulate my behavior. Which is not how you should feel in your community.

Similarly, Eileen, a long-term DC resident who has worked with youth and families in Columbia Heights and the surrounding neighborhoods since high school, commented, "I love these people who act like you're not there. I'm like you know—I've been in this building longer than you've been here. So . . . if they don't speak to you, then you're one of the neighborhood—that's a good sign. They ignore me! I'm to be reckoned with."

Kids in the neighborhood particularly see the changes on the street. Like Catharine's cousins, the students Eileen works with find the changes to the public spaces challenging. She explained:

For older kids, I think it's a very alienating environment . . . I mean there are kids who have fully adapted to it and see themselves as future leaders and whatever, but you know, part of it is that as kids go away to college I think very few of them come back to the neighborhood because there really isn't a neighborhood to come back to . . . and they see their families struggling within that community to stay within the community, to hold onto what's left of—the reason their parents moved here.

She further explained that some of the kids have responded negatively by engaging in theft and other predatory behavior in the neighborhood because they do not feel that the neighborhood is for them anymore.

Hanging Out

The feeling that public spaces are no longer spaces for long-term residents is acutely felt by residents—largely African American and Latino—who hung out in the parks in Columbia Heights. There are several small parks within the neighborhood with very different trajectories. For example, the Trolley Turnaround Park, which had a history of being a hangout place in the neighborhood, was considered by the new residents surrounding the park as a place for drunks, drug users, and the homeless. The playground equipment, they argued, was unusable because people were sleeping or defecating on or under them. However, this perspective was contested by other parents—particularly those who had been in Columbia Heights before the redevelopment—who said that the people hanging out in the park were respectful and moved when asked.

Many newer residents—most of whom are White—argued for a massive change in order to modify these behaviors or remove those who hung out in the parks. They wanted the park to be primarily for the growing number of families with children. The city told organizers that they needed to get new people into the park in order to start the process. By the time meetings with the city about the design of the park began, there was a large constituency of interested users who could testify about their desire for a new space and increased police enforcement. Police argued that there was no law against loitering and that the current users had a right to use the space, seeming reluctant to arrest the older users of the park. New residents complained that the police could arrest the men for public drinking if nothing else. Police in the community know the park users well, but they are limited in what they can do to arrest the users unless they actually see alcohol being consumed. Police also have struggled to balance new residents' concerns about nuisance crimes such as public drinking, sleeping in the alleys, or public urination with more serious ongoing violent crime and prostitution in other parts of the neighborhood.

Older users of the park who showed up to the meetings wanted to have bathrooms installed, similar to what had been done at another park nearby. However, the idea was rejected by both new neighbors and city officials who believed bathrooms invited crime. A blog reported on the planning meeting in which design options for the park were unveiled. One comment summed up the meeting.

> Someone raised the issue of why tables were being put in the park if we were trying to make it not a "drunk park." . . . Representatives of the local church and others who reported trying to help the drinkers reacted pretty negatively to the 'no tables' discussion saying that "tables don't make people drink alcoholism does" . . . This discussion sort of disintegrated with parents expressing concerns that tables attract the drunks and make the park unfriendly for children and church reps insisting that we need to talk about long term solutions to social problems, not about tables.

In spite of the efforts of previous users of the park, Trolley Turnaround Park was redeveloped dramatically. It is fenced and closes at 9 p.m., the play equipment is intended for children under the age of 10, and the play equipment is fenced in on the west side of the park. At the southeast corner, there are two unshaded permanent tables with checkerboards on them and four concrete seats. The entire park has a low wall intended for seating, with planters along the edges. The designers used a historic streetcar theme with enlarged replicas of the tokens accepted on the original DC streetcars that stopped running in 1964 on the fencing, brick accents where the tracks would have been, and pictures and interpretive signs about the trolley's history in the neighborhood before the 1968 riots, consistent with the before and after narrative of the neighborhood history. However, as one former park user complained, "you can't do anything in that park now—it's not for adults anymore."

Now, the children's playground at the park is packed with children, parents, and nannies of many ethnicities as well as older children kicking soccer balls or throwing footballs in the small open space in the park. During the day, quiet groups of adults hang out to play cards, have business meetings, or eat lunch. Because of community pressure, a police officer on a motorcycle is assigned to the park and hangs out either on one of the low walls or on the corner outside the gates. Organizers of the "Friends of the Trolley Turnaround Park" have seen a positive difference, and have not noticed any of the old behavior that drove the redevelopment process. Many new residents look at the park as a positive example of the power of mobilization while others see it as a sign of the neighborhood's growing gentrification.

Like the Trolley Turnaround Park, the 14th and Girard Street Park, in the heart of the neighborhood, has been a social space for African Americans in Columbia Heights since the late 1960s. Current users of the park proudly state that they've been hanging out in the park "since before it was a park—since it was an apartment building." The current park space did not become a park until the late 1970s, according to current users who hung out in and around the apartment building when it still stood there. When the current space transitioned from an apartment building to a park, it consisted of tables in the front and a basketball court in the back.

Tall, old trees obstructed the view from 14th Street from police monitoring park activities, but shaded the tables for park users. A low wall where park users would sit and hang out divided the table area from the basketball court. There were no bathrooms, so the men used a corner at the edge of the basketball court. On rainy days, the poor drainage turned that corner into a cesspool, and on hot summer days the smell from the corner would fill the park and the surrounding sidewalks. A longtime park user who was employed in construction work at the site of the new Metro stop in the mid-1990s occasionally brought lime to spread over the corner to reduce the smell and improve sanitation.

As crack and heroin infiltrated Columbia Heights in the 1970s and 1980s, the park gained a tough reputation like the neighborhood that surrounds it. Park users said there was often a threat or reality of violence among park users over drug, gang, or interpersonal disputes. The area around the park was known for crime, attributable in part to poorly managed housing developments near the park on 14th Street. Over the years, the park received significant complaints about noise, public drinking, public intoxication, litter, and gambling. Although these threats waned as the users of the park aged and harder drugs declined citywide, the park's reputation among newer neighbors has endured. One housing developer of a nearby parcel of land complained that the park made selling condominium units in the new building difficult. Park users, conversely, fondly remember how they used to hang out till 3 a.m. drinking and smoking and playing cards or seeing neighbors who felt like family. Although they acknowledge that there were—and still are—some people you "can't trust" in the park, it is also integral to their sense of community.

Newer residents counter that they do not feel safe approaching the park. However, there is always significant debate between listserv participants about the park—with some suggesting the park is harmless and that complainers should participate in park activities such as chess, cards, eating lunch in the park, and talking with the people who hang out there. Other residents argued for strict enforcement of public drinking and public urination laws in the park. As one outspoken community member wrote on the neighborhood listserv in 2001 in response to a deluge of complaints from passersby: "I don't think there is much to worry about in that park. That crowd has been there for at least 15 years."

In 2006, $2.1 million was allocated for green spaces in Columbia Heights—$250,000 was earmarked for the renovation of the 14th and Girard Park. A year later, the city hosted three community meetings to allow neighborhood residents the opportunity to voice their opinions about what the park should look like. Many new residents who were disgusted by how the park was used before its renovation argued for a dog park on the neighborhood listserv and in public meetings. At the public meeting, park users also showed up to share their opinions on what they believed the park needed. Particularly affronted by the idea of taking "our park" and turning it into a dog park, one park user and 35-year resident of Columbia Heights testified, "you care more about a dog's shit than you do about human beings!" He believed that the neighborhood was more interested in amenities for dogs than for neighbors who used the park. Generally, park users at the 14th and Girard Street Park, like those at the Trolley Turnaround Park, felt that the only thing missing from the old park were bathrooms. These repeated comments suggest that, consistent with both common sense and literature, park users did not want to urinate in public, but felt that was the only option because there were no other public bathrooms. The idea that one should not hang out at a park long enough to need a bathroom was taken as a fact by those who opposed bathrooms in the parks in the neighborhood. However, long-term hanging out in the parks of Columbia Heights is a normal activity for many, particularly older, African Americans.

In the end, the park was redeveloped with two bathrooms, more open space, and a splash pad for young children. Like the Trolley Turnaround Park, the park is now fenced and closes at 9 p.m. when staff from the Department of Parks and Recreation (DPR) come to lock the gates. Unlike the Trolley Turnaround Park, the park users are largely the same. But in the meantime, the buildings surrounding the park have changed dramatically. One of the most notorious buildings, Meridian Park Terrace, was redeveloped by Somerset Development, a mission-driven developer who actively works to build bridges between Section 8 residents and neighbors, and provides support services to the residents. Buildings on every side of the park have been renovated or rebuilt with a mix of income restrictions, including market rate, deed restrictions, and Section 8 subsidies, as well as a building for very low-income seniors. The design of the park supported the long-term users' vision of the park while incorporating mechanisms for park management by fencing the park and closing it at sunset. However, new residents continue to express fear and discomfort over the public drinking and hanging out by African American seniors in the park.

The summer after finishing fieldwork in Columbia Heights, I returned to 14th and Girard. I arrived in the midst of an altercation between the residents and three police officers. According to the park users, one of the officers had arrived in the park and started pouring out cups, searching bags, and threatening bans from the park for public drinking. The park users complained loudly until another officer arrived on a bicycle. A supervisor arrived from the district office to defuse the situation. No charges were filed, but harassment by police had become more frequent throughout the two years I was involved at the park. The times I was in the park, the police hung out, parking their bicycles or motorcycles in the middle of the park, but park users told me about times when the police came to fine people for public drinking and ban them from the park. This was the first time I had seen it, and to park users, this interaction was more egregious. It may have been the result of complaints from new neighborhood residents who continue to see the park as dangerous and disorderly and complain to other neighbors over the neighborhood listserv and in community meetings. Long-term users continue to use the park, threatening the feelings of safety and comfort of new residents who believe public drinking should be confined to a bar patio or backyard, rather than a public park.

Another way in which hanging out in public spaces has felt threatening to new neighbors is the practice of men commenting on women who walk by. Outside of 14th and Girard, some of the older men—most are 70 or older, some have walkers and canes—sit on a low wall by the gate to hang out. They chat to each other and to passers-by. When women pass, they typically say, "hey, baby." Sometimes the men make other comments—"you got it goin' on, girl," or similar. Many White women ignore the comments but look uncomfortable. Black women often respond jovially or with a thank you. However, as Ed explained after the police officers started cracking down on the men sitting on the wall, "It's not like it's young guys causing trouble—you have to be at least 70 to sit out there . . . and if you were really trying [to pick up women], that's not how you'd do it." Typically, police will make them move and they will migrate to an inside bench and return to the wall the next day.

In the northwest part of the neighborhood, young White women reported feeling threatened or uncomfortable by groups of Black men and Latinos hanging out. One woman related a story about how a group of Latinos hung out on a corner near her house. When she complained to police about the loitering, they told her that the men hung out there after work and went home. She explained that her friends felt uncomfortable getting out of their cars on that side of the street. After she discovered that they hung out all day and drank, she e-mailed her neighbors, who were less receptive to her complaints, suggesting that she meet them or let it go rather than calling the police. A police officer in the neighborhood argued that the police struggle to balance responsiveness to complaints of loitering and public drinking with the need to respond to more serious crimes like violence and prostitution, which continue in parts of Columbia Heights.

Discussion

For many who were involved in the redevelopment of Columbia Heights, from the District government and the development community, it was a success. Columbia Heights' redevelopment has been celebrated by the Urban Land Institute and the Congress for New Urbanism. The Ward 1 city planner (who is responsible for Columbia Heights) receives a high volume of requests from student researchers who want to use the neighborhood as a case study for successful redevelopment. Even newer affluent residents who critique both the design and clientele of DCUSA praise the transformative power of the redevelopment.

The alternative to gentrification in the District is often boiled down into some form of an oversimplified response: "Should we have done nothing?" I did not meet anyone who had lived in the neighborhood for more than a decade who missed the violence of the neighborhood. For many long-term residents, the sit-down restaurants, shopping, and reductions in violence were welcome changes from the neighborhood's past. But it is more complicated than a simple either-or binary. To long-term residents, violence, illegal activity, and blight were only one part of the neighborhood from 1960 to 2000. However, they are hallmarks of the narrative adopted by residents who have arrived since 2000. Unfortunately, it means that all behaviors and people associated with that era of Columbia Heights are implicated as challenges to the forward momentum of home sales prices, high-end amenities, and safety.

While the District government, neighborhood activists, and residents employed the best practices in community involvement, affordable housing, transportation, and sustainability available at the time, the displacement of the residents who stayed has become social and cultural, rather than physical. The narrative of dysfunction that emerged about Columbia Heights combined with the historic socioeconomic and racial segregation of US cities is used to justify the removal of visible traces of 1960–2000 Columbia Heights and sanitize the neighborhood to fit the image of an economically viable and safe neighborhood from the perspective of new, largely homeowner households.

In Columbia Heights, the "right to the city" has been promoted through the preservation of affordable housing, meaning that many long-term residents of the neighborhood have control of their own buildings and homes. This preservation of private and collective spaces (single-family homes and apartment buildings, respectively) was done through programs such as property tax reductions, TOPA, city-funded tenant organizers, and subsidies for rental housing. For many policy makers, this was the extent of what was necessary to address gentrification and redevelopment. The poverty and socioeconomic isolation that characterized Columbia Heights from the perspective of the District government had been deconcentrated, giving the long-term residents access to a connected neighborhood with new jobs, new services, and safer streets. The more than 2,200 units of long-term income restricted housing in the neighborhood prevented the wholesale gentrification of Columbia Heights. It was assumed that the creation of a mixed-income neighborhood would yield positive results for all residents in the form of social and economic integration.

However that integration has been challenged by the diluvial narrative of riots and redevelopment, which suggests that the neighborhood was wealthy, White, and economically viable before the riots, went through a dark forgettable era after, and has been brought back through development and gentrification to economic viability and relevance. As Goldsmith (2002) suggested, this narrative's race and class dynamics are compounded through the preexisting bias of many new residents and the impact of generational socioeconomic and racial segregation. These biases, largely developed through popular media images of poor and minority communities, have added challenges to neighborhoods experiencing gentrification.

It also raises questions about the potential of mixed-income redevelopment policies for improving the outcomes and empowerment of low-income households. David Harvey argues that the right to the city is not just a right to stay, as is suggested through the focus on mixed-income housing development. Instead, it is a right to be an active part of shaping the community—or as Harvey suggests, "the right to change ourselves by changing the city" (2008, p. 315). Planning and policy interventions for public spaces have largely favored new-resident preferences to the exclusion of long-term residents, effectively dismantling their right to shape the community. Instead, planners and new residents threw out the proverbial baby (socializing) with the bathwater (illegal activity) by marginalizing the locations for hanging out.

The clearest example of this is the redevelopment of the Trolley Turnaround Park, as compared to the 14th and Girard Street Park. While both illustrate a change in practices in the neighborhood, the Girard Street redevelopment respected the positive aspects of the community of park users while trying to address questions of safety and nuisance by closing the park at night and increasing street-level visibility. At the Trolley Turnaround Park, long-term users no longer felt comfortable hanging out. In fact, the design suggested that the outdoor culture of hanging out is no longer appropriate for the community, raising the question of where low-income residents in Columbia Heights can spend time outside in community with their neighbors. This concept has been reinforced in parks throughout the neighborhood, and aside from 14th and Girard, amenities that encourage hanging out in public for more than a lunch or to watch children play have been discouraged through physical designs that change the neighborhood's social spaces.

These changes to the social spaces of Columbia Heights are reinforced by the expectations of new residents that define the ways public spaces are used. Most of the long-term residents I interviewed suggested Columbia Heights has an outdoor culture in which neighbors acknowledge each other—often through a short hello. Hanging out for extended periods of time—whether due to heat, unemployment, retirement, night shift, or childhood—is a normal activity. While some residents may be involved in illegal activity, they do not represent the bulk of the Columbia Heights residents who hang out. However, as new residents demand increased enforcement to address issues that make them feel uncomfortable, like Catharine's nephews or the teens Eileen works with in the neighborhood, they are implicitly determining who belongs there. By calling police on neighbors who are not involved in illegal action in public spaces, it increases harassment and the ongoing sense that the neighborhood no longer belongs to those who have been there for decades. This includes African American residents who were raised there or have been in Columbia Heights since moving from the rural South or Southwest DC in the 1950s, and Latinos from Central America or from other changing parts of the city in the 1980s. While none of them want a return of the violence and city neglect that was pervasive in Columbia Heights throughout the last quarter of the 20th century, there is a sense of loss for the community and the individual lives that had been built and sustained in spite of that violence.

The answer to "should we do nothing?" or "how do long-term residents feel about Columbia Heights now?" is the same: it's complicated. Redevelopment in DC has employed some of the most effective tools to address the built environment, preservation of affordable housing, and the creation of new affordable units. However, neighborhood-as-social-space must also be considered in a neighborhood's redevelopment, along with place making. The preservation of entire buildings comes close, but with it must come an acknowledgment by all parties involved that preservation is not just units of housing—but of communities, or social spaces that exist within the physical boundaries of the neighborhood.

Note

1 The official name for the National Park Service–owned park is Meridian Hill. However, many long-term African American residents call it Malcolm X Park. In one discussion with residents. many explained, "that's what we call it." Activists and District government have tried to change the name since 1969, but the federal government has rejected the change.

References

96th Congress Testimony of Marion Barry. (1980, September 4). H Con Res 420: To Disapprove Rental Housing Conversion and Sale Act of 1980. *Oversight Hearing and Markup Before the Committee on the District of Columbia.* Washington, DC.

Anderson, E. (2012). *Cosmopolitan canopy: Race and civility in everyday life.* New York, NY: W.W. Norton & Company.

Baker, D. (2010, April 17). *ULI 2010 Awards for Excellence: Congratulations Columbia Heights.* Retrieved March 22, 2011, from D Blog: www.db-work.com/blog/2010/04/uli-2010-awards-for-excellence-congratulations-columbia-heights/.

Briggs, X., Popkin, S., & Goering, J. (2010). *Moving to opportunity: The story of an American experiment to fight ghetto poverty.* Oxford, UK: Oxford University Press.

Cherkasky, M. (1996/1997). For sale to colored: Racial change on S Street NW. *Washington History*, 40–57.

Cisneros, H.G. (2009). *From despair to HOPE: HOPE VI and the new promise of public housing in America's cities.* Washington, DC: Brookings Institution Press.

Clement, B. (2004/2005). The white community's dissent from "Bolling." *Washington History*, 86–109.

Columbia Heights citizen unit has history of achievements. (1955, March 2). *The Evening Star, Washington, DC*, pp. A–12.

Columbia Heights Citizens' Association. (1904). A statement of some of the advantages of beautiful Columbia Heights: A neighborhood of homes. Washington, DC.

Community Services Advisory Committee (CSAC). (1973). *Operation plan for the 14th Street urban renewal area*. Washington, DC.

Congress for the New Urbanism. (2009, March 25). *CNU announces 2009 Charter Award recipients*. Retrieved May 10, 2011, from Congress for the New Urbanism: www.cnu. org/node/2750.

Crenson, M. (1983). *Neighborhood politics*. Cambridge, MA: Harvard University Press.

Davis, J.E. (1991). *Contested ground: Collective action and the urban neighborhood*. Ithaca, NY: Cornell University Press.

Day, K. (2003). New urbanism and the challenges of designing for diversity. *Journal of Planning Education and Research, 23*, 83–95.

Dear, M. (2002). Preface and Chapter 1, "The Resistable Rise in the L.A. School. In M. Dear, *From Chicago to L.A.: Making Sense of Urban Theory*. Thousand Oaks, CA: Sage Publications.

Department of Housing and Community Development. (2009). *DHCD Funded Projects*. Retrieved November 2009, from Department of Housing and Community Development: https://octo.quickbase.com/db/bit4kvfmq.

Franklin, B.A. (1968, April 7). Capital put under 4 PM curfew. *The New York Times*, pp. 1, 62.

Freeman, L. (2006). *There goes the 'hood: Views of gentrification from the ground up*. Philadelphia, PA: Temple University Press.

Goering, J. (2005). The MTO experiment. In X. de Souza Briggs & W.J. Willson (Eds.), *The geography of opportunity: Race and housing choices* (pp. 127–149). Washington, DC: Brookings Institution.

Goetz, E.G. (2013). *New Deal in ruins: Race, economic justice, and public housing policy*. Ithaca, NY: Cornell University Press.

Goldsmith, W.W. (2002). From the metropolis to globilizations: The dialectics of race and urban form. In S.F. Campbell (Ed.), *Readings in urban theory* (pp. 129–149). Malden, MA: Blackwell.

Harvey, D. (1996). *Justice, nature, and the geography of difference*. Malden, MA: Blackwell.

Harvey, D. (2008a). *Social justice and the city*. Athens, GA: University of Georgia Press.

Harvey, D. (2008b). The right to the city. *New Left Review*, 23–40.

Hyra, D. (2008). *The new urban renewal: The economic transformation of Harlem and Bronzeville*. Chicago, IL: The University of Chicago Press.

Jackson, K.T. (1985). *Crabgrass frontier: The suburbanization of the United States*. New York, NY: Oxford University Press.

Jackson, M.I. (2008). *Model city blues: Urban space and organized resistance in New Haven*. Philadelphia, PA: Temple University Press.

Jaffe, H., & T. Sherwood. (1994). *Dream city: Race, power, and the decline of Washington, DC*. New York, NY: Simon & Schuster.

Julian, E.K., & McCain, D.L. (2009). Housing mobility: A civil right. In C. Hartman, & G.D. Squires (Eds.), *The integration debate: Competing futures for American cities* (pp. 85–98). New York, NY: Routledge.

Kleit, R.G. (2005). HOPE VI new communities: Neighborhood relationships in mixed-income housing. *Environment and Planning, 37*, 1413–1441.

Kruse, K.M. (2007). *White flight: Atlanta and the making of modern conservatism.* Princeton, NJ: Princeton University Press.

Manzo, L.C., Kleit, R.G., & Couch, A. D. (2008). "Moving three times is like having your house on fire once": The experience of place and impending displacement among public housing residents. *Urban Studies, 45*(9), 1855–1878.

Mitchell, D. (2003). *The right to the city: Social justice and the fight for public space.* New York, NY: The Guilford Press.

Newman, K. (2004). Race, politics and community development in US cities. *The Annals of The American Academy of Political and Social Science,* 34–48.

Paige, J.S. (1983, May). Safe, decent and affordable: Citizen struggles to improve housing in the District of Columbia. *Studies in DC History and Public Policy.*

Park, R. (1984). *The city: Suggestions for the investigation in the urban environment.* Chicago, IL: The University of Chicago Press. (Original work published 1925).

Rosenbaum, L.S. (2000). *Crossing the class and color lines: From public housing to white suburbia.* Chicago, IL: The University of Chicago Press.

Rubin, H.J. (2000). *Renewing hope within neighborhoods of despair: The community-based development model.* Albany, NY: State University of New York Press.

Ruble, Blair. (2010). *Washington's U Street.* Washington, DC/Baltimore, MD: Woodrow Wilson Center Press/John Hopkins University Press.

Smith, N. (1979). Toward a theory of gentrification: A back to the city movement by capital not people. *Journal of the American Planning Association, 45*, 538–548.

Stone, C. (1989). *Regime politics governing Atlanta, 1946–1988.* Lawrence, KS: University Press of Kansas.

Talen, E. (2002). Beyond relativism: Reclaiming the search for good city form. *Journal of Planning Education and Research, 22*, 36–49.

Twelvetrees, A. (1989). *Organizing for neighborhood development.* Brookfield, VT: Avebury.

United States Census. (2010). *American Factfinder.* Retrieved April 14, 2011, from US Census: http://factfinder2.census.gov/faces/nav/jsf/pages/index.xhtml.

Venkatesh, S.A. (2006). *Off the books: The underground economy of the urban poor.* Cambridge, MA: Harvard University Press.

Washington Architectural Foundation. (1997). *A community-based plan for the Columbia Heights Metro Station area.* Washington, DC: Washington Architectural Foundation.

Weil, M. (1968, April 20). 7th Street's "different people". *The Washington Post,* p. B1.

White, J., Freundel Levey, J., Fulwood Jr, I., Rosen, L., Ali, V., & Guyot, L. (2008, April 2). The DC riots: 40 years later. (K. Nnamdi, Interviewer).

14

A TALE OF TWO THEATRES

The Implications of Redevelopment and Gentrification on Community Anchors and Identity in U Street/Shaw

Allison Heck

In 2005, DC's City Council adopted the *DUKE Plan* (*Duke Plan*) as a vision for redeveloping the U Street/Shaw neighborhood by drawing from the neighborhood's historical period of "Black Broadway" between 1910 and 1948 as a place brand. The community would be recreated into multiple sub-neighborhoods that could serve as small-scale attractions for new residents and visitors. Noted for its inclusion of more than 500 residents in the planning process, the *Duke Plan* identified cultural landmarks, such as the Howard and Lincoln Theatres, as anchors for destinations, plazas, and transit-oriented development. Anchors serve as place markers that support the "Black Broadway" brand that celebrated the African American history, culture, and political accomplishments of the time period, including but not limited to, Duke Ellington, Thurgood Marshall, and Carter G. Woodson, to name a few.

The Lincoln and Howard Theatres were identified as key attractions for residents and visitors as well as economic engines to promote ancillary entertainment-based ventures along the U Street corridor. The story of each theatre outlines how governance and the process of redevelopment dealt with pressures between commercial growth and community concerns regarding theatre ownership, mission, and audience in a manner that produced a particular "authentic" U Street/Shaw African American identity. The debates described in this chapter surrounding each theatre's renovation and management also portray the ongoing issues of gentrification related to race and class within DC identity politics and heritage. Both the Howard and Lincoln Theatres opened in the early 1900s to serve the Black population living in the city because of segregation. As each theatre underwent reconstruction, the stakeholder engagement became a point of political contention concerning the intended use, programming, and audience of each theatre. The findings from this study contribute to the existing literature regarding the potential impacts of different anchor types as community economic development catalysts.

Blurring the Lines of Economic, Cultural, and Social Anchor Theory

Anchor institutions have the potential to become the backbone of a neighborhood socially and economically as sites of stability and "change agents" (Taylor & Luter, 2013). Within the literature, three distinct forms of anchors are defined: economic, social, and cultural. However, an analysis of the Howard and Lincoln Theatres provides a practical and theoretical bridge between these disparate anchor definitions while also illuminating how authenticity is negotiated in terms of cultural landmarks.

Economic Anchors

Economic anchors are large, immobile firms that play an integral role in the local economy and often promote mutually beneficial community relationships (Porter & Kramer, 2011; Taylor & Luter, 2013). Anchors are place-based, dedicated to serving a particular area, or feel a historical rootedness and tie to the surrounding neighborhood (Birch, 2007; Kordesh, 2002). Higher educational institutions such as Howard University located near the U Street/Shaw neighborhood have traditionally been identified as economic anchors. Recent literature extends the definition of immobile anchor institutions to city libraries, museums, and performance complexes such as theatres that often become embedded in the cultural identity of a neighborhood (Maurrasse, 2007 as in Taylor & Luter, 2013).

Social Anchors

In a similar vein, social anchor theory (SAT) contends that communities inherently have a certain number of social institutions that anchor social networks creating neighborhood identity, associations, and linkages (Clopton & Finch, 2011). Social anchors are defined as "any institution that supports the development and maintenance of social capital and networks at the community level and provides an attachment for the collective identity of the community" (Clopton & Finch, 2011, p. 70). These institutions connect community members across demographic identities, bridging social capital while also developing a unique place-based identity. Thus, social anchors are centers for social capital development at the neighborhood level and integral to redevelopment efforts.[1] Social anchors allow communities to cement an authentic identity by preserving community attributes through "a consistent marker of identification" (Clopton & Finch, 2011, p. 74).

For example, the renovation of the Lincoln and Howard Theatres had the potential to support the larger place brand of U Street/Shaw as a revitalized "Black Broadway."

Cultural Anchors

Cultural anchors are arts- or culture-based institutions that serve as umbrella organizations, brokers, or gathering spaces for cultural activities. Cities have repeatedly leveraged cultural anchors as means for redevelopment (Clark, 2011). Cultural anchors may also monitor and safeguard the cultural clusters—social networks based in the productivity of cultural products—from displacement. As cultural anchors, institutions like the Lincoln and Howard Theatres may have the ability to advocate for place-based, people-based neighborhood revitalization.

The literature on anchor institutions is divided among subdisciplines such as economic development, community development, and cultural development. In practice, anchor institutions can breach the definitions outlined by each of these disciplines as cultural economic engines that also serve as nodes for social capital networks. The trials and successes of both the Howard and Lincoln Theatres bridge these distinct theoretical lines, providing a much-needed case study in the use of community cultural landmarks as anchor institutions in redevelopment.

Theatres as Community Anchors

The theatres in U Street/Shaw have repeatedly been identified as past, current, and future community anchors (DCOP, 2005; Ruble, 2010). At a public meeting discussing the Howard Theatre, a long-term resident recalled that his father, in his youth, would sell sandwiches to projectionists outside the theatres, attend shows, and mingle among the celebrities who frequented the venues (Shaw Library, 2010). The theatres served multiple purposes such as bridging social networks between lower- and higher-class people, serving as formal and informal economic anchors, and continually solidifying and communicating a particular cultural identity. Years later, city and community officials hoped the restoration of these theatres would rejuvenate the multifaceted roles the landmarks had once provided in U Street/Shaw.

The architects of the *Duke Plan* chose to focus on the Lincoln and Howard Theatres as community anchors in the revitalization of U Street/Shaw. Not only could the theatres serve as cultural heritage touchstones, but their ability to once again attract popular acts could increase the number of visitors to the corridor. The theatres could achieve a number of economic development outcomes by boosting tourism, serving as a venue for outreach and community events, incubating new talent, being a community center for artists, and building social networks and a collective identity. The first goal of the Duke Plan was "Filling the Gap" between the two theatres to establish a "mixed-use destination" strategy (DCOP, 2005, p. 8). Much emphasis was placed on the Howard Theatre, which continued to lay vacant and infested with rats, while the Lincoln had been restored in the early 1990s, but lacked patrons (ANC1B, 2010). The renovation trajectory for each theatre will be discussed by addressing the theatre's history, focus in the *Duke Plan*, actions taken, and an analysis of the project's ability to serve as a community anchor.

Howard Theatre: A Deregulated Economic Success?

On April 12, 2012, a large crowd gathered in front of the recently restored façade of the Howard Theatre. The theatre is located near the east end of the U Street corridor near the western boundary of Howard University. The neighborhood here has maintained its identity and long-term residents more so than other areas of U Street/Shaw. However, there are signs of significant changes in business ownership and resident demographics since the city implemented its vision for the area within the past eight years. The Howard Theatre served as a form of architectural and cultural preservation that would retain the heritage of this soon-to-be changed community. Reopening the theatre required a large investment from both public and private entities focused on a market analysis-driven approach.

History of the Howard Theatre

Opened in 1910, the Howard Theatre was the first theatre in the nation for African Americans and quickly became known as a premiere theatre for live entertainment (Ruble, 2010). As the "Theater of the People," the venue drew White and Black audiences and was a huge success, running multiple performances a day throughout the 1940s and 1950s that featured nationally known and local musicians (McQuirter, 2003). The theatre began to suffer as many residents moved to the suburbs in the 1950s and 1960s, and closed after the 1968 riots. The theatre reopened briefly in 1975, but closed shortly afterward. By the early 2000s, the Howard Theatre had been dormant for nearly 20 years with a crumbling façade, leaking roof, and rundown interior.

Those involved in the Duke Plan saw the Howard Theatre as a potential community anchor that could revive the crime-ridden and undesirable 7th and T Street corridor that many residents viewed as a place to actively avoid (Card, 2012; Nadeau, 2012; Pomeroy, 2012). The Howard Theatre would serve as the anchor for a reimagined "Howard Theatre Sub-District" that included the redevelopment of the theatre and associated plaza (to be known as Ellington Plaza) as well as the development of neighboring sites as mixed-use office-retail and work spaces (DCOP, 2005). According to the plan, the Howard Theatre Sub-District would be:

a vibrant center focused upon a revived Howard Theatre. The theatre will be restored to its original and historic façade and will be well-programmed with local and national performers who attract day and night patrons. . . . Performances will be affordable to patrons who will be a range of local residents, visitors and tourists.

(DCOP, 2005, p. 14)

Using a market analysis approach, the Duke Plan recommended reconstructing the interior of the Howard Theatre as a 500- to 600-person space with additional uses including a museum, restaurant, and gift shop (DCOP, 2005). The realization of this vision would face city budget constraints, private-public partnership negotiations, a few scandals, and an economic downturn.

Restoration of the Howard Theatre

The restoration of the Howard Theatre took on a deregulated development model that combined city resources with private and nonprofit investments. In doing so, pressures were to not only restore the Howard, but restore it in a market-savvy manner that would reap economic benefits for investors. Shortly after the Duke Plan had been adopted, Howard Theatre Restoration, Inc. (HTR) was formed as a 501(c)(3) organization that would work in partnership with city government and other entities to restore the Howard (HTR, 2013). Because of the economic downturn, the ability to fundraise for the project became difficult. Rather than pursue a public-private partnership (e.g., a P3), both the city and HTR openly pursued the project as a P5 project that collaborates among neighborhood residents, philanthropic, public, private, and nonprofit sectors, creating a diverse web of stakeholders. The primary stakeholders included the city, which provided staff, political support, and roughly $8 million, while the HTR worked with the Ellis Development Group (EDG) to manage the restoration (HTR, 2013). The HTR continued its involvement throughout the process as the owner of the renovated theatre and financial manager.

The project took $29 million and seven years to complete (EDG, 2011). The multi-sourced financial deal included city, private, and nonprofit resources. The city contributed $8 million in the form of a grant from the Deputy Mayor for Planning and Economic Development's Office along with a $4 million TIF bond and a historic tax credit. The city's financial contribution was the first of its kind. This significant contribution was used in coordination with a $7.1 million equity investment from US Bank and $5 million construction loan from Eagle Bank. Additional support came from the National Park Service's Save America's Treasures Program ($350,000), Hampton Roads Ventures ($10,000), and Mid-Urban Atlantic ($5,000), as well as smaller contributions from Howard University, the Philip Graham Fund, and individual donors. Finally, DC Housing

Enterprises, a nonprofit subsidiary of the DC Housing Authority, provided new market tax credits and an allocation investment of $11,000 (DC Housing, 2013; EDG, 2011).

The EDG is headed by Roy "Chip" Ellis and his brother, Malik, both Black, multigenerational Washingtonians. In 2008, Chip Ellis signed a 75-year lease to rehabilitate the theatre and also hired a fundraising consultant (Castro, 2010; Plumb, 2008). Just one year later, the HTR board was under scrutiny because of the lack of separation between board members and those providing services to and being paid by HTR funds. The nonprofit was subsequently audited by the Deputy Mayor of Planning and Economic Development (O'Connell, 2009). These allegations of conflict of interest do not diminish the final result of the fully restored theatre, but call into question the relatively small network involved in the restoration.

The reconstruction of the Howard Theatre began in 2010, prior to the finalization of the project's budget. At the event at the Shaw library that December, Ellis (2010) described his passion for the theatre and how it could once again serve as an anchor in the community that would bridge young and old audiences through events and a museum, stating, "it is just way too important to lose [the Howard's history]. . . . We have a wonderful opportunity to really tell our story." In 2011, Ellis and the HTR held a press event to show the progress on the reconstruction. The press reports provided accounts of the newly completed interiors that afforded room for 650 to 700 people seated or 900 to 1,000 standing, including a renovated stage with DJ booths and a new basement with bathrooms, green room, dressing room, and kitchen. Seventeen windows from the original façade were restored while aspects of the 1910 and 1940 façade were combined to give the theatre new life (Muller, 2011). The lack of parking associated with the Howard Theatre was solved by providing parking at an adjacent development that was also overseen by Ellis (ANC1B, 2010).

On April 12, 2012, members of the city, EDG, HTR, and other contributors stood proudly in front of the fully restored theatre. The HTR lived up to its goal of restoring the theatre as "[n]either identical to, nor different from the old theatre, but rather a state-of-the-art continuum" (HTR, 2013). HTR brought in New York-based operator Blue Note to manage the operations and programming for the theatre. The theatre regularly books African American live entertainment, including gospel brunches on Sundays, combined with making the space available for community events (Howard Theatre, 2013). Ten-year U Street/Shaw resident and community politician Brianne Nadeau commented:

> Brianne: That was something the ANC [1B] . . . tried to support as much as we were engaged. . . . I mean how great is it? That that [the Howard Theatre] is open? I mean, it's beautiful and *it's like a beacon of rejuvenation*, you know?
> (Nadeau, 2012, emphasis added)

FIGURE 14.1 Dilapidated Howard Theatre. From: Derek Hyra.

FIGURE 14.2 Restored Howard Theatre and Ellington Plaza. From: Author.

The restoration of the Howard Theatre was, as Brianne stated, "a beacon of rejuvenation" for the remaining section of the U Street corridor that had not realized its redevelopment potential. The restoration of the theatre and nearby parcels created a more welcoming public space. However, the changes to the neighborhood resulting from this redevelopment project call into question the ability for the Howard to serve as a community anchor rather than simply an economic anchor (see Figures 14.1 and 14.2).

Community Anchoring and Growth Versus Equity at the Howard Theatre

The market-oriented approach employed to renovate the Howard creates an environment in which the theatre must continue to place greater emphasis on economic profit rather than community outreach. The stakeholders involved, management structure, programming, and resident displacement associated with the project are evidence of a pro-growth agenda.

The Duke Plan process had a high participation rate during which residents expressed a desire to see the Howard Theatre restored to its former glory as a community anchor that positively benefited the existing neighborhood. In order to see this project realized, the city and HTR had concentrated on fundraising more so than community involvement. The stakeholders who contributed the most financial capital (besides the city and HTR), were global financial institutions interested in seeing a return on investment. Therefore, when it came time to find a theatre operator, a well-known successful operator outside of the DC area was chosen to ensure that the theatre would generate a profit. During an interview with Natalie Hopkinson (2013), a scholar of U Street/Shaw's musical heritage, she states, "Local acts don't have as much access. New York promoters are not interested . . . in the indigenous culture." The choice for a non-DC-based operator calls into question the Howard Theatre's ability to serve as a social anchor in the community as few local acts can gain access to the venue. Yet the programming at the Howard Theatre has remained centered on African American entertainment, maintaining the cultural anchor status of the theatre and possibly one of the last large performing arts spaces on the corridor that actively attracts nationally known African American acts. The theatre also hired a nonnative celebrity chef, Marcus Samuelsson, to design the dining menu and prohibition-style cocktail list in order to attract higher-income clientele (Frederick, 2012). Hopkinson's comment suggests the theatre's programming emphasizes acts that will attract those who live beyond DC. The theatre's intended audience spurs questions of who actually will frequent the renovated Howard Theatre in the wake of gentrification in this section of the neighborhood.

Howard Theatre is located just one block from the largest agglomeration of place-based Section 8 housing that remains in the neighborhood. The majority of these buildings are homes to long-term residents. Recently, a number of the buildings have concluded their 30-year leasing contracts with the federal government that provide the ability for lower-income residents to afford to live there. The conclusion of the contract gives management companies the option to change their buildings to market-rate buildings, which would force low-income residents out of their homes as they would not be able to afford the new market-rate rents. Lincoln Westmoreland II, one of the larger complexes with 121 units located on 8th Street, NW between R and S Streets, announced in January 2013 that the management company would exit the Section 8 program in May of the same year (EastShawDC, 2013). While the Howard Theatre's restoration marked a rebirth of a "Black Broadway" landmark, many long-time residents are now being pushed out because of the forces associated with its redevelopment. Ellis' other project, Progression Place, above the Shaw/Howard University Metro stop, will house a mixed-use building including office space for the United Negro College Fund. The development also includes 205 housing units, of which only one quarter will be priced for low- to moderate-income residents who make 60% to 80% of the average median income (Neibauer, 2012a). These changes make benefits of the Howard Theatre's restoration to long-term community residents hard to find.

In comparison, outreach efforts of the Howard Theatre have proven HTR and Ellis have made good on some of their promises. An "Oral History Day" hosted at the theatre launched a project to document the history of the art and cultural community related around the Howard (HTR, 2012). While there is no evidence of a subsidy for low-income residents for tickets, the price for attending Howard Theatre events is fairly affordable (Howard Theatre, 2013). The theatre also offers reduced rates for space rentals to nonprofits for community events. The restoration created 100 permanent jobs, 40 of which were held by local DC residents. One hundred construction jobs were generated, with 10 of those set aside for public housing residents. Twenty-eight permanent jobs were also set aside for public housing residents (NDC Academy, 2013). In order to realize its potential as a community anchor, the Howard Theatre must continue to engage in such partnerships and programs to build its capability to bridge social capital. The issue remains that the displacement of large numbers of long-term, low-income residents will result in a dearth of an indigenous community for the Howard to serve. The project's economic viability has potentially come at the cost of losing place-based, long-term social networks within the neighborhood.

Lincoln Theatre: U Street/Shaw's Lost Jewel and the Trials of Community Ownership

Opened as a first-run movie house in the early 1920s, the Lincoln had been one of the largest theatres in Washington, DC that served the Black population. Despite a 1990s restoration, the Lincoln "did not lead or even seem to ride the crest of this cultural and redevelopment wave" that occurred along the U Street corridor despite it being located at a prime commercial location (Clark, 2012). The ongoing saga of keeping the lights on at the Lincoln illustrates the struggles of community ownership of an anchor with limited outside financial support.

History of the Lincoln

The Lincoln Theatre opened in 1922 as a vaudeville and silent theatre, but the majority of its life was spent as a first-run movie house (Ruble, 2010). The theatre also had a club called the Cotillion Room, which was one of the only places in DC during the 1920s and 1930s where Blacks and Whites could dance together (WAMU, 2010). The Lincoln struggled in the 1950s and after the 1968 riots, leading to its closure in 1982 (Thomas, 2012). In the early 1990s, a developer's failed attempt to revitalize the theatre and surrounding parcels prompted the city to purchase the Lincoln and complete renovations (Dedman, 1990). During this process, the Lincoln Theatre Foundation (LTF) was established comprised of a group of concerned citizens. The city hoped to reopen the theatre and bestow management and operation responsibilities to the Lincoln Theatre Foundation.

The Lincoln Theatre (displayed in its current restored state in Figure 14.3) held a grand reopening in 1994 (Mills, 1993). The renovation was funded by a $4 million loan from the US Department of Housing and Urban Development in 1989 and a total of $9 million more from the city to complete the restoration. The LTF was committed to showcasing African American talent and hosting events including The Duke Ellington Jazz Festival beginning in 2005 and the immensely popular *Sophisticated Ladies* in 2010, a music revue centered on Duke Ellington's work (WAMU, 2010). Despite these successes, the theatre was closed the majority of the time and made most of its revenue from local rentals to community groups (Brown, 2012). In order to offset the Lincoln's revenue gaps, the city often provided small capital injections ranging between $250,000 and $500,000 to help keep the theatre afloat (Graham, 2012).

The Duke Plan marks the Lincoln Theatre as a neighborhood anchor, but provides little additional funds to rejuvenate the area further. The "Lincoln Common Sub-District" included the west section of U Street with the Lincoln Theatre and Metro station serving as its center. The city recommended making the place more

FIGURE 14.3 The Restored Lincoln Theatre in April 2010. From: Author.

pedestrian friendly and creating a place for street events (DCOP, 2005, p. 31). In 2007, the LTF informed Mayor Adrian Fenty that the theatre might have to close permanently, causing the DC government to commit another $200,000 and a possible annual budget allocation to maintain theatre operations (Ruble, 2010). In 2011, Councilmember Jim Graham publicly announced the theatre was broke and asked for additional funds. As acting mayor, Vincent Gray responded by stating the city would assume ownership and bestowed management to the DC Commission on the Arts and Humanities (DCCAH) until the theatre had a sustainable business model (Neibauer, 2012b).

Restoring the Management and Operations of the Lincoln: The Tension Between Community Ties and Profits

In late 2011, the financial future of the Lincoln Theatre was abysmal. The stakeholders involved in creating a path to economic stability for the Lincoln were faced with resurrecting a troubled community anchor by abandoning its status as a social network hub. The positions of each stakeholder, the LTF and the city, will be discussed in order to understand the complexity of the Lincoln Theatre's government makeover followed by an analysis of the path chosen to structure the theatre.

The Lincoln Theatre Foundation (LTF)

The LTF had operated the Lincoln Theatre for roughly 20 years. Members of its board included some of the longest-running Black-owned businesses and residents of the U Street corridor. Both Rick Lee of Lee's Flower Shop and Kemal Ben Ali, the son of Ben's Chili Bowl's founder and current restaurant manager/co-owner, each held a position on the Foundation's board and had served as chairman. The LTF had been publicly ridiculed as mismanaging the Lincoln financially and programmatically throughout 2011 and 2012 (Neibauer, 2012b). At a July 9, 2012, public meeting to discuss the theatre's future, former members pointed out the issues surrounding the Lincoln Theatre were not problems that could easily be solved under the purview of the LTF or any other entity (Ali, 2012; Lee, 2012). These problems included the ongoing rental revenue problems faced by acting-manager Darlene "Star" Brown (2012), who stated she had seen a decline in community organization rentals at the Lincoln and struggled to program and fundraise for the theatre. The rental revenue did not generate enough, if any, profits that could be put toward in-house programming. Amidst these obstacles, the LTF worked to retain the theatre as a community anchor.

When the city took over the theatre in 2011, the majority of the staff was laid off except for the general manager. The former staff primarily consisted of long-time residents who helped maintain the theatre as volunteers. The role the Lincoln served as a social and, to a certain degree, a cultural anchor continued through its darkest days. The LTF lobbied the city to keep management in the community or outsource operations to a commercial presenter with subsidies to the community to maintain the theatre's presence as an anchor institution (Schwartz, 2012).

The City and the DC Commission for the Arts and Humanities (DCCAH)

The city was tired; tired of holding onto a sinking ship and receiving criticism for it by the public and the press (Freed, 2013; Neibauer, 2012b, 2013; Schweitzer, 2012). Mayor Gray's stance to transfer management and operations of the Lincoln to the DCCAH represented the end of the city's patience with the LTF and its financial struggles. With the Howard Theatre opening its doors in April 2012, the city felt it was time to make sure the vision of both theatres as anchors outlined in the Duke Plan was finally realized. The city's plan was threefold: 1) stabilize the theatre financially; 2) find a partner who could make the theatre profitable; and 3) maintain some semblance of community engagement.

While the city was primarily interested in establishing economic stability, DCCAH seemed to understand the social and cultural importance of the theatre to long-term residents (Bettman, 2011). In a conversation with Moshe Adams,

DCCAH's Director of Grants and Legislative Affairs, he describes the commission's sensitivity to community input during the summer of 2012:

> Moshe: It [The Lincoln] is a very unique space. . . . It's just more of a neighborhood theater . . . the community has traditionally felt a part of it because there was a nonprofit that was heading it and now we want that same community involvement. . . . This is their 3rd generation of being in U Street and now they see all this stuff happening and they are feeling pushed out. So to give them that voice, it's just invaluable. I think with U Street it's a bit different because with all the new developments what I see is people are holding on, I think neighborhood folks are holding on to what they can.

The LTF and residents appreciated the nuanced approach to community involvement. However, the DCCAH received clear orders from the mayor indicating the commission did not have autonomy in its decision making for the future of the Lincoln Theatre. It was clear the city was committed to finding a new operator to start generating profits for the venue.

Go Big or Go Home: The City's Commitment to Economic Anchoring

On August 3, 2012, the DCCAH released a request for proposals (RFP) for a new operator. Then, nothing happened. The Lincoln remained quiet outside of the revamping of the venue's HVAC and sound system. In December 2012, DCCAH released a second RFP as it found the first RFP did not have quality applicants.[2]

The setbacks did not deter DCCAH's attempts to elicit community engagement in the decision-making process, but its efforts to do so were met with criticism. A community meeting was held on February 26, 2013, at the Lincoln Theatre during which DCCAH was not able to provide specifics regarding how comments would be integrated into the decision-making process and could not provide answers to specific queries on the applicants (DCCAH, 2013a; Schweitzer, 2013). Those in attendance expressed their desire for the theatre to retain its community-oriented spirit as a space for local artists, nonprofit organizations, and youth programs (Freed, 2013). A major concern was the Lincoln's ability to complement rather than compete with the beautifully restored Howard Theatre down the street. One woman commented, "We don't need the Howard Theatre to put us to shame anymore . . . we need to wake up" (Schweitzer, 2013). The majority of those who attended the meeting left with their questions unanswered and feeling a lack of transparency in the city's decision-making process.

Two months later, in April 2013, DCCAH announced it had selected a new operator for the Lincoln Theatre, whose proposal included a resume of quality arts programming and commitment to helping the venue "support the financial wherewithal for the Theatre independent of District government funding" (Neibauer, 2013). On June 27, 2013, Mayor Gray announced that I.M.P. (standing for It's My Party), owners of the 9:30 Club located at 815 V Street, NW had been selected as the theatre's new operator (DCCAH, 2013b).

I.M.P.'s owners, Seth Hurwitz and Richard Heinecke, had a proven track record as independent promoters within the Washington Metro Area (Reinink, 2012). Hurwitz and Heinecke have conducted business in the neighborhood since the late 1990s when the 9:30 Club moved from downtown DC to the U Street corridor. Yet I.M.P. is not a choice that represents the mission of promoting African American live entertainment as desired by both the LTF and community residents who were present at the DCCAH public forum. Rather, I.M.P. is well-known for booking rock and "alternative" bands associated with the musically inclined lifestyle of young urban professionals/gentrifiers (LeBlanc, 2009). Hurwitz stated his elation with I.M.P.'s selection as the Lincoln's long-term operator, but did not show a dedication to provide future programming for its former core audience. "To be able to make this more a part of people's lives here again is an opportunity that is truly a privilege. . . . The Lincoln is just too cool not to do" (Hurwitz, 2013 as quoted in DCCAH, 2013b). The choice of I.M.P. by the city indicates the ongoing transition of power, culturally, and economically, from long-term African American residents to first- and second-wave gentrifiers.

Community Anchoring and Growth Versus Equity at the Lincoln Theatre

The LTF's struggle indicates the commitment and dedication required to maintain a community anchor. For the city it seemed that the ability for the venue to function independently financially was far more important than maintaining community ownership and engagement. For some, the re-imagination of the theatre by I.M.P. is long overdue, but calls into question *who* will be the audience for the theatre. The Lincoln is a formidable façade that directly faces the entrance of the U Street/Cardozo Metro stop and is also aptly positioned next to one of the largest tourist draws on the corridor, Ben's Chili Bowl. The potential for the Lincoln to draw in a large crowd, no matter its origin, is a highly desirable asset for the city and I.M.P.

The ability for the Lincoln to serve as a community anchor may have passed. With the LTF now defunct, it continues to have concerned stakeholders with no clear authority or role in the theatre's future. In this case, the ability to balance cultural, social, and economic anchoring proved too difficult a task for either stakeholder (LTF or the city). The city's actions continue to show a penchant for economic vitality above all else in its stakeholder role along the U Street corridor.

Comparing the Howard and Lincoln Theatres as Community Anchors

Community anchors carry a heavy burden. They serve as touchstones of a neighborhood's cultural identity, social network hubs, and local economic engines. The Lincoln and Howard Theatres developed their positions as community anchors organically because of the limitations segregation placed on access to entertainment and other opportunities for the local Black community. Once segregation ended, the theatres floundered to identify their new role and market within the city, with each eventually closing its doors. Proactive citizens concerned with the preservation of cultural landmarks turned the spotlight back on these institutions and their importance within the community. The path of rejuvenation for both the Howard and Lincoln Theatres reveals the differences in each venue's physical attributes and interactions with the city that informed the redevelopment process and ability to serve as a community anchor.

The physical footprints of each theatre had repercussions on the ability for each governing foundation, HTR and LTF, to manage and program their venues in a marketable manner. The smaller space and addition of a kitchen to the Howard Theatre make the newly renovated space more marketable for a wider variety of events. The Lincoln has a large physical footprint and permanent seating arrangement that restricts the types of events that can occur in the space.

The city's attitude and relationship with each theatre is also different. The Howard Theatre had the city's formal backing prior to the adoption of the Duke Plan, but the adoption of the plan cemented the city's commitment to redevelopment. The city put a great deal of effort behind the realization of the Howard Theatre's restoration as a state-of-the-art facility including staff, energy, and the creation of an innovative financing package (EDG, 2011). Comparatively, the Lincoln Theatre was a project the city never wanted. The theatre was acquired as part of a government bailout of a failed redevelopment and restoration plan. The city put just enough resources into the theatre to see it restored, but left out key infrastructural improvements that would create a modern performance venue (Brown, 2012). Once the restoration was complete, the city quickly handed over the management and operation of the theatre to a nonprofit group, providing little to no additional resources. The city finally addressed the theatre once the Howard Theatre's finances and project timeline were finalized. The selection of new operator, I.M.P., indicates the Lincoln Theatre will follow the Howard Theatre's programming emphasis on nationally known acts. In both cases, the social hub aspects of the theatres were not considered on equal footing with economic growth.

The commonality the Lincoln and the Howard Theatre previously shared was a commitment to artistic programming for the African American community. Both institutions served as cultural anchors for the reimagined, redeveloped "Black Broadway" described in the Duke Plan. The choice of I.M.P. as operator of the Lincoln Theatre cuts the venue from its African American live entertainment roots. Instead, the city chose to diversify. The Howard Theatre will become the center for preserving African American live entertainment, while the Lincoln Theatre can be reimagined to draw in large audiences including new residents and outsiders.

The ability for each venue to continue to reach out to long-term residents and organizations may be critical in maintaining generational social networks and bridges between new and old residents. In her experience of the "sneak peek" of the Howard Theatre, *Washington Business Journal* contributor Jennifer Nycz-Connor (2012) wrote, "Because even with all the changes, the heart of the Howard remains the same. Just renewed for all." In the simplest of terms, this rose-colored interpretation of the theatre's restoration does not touch on the politics in which it is immersed. The greatest tragedy for community members would be if the these theatres are employed as surface-level interpretations of what once was without engaging in a critical discussion of the neighborhood's history and social contributions or attempting to build on the social ties and collective identity that they once promulgated within the community.

Conclusion

For both the Howard and Lincoln Theatres, the "Black Broadway" brand outlined in the Duke Plan became the impetus for the recent reincarnations of the theatres as anchor institutions of a cultural destination district, but neither currently fulfills the role of community anchor within the neighborhood. A community anchor provides a place that serves as a bonding and bridging social network hub that validates collective neighborhood identity while providing opportunities for economic advancement and profitability, particularly related to the creative industries and preservation. The Howard Theatre can balance economic anchoring for the redeveloped 7th Street, NW corridor as well as serve as a potential cultural anchor. In comparison, the Lincoln has been the lynchpin of a long-term resident social network for years that was recently dismantled without a new organizing mission. The theatre's future as an economic and cultural anchor is uncertain, but will most likely come at the price of its social anchor role.

This work's contributions to anchor theory suggest that community anchoring requires a diverse set of committed stakeholders who draw on a place-based institution as inspiration for community benefits and sociality. Particularly within cases of arts-related anchors, issues of growth in the form of economic viability and equity in terms of social and cultural representation often are at odds with one another. In cases where anchors are city-owned or subsidized, the city should actively engage the community in its plans to ensure that community buy-in and social anchoring is not compromised throughout the project planning and implementation process. It is imperative for neighborhood organizations managing anchors to focus on fundraising, securing city funds, and leveraging social network ties to maintain place-based ownership over operations and programming. If this does not occur, there is a high chance that the community will lose control over the anchor.

Notes

1 Social anchoring can have negative effects. Social anchors may become insular social networks that result in hyperbonding among community members that can negate community development and lead to social capital fragmentation (Abbott, 2008; Clopton & Finch, 2011).
2 The second RFP revealed the city had chosen to lease rather than license the theatre to a commercial or nonprofit operator for 5 to 10 years, with one five-year option for renewal. The desired applicants were required to have at least 10 years of experience operating venues with at least 400 seats (Neibauer, 2012b).

References

Abbott, A. (2008). Communicative Planning in Revitalization Efforts: A Case Study of East Gainesville, Florida. (Master's thesis). Gainesville, FL: Univesity of Florida.

Ali, K.B. (2012). Public comments made at "Oversight Roundtable of the Small and Local Business Development Committee on Developing a Sustainable Operational Model for the Historic Lincoln Theatre," July 9, 2012, John A. Wilson Building, Room 500, 1350 Pennsylvania Avenue, NW, Washington, DC.

ANC1B. (2010, July 1). Transcript of ANC1B Monthly Meeting. Washington, DC.

Bettman, R. (2011). D.C.'s historic Lincoln Theater and the trickle-up effect. *Huffington Post, DC Impact*. Retrieved from www.huffingtonpost.com/robert-bettman/dcs-historic-lincoln-thea_1_b_1009503.html.

Birch, E.L. (2007). The draw. *Next American City, 15*, 28–58.

Brown, D. "Star." (2012). Public comments made at "Oversight Roundtable of the Small and Local Business Development Committee on Developing a Sustainable Operational Model for the Historic Lincoln Theatre," July 9, 2012, John A. Wilson Building, Room 500, 1350 Pennsylvania Avenue, NW, Washington, DC.

Card, B. (2012, August). Interview with Brian Card.

Castro, M. (2010, March 22). Howard Theatre's ongoing drama. *Washington Business Journal*. Retrieved from www.bizjournals.com/washington.

Clark, T. (Ed.). (2011). *The city as entertainment machine*. New York, NY: Lexington Books.

Clark, T. (2012). Public comments made at "Oversight Roundtable of the Small and Local Business Development Committee on Developing a Sustainable Operational Model for the Historic Lincoln Theatre," July 9, 2012, John A. Wilson Building, Room 500, 1350 Pennsylvania Avenue, NW, Washington, DC.

Clopton, A.W., & Finch, B.L. (2011). Re-conceptualizing social anchors in community development: Utilizing social anchor theory to create social capital's third dimension, *Community Development, 42*(1), 70–83.

DC Housing. (2013). DC Housing Enterprises (DCHE). Retrieved from www.dchousing.org/?docid=211.

Dedman, B. (1990, September 7). Shaw Group files for bankruptcy; developer Cohen's project falters. *The Washington Post.*

District of Columbia Commission on the Arts and Humanities (DCCAH). (2013a, February 26). Recorded comments from Lincoln Theatre community meeting on Tuesday, February 26, 2013. Retrieved from DCCAH website: http://dcarts.dc.gov/.

District of Columbia Commission on the Arts and Humanities (DCCAH). (2013b, June 27). Mayor Vincent G. Gray announces the winning bid for the historic Lincoln Theatre. Retrieved from http://dcarts.dc.gov/release/mayor-vincent-c-gray-announces-winning-bid-historic-lincoln-theatre.

District of Columbia Office of Planning (DCOP). (2005). *The DUKE Plan Final Report.* Retrieved from: http://ddot.washingtondc.gov/ddot/cwp/view,a,1249,q,642946.asp on April 14, 2010.

EastShawDC. (2013, January 28). Lincoln Westmoreland II to exit Section 8 program in May. [Web log post]. Retrieved from http://eastshawdc.blogspot.com/2013/01/lincoln-westmoreland-ii-to-exit-section.html.

Ellis Development Group (EDG). (2011). Howard Theatre restoration closes $29 million deal reviving the nation's oldest African American theatre. Press Release, June 1, 2011. Retrieved from www.howardtheatre.org/Press_Releases/Howard-Theatre-Restoration-Closes-$29M-Deal.pdf.

Ellis, R. "Chip." (2010, December 8). Comments made at the Howard Theatre Shaw Library event, Washington, DC.

Frederick, M. (2012, February 22). Howard Theatre to reopen with celebrity chef menu. *Washington Business Journal.* Retrieved from www.bizjournals/com/washington.

Freed, B. (2013, February 27). Arts commission gives few answers to public questions about Lincoln Theatre's future. Retrieved from http://dcist.com/2013/02/arts_commission_gives_few_answers_t.php.

Graham, J. (2012). Public comments made at "Oversight Roundtable of the Small and Local Business Development Committee on Developing a Sustainable Operational Model for the Historic Lincoln Theatre," July 9, 2012, John A. Wilson Building, Room 500, 1350 Pennsylvania Avenue, NW, Washington, DC.

Hopkinson, N. (2013, March). Interview with Natalie Hopkinson.

Howard Theatre. (2013). The Howard Theatre. Retrieved from http://thehowardtheatre.com/.

Howard Theatre Restoration. (2012, November 2012). Howard Theatre Oral History Project. Retrieved from www.howardtheatre.org/Press_Releases/HTR_OHD_Press_Release.pdf.

Howard Theatre Restoration. (2013). Howard Theatre Restoration. Retrieved from www.howardtheatre.org/home.html.

Hurwitz, S. (2013, June 27). Comments provided in: District of Columbia Commission on the Arts and Humanities (DCCAH). (2013b, June 27). Mayor Vincent G. Gray announces the winning bid for the historic Lincoln Theatre. Retrieved from http://dcarts.dc.gov/release/mayor-vincent-c-gray-announces-winning-bid-historic-lincoln-theatre.

Kordesh, R. (2002). *Illinois workforce advantage: State of Illinois place-based community development initiative.* Retrieved from www.community-wealth.org/_pdfs/articles-%20publications/anchors/paper-kordesh.pdf.

LeBlanc, L. (2009, April 20). Industry profile: Seth Hurwitz. Retrieved from www.celebrityaccess.com/news/profile.html?id=456.

Lee, R. (2012). Public comments made at "Oversight Roundtable of the Small and Local Business Development Committee on Developing a Sustainable Operational Model for the Historic Lincoln Theatre," July 9, 2012, John A. Wilson Building, Room 500, 1350 Pennsylvania Avenue, NW, Washington, DC.

Maurrasse, D. (2007). *Leveraging anchor institutions for urban success.* Chicago, IL: CEOs for Cities. As described in Taylor, H.L., & Luter, G. (2013). *Anchor institutions: An interpretive review essay.* University of Buffalo: Anchor Institutions Task Force. Retrieved from www.margainc.com/files_images/general/Literature_Review_2013.pdf.

McQuirter, M. (2003). *African American Heritage Trail, Washington, DC.* Washington, DC: Cultural Tourism DC. Retrieved from www.culturaltourismdc.org/sites/default/files/pdf/AAHT_OCT_07_FINALsp.pdf.

Mills, D. (1993, September 17). A right turn on U Street; mayor & Co. get a sneak peek at renovated Lincoln Theatre. *The Washington Post.*

Muller, J. (2011, December 21). Once great Howard Theatre will be great again. [Web log post]. Retrieved from greatergreaterwashington.org/post/13095/once-great-howard-theatre-will-be-great-again/.

Nadeau, Brianne (2012). Interview with Brianne Nadeau.

National Development Council (NDC) Academy. (2013). Community Development. Retrieved from ndcacademy2013.org/uploads/NDC_Top_6_Final.pdf.

Neibauer, M. (2012a, June 15). With $2.7M loan, D.C. aid to Progression Place increases. *Washington Business Journal.* Retrieved from www/bizjournals.com/washington.

Neibauer, M. (2012b, December 12). D.C. offers historic Lincoln Theatre for lease. *Washington Business Journal.* Retrieved from www/bizjournals.com/washington.

Neibauer, M. (2013, April 22). D.C. selects new Lincoln Theatre operator. *Washington Business Journal.* Retrieved from www/bizjournals.com/washington.

Nycz-Conner, J. (2012, April 20). The Howard Theatre is back and in business. *Washington Business Journal.* Retrieved from www/bizjournals.com/washington.

O'Connell, J. (2009, February 2). Ethics questions dog Howard Theatre Organization. *Washington Business Journal.* Retrieved from www/bizjournals.com/washington.

Plumb, T. (2008, December 18). Howard Theatre gets $350,000 grant. *Washington Business Journal.* Retrieved from www/bizjournals.com/washington.

Pomeroy, S. (2012, August). Interview with Scott Pomeroy.

Porter, M., & Kramer, M. (2011). Creating shared value. *Harvard Business Review, 89*(1/2), 62–77.

Reinink, A. (2012). 50 fascinating people, places, & things: Seth Hurwitz. *Bethesda Magazine.* Retrieved from www.bethesdamagazine.com/Bethesda-Magazine/November-December-2012/50-Fascinating-People-Places-Things/Seth-Hurwitz/.

Ruble, B. (2010). *Washington's U Street: A biography.* Washington, DC: Woodrow Wilson Center Press.

Schwartz, B. N. (2012). Public comments made at "Oversight Roundtable of the Small and Local Business Development Committee on Developing a Sustainable Operational Model for the Historic Lincoln Theatre," July 9, 2012, John A. Wilson Building, Room 500, 1350 Pennsylvania Avenue, NW, Washington, DC.

Schweitzer, A. (2013, February 27). Lincoln Theatre community meeting: Way to blow it, DCCAH. *Washington City Paper.* Retrieved from www.washingtoncitypaper.com/blogs/artsdesk/general/2013/02/27/lincoln-theatre-community-meeting-way-to-blow-it-dccah/.

Schweitzer, A. (2012, March 27). Should the District sell Lincoln Theatre? *Washington City Paper.* Retrieved from www.washingtoncitypaper.com/blogs/artsdesk/theater/2012/03/27/should-the-district-sell-lincoln-theatre/.

Shaw Library. (2010, December 8). Public comments by audience at Howard Theatre Shaw Library event on December 8, 2010. Washington, DC.

Taylor, H.L., & Luter, G. (2013). *Anchor institutions: An interpretive review essay.* New York: Anchor Institutions Task Force and Marge, Inc.

Thomas, L. (2012). Public comments made at "Oversight Roundtable of the Small and Local Business Development Committee on Developing a Sustainable Operational Model for the Historic Lincoln Theatre," July 9, 2012, John A. Wilson Building, Room 500, 1350 Pennsylvania Avenue, NW, Washington, DC.

WAMU. (2010). Transcript of Sophisticated Ladies Discussion. Retrieved from wamu.org.

15

H STREET, MAIN STREET, AND THE NEOLIBERAL AESTHETICS OF COOL

Brandi Thompson Summers

An April 2014 *New York Times* article describes Washington, DC's H Street, NE corridor as once a predominantly low-income, Black neighborhood that is now "increasingly mixed, racially and economically, as row houses within a block or two of the corridor undergo upscale renovations, property values rise and ethnic restaurants and fashionable pubs proliferate" (Meyer, 2014). The location of the H Street corridor is a particularly attractive space for commercial and residential development because of its proximity to Union Station (where the closest Metro stop resides) and because it is within commuting distance from Penn Quarter, Downtown, and other popular neighborhoods. The corridor is a hub of transition and transference as the Metro buses that ride along H Street and those that stop at the high-traffic corner of 8th and H Streets connect the H Street corridor with other destinations in the District as well as other cities in the region. Known as one of three neighborhoods devastated by riots following the 1968 assassination of Dr. Martin Luther King Jr., in 2011 H Street was named *USA Today*'s top "up and coming" neighborhood. In recent years, community organizations and government agencies have placed significant efforts into the rebuilding and rebranding of the H Street corridor—now called the Atlas District—privileging "diversity" and the possibility of a global community.

The transformation of the H Street corridor, in many ways, has followed a common gentrification model that has taken place in urban centers across the United States. Popular conceptions of gentrification involve the replacement of poor and working-class urban residents with middle- and upper-middle-class households. Adding race to this equation, gentrification is also understood as involving the displacement of lower-income Blacks and other people of color with White newcomers who possess higher incomes. In spite of multiple definitions of gentrification, most scholars and the general public can abstractly account for feelings of neighborhood change—sometimes signaled by the appearance of a new Starbucks. It is when revitalization and reinvestment strategies are accompanied by gentrification that the overall impact on communities becomes more complicated since most residents see the benefits of improved physical and economic conditions and services.[1]

In this chapter, I argue that the category of diversity has performed subtle yet significant discursive work in the development of H Street. Furthermore, I highlight the relationships among race, diversity, belonging, and urban development in the historical devaluation of H Street as a Black space, and its revaluation as an emerging multicultural neighborhood. In terms of the racialization of space, I also explore how discourses of diversity and neoliberalism shape what and who are deemed un/desirable and I identify how these discourses legitimate practices of racial inequality without naming race. By using diversity to map the space, I argue that the development of H Street places emphasis on a specific ideology of difference as multiculturalism and diversity in the spread of neoliberalism. Given the history of the neighborhood, this chapter considers the remaking and literal embodiment of H Street as a space of diversity. H Street's remaking requires changes to the prevailing narrative that defines the neighborhood as a Black ghetto, or area of urban blight, to a more desirable narrative of a diverse, multicultural welcoming space. Therefore, this chapter investigates how diversity has been discursively sutured to this neighborhood to produce a brand new spatial identity.

Borrowing from Brenda Weber's formulation of post-Katrina New Orleans as a "body in distress that can only be effectively 'healed' through the design ministrations offered by the experts who populate makeover television," I call attention to the location of Blackness in a neoliberal context by positioning the post-riot H Street corridor as an afflicted Black social body restored only by the mobilization of diversity (Weber, 2010, p. 179).[2] In other words, diversity acts as the antidote to Blackness. Blackness is deemed excessive and unwieldy if not disciplined, managed, contained, or deployed for proper use.

While the rebuilding and transformation of a neighborhood requires traditional economic components like labor and capital, as Sharon Zukin argues, "it also depends on how they manipulate symbolic languages of exclusion and entitlement" (1995, p. 7). The aesthetic appearance or "feel" of a city reflects "decisions about what—and—who should be visible and what should not, on concepts of order and disorder, and on uses of aesthetic power" (Zukin, 1995, p. 7). The H Street corridor was once signified by the local media, local officials, and some residents as a poor, Black ghetto but has been reimagined to attract individuals with cosmopolitan tastes who value diversity. Now "constructed multicultural urbanity" is used to attract new affluent residents, visitors, businesses, and developers (Hackworth & Rekers, 2005, p. 232).

Despite narratives and representations that equate diversity and equality for all, the process of (re)valuing H Street reveals the embeddedness of neoliberalism in its transformation—"where a logic of seemingly [race-] neutral market competition in the context of state absolution prevails" (Weber, 2010, p. 179). In other words, the state has no bearing on dismantling systemic racial inequalities exacerbated by free market competition. Weber's makeover metaphor is useful in conceptualizing how the old "Black" H Street, as a site of chaos, disorder, and pathology, required not only the rehabilitation of the physical space, but also of symbolic codes of Blackness through the lens of a neoliberal project in the purported age of colorblindness and post-racialism. What manifests in the remaking of Blackness on H Street is that the area has not been purged of symbols of Blackness; instead Blackness is transformed to become palatable and consumable while some of the constructed edginess remains—to add excitement.

This chapter begins with a conversation about the emerging themes of devaluation and revaluation and the deployment of "diversity" to discursively produce post-riot H Street as a multicultural space, rebuilt by innovative entrepreneurial pioneers. I then discuss the ways "diversity" is institutionalized as a valuable social commodity to market. I end this chapter by analyzing the politics of aesthetics and belonging. In other words, I discuss how the marking of Blackness through aestheticization of space and race contributes to H Street's structuring as both universal and exclusive.

What Goes Down, Must Come Up: Devaluing and Revaluing the H Street Corridor

Several years of failed investment schemes plagued the H Street corridor following the 1968 riots until the beginning of the 21st century. As the neighborhood grew increasingly poorer and blacker, the closure of several key retail stores in the 30 years following the riots left large gaps in its streetscape. H Street redevelopment plans in the 1970s originally included significant involvement and placed decision-making power in the hands of local groups led by Black residents and community leaders. The rebuilding of H Street was seen as an opportunity for the Black community to control the money, jobs, and political power—an element many Black leaders felt was missing in DC (Jacoby, 1969). Organizations like Change, Inc., the Model Cities Commission, the Near Northeast Community Improvement Corporation, and the People's Involvement Corporation requested access to local and federal funds to rebuild the tarnished corridor. Black residents living in the area wanted the corridor to be planned by Black developers, built by Black architects, and refreshed with local Black-owned businesses, who they believed could adequately meet the needs of the predominantly working-class, Black neighborhood that lacked political and economic support from the local and federal governments (Levy & Downie, 1970). Nevertheless, plans to refurbish

H Street as a Black-developed and Black-operated commercial corridor were later deemed economically impractical and unfeasible. Following the failure of lukewarm government-led efforts to revive the area, H Street, devalued as a Black, poverty-stricken, blighted ghetto, was considered hopeless and stagnant by lending institutions, developers, small business owners, local government officials, and media outlets. The area was not worthy of investment or habitation.

Not until Mayor Anthony Williams' administration in the early 2000s did changes take hold and H Street attract a number of investors, restauranteurs, and developers. The Williams administration primarily stressed neoliberal development strategies that encouraged economic growth through the proliferation of public-private partnerships. Rather than emphasize an expanded role for the local government, several of the programs introduced by the administration, like the Main Streets and Great Streets initiatives, largely supported entrepreneurial efforts toward small business growth. These initiatives limited the local government's role in providing various services for its residents, in favor of free market approaches to economic development.

The early 2000s saw a turning point in gentrification processes across the country—a particular kind of gentrification that commodified ethnic diversity, transforming it into a feature that brought added symbolic value to living there and increased economic value to real estate prices. Neighborhoods like the H Street corridor are appealing "for the capital that it may attract, never for the value it already represents to residents because of the histories, meanings, and value that it may sustain or help produce" (Dávila, 2012, p. 11). For example, in my 2010 interview with Shauna, a young White woman in her 20s who moved from northern Virginia to H Street's "Atlas District," she explained that she and her husband chose to purchase a home there primarily because they believed they could benefit financially from the increased value that would come as a result of the forthcoming streetcar. They surmised that streetcar service, even the promise of a streetcar, would presumably lead to the success of neighborhood businesses and increased property values. Furthermore, she extolled the increasing diversity that the neighborhood was experiencing as a clear virtue and a sign of positive change.

Renewed energy around the development of H Street in the 2000s—and the process of its revaluation—placed particular emphasis on the corridor as a welcoming space of diversity. These efforts have not gone unrecognized. Besides its designation in *USA Today* as the top US neighborhood to explore, in 2012, *Forbes* magazine ranked H Street number six on its list of "America's Hippest Hipster Neighborhoods" (behind other popular, "diverse," and controversial gentrified neighborhoods like the Mission District in San Francisco and the Williamsburg neighborhood in Brooklyn). Several stories about H Street's transition suggest that early signs of gentrification—cleaning up trash in the neighborhood, implementing various aesthetic improvements to the streets, increased law enforcement presence—have been understandably welcomed by older Black residents and store owners (Meyer, 2007; Schwartzman, 2006; Sullivan, 2014). Despite national attention and local praise for the transition and aesthetic appeal of H Street, many of the problems that Black residents faced since the 1950s—poverty, inconsistent and insufficient city services, limited retail options, lack of employment opportunities—continue to plague its longtime residents. In fact, some residents complain about the influx of restaurants and bars on H Street and limited retail options for Black (working-class) customers (Young, 2012a). Others see the changes on H Street as part of a strategic ploy to rid the area of Black residents in favor of Whites—who fled the city for the suburbs in the aftermath of the riots (Schwartzman, 2006; Young, 2012b).

The absence of a welfare state and the minimized role of the state as protector/provider requires people to learn to govern themselves. The state no longer supports groups against oppressive conditions—the state's revised role is to support individuals and monitor social responsibility—therefore public space becomes a showcase for the entrepreneurial. Using this logic, the history of the H Street revival following the 1968 riots points to an ineffectual local government and unruly people who were unable to fix the neighborhood's problems. Ineptitude, absence, and neglect from the local government required the involvement of private sources, sometimes in collaboration with public sources. This is especially relevant in terms of business ownership. Small Black businesses have increasingly had a difficult time remaining on H Street. While some believe the business owners must conform and "learn to be like White businesses" in order to thrive in the corridor, others recognize that Black businesses are priced out as the taxes have tripled and quadrupled because H Street has become more popular.

The Charm and Value of Diversity

Multiculturalism, and its logic of difference, orders and contributes to the corridor's political economy. Culture and economics are not mutually exclusive categories; in fact, in these neoliberal times, culture and commerce are co-constitutive. As evidenced by the content of and dramatic increase in media attention, commercial development, and financial investment to the corridor, current value on H Street is abstractly conceived through material and symbolic representations of diversity, hipness or coolness, global cultures, and authenticity. These discursive representations affect the resources the area receives. Resources like policing, surveillance, national media attention, and visits by political figures and celebrities increase as the area is deemed more desirable. Various actors (government, investors, residents) rely on representations of a neighborhood to direct funds and development. The importance of diversity and cultural consumption intensifies social and economic inequities by valorizing diversity in particular areas to make previously undesirable spaces popular.

Diversity is incorporated as part of the vision for H Street's future in the District's official strategic plan drafted by the Office of Planning. In the early 2000s, the DC Office of Planning held multiple community meetings seeking input from local residents about their vision for the corridor. From these discussions emerged the theme "Respect for History, Heritage, and Diversity" for the purpose of land use, zoning, and development as a "shared vision" between residents and the local agency. According to the report, the neighborhood's history, heritage, and diversity already provide "a strong foundation" for the corridor's future (DC Office of Planning, 2004, p. 32). Throughout the plan, the term *unique* is used multiple times to describe the corridor's social and physical environment. In addition to emphasizing the purported economic benefits of historic preservation and heritage tourism, *diverse* is one of the few descriptive terms also used to characterize the space.

In her account of how organizations and institutions use the language of diversity as a mode of celebration and value, Sara Ahmed argues that diversity ultimately adds value to whatever it has been attributed to. In particular, she maintains that diversity can be understood in market terms. Ahmed describes this stylization of pluralism as a Benetton mode of diversity, "in which diversity becomes an aesthetic style or way of 'rebranding'" a particular space, institution, or organization (2012, p. 53). The enactment of diversity on H Street appears in different forms—on official statements, in photographs, and so forth. H Street branding efforts fall in line with what Leland Saito (2009) describes as the outcome of the decline of manufacturing in US cities. He speaks of the increasing importance of cultural production in the economic growth of urban centers in its ability to attract business and spur tourism.

The 2013 H Street neighborhood profile brochure produced by the Washington, DC Economic Partnership (WDCEP), a public-private partnership that specializes in promoting DC business opportunities, provides general information about the corridor. In the organization's attempt to attract business, the brochure enumerates the advantages of H Street's cultural diversity and proclaims the street has "returned to its roots as a thriving, commercial hub, and is home to a diverse, cohesive community." The brochure goes on to describe some of H Street's attributes: "A revitalized visual and performing arts scene, hip bars and restaurants, art galleries, music venues and a boom of high-end condos and apartments are quickly reshaping the historic corridor" (WDCEP, 2013). As Asch and Musgrove (2012) argue, public-private partnerships like WDCEP are in alignment with investors and hipsters who "highlight H Street's early 20th century heyday as a bustling, working-class commercial strip—a history that sells well as entrepreneurs seek to revive its commercial success by catering to a clientele interested in a gritty 'authentic' experience." Instead of being overlooked, the Black and working-class history of the neighborhood is embraced and commoditized. Therefore, the value of diversity is in the construction of a thriving, "cohesive," hip, and upscale community that supposedly dissolves tensions between longtime residents and newcomers—all while respecting the history of the neighborhood.

The frustrations some longtime Black residents experienced were highlighted in a February 2012 *Washington Informer* article. The piece describes complaints these residents have with the demographic shift of H Street. Where H Street merchants previously "catered to the tastes of Blacks, [they] now cater to others" (Young, 2012b). Furthermore, some Black residents resent the increasing presence of bars and restaurants along the corridor because "they are not offering any of the Black men a job" (Young, 2012a). Similarly, Black business owners along the corridor have expressed concerns that the changes to H Street, and the implementation of large-scale projects like the streetcar development plan, lead to "discriminatory tactics aimed at forcing minority operators out of business" in favor of White entrepreneurs (Rowley, 2011). It is important to mention here that I mark the shift away from Black enterprise (and aesthetics) on H Street not to memorialize a glorious Black past, but instead to indicate the particular ways that governing, markets, and style are now organized around diversity. This matters because narratives about the diversity of the H Street corridor impact how bodies move through the space. These discourses shape what spaces and people are cool, safe or unsafe, and which establishments and bodies belong.

In order to retain its new value, H Street must be constructed as an ideal space for investment—a place where people should spend their money, where difference does not threaten the seamless narrative of hip, cool authenticity, and be a haven for the (upper-) middle class away from sterile, predominantly White neighborhoods like Georgetown in Northwest DC. Over the past decade, the H Street corridor has experienced significant growth in entrepreneurial retail capital, or what Zukin and her colleagues (2009) describe as "boutiques." They define new entrepreneurial capital as small businesses (local chains or individually owned stores), "with a recognizably hip, chic, or trendy atmosphere, offering innovative or value-added products (e.g., designer furniture or clothing, gourmet food) and enjoying a buzz factor in promotion, including heavy press coverage and online presence" (Zukin et al., 2009, p. 58).

In a conversation with Mark Johnson, the co-owner of Hunted House, a vintage furniture store located on H Street between 5th and 6th Streets that resells unique items from local auctions and estate sales, he stated that he and his business partner decided to move their store from the trendy 14th and U Street Corridor (where several other established vintage furniture stores reside) to H Street in 2012. Mark shared that the rent is significantly higher on H Street; however, they decided to relocate because it was "the place to be." In their two years, business has been relatively steady, however not incredibly successful. Mark said he believes there is a solid customer base for the products he sells around the "Atlas Corridor" and his most frequent customers are nearby residents. In contrast to older retail stores, boutique businesses like Hunted House constitute a strong discourse of change and represent a shift to "social" entrepreneurialism, where business owners attempt to draw from the aesthetic tastes of the new residents.

Vestiges of H Street's yesteryear are represented by stores like Murry's, located on 6th and H Streets. Identified on a large placard as "your neighborhood food store," Murry's survived some of H Street's most challenging times—poverty, gang violence, illegal drug distribution, and the ravages of drug addiction. While customer service is attentive and friendly, Murry's is like many grocery stores in low-income communities that carry a small selection of fresh fruits and vegetables, and a wide variety of packaged, processed food choices. The prices are steep compared to the nearby local grocery chain, Giant, or online grocery shopping services like Peapod. The white, one-story building, surrounded by steel gates erected to prevent shoppers and neighborhood dwellers from stealing shopping carts, does not fit the distinctive architectural aesthetic of H Street's refurbished Victorian dwellings. Like the Safeway store that inhabited the space before it, the wooden bench in front of Murry's serves as a social gathering place for older Black men, and a place of solitude for others who wish to relax and read the daily newspaper.

The building that houses Murry's, its accompanying parking lot, and the neighboring five-story H Street Self-Storage facility will be demolished and replaced by a 101,000 square foot mixed-use development anchored by a Whole Foods Market. In the case of the Murry's/H Street Self Storage construction/demolition project, the designated Advisory Neighborhood Committee (ANC) worked with representatives from Insight Development (who bought the land) to "create a design that complements the historic fabric of H Street NE." In a February 2013 letter addressed to the DC Zoning Commission secretary, the ANC 6A chairperson emphasized the committee's work with Insight Development, and its conditional approval of the construction if the developer agrees to preserve the corridor's "historic building fabric" and support the proposed designation of H Street as a historic district.[3] While ANCs play a large role in the neighborhood's development planning, they do not directly impact policy. Nevertheless, the destruction of the buildings that house Murry's and H Street Self-Storage removes an aesthetic that is "incongruous with the spirit of authenticity" the committee hopes to restore in its imaginative reconstruction of H Street's past (Zukin, 1987, p. 135).

Desire for retail businesses, like Whole Foods Market, that serve an upper-middle-class customer base rather than service businesses that cater to a largely working-class Black consumer, exposes a clear contradiction of neoliberalism: "its praise for entrepreneurship and individual agency in economic matters at the same time that it is characterized by the growing policing and restricting of the populations that have historically been most entrepreneurial" (Dávila, 2012, p. 49). Furthermore, changes to H Street's commercial landscape (including the introduction of a Whole Foods Market) resemble other contemporary "revitalized" urban spaces that can be "paradoxically characterized by the simultaneous celebration of diversity on the one hand, and increasing isolation, boundaries, and separation between social groups on the other" (Walks, 2006, p. 471). This shift can be explained, in part by the infiltration of diversity discourses by neoliberal market logics, and by "the aestheticization processes which work to naturalize landscape tastes and to reify neighborhood forms and cultural difference" (Walks, 2006, p. 471). Not only are the processes of natural landscape tastes aestheticized, but also racial difference itself, in the form of "diversity." For example, Whole Foods Market's mid-Atlantic regional president spoke of the synergies between the Whole Foods brand and H Street. He specifically highlighted H Street's demographics as representing what Whole Foods values: "That neighborhood reflects a lot of what Whole Foods is about—diversity, passion for food, history. Things like that. That's what we are too. We are so in tune with that. That sense of community and pride" (O'Connell, 2013). A press release announcing the new store also references the corridor's diversity as an attribute and implies that diverse communities with diverse, commodifiable cultural opportunities can benefit both old and new residents. The press release states:

> The H Street Corridor is a thriving hub of diversity and cultural richness—a perfect match for Whole Foods Market's goal to support each and every community we're in. . . . Whether you're a long-time resident or new to this neighborhood, we are proud to have the opportunity to join you and help write the next page of history. Being among the flourishing food scene, cultural offerings of the arts district and the exciting mix of residents will make Whole Foods Market a great partner to those in the community.

Here we see diversity used by Whole Foods as a way to accrue value for both the Whole Foods brand and the H Street corridor's brand. So, in the case of H Street, the neighborhood is both seen and aesthetically valued as a diverse space to corporate interests.

The Corner: 8th and H Streets

The concept of diversity, and its role in the reimagining of H Street, is not necessarily rooted in assorted demographic representation, but a discourse of diversity. Blackness is a necessary component of diversity—it indicates our successful transition into a post-racial social climate—and therefore Black bodies must be present to add to this diverse space. For H Street, the 8th and H intersection is an important site for the corralling of Blackness—managing the excess of Blackness—in a specific location.

The intersection, located in the center of the corridor, served as an important juncture from the early to mid-20th century when the streetcar was originally in service. Because of its centralized location, a robust commercial cluster developed at the corner of 8th and H Streets in the early 1900s (DC Office of Planning, 2004, p. 5). 8th and H Street was, and continues to be, a center of activity and a meeting place along the corridor. Nevertheless, the intersection has had a particularly sordid recent history. It was from this location that the "8th and H Street Crew" got its name. Sixteen members of the "crew" were charged with the October 1, 1984, slaying of 49-year-old Catherine Fuller—often described as the most brutal murder in the city's history. The unprecedented arrest of the 16 youths allegedly involved in Ms. Fuller's murder represented the criminalization of young Black males that took place at an alarming rate in urban centers during this violent era.

Attempts to relieve this intersection from its reputation as the gathering place of the 8th and H Street Crew came in the form of several plans for commercial redevelopment. The H Street Connection shopping center that begins at the southeast corner of 8th and H opened in 1987, at that time heralded as the centerpiece of redevelopment efforts on H Street. Its grand opening brought Mayor Barry, City Council members and two marching bands, in part to celebrate the arrival of a Dart Drug store built on the site where Catherine Fuller was murdered in 1984, but also to mark a turning point in the transition of the neighborhood (Marcus, 1987).

By the 1970s and 1980s, this intersection resembled what John Jackson describes as a "reconfiguration of public space" that evolved after the introduction of the welfare state. He says:

> The welfare state starts the process [of exclusive publicness] by evacuating privacy from the home, turning what was once intimate seclusion into a matter of public record, especially as social workers document the presence or absence of men in welfare recipients' homes. In this context, access to privacy becomes a solely bourgeois privilege, and when this publicness is all one is allowed, privatization of public space may be the only obvious riposte. Flip-flopped feet on concrete sidewalks, bright pink rollers in unkempt and auburn-streaked hair, the slouchiest of stoop-sitting—they all assert a very powerful counter-privatization.
>
> (Jackson, 2005, p. 54)

In the 1980s, the corner housed a "dismal, trash-littered park [that was] used by neighborhood residents, young and old, as a place to play cards, to shoot the breeze, smoke, drink and talk" (Sargent, 1984, p. A38). The intersection is now the city's highest bus transfer point—the number one bus transfer location in the District, and is a central gathering place for lower-middle class and working-class Black city dwellers. The bus stops at the 8th and H Street intersection act as repositories for hundreds of people to congregate every day to travel to other parts of the city.

DC's Department of Transportation has worked with the Rappaport Company, developer for the project, to protect the 8th and H intersection because it is deemed "an amenity at present" (DC Zoning Commission, 2010, p. 128). Preserving the bus transit transfer point in its current location cannot be framed as a strategy to help poor and working-class Black people maintain viable, afford-able options for transportation. Instead it is recognized as part of a wider system of transportation that serves as a universal necessity for all city residents to benefit from the walkability of the neighborhood.

Eighth and H is currently flanked by several businesses that presumably appeal to working-class visitors like a drug store, athletic shoe store, a 7–11 conve-nience store, a McDonald's restaurant, a Chinese carryout, a liquor store, and a check-cashing facility. Because the intersection is known for its high volume of Black bus riders who travel across the river to Anacostia, Blackness can be contained on this corner as the riders socialize and wait for their transit. With the shifting economic conditions of the corridor catering to more affluent patrons, these Black bodies are not invited to stay for long, only to share the space momentarily.

The DC Zoning Commission approved plans to demolish the one-story, suburban-style shopping center and build an eight-story, mixed-use residential and commercial property in its stead. Various reader comments on blogs that dis-cuss the redevelopment of the shopping center include those from self-described area residents who still avoid walking past 8th Street "due to the large numbers of people who hang out on the corners" and others who avoid taking the bus alto-gether because the intersection is "just too sketchy, especially at night."[4] Although unsaid, race, in this way, operates as a cultural scheme for the production of dif-ference (and danger), of which Blackness is the chief signifier. At the 8th and H intersection, the fear of looming, "sketchy" Black men and women on a busy street corner surrounded by commercial establishments, produces Blackness, like fear, as an aesthetic category (Zukin, 1995, p. 42). Although Sharon Zukin argues that race and ethnicity survive "on the politics of fear by requiring people to keep their distance from certain aesthetic markers" like baggy jeans and shaggy or shaved heads (Zukin, 1995, pp. 41–42), I would argue that it is the aesthetic markers themselves, not fear, that produce Blackness as style. In this way, the pres-ence of these Black bodies reflects a different narrative than how a "Black" space would be identified in the past. Their presence is now valued as visible evidence of multiculturalism—even by those who describe the area as "sketchy."

In comparison to the diversity of races and classes found at the eastern and western ends of the H Street corridor, the intersection of 8th and H Streets is noticeably less heterogeneous providing clear markers of working-classness and poverty. Prior to the closing of the DC Economic Security Administration and Family Services Administration offices in 2013, the space that stretched between 6th and 8th Streets was often inhabited by scores of Black people, both young and old, perched outside the building, most likely waiting to be seen by agency representatives who provide family care and financial aid for poor DC residents. On most days, the dwellers, standing casually, looked disheveled. Women stood alongside their children, chiding them stringently. Young Black women in long, colorful weaves, platform shoes, decorated nails, and knock-off designer bags would stroll up and down the street as young Black men standing near the bus transfer stops would call out to them.

In order for the narrative of diversity and inclusion on H Street to survive and thrive (for developers, planners, and local government agencies to attract more attention to the corridor), Blackness—as a form of difference and variable of multiculturalism—must be explicitly visible. The containment of Black presence at the 8th and H intersection makes Blackness less intimidating since the representation of Blackness is intimately reduced to the body. Herman Gray argues that trouble arises when this difference "aligns with the history of subordination and collective struggles for freedom, and becomes the basis for attachment to indecipherable others desirous of social justice" (2013, p. 780). Consistent with a neoliberal logic of diversity and difference, "race is visible but emptied, made an exception, not the matter" (Gray, 2013, p. 780). Therefore, because Blackness is *hyper*visible, "it is unremarkable, pervasive, and, in the face of differently valued and desirable immigrants of color [blackness is] perhaps even pedestrian" (Gray, 2013, pp. 780–781). Furthermore, as Zukin notes, social diversity is managed through the explicit visual representation of different racial and ethnic groups. This acknowledgement can reflect on a visual recognition of "past" oppression since "establishing a visual order of cultural hegemony seems to equalize by identifying and making formerly 'invisible' social groups visible" (Zukin, 1995, p. 274). The presence of Black bodies congregating around 8th and H do not necessarily point to the social and economic disparities between the longtime Black residents and newer White residents who inhabit the neighborhood, but instead shows evidence of H Street as a welcoming, inviting space for all—while maintaining a modicum of edginess and perceived danger.

This discursive tethering of Blackness to the corner of 8th and H is also exemplified by critiques of those moments when Blackness spills out beyond the corner's designated borders. For instance, reports of a shooting that took place on December 21, 2012, in front of the DTLR clothing store at 9th and H Streets after the release of Nike's newest Air Jordan basketball shoes brought about dozens of implicit and explicit online comments about Blackness on H Street. The incident was reported on several local Web sites and blogs, as well as in the *Washington City Paper*. Photographs accompanying the story showed a large crowd of young Black men and women queuing up as police officers erected tape along the perimeter of the building.

On the Web site dcist.com, several of the comments posted by viewers expressed their dismay that such an event could take place in 2012, and is instead reminiscent of H Street in the 1980s and 1990s. One commenter, "cardozomite" said: "I bet someone was playing Go-Go Music, too." Others questioned and analyzed Black "culture" and asked why Black people are so fixated with basketball shoes and "do they spend as much on business shoes or clothing?" This practice of indexing or coding race of this sort "rearranges the importance of racism and pitches its reality toward some group dysfunction" (Davis, 2007, p. 351). These critiques of the "culture" of Blackness as irrational and irresponsible are attempts to explain why Black people "choose" to purchase needless accessories rather than adorn themselves with apparel that enables them to take on the appearance of productive, laboring citizens. Indeed, this view of the limits of Black culture illustrates the myth of American exceptionalism under capitalism as it highlights the idea that any individual can choose to shed culture and cultural practices that limit their access to the American Dream. Rather than interrogating the social and economic conditions that encourage multibillion-dollar global brands like Nike and the National Basketball Association (NBA) to target young, working-class and poor people of color to purchase their goods by idealizing (proximity to) basketball as a way to transcend poverty and achieve wealth and fame, the post-race neoliberal logic invites spectators to harp on the outdated ills of Black culture.

Although the intersection of 8th and H Streets operates as a vital transfer point for public transportation, the sidewalk is used as what John Jackson (2005) might call a form of counter-privatization. In *Real Black*, Jackson offers a useful discussion about public and private life in Harlem. Private spaces previously existed within the home, but with the introduction of the welfare state, private became synonymous with the street, since the state's management and surveillance of the poor turned "what was once intimate seclusion into a matter of public record" (Jackson, 2005, p. 54). The street became the location where previously private activities and transactions took place. As a result, "access to privacy becomes a solely bourgeois privilege, and when this publicness is all one is allowed, privatization of public space may be the most obvious riposte" (Jackson, 2005, p. 54). Like in Harlem, gentrifiers who have begun to move into the neighborhood surrounding H Street deem such behavior inappropriate. One longtime Black resident, George David Butler, spoke to the *Washington Informer* about his dismay at changes to the corridor. Butler spoke of an afternoon in 2011 when police arrived at the Sherwood Recreation Center "because the new members of the community complained the annual Father's Day celebration at Sherwood was too noisy." While the event served as an important celebration for longtime residents in their quest to build (or perhaps maintain) social cohesion, the fête, put on by H Street merchants, "has taken place over the past 30 years without incident" (Young, 2012b).

Conclusion

For years, many Black Washingtonians have talked about "The Plan" to remove Black people from DC, and while there is little evidence to support an *explicit* strategy to do so, changes to the lived environment seem to favor residents with more access to capital. In the redevelopment of the H Street commercial corridor, "diversity" is used to attract businesses, customers, and tourists to the area.

Diversity discourse makes Blackness one of many inflections while H Street acts as a neoliberal zone that sustains neoliberal reforms and affirms Blackness by using it as an entrepreneurial machine of development. It is through the work of diversity that H Street emerges as a hip, yet edgy district. Nevertheless, while diversity evokes difference, it does not provide commitment to redistributive justice.

Neoliberal discursive logic stitches multiculturalism (in the form of Black, brown, and White bodies, and global cuisine) into discourses of urban renewal and American progress. Therefore, conflicts, deep antagonism, racism, and the workings of capitalism that accompany gentrification are masked and muted through a desire to create a stable, coherent, unified, and digestible narrative. Infusing a desire for "diversity" into the reimagining of urban space allows for the local government, developers, entrepreneurs, and new residents to ignore the conditions that made the H Street corridor Black and poor in the first place. While the intentions to redevelop the area are not to displace Black residents, local efforts to construct a "multicultural urbanity" attract a diverse sampling of young, upwardly mobile professionals (Hackworth & Rekers, 2005). Emphasis on (cultural) diversity replaces social justice issues with the notion that a successful commercial corridor will be universally beneficial despite the fact that the largely poorer, Black residents will no longer be able to afford not only housing, but also the services and dining options along the corridor. A consequence of a diverse space is often the disinviting of Black residents.

H Street is a place where difference acts as an enhancement. In light of H Street's violent past, the narrative describing its history must reinvent itself in order to write the violent times away and repurpose the neighborhood for a new market and a new time. Nevertheless, the trace is present, even in the most aggressive attempts to eschew the past. It is through statements about diversity (as introduced by Whole Foods, the DC Office of Planning, Main Streets programs, etc.) that the political economy of the H Street corridor is organized. Racism and other forms of inequality that take place here are not overt, but subtle, where euphemisms like "creativity," "diversity," and "cultural vibrancy" are used to disinvite. H Street remains raced and the management of Blackness produces a specific form of inequality in a different guise. In other words, it is not simply the production of Blackness that has now been claimed in the name of diversity and multiculturalism on H Street, rather it is the production of Black inequality and disadvantage.

Notes

1 My use of the term *revitalization* borrows from Kennedy and Leonard, who define it as "the process of enhancing the physical, commercial and social components of neighborhoods and the future prospects of its residents through private sector and/or public sector efforts. Physical components include upgrading of housing stock and streetscapes. Commercial components include the creation of viable businesses and services in the

community. Social components include increasing employment and reductions in crime" (2001, p. 6).

2 In addition to Weber's study, there are similar analyses of urban reinvention in New Orleans (Thomas, 2009; Woods, 2009) and New York (Greenberg, 2008).

3 This emphasis on the preservation of H Street's historic architectural aesthetic is in accordance with the 2003 H Street Strategic NE Development Plan, drafted by the DC Office of Planning, which implemented a branding plan to H Street that divided the corridor into three distinct parts: between 2nd and 7th Streets is urban living; between 7th and 12th Streets is commercial retail; and between 12th and Bladensburg is arts and entertainment (DC Office of Planning, 2004).

4 www.popville.com/2013/06/foot-locker-closing-in-october-at-8th-and-h-street-ne/.

References

Ahmed, S. (2012). *On being included: Racism and diversity in institutional life*. Durham, NC: Duke University Press.

Asch, C.M., & Musgrove, G. D. (2012, October 19). Not gone, not forgotten: Struggling over history in a gentrifying D.C. *The Washington Post*. Retrieved from www. washingtonpost.com/blogs/therootdc/post/not-gone-not-forgotten-struggling-over-history-in-a-gentrifying-dc/2012/10/18/09ad8c24–1941–11e2-b97b-3ae53cdeaf69_blog.html.

Dávila, A. (2012). *Culture works: Space, value, and mobility across the neoliberal Americas*. New York, NY: New York University Press.

Davis, D. (2007). Narrating the mute: Racializing and racism in a neoliberal moment. *Souls: A Critical Journal of Black Politics, Culture, and Society, 9*(4), 346–360.

District of Columbia Office of Planning. (2004). *Revival: The H Street NE Strategic Development Plan*. Washington, DC: Government of the District of Columbia.

District of Columbia Zoning Commission. (2010, July 19). *Zoning Commission Public Hearing*. Washington, DC: District of Columbia Zoning Commission.

Gray, H. (2013). Subject(ed) to recognition. *American Quarterly, 65*(4), 771–798.

Greenberg, M. (2008). *Branding New York: How a City in Crisis Was Sold to the World*. New York, NY: Routledge.

Hackworth, J., & Rekers, J. (2005). Ethnic packaging and gentrification: The case of four neighborhoods in Toronto. *Urban Affairs Review, 41*(2), 211–236.

Jackson, J. (2005). *Real black: Adventures in racial sincerity*. Chicago, IL: The University of Chicago Press.

Jacoby, S. (1969, March 15). Battle rages for control of riot-area renewal. *The Washington Post*, p. B1.

Kennedy, M., & Leonard, P. (2001). *Dealing with Neighborhood Change: A Primer on Gentrification and Policy Choices*. Washington, DC: The Brookings Institution.

Levy, C., & Downie, L., Jr. (1970, April 5). The lights are still out from riots: First in a series. *The Washington Post*, p. A1.

Marcus, R. (1987, May 10). Northeast redevelopment is hailed as H Street shopping center opens. *The Washington Post*, p. D3.

Meyer, E. (2007, December 2). Signs of recovery in a "riot corridor." *The New York Times*. Retrieved from www.nytimes.com/2007/12/02/realestate/02nati.html?pagewanted=all&_r=0.

Meyer, E. (2014, April 15). Washington retail district's future rides on streetcars. *The New York Times*. Retrieved from www.nytimes.com/2014/04/16/business/washington-retail-districts-future-rides-on-streetcars.html?_r=0.

O'Connell, J. (2013, November 5). Whole Foods Market signs lease for H Street NE store and eyes another at Walter Reed. *The Washington Post*. Retrieved from www.washingtonpost.com/business/capitalbusiness/whole-foods-market-signs-lease-for-h-street-ne-store-and-eyes-another-at-walter-reed/2013/11/05/cf22eaa4-4649-11e3-bf0c-ceb f37c6f484_story.html.

Rowley, D. (2011, March 16). H street revitalization hits a snag. *The Washington Informer*. Retrieved from http://washingtoninformer.com/news/2011/mar/16/h-street-revitalization-hits-a-snag/.

Saito, L. (2009). From "blighted" to "historic": Race, economic development, and historic preservation in San Diego, California. *Urban Affairs Review, 45*, 166–187.

Sargent, E. (1984, December 13). Desolate NE intersection gave name to the "Eighth and H Street Crew"; some youths see street crime as only alternative. *The Washington Post*, p. A38.

Schwartzman, P. (2006, April 4). Whose H street is it, anyway? *The Washington Post*. Retrieved from www.washingtonpost.com/wp-dyn/content/article/2006/04/03/AR2006040301762.html.

Sullivan, L. (2014, January 22). Gentrification may actually be boon to longtime residents. *National Public Radio*. Retrieved from www.npr.org/2014/01/22/264528139/long-a-dirty-word-gentrification-may-be-losing-its-stigma.

Thomas, L. (2009). "Roots Run Deep Here": The Construction of Black New Orleans in Post-Katrina tourism narratives. *American Quarterly 61*(3), 749–768.

Walks, R. A. (2006). Aestheticization and the cultural contradictions of neoliberal (sub) urbanism. *Cultural Geographies, 13*(3), 466–475.

Washington DC Economic Partnership. (2013). DC neighborhood profiles 2014: H Street, NE. Washington, DC: Washington DC Economic Partnership. Retrieved from www.wdcep.com/wp-content/uploads/2010/08/hstreet.pdf.

Weber, B. (2010). In desperate need (of a makeover): The neoliberal project, the design expert, and the post-Katrina social body in distress. In D. Negra (Ed.), *Old and new media after Katrina* (pp. 175–201). New York, NY: Palgrave Macmillan.

Woods, C. (2009). Katrina's World: Blues, bourbon, and the return to the source. *American Quarterly 61*(3): 427–453.

Young, J. (2012a, January 19). D.C. residents call for fewer bars on H Street. *Washington Informer*. Retrieved from http://washingtoninformer.com/news/2012/jan/19/dc-residents-call-for-fewer-bars-on-h-street/.

Young, J. (2012b, March 12). H street NE corridor struggles for identity. *The Washington Informer*. Retrieved from http://washingtoninformer.com/news/2012/feb/02/h-street-ne-corridor-struggles-for-identity/.

Zukin, S. (1987). Gentrification: Culture and capital in the urban core. *Annual Review of Sociology, 13*, 129–147.

Zukin, S. (1995). *The cultures of cities*. New York, NY: Wiley.

Zukin, S., Trujillo, V., Frase, P., Jackson, D., Recuber, T., & Walker, A. (2009). New retail capital and neighborhood change: Boutiques and gentrification in New York City. *City & Community, 8*(1), 47–64.

16

REPRESENTATIONS OF CHANGE

Gentrification in the Media

Gabriella Modan and Katie Wells

Introduction

In a recent story about gentrification on a local Washington, DC radio station, residents and pundits spoke to reporters and offered up the following definitions of gentrification:

the forced move of a large group of persons

when the people who are living in their own city don't have enough to pay for housing in their own city because of new people coming in

a natural, demographic, and commercial change in a city

a market-driven change in a neighborhood where housing stock that may not be in great shape, may not be of great value, becomes a place where new-comers to the city, want to settle down.

What's striking about these quotes is the way the speakers characterize gentrification as a trend that is natural and caused by some abstract phenomenon. Even in the case where some causative agent is implied, as in the forced move of a large group of persons, there is no hint about who or what might be responsible for it.

Washington, DC's gentrification has been a topic of much media attention in the past few years, from journalists writing for the homegrown newspapers *City Paper*, *The Washington Post*, and *Intowner* to online sites like *Slate*, *Forbes*, and even *Al Jazeera*. This coverage tends to focus on the semiotics of urban change: the new contrasting landscapes, flaring racial tensions, preferences, and lifestyle choices of young professionals with disposable incomes. What the writers[1] leave largely unexamined are the roots of this change. In DC, as elsewhere, actors in the public and private sectors have endeavored over time to shape DC into a city attractive to investors and upper-income residents. The changes that have helped to make the current landscape of luxury condominiums, wine bars, yoga studios, and Asian-fusion tapas restaurants were not inevitable. Rather, they are the effect of concerted and contested place-making efforts among the city's leaders, businesspeople, and residents.

This chapter illustrates how media representations of gentrification render invisible the place-making efforts of such players by grammatically obscuring their roles in producing the city's current gentrified landscape. Media representations powerfully mold the world; they shape what we see and how we imagine the world to be. As Susan Ehrlich notes, "our experience of reality is mediated by language and the particular perspective it entails" (2001, p. 36). Public discourses, in other words, both reflect and promote particular values and sets of power. In DC, media discourse powerfully shapes what is possible to say and what the criteria of truth are in conversations about urban change.

We use the tools of critical discourse analysis to elucidate how media writers, whether consciously or unconsciously, grammatically manipulate agency, thereby promoting and making commonsensical the view of gentrification as a spontaneously occurring phenomenon. Understanding the linguistic mechanics of this process lays bare the "manufacture of consent," that is, how people come to understand a particular set of relations as simply common sense, or just the way things are (Herman & Chomsky, 1988; Lippman, 1922). Revealing the linguistic mechanics is the first step in rewriting this discourse and reframing gentrification in the popular imagination. Understanding how urban change is portrayed and discussed in media stories is critical for making sense of contemporary life in DC, and for confronting and changing its inequitable place-making processes.

Economic Deconstructions and Critical Discourse Analysis

Researchers in geography, anthropology, and linguistics have made clear the hazards of discourses that cast economic, cultural, and political systems as autonomous entities rather than structures driven by the decisions of powerful individuals. For example, economic geographer J. K. Gibson-Graham (2006) argues that the popular notion of the Economy (with a capital E) is a historically and socially constructed idea that has been deeply shaped by relationships of power. Political cartoonists, reporters, and policy makers routinely represent the Economy as a mysterious and uncontrollable force that governs us, that we don't have the power to transform or manage. In reality, of course, economic processes are the product of collective decisions made every day by a host of institutional decision makers who establish the preconditions for economic processes such as health care, education, currency, and law. However, dominant economic discourses often prevent researchers, policymakers, and citizens from noticing the various acts and individual beliefs that actually constitute economic processes.

Similarly, in her ethnography of Wall Street investment bankers, anthropologist Karen Ho (2009) makes the point that "market forces" seem to be abstract and mysterious simply because researchers or journalists have not investigated in depth just how market forces come to be. As Ho argues, the financial and cultural phenomena that coalesce into "market forces" stem from specific acts and beliefs of investment bankers, including their values about job security for themselves and for the companies they invest in and for.

While Gibson-Graham and Ho focus exclusively on the content of discourse, anthropologist Micaela di Leonardo (2000) alludes to discourse structure in her critique of William Julius Wilson's analysis of the "underclass." Di Leonardo takes Wilson to task for what she calls *passive verb political economy*, whereby Wilson "blame[s] an agentless 'deindustrialization' for contemporary Black poverty—effacing racism, the widening gulf between rich and poor, and the public policies that have maintained them" (p. 319).

Where Di Leonardo uses *passive verb political economy* to refer to a general style of discussing poverty, discourse analysts would examine such discussions from a more micro-level perspective, attending in detail to the grammatical structures speakers and writers use that obscure the agents responsible for the actions and outcomes under discussion. These structures include but are not limited to passive verbs. (This is in fact the case in the discourse Di Leonardo critiques; grammatically, *de-industrialization* is a nominalization, not a passive verb.)

The utility of micro-level attention to the mechanics of language can be seen in critical discourse analysts' work on grammatical agency. Cornelia Ilie writes that agency "represent[s] a structural feature that may be used to express ideological positions by attributing to the participants specific kinds of involvement in and responsibilities for actions and events" (1998, p. 59). In her analysis of the speeches by Romanian dictator Nikolai Ceaușescu, Ilie found that Ceaușescu (or his speech writers) systematically reshaped agentive relationships, for example by casting documents, rather than people, as agents of change. In another study, Tony Trew (1979) noted that British newspaper writers differed in their attribution of agency in their reports of police shootings in Rhodesia, casting the police grammatically as alternately more or less responsible for shooting rioters.

The effect of such strategies can be profound; as Nancy Henley, Michelle Miller, and Jo Anne Beazley (1995) found, people reading passive voice sentences describing sexual assault attributed less agency to the assaulter than they did in equivalent active voice sentences, and they attributed less harm to the victim. Similarly, Susan Ehrlich (2001) found that when a defendant in a sexual assault case used features such as passive voice and nominalization, the judges did not find him responsible for initiating the sexual acts that were said to have occurred.

Gentrification Fundamentals

Contemporary gentrification, which scholars sometimes call state-led, municipally managed, or revanchist (revengeful), follows broad political and economic shifts in the last quarter of the 20th century, whereby government actors deregulated existing markets, bankers developed and expanded newer and riskier markets, corporate businesspeople became involved in development, and state government officials put greater emphasis on local tax revenues (Davidson, 2008; He, 2007; Murphy, 2008; Slater, 2004). In the wake of deindustrialization and a global recession, city government officials across the United Kingdom and North America have created urban policies under the belief that self-regulated markets will solve economic and social problems (Block, 2008, p. 170). City government officials rolled back government provisions while rolling out opportunities for the private sector (Peck & Tickell, 2002). Officials touted policies to attract wealthier residents as answers to depleted tax bases, abandoned properties, poverty, and crime (Smith, 2002). Those devising such policies deemed manufacturing and blue-collar labor "things of the past" (Slater, Curran, & Lees, 2004, p. 1147).

Since the mid-1990s, state and federal policy makers, who shrank federal programs, have increased pressure on local government leaders to generate tax revenues through gentrification. At the same time, local-level politicians' defunding of public housing programs allowed them to repurpose the land on which public housing stands (Smith, 1982, 1996). To spur private property market investments and remake working-class and vacant areas, city government leaders funded infrastructure projects like office buildings, private recreation facilities, and retail complexes (Hackworth & Smith, 2001). Through policies like tax abatements, zoning concessions, building permits, and selling tax-deficient and abandoned properties, such leaders have supported major real estate capital and helped to morph gentrification into a systematic process. And, rather than addressing the policies that propel the concentration of poverty in urban areas, they approached poverty concentration itself as a problem and promoted mixed-income development as the solution (Crump, 2002; Newman & Ashton, 2004).

As government leaders' public policy decisions became central to the expansion of gentrification, so too did gentrification become central to the direction in which these players chose to take urban policy. It has become axiomatic that city governments should directly engage in real estate development (Hackworth, 2007, p. 130). Neither liberal nor conservative policy makers have been willing to consider the de-commodification of housing. In ways that could not have been foreseen in the 1960s, gentrification has evolved into a mainstream public policy strategy for cities worldwide and one of the most prominent characteristics of urban space. Where 40 years ago policy makers saw gentrification as a problem for urban policy, today they cast it as a solution (Lees & Ley, 2008; Smith, 2002). Gentrification, "the production of space for—and consumption by—a more affluent and very different incoming population," is the defining feature of contemporary cities (Slater, 2004, p. 1142).

Gentrification cannot be explained by economic restructuring alone, however (Ley, 1986). Structural explanations of gentrification make the most sense when they are melded with analyses of cultural symbols, social forces, and identity politics (Zukin, 1995). Culture is a powerful force of change in the urban landscape (Mitchell, 1999). As Eugene McCann writes, "The politics of local *economic* development must, then, be understood as always, simultaneously, the *cultural* politics of making meaning, making a living, and making place" (2002, p. 397, emphases in original). The production of gentrified landscapes, areas of poverty and limited investments that became sites of commodification and reinvestment, can be traced to the actions, politics, aesthetics, and consumption preferences of a group of residents employed in the arts, media, nonprofits, social services, education, and social sciences (Ley, 1996). Changes in labor markets, like the rise of the service-based industry and its new middle class, the aging of the Baby Boomers, and the cultural turn away from suburbs, cultivated new ideas about how to best organize daily life and contributed to the production of gentrification (Stabrowski, 2014). Thus, gentrification has not only a financial logic but an ideological one.

2011 as a Key Moment

In Washington, DC, 2011 was a watershed year for gentrification discourse. Talk about urban change in the media mushroomed around three key events. In March, the US Census Bureau released decennial data showing that DC was undergoing a dramatic demographic shift. As White residents moved to the city in increasing numbers and Black residents moved (or were pushed) out of DC, the city was becoming Whiter. The number of Black residents dropped by 40,000 between 2000 and 2010 alone.

In April, a play about gentrification won the Pulitzer Prize, and the Woolly Mammoth Theater, where the play had one of its first national runs, announced a summer reprisal with a series of audience discussions about urban change. Penned loosely as a response to *A Raisin in the Sun*, the play *Clybourne Park* explored what happens when a wealthy White couple moves into a mostly Black neighborhood in a contemporary American city.[2] In the fall, the Occupy Wall Street movement gained popularity and brought mass attention to economic inequality and inequitable access to public spaces in cities. The Occupy DC movement staged a three-month takeover of the downtown McPherson Square Park.

Alongside the Census Bureau findings and the *Clybourne Park* reprisal, the Occupy movement helped to fuel discussions among DC residents and media writers about who should be able to live in the city, how decisions on urban development should be made, and whether gentrification was a process to be welcomed. For instance, one *City Paper* article, "Confessions of a Black Gentrifier," was posted 129 times on Twitter and discussed in numerous local blogs and neighborhood listservs from DC to New York to Southern California. This essay became the material of informal conversations across the city,[3] and was assigned in university classes, mentioned in academic journal articles and a property law blog, promoted by social justice organizations like Social Justice Camp DC, and picked up by larger publications such as *The Atlantic Monthly*.

Methods

To gain a detailed understanding of gentrification discourse in DC, we turn to empirical data from 2011 articles discussing gentrification in *The Washington Post* and *The Washington City Paper*, two local media sources that have large circulation, are freely available online, and often see their stories widely picked up in other local media sites such as blogs and neighborhood listservs. In these sources we identified all mentions, descriptions, and explanations of gentrification, transformation, development, and change, including demographic shifts, changes to the built environment, and changes in real estate prices. We then examined recurring themes and grammatical patterns and their implications for commonsensical understandings of gentrification.

Linguistic Strategies in the Media

Throughout the stories in *The Washington Post* and the *City Paper*, writers frame gentrification as a simple, natural, cultural, and agentless phenomenon. The linguistic strategies that contribute to this characterization are both thematic and structural. Thematically, gentrification is cast as a cultural phenomenon, whereby individual gentrifiers bring cultural preferences and practices with them that clash with those of the people already living in gentrifying neighborhoods. Alongside these content themes are five grammatical structures (detailed later in this chapter) that contribute to agentless constructions.

In pointing to these linguistic devices, we are not implying that such constructions should never be used in discussions about gentrification. Our goal, rather, is to stress the prevalence and interaction of these features in concert with the absence of other thematic and grammatical means of describing gentrification. Together, these linguistic choices work to obscure the real agents of gentrification.

Gentrification as Cultural Phenomenon

As with the quotes that started this chapter, a common method of introducing gentrification is to present lay definitions of the subject. These definitions often characterize agents of gentrification as the people moving into neighborhoods targeted for gentrification, with a focus on their race, class, and/or predilections vis-à-vis the neighborhoods into which they're moving. In the *City Paper* article on "Confessions of a Black Gentrifier," the author quotes two self-identified middle-class Black residents of Anacostia explaining their take on gentrification:

> I used to think [gentrification] was about race—when white people moved into a black neighborhood. . . . Then I looked up the word. It's when a middle-class person moves into a poor neighborhood.

> Actually I thought it was if you see a white guy in Anacostia, listening to an iPod, jogging or walking a dog!

Race, class, and yoga studios play a large role in media stories about gentrifying neighborhoods. They are some of the most easily observable sociopolitical correlates of gentrification, and they surely make an iterative contribution to attractiveness of neighborhoods (iterative in that real estate investment, house flipping, and other land/property-based activities often preceded or at least co-occurred with new middle-class DC residents moving in). However, the personal choices of individuals to move into neighborhoods where they have more economic and/or symbolic capital than current residents do not adequately explain how gentrification happens. The focus on semiotic signifiers of race and class, the fears of displacement they evoke, and the tensions they cause in gentrifying neighborhoods, while important for understanding DC's cultural politics, obscures the crucial role of political and business players in creating, sustaining, and strengthening gentrification.

In our data, the markers of gentrifying neighborhoods are very frequently written on the bodies of residents. In addition to race (overwhelmingly White in these stories), and class (some version of "middle-class," "wealthy," or "well-off"), other signifiers include age ("young," but otherwise unspecified), exercise preferences, food ways, architecture, and clothing:

> Young families and urban gentrifiers have remodeled the Victorian townhouses that line Bloomingdale's streets. Yoga District took up residence next to the mini-mart and, a few years ago, the Big Bear Café opened in a former bodega.

> A group of young Black professionals in Anacostia has gathered over spinach-strawberry salad and white wine, when the conversation turns, as it often does, to what they call the "G-word": gentrification.

> . . . Sariane Leigh, 33, who writes a blog called *Anacostia Yogi*, putting her hand on her hip and waving a sweet-potato fry for emphasis.

> The change that had occurred in four short years was stark. To put it bluntly: There were White people, everywhere.

> But a young black gentrifier gets lumped in with both groups [gentrifiers and long-term Black residents], often depending on what she's wearing and where she's drinking.

In stories about gentrification, writers also use elements of the built environment to signal gentrified spaces. These include commercial eating and drinking establishments, yoga studios and lifestyle establishments, and dog parks:

> Still, he shakes his head as he describes the changes he's seen come to the city, like dog parks, which he first began noticing in 2007.

> But gentrification makes people feel like they don't belong in certain places. Not everyone can regularly afford $15 cocktails at Room 11.

Nowhere is the characterization of gentrification as a cultural phenomenon clearer than in a journalist's comment about an article he had written, in which he discussed bike-share stations and organic markets together with tax breaks to developers and unequal development. When another journalist asked him about this story, he said,

> It's not really a story about gentrification. . . . That's sort of incidental. It's about the fact that the structural inequalities we see in the rest of the country are replicated in DC, despite its supposed "immunity" to recessions.

In these remarks, we see a bifurcation made between gentrification and the structural inequality of uneven development.

A clear example of the use of race as a semiotic or cultural marker is in the commonly occurring metaphor of Washington, DC as Chocolate City, often contrasted with new characterizations as a city with a "vanilla swirl," and often explicitly linked to Parliament Funkadelic's 1975 anthem of the same name:

> So "Chocolate City" is melting, getting a vanilla swirl, turning into a white chocolate macadamia nut cocoa ball. Oh, so bittersweet. . . . But Chocolate City was not just about numbers. It was a feeling, a state of mind, a taste and tempo unique to a place and time. Roberta Flack at Mr. Henry's, Smokey Robinson at the Carter Baron, late nights at the Foxtrappe Club. In the 1970s, black residents in a post-riot town made their move from the "streets to the suites," while Parliament Funkadelic captured the pride, power and sense of newfound freedom in a song called Chocolate City.

> "The Parliament song 'Chocolate City' pinned a label on the city," said poet E. Ethelbert Miller, a leading figure in Washington's black arts community. "Well, chocolate melts. . . . We're seeing the eroding of a community. If you're a black person accustomed to a way of life, that way of life is coming to an end."

These excerpts and their mentions of a state of mind or a way of life cast gentrification (described as the root cause of these shifts) as a primarily cultural phenomenon. The focus on cultural markers of gentrification serves either to portray long-term Black residents in a deeply nostalgic light, or to characterize new wealthy and/or White residents as alien entities with incomprehensible ways.

The Mechanics of De-agentification

By far the most common characterizations of gentrification cast this phenomenon not as the result of specific people's actions—for example, "developers and government officials are gentrifying a neighborhood"—but rather as a natural and agentless force. This texture of non-agency emerges through five linguistic strategies that form a hierarchy of agency: constructions in which the roles of agents, receivers of actions, or other involved entities are switched around or *remapped*; passive voice constructions with deleted agents; passive voice constructions with agent mentioned; underspecified agents; and explicit agents.

Agency is an example of what linguists call a semantic role. Briefly put, semantic roles are the relationships that entities have to actions in which they're involved. Relevant for our data are the following semantic roles (based on Larson, 1984 and Radford, 1988):

Agent—volitional instigator of an action (**Sandy** opened the door.)

Experiencer—entity experiencing an action (**Sandy** felt the wind.)

Patient—entity affected by an action (**Sandy** opened **the door.**)

Locative—place where an action occurs (**Sandy** opened the door in **the hallway.**)

Resultant—entity that undergoes change caused by an action (*When Sandy opened the door,* **the glass** broke.)

As Tables 16.1 and 16.2 show, in the data we analyzed, writers remapped multiple semantic roles to fill the place of agent.

Semantic Role Remappings

TABLE 16.1 Semantic Role Remappings

1	Locative becomes agent	*The site* is to bring a grocery and other retailers to Georgia Avenue and V Street.
2	Resultant becomes agent	*The 10-year [population] growth spurt* has brought in residents with more income and education.
3	Resultant becomes experiencer	*The changes occurring* in the District are not just making the city economically richer but more culturally diverse.
4	Patient becomes experiencer	*Rents* became out of reach.
5	Patient becomes agent	*The streetcar* is going to cause gentrification over the long term

Voice and Agents

TABLE 16.2 Voice and Agents

6	Passive voice with no agent	Existing apartments *were being converted* into condominiums.
7	Passive voice with agent	[L]iving in the city is cool again, thanks in no small part to development *incentivized by government investment*.
8	Active Voice with Underspecified agent	. . . *trends* have redefined realities for neighborhoods.

While all of these remappings occurred in our data, in the interests of space we focus on writers' remappings of resultant roles onto experiencers and agents.

Resultants onto Experiencers

Through this strategy, writers frame the effects of real-world agents' actions as happening of their own accord. Such sentences arguably do the most to reframe real-world semantic relations, because they provide no grammatical slot for an agent; change simply happens, much like spontaneous combustion.

> . . . **development has flourished** and trends have redefined realities for neighborhoods.

> . . . a succession of mayors has recognized and tried to accommodate **the changes** they saw **coming**; changes driven more by economics than by race.

> **The changes occurring** in the District are not just making the city economically richer but more culturally diverse.

> Lauren Dennis moved to a **changing Petworth** [that] she has watched **continue to transform** around her.

> **The change that was coming** needed more people at the table.

The last sentence just cited is an interesting example of just how naturalized this gentrification discourse is. It occurs in an article about a community group who is becoming involved in city leaders and developers' efforts to reshape their neighborhood. Despite the fact that this group's main goal is to be agentive, and that the article's writer reports on many developments in the neighborhood that they've been responsible for or intervened in, the writer nevertheless uses the non-agentive pattern in which nobody was causing the change. Furthermore, in the larger sentence, the phrase *the change that was coming* is anthropomorphized as an entity sitting at the decision-making table. (Compare this sentence to "The developers and politicians needed more people at the table.")

Remapping Resultants onto Agents

Throughout the data, phenomena like demographic shifts or gentrification itself are portrayed as the agents of change, rather than as results of change. For example:

> The demographic change results from almost 15 years of **gentrification** that has transformed large swaths of Georgia Avenue.

> **The 10-year [population] growth spurt** has brought in residents with more income and education.

In the first example, *gentrification*, which is the result of various political, economic, and cultural actions, is cast as the cause of demographic change and transformation that are the result of the same political, economic, and cultural actions. In the second example, *residents* is cast as the patient on which the agentive *10-year growth spurt* acts. In reality, however, the 10-year growth spurt is basically synonymous with new residents coming to the city; the number of new residents who came to the city *constitutes* the 10-year growth spurt. Rather than one acting on the other, then, they are different instantiations of the same phenomenon, a phenomenon caused by parties and activities left unexplained.

Throughout the data, terms like *demographic change*, *trends*, *transformation*, and *gentrification*—terms that are abstract and essentially synonymous, are being used to explain each other. If we were to reverse agent and patient in these sentences—for example, "Residents with more income and education have brought a 10-year growth spurt," or "The gentrification results from almost 15 years of demographic change"—the sentence meanings change minimally, showing the writers' arbitrary assignment of agent and patient roles.

Passive Voice

Next on the hierarchy of agency are passive voice constructions. Because these sentences provide an optional slot for an agent, they at least allude to the existence of an agent, even if the agent is not specified.[4]

> They have the opportunity—before **projects are approved** and businesses are ready to move in—to influence the forces of progress.

> The historic **Howard Theatre is being refurbished** near the Shaw-Howard University Metro station, and across the street, construction has begun on the mixed-use Progression Place.

When the agents of the change are explicitly mentioned in sentences, passive voice constructions are less powerful in obscuring the real agents of activities. In our corpus, we had only a few examples of this strategy. For instance:

... [L]iving in the city is cool again, thanks in no small part to development **incentivized by government investment.**

While this construction provides more agency than passive sentences without explicit agents, it still conveys less agency than an active voice construction like "Government leaders have invested money to incentivize developers, and that has contributed to making living in the city cool again."

Underspecified and the Occasionally Named Agents

Conveying more agency than passive voice sentences are active voice sentences with vague, abstract agents. The meaning of such abstract terms can be fluid, slippery, and shifting from context to context (cf. Blommaert & Verschueren, 1998; Gal & Kligman, 2000; Modan, 2008). While agency was mitigated in the previous examples through grammatical structure, in this case it's the inherent meaning of the word that leads to obscuring agency.

> **The economy and other forces** play a role beyond what residents can control.

> I'd come home from school and ask, "when **they** build that?". . . referring to shiny new luxury condos or stores or restaurants.

> ... [T]**rends** have redefined realities for neighborhoods.

These sentences provide no information that might enable a reader to understand what forces, trends, or people are behind the actions described.

Explicit Agency

In the data we see three groups of agents: residents, mayors, and developers. As with the patterns discussed earlier in this chapter, it's necessary to analyze who is named as agents for what kinds of actions. When writers name agents of gentrification, they most frequently depict them as wealthy and/or White residents moving into (usually Black) neighborhoods. Writers cast these residents, in and of themselves, as the impetus behind Black residents moving out. Rising housing costs are sometimes mentioned, but with no explanation about how housing costs came to be rising.

> Although she's part of **the influx of young, White professionals,** "I feel a sense of guilt for the effect it has had on the families in the neighborhood," she said.

> The simple truth: **People moving** in have the bucks to buy.

> And because we live in a "nation of cowards" (as US Attorney General Eric Holder put it) where perhaps the only thing harder to talk about than race is

class, it's unsurprising that worries about gentrification boil down to **White versus Black**, instead of **educated and privileged versus uneducated and underserved**.

The conversation about the phenomenon remains a strict narrative of **young Whites displacing Blacks** who have lived here for generations.

Gentrification is always a delicate topic, especially in a city where it usually has meant **well-to-do Whites buying up affordable houses** in predominantly Black neighborhoods.

He said many "For Sale" signs in historic Anacostia are tagged with the graffiti, "**No Whites**," which "means that a small minority fear **being pushed out of their homes**" by gentrification.

This last example is a particularly eloquent illustration of the equation of gentrification with White people buying property in Black neighborhoods.

In the few cases when media writers mention the real-life agents of the activities and policies that contribute to gentrification, more often than not they portray these players as *responding to change*, rather than *causing* it. Some examples:

Both [Mayor Williams and Mayor Fenty] have also **tried to accommodate change** by working to improve the quality of government, by making neighborhoods more hospitable[,] and by building a vibrant, income-generating downtown to sustain growth.

[The community group] ha[s] a large enough presence **to apply pressure on city leaders** and do their own deal making to ensure that the Northwest DC neighborhood becomes what residents want.

We found only a few instances when writers named the real-life agents of change, such as government leaders and developers, as promoters of gentrification:

Anthony A. Williams, who oversaw some of the most dramatic growth during his two terms as mayor, sounded bittersweet as he recalled his effort to attract new residents and businesses to generate revenue for a city in decline.... "When you're in public service you're there to promote diversity and harmony. But, on the other hand, you want to help your city economically," he said. "Sometimes, they come at cross purposes."

Developers made several offers for her property, on a leafy stretch of Historic Anacostia on Talbert Road and Mount View Pl. But she refused to sell.

Through the grammatical strategies outlined earlier, the role of government leaders, policy makers, and developers is discursively obscured by the actions of individual city residents or abstract concepts such as "trends" or "changes." As a consequence, the accountability of these real players is erased from commonsense understandings of gentrification.

Conclusions

Collectively, the linguistic strategies of underspecifying the agents of change, employing passive voice constructions, remapping semantic roles, and casting gentrification as a cultural practice contribute to the portrait of gentrification in Washington, DC as an agentless process. This assemblage of features has ideological effects, one of which is an erasure of responsibility. As a result of their obfuscation of agency, the writers of these stories dislodge gentrification from structural forces, aligning it with cultural preferences and lifestyle trends, and engendering an oversimplified view of contemporary urban life.

When writers' agentive choices make it seem commonsensical to think of gentrification as an autonomous force of nature, it is difficult to intervene in the process. Like actual forces of nature such as hurricanes, the commonsensical role for people is one of responding to the results of the force, rather than proactively shaping the process, as we saw in the data with the mentions of mayors who were cast as responding to—rather than paving the way for—gentrification.

Writing about gentrification in a style that obscures agency is so naturalized that we found it difficult ourselves to systematically structure our prose so as to include the agents of the processes we were discussing. We have endeavored to use active voice and provide human agents wherever there was no stylistic or comprehension-based imperative to do otherwise. Undoubtedly we've missed a few instances. But our goal in this analysis, as well as in our linguistic choices, has been to make some headway in denaturalizing these prevalent ways of discussing gentrification in public discourse. We believe that awareness of the linguistic choices we make and their ideological effects is the first step in reframing gentrification as a result of political, economic, and cultural actors. Such a reframing would enable a stronger focus in media and other public and casual discourse on the causes of the structural inequalities that have led to gentrification and that gentrification continues to foster.

Notes

1 We recognize that newspaper writing is a collaborative process involving writers, researchers, and editors, among other parties. For ease of reading, we use the term *writers* as a gloss for all these participants in the writing process.
2 The original story, *A Raisin in the Sun*, takes place in the 1950s and follows a wealthy Black family who buys a house in a mostly White neighborhood.

3 We make this observation based on the numerous conversations we overheard or were drawn into around the city referencing this article.

4 There is an optional slot for a prepositional phrase starting with *by*, as in "The door was opened *by Sandy*."

References

Block, F. (2008). Swimming against the current: The rise of a hidden developmental state in the United States. *Politics Society, 36*, 169–206.

Blommaert, J., & Verschueren, J. (Eds.). (1998). *Debating diversity: Analysing the discourse of tolerance*. London, UK: Routledge.

Crump, J. (2002). Deconcentration by demolition: Public housing, poverty, and urban policy. *Environment and Planning D: Society and Space, 20*(5), 581–596.

Davidson, M. (2008). Spoiled mixture: Where does state-led "positive" gentrification end? *Urban Studies, 45*, 2385–2406.

Di Leonardo, M. (2000). *Exotics at home: Anthropologies, others, and American modernity*. Chicago, IL: The University of Chicago Press.

Ehrlich, S. (2001). *Representing rape: Language and sexual consent*. London: Routledge Press.

Gal, S., & Kligman, G. (2000). *The politics of gender after socialism*. Princeton, NJ: Princeton University Press.

Gibson-Graham, J. K. (2006). *A postcapitalist politics*. Minneapolis, MN: University of Minnesota Press.

Hackworth, J. (2007). *The neoliberal city: Governance ideology and development in American urbanism*. Ithaca, NY: Cornell University Press.

Hackworth, J., & Smith, N. (2001). The changing state of gentrification. *Tijdschrift Voor Economische En Sociale Geografie, 92*(4), 464–477.

He, S. (2007). State-sponsored gentrification under market transition: The case of Shanghai. *Urban Affairs Review, 43*, 171–198.

Henley, N., Miller, M., & Beazley, J. (1995). Syntax, semantics, and sexual violence: Agency and the passive voice. *Journal of Language and Social Psychology, 14*, 60–84.

Herman, E. S., & Chomsky, N. (1988). *Manufacturing consent: The political economy of the mass media*. New York: Pantheon.

Ho, K. (2009). *Liquidated: An ethnography of Wall Street*. Durham, NC: Duke University Press Books.

Ilie, C. (1998). The ideological remapping of semantic roles in totalitarian discourse, or, how to paint white roses red. *Discourse & Society, 9*(1), 57–80.

Larson, M. L. (1984). *Meaning-based translation: A guide to cross-language equivalence*. Landham, MD: University Press of America.

Lees, L., & Ley, D. (2008). Introduction to special issue on gentrification and public policy. *Urban Studies, 45*, 2379–2384.

Ley, D. (1986). Alternative explanations for inner-city gentrification. *Annals of the Association of American Geographers, 76*, 521–535.

Ley, D. (1996). *The new middle class and the remaking of Central City*. Oxford, UK and New York: Oxford University Press.

Lippmann, W. (1922): *Public opinion*. New York: Macmillan.

McCann, E. J. (2002). The cultural politics of local economic development: Meaning-making, place-making and the urban policy process. *Geoforum, 33*(3), 385–398.

Mitchell, K. (1999). What's culture got to do with it? *Urban Geography, 20*(7), 667–682.

Modan, G. (2008). Mango fufu kimchi yucca: The depoliticization of "diversity" in Washington, D.C. discourse. *City & Society, 20*(2), 188–221.

Murphy, L. (2008). Third-wave gentrification in New Zealand: The case of Auckland. *Urban Studies, 45*, 2521–2540.

Newman, K., & Ashton, P. (2004). Neoliberal urban policy and new paths of neighborhood change in the American inner city. *Environment and Planning A, 36*, 1151–1172.

Peck, J., & Tickell, A. (2002). Neoliberalizing space. *Antipode, 34*(3), 380–404.

Radford, A. (1988). *Transformational grammar: A first course.* Cambridge, UK: Cambridge University Press.

Slater, T. (2004). North American gentrification? Revanchist and emancipatory perspectives explored. *Environment and Planning A, 36*(7), 1191–1213.

Slater, T., Curran, W., & Lees, L. (2004). Gentrification research: New directions and critical scholarship. *Environment and Planning A, 36*(7), 1141–1150.

Smith, N. (1982). Gentrification and uneven development. *Economic Geography, 58*(2), 139–155.

Smith, N. (1996). *The new urban frontier: Gentrification and the revanchist city.* New York, NY: Routledge.

Smith, N. (2002). New globalism, new urbanism: Gentrification as global urban strategy. *Antipode, 34*(3), 427–450.

Stabrowski, F. (2014). New-build gentrification and the everyday displacement of Polish immigrant tenants in Greenpoint, Brooklyn. *Antipode, 46*, 794–815.

Trew, T. (1979). Theory and ideology at work. In R. Fowler, R. Hodge, G. Kress, & T. Trew (Eds.), *Language and control.* London, UK: Routledge/Kegan Paul.

Zukin, S. (1995). *The cultures of cities.* Malden, MA: Blackwell.

CONCLUSION

Contesting Change and Legacy: Lessons from the DC Story

Blair A. Ruble

Howard Gillette began this volume with an account of his life in Washington, DC over a three-decade period beginning in 1975. The city had already changed substantially as a consequence of the civil violence following the assassination of Reverend Martin Luther King Jr. in April 1968. That carnage had been provoked, in part, by the dramatic demographic changes that had taken place in the city following World War II, connected with the distinct yet interactive processes of suburbanization and desegregation. The evolution of the Gillettes' block in Mount Pleasant was only slightly less dramatic after they moved in. The "cluster of households occupied by refugees from postwar Czechoslovakia" gave way to a substantial African American neighborhood that, in turn, underwent a real estate revival drawing Whites back with a considerable Hispanic presence growing and dissipating—all within the span of a few years. From the time the Gillettes moved on, to the arrival of their son a few years later, Mount Pleasant had become home to a new bourgeoisie, the so-called millennials such as their own son.

The transformation sweeping through the Gillette's corner of Mount Pleasant was no more dramatic—and arguably less so—than what was happing in every Washington, DC neighborhood. Tens of thousands of White residents fled the city during the quarter century following World War II. By the time the White population stabilized, African Americans began to move out to the suburbs (many out of choice; some out of necessity). New Hispanic, African, and Asian immigrant communities took root, followed by the arrival of a wave of largely young, predominantly, although not exclusively, White professionals following the turn of the millennium.

These shifting social patterns accompanied economic change in which long-term government employment—long a stable base for the District's Blacks and Whites together—gave way to an expanding private sector, which, even when based on the largess of federal contracts, nonetheless lacked the security of the Civil Service. Washington, DC did not de-industrialize as many older US cities had as much as it jumped into a postindustrial era. As Derek Hyra has argued, the Washington, DC metropolitan area has become a prototype for the postindustrial American metropolis (Hyra, forthcoming).

This volume amplifies the reality that the District of Columbia is a much more vibrant, vital, and changing urban center than tourist postcard scenes of munificent parks and public spaces might suggest. DC has been a city traumatized by change since World War II came to an end. As long-standing social and racial conventions collapsed, hundreds of thousands of newcomers inundated the region, and tens of thousands of locals were moving from one neighborhood to another. The human mind changes more slowly than social reality. As sagacious Argentine novelist Jorge Borges has written, "the picture of the city that we carry in our mind is always slightly out of date" because the city has already changed before we recognize it (1998, p. 352). The result is a sensibility driven by the fluidity of urban life in DC in which bottom-up responses to change collide with top-down policies; all against a backdrop of persistently dated mental constructions about what DC is and can be.

All cities have to reinvent themselves or die, and how they do so is bounded by the past. Consequently, tensions persist between change and legacy. Each of the contributions to this volume relates to this commanding theme of rapid transformation and cognitive persistence. Clashing forces—evident in the work presented here—form a solid foundation for what might be considered a singularly DC "school" of urban studies. The contributors to this volume accentuate the speed and depth of Washington, DC's transformation along four dimensions: demography, economics, public policy, and identity.

Demographic Change

For longtime DC residents, the profound forces sweeping across the city are visible by simply looking around. Where once streets were full of working-class and middle-class Blacks, and multigenerational families, now increasingly uniform young, visibly prosperous White professionals fill sidewalks. Traditionally White neighborhoods to the north and west have become home to visible minorities—although more often Hispanic and Asian rather than African American. Everyone's mental map of where one is "supposed" to be is discernibly out of date as a consequence of dramatic changes in who lives where.

According to the US Census, the District's population increased from 663,091 in 1940 to an all-time high of 802,178 a decade later (US Bureau of the Census, 2005). The city began to lose residents to the surrounding suburbs soon thereafter. By 1970, the District's population had fallen to 756,510 before collapsing to a low of 572,059 in the 2000 US Census and rebounding to more than 600,000 at present (US Bureau of the Census, 2013, 2015). This roller-coaster demographic portrait captures only one segment of Washington, DC's transformation. A quickly changing racial balance is perhaps of even greater significance. The District of Columbia's population was 28.2% African American in 1940, 53.9% in 1960 (Washington, DC became the first major American city to be majority African American around 1956), and 71.1% in 1970. The racial balance began to shift during the 1980s as the White population stabilized and then grew against a backdrop of Black suburbanization. By the early 2000s, Washington, DC's population was no longer majority African American. Nor was it majority White as Hispanics and others accounted for around 15% of the population.

These overall trends were accompanied with a rapidly shifting economy that attracted increasingly well-educated professionals into the city. Georgetown University historian Maurice Jackson (2012) notes, however, that not all groups shared rising income levels. At present, the median income is $101,000 for DC Whites and $39,000 for DC Blacks. Often described as "gentrification," in fact these processes of profound demographic change are of long duration and profound meaning as they create a context in which rapid transformation rather than stability is normal. Over the past handful of decades, Washington, DC has matured from a large "Southern town" to a giant metropolitan region that is home to more than 9 million people stretching from the Mason-Dixon Line separating Maryland and Pennsylvania to near the Virginia state capital of Richmond, and from the Blue Ridge Mountains eastward beyond Chesapeake Bay.

Kathryn Howell's work on Columbia Heights underscores the impact of such rapid and extensive demographic change on the city; and, as she notes, the relationship between the city's long-term residents and these dramatic demographic fluctuations is "complicated." The socioeconomic profile of even a relatively well-defined neighborhood such as Columbia Heights—which is located next door to Howard Gillette's Mount Pleasant—has metamorphosed beyond recognition many times over. It has done so despite the reality that, as Howell argues, "the District of Columbia government, neighborhood groups, housing advocates, and developers instituted some of the best practices in urban planning and housing policy." Moreover, as one of her respondents, Melissa, notes, the commitment to the neighborhood runs deeper than policy. There is, in Melissa's words, a "strong sense of 'but this is where my people are from. I don't want to leave, and I'm going to stand my ground.'"

Brett Williams takes the argument further in writing about the present "supergentrification" of the Southwest Washington Waterfront. For Williams, "gentrification inadequately captures the dialectics of investment and abandonment, development and displacement, accumulation and dispossession that shape urban life and property relations." She passionately argues against the displacement of poor communities so evident in the story of Southwest Washington, DC.

Speaking of the importance of social networks, Williams is concerned about the ways demographic change shatters social networks, isolates people, and destroys fragile ecosystems that once sustained residents.

The dislocations of neighborhood change chronicled by so many contributors would demand aggressive policy responses if they were viewed as the consequences of concerted private action sanctioned by public policy. They are more difficult to reign in once they are conceptualized as natural consequences of impersonal urban processes beyond the control of local authorities.

Gabriella Modan and Katie Wells argue that the identification of the underlying forces driving gentrification as "caused by some abstract phenomenon" is itself a product of concerted action. While the city's recurring pattern of privately financed neighborhood revitalization is portrayed by journalists as worthy of attention, observers all too often focus on the semiotics of change and choose to ignore its structural roots. The discourse on gentrification has become sterilized by a conversation that obscures agency. Gentrification just happens; therefore, there is nothing that can be done about it.

Important for appreciating the urban condition at the outset of the 20th century, the contributors to this volume reveal the District of Columbia to be an excellent research venue for exploring the importance of demographic transformation. They highlight the traumas of displacement and disenfranchisement that often accompany the ebb and flow of different social groups through a particular neighborhood and city.

These profound social changes, in turn, rest on equally profound revolutions in city and regional economies. Most prominently, this volume is replete with actors who make change happen. If agency remains too obtuse when speaking of demographic change, the drivers of economic change make it all the more visible in the DC story.

Economic Change

The transformation of the Washington, DC economy from that of a government company town to a postindustrial powerhouse is evident in the evolution of the city and regional employment structure. While the number of jobs in DC has risen from 650,320 to 751,580 between 2000 and 2014, the number of federal positions has declined during the same period from 210,670 to 188,510 (Fuller, 2014). This shift in the city's traditional employment patterns becomes more pronounced once suburban employment—which stands at more than 3 million at present—is brought into the analysis.

Since the beginning of this century, the greatest expansion within the DC employment profile has taken place in the professional and business services and education and health services sectors. Such growth is visible in the expansion of the District's gross regional product from $78.3034 billion in 2009 dollars to $106.0363 billion. This expansion supports the proposition that DC and the Washington, DC region have become model postindustrial economies, among the most successful in the United States.

George Mason University's Stephen S. Fuller (2014) has noted elsewhere that such growth is highly dependent on procurement contracting by the federal government, which rose by 181% during the first decade of this century. As powerful indicators of expanding economic success as these data may be, the social realities linked to a move away from traditional civil service employment to federal contracting are substantial. The once secure job tenure policies of the federal government that long have sustained Washington, DC's African American community have given way to more tenuous employment opportunities. New job market realities only add extra stress to communities that are vulnerable to rapid demographic change.

New actors have emerged in the District as the federal government shifts its approach toward the public service workforce. The corporate sector has played a greater role in shaping the city and its economy than ever before. Susanna Schaller's examination of "Business Improvement Districts" (BIDs) speaks to the new and powerful role the District's business community plays. BIDs are hardly unique to Washington, DC, having emerged from the neoliberal consensus of the late 1980s and 1990s about the need to leverage public and private resources to reinvigorate urban neighborhoods (and raise land values for real estate developers). Their impact, though, has been particularly striking in a city such as Washington, DC that was planned from the outset to represent the physical and symbolic embodiment of national values and notions of public good.

Schaller demonstrates that BIDs have emerged as a potent mechanism for mobilizing the private resources released by the sorts of economic changes that Fuller described to demarcate urban physical and social environments. By concentrating on the reestablishment of civility in the public realm, BIDs often ignore the structural factors that created the very conditions that made them appear necessary in the first place.

Margaret Cowell and Heike Mayer explore a more explicit public-private intervention into the District's economic and spatial development by turning attention to one of the largest development projects in the city's history, the creation of a new headquarters for the Department of Homeland Security on the site of the St. Elizabeths Hospital campus in Anacostia. Among the most disenfranchised areas in the entire city, the surrounding neighborhood has been largely bypassed by the transformational forces so visible in many of the areas under examination here. The decision to place the headquarters campus for a major federal agency on the St. Elizabeths' site will bring thousands of new workers commuting to the area. Can it create new opportunities for those already there? Can anchor institutions elevate their host communities? Or will they transform them by displacing those long in place? Federal and District authorities have tried assiduously to align the goals of the Department of Homeland Security with those of the local community. This would not have happened without attentive planning and concerted effort. Whether they have succeeded remains to be seen.

Policy Change

As profound as shifting demographic and economic forces have been in shaping Washington, DC since World War II, study of the District and its metropolitan region in many ways powerfully highlights the importance of public policy in creating urban realities. Washington is, of course, a capital city and, therefore, never far from the purview of national as well as local policy makers.

Christopher Klemek's chapter comparing the perceived exceptionalism of Paris and Washington, DC sheds light on the special challenges of national capitals. National policy makers and authorities in capital cities are disturbed by the specter of "dangerous locals" who make demands that challenge national assumptions. Capital cities such as Paris and Washington, DC come to be viewed as "exceptional," and their residents become so "exceptional" that they can be denied the very civil rights granted to other citizens. Paris and Washington, DC offer exemplars of how major forces shaping national urban morphology—such as suburbanization—become transformed in capital cities into national challenges. Despite the enfranchisement of local residents in both cities at the end of the past century, Paris and Washington, DC have proven themselves too volatile to leave alone.

National capitals also can come to serve as convenient sites for policy experimentation. Conveniently located in the backyards of national governments, capital cities offer state authorities and bureaucrats opportunities for experimentation too close at hand to ignore. The District of Columbia has provided just such a target of opportunity for policy mavens from the time of Reconstruction through late-20th-century neoliberalism. This was especially the case during the 1960s at the height of the American Great Society experiment when, as Bell Julian Clement demonstrates, national goals aligned with local grassroots organizations to produce an especially fertile proving ground for urban social innovation. This dynamic period left "a city full of progressive promise, teetering hopefully on uncertain foundations."

The establishment of limited home rule both emerged from and continued the legacy of Great Society thinking. The upheavals of the next quarter century suggest that the policies of the era were at best incomplete. The locals so feared, as Klemek argues, were indeed "dangerous;" and the foundations, as Clement suggests, remained too "uncertain." The initial home rule experiment ended with the congressional imposition of the Financial Control Board in 1998. By exercising control over District finances, congressional overseers underscored the reality that public policy more often than not is a consequence of budgets and public expenditures.

Natwar Gandhi, James Spaulding, and Gordon McDonald's authoritative evaluation of the evolution of DC public finance since 1998 reveals the growth of DC's overall financial resources to have been directly related to population growth and economic expansion. The use of public funds evolved as their availability grew. In general, they report a broad shift in municipal budgets toward human resources–based development. In particular, they identify how public expenditures are allocated in such policy areas as education and housing as a new political battleground between new and old DC. They indicate the limits to the ability of municipal government to respond to structural challenges. As they conclude, "increasing revenues and budgets have not masked persistent poverty and the widening inequality of income in the city."

The study of DC thus highlights not just top-down approaches to urban governance but also the importance of the crucial middle ground where policies established from above meet bottom-up responses from residents and communities. Johanna Bockman's study of the cooperative movement demonstrates how, "long before formal home rule began, DC residents established consumer, worker, financial, purchasing, and housing cooperatives." This movement enabled District residents to expand autonomous realms within the Federal City in which they could shape their own communities and destinies.

Identity Change

The profound and rapid demographic, economic, and public policy changes that have swept across DC in recent decades have led to equally profound conflicts over city, neighborhood, community, and individual identity. What does it mean to be a Washingtonian if, as Derek Hyra (forthcoming) has observed, Washington, DC has evolved from "chocolate city" to "cappuccino city"? The shifting top-down and bottom-up dynamics identified in this volume lead to a constant renegotiation of meaning among neighborhood, "downtown" (i.e., business community), regional (suburbs), national, and global interests.

Many of these tensions lie beneath the complex tales surrounding the rebirth of two of African American Washington, DC's most important theaters: the Lincoln and Howard Theatres along the U Street corridor. Allison Heck's chapter places these projects within the context of the literature on anchor institutions in community redevelopment. In part, the 2005 DUKE Plan for redeveloping the U Street/Shaw neighborhood raises similar questions to those Cowell and Mayer explore in relation to the construction of a headquarters campus for the Department of Homeland Security in Anacostia. In this instance, the challenges posed by the development and use of these major historical and cultural landmarks are accelerated by questions of race, class, and identity.

As Heck's discussion illustrates, community anchor institutions carry burdens beyond their economic function. They redefine—and are redefined by—cultural identity and become social network hubs that provide a context for how residents think about themselves. In cities as historically divided by profound conflicts over identity—Black versus White, international hub versus national symbol, national capital versus hometown—conflicts over identity are omnipresent and define all range of initiatives, such as economic development schemes, that begin as being about something else—such as race.

Identity conflicts frequently become attached to shifting symbols, as is the case of bicycling in Washington, DC. In addition to the ongoing tensions that inevitably arise as cars, cyclists, and pedestrians vie for access to the same streets and sidewalks, bicycling in Washington, DC has come to be seen by many long-term residents as evidence of a reorientation of municipal policy toward the demands of newly arriving, upwardly mobile, young professionals: the so-called millennials. Ralph Buehler and John Stowe record the significant embrace of cycling as a means of transportation throughout the Washington, DC region. Yet, as they note, "area cyclists are predominantly male, between 25 and 65 years old, White, and from higher-income groups." For this reason, a means of conveyance becomes a symbol of disruptive social and cultural change. Riding a bike—or not—in Washington, DC is an expression of contested identities.

Conflicts over bicycling reflect equally divided conceptions over the meaning of the city and community as well as the use of public space. Brandi Thompson Summers reveals in her examination of the conversion of H Street, NE from "riot corridor" into a new center of "cool" that the essential meaning of such concepts as "diversity" is contested in a changing and divided Washington, DC. "Blackness" is as essential to any appreciation of H Street as "cool" and yet, as Summers argues, that same Black presence must be contained and pacified.

Washington, DC's African American intellectuals have resisted such containment and pacification from the city's founding. Home to a large African American community (slave and free) from the beginning, Washington, DC saw its Blacks open churches, create a nascent school system, and establish the first YMCA organized for Blacks before the Civil War. The community's intellectual elite—led by ministers, teachers, and professors—carried the tradition forward. Carter G. Woodson in many ways established the field of African American history from a townhouse near Washington, DC's U Street.

Woodson was embedded in a community of towering thinkers who helped to define the underpinnings for conceptions of Blackness that could not be delimited and placated. Michelle C. Chatman's exploration of Pan-Africanness within the shadow of the US Capitol is essential to discussions of identity conflict in DC as it brings an essential dimension of Washington, DC's African American thinking forward to the contemporary era. In doing so, she underscores how fundamental debates over Blackness are to identity within the context of Washington, DC.

The Washington African American community drew on a wide variety of arts and letters to express its deeply held views even as the city's Black population was denied the elementary grounding of democracy: the right to vote. As Maurice Jackson reminds readers, Washington's music culture has long provided a powerful outlet for expressing discontent with the current state of affairs in the city. Dating from the early twentieth century through the first years of the twenty-first, musicians — beginning with James Reese Europe and Marion Cook; continuing with Duke Ellington and Ahmet Ertegun; enriched by engagement with Marian Anderson and Billie Holiday; and later Marvin Gaye and Gil Scott-Heron — have given voice to the city's deepest grievances. This tradition continues today even as the rhythm has changed to Go-Go and Hip-Hop.

The challenges posed by conflicts over identity, economic, and political power are not unique to Washington, DC, or even the United States. As Amanda Huron reveals in her comparison of inner-city self-help in Washington and Johannesburg, the DC story is universal even as it remains local. Lessons learned in Washington, DC can beneficially inform urban development elsewhere; and vice versa. The challenges of social displacement and exclusion; or economic growth and vitality; of affordability and opportunity are shared by cities around the world.

A DC School of Urbanism?

Chris Myers Asch and George Derek Musgrove's chapter places the changes of a neighborhood such as Summers' H Street, Howell's Columbia Heights, Williams' Southwest Waterfront, Cowell and Mayer's Anacostia, Heck's U Street, and Gillette's Mount Pleasant into the broader sweep of "gentrification" in DC which, it turns out, dates back a century. They argue that the present period of development and displacement is a fourth wave of "private revitalization" to wash over the city. By tracing waves of change that engulfed Georgetown, Capitol Hill, Foggy Bottom, Kalorama, Capitol Hill, Hill East, Logan Circle, Dupont Circle, Mount Pleasant, Adams Morgan, Shaw, and LeDroit Park—and now heading to Petworth and Anacostia—Asch and Musgrove reveal that private development and social displacement are commonplace in a city all too often conceptualized as a federal preserve.

By asking if the city is "headed for some bad trouble," Asch and Musgrove underscore the city's deep fissures that repeatedly have led to sudden outbursts of civic unrest and violence. Hometown DC—as opposed to the tourist Washington, DC—experienced major civic rebellions in 1919, 1968, and 1991, as well as a continuous flow of less dramatic confrontations. In a city as buffeted throughout its history by deep and systemic change as Washington, DC, rebirth and forfeiture are intimately connected. This unending interplay of enhancement and loss—change and legacy—is what makes the District of Columbia of outstanding importance for the study of the urban condition over time.

Collectively and individually, the contributors to this volume outline the contours of a set of sensibilities and concerns that blend together to create a distinctive "DC school of urbanism." Their perspectives revolve around the challenges posed by life in a city that at one and the same time is a 21st-century economic powerhouse drawing on the contradictions of 20th-century class and race relations as mediated through 19th- (and even 18th-) century political structures. As this volume demonstrates so powerfully, Washington, DC is a city urban researchers can no longer afford to ignore.

References

Borges, J. (1998). Unworthy. In *Collected fiction*. New York, NY: Penguin.

Fuller, S. (Presenter) (2014, October 7). Federal spending fuels the Washington region's new economy. *Conference on a post-industrial powerhouse: Growth and inequality in our nation's capital*. Lecture conducted from American University Metropolitan Policy Center and Woodrow Wilson Center Urban Sustainability Laboratory, Washington, DC.

Hyra, D. (forthcoming). *Making the gilded ghetto: Race, class and politics in the cappuccino city*. Chicago, IL: The University of Chicago Press.

Jackson, M. (2012). Pricing the soul out of Washington, DC. *The Chronicle of Higher Education*. Retrieved April 3, 2015, from http://chronicle.com/article/Pricing-the-Soul-Out-of/132259/.

US Bureau of the Census. (2005). District of Columbia—race and Hispanic origin: 1800 to 1990. (www Census.Gov/population/twps0056/table 23.pdf).

US Bureau of the Census. (2013). Washington-Baltimore-Arlington, DC-MD-VA-WV-PA Combined Statistical Area. (www.census.gov/popest/data/metro/totals/2012/tables/CBSA-EST2012–02.xls).

US Bureau of the Census. (2015). State and county quick facts. (quickfacts.census.gov/qfd/states/1100.html).

CONTRIBUTOR BIOGRAPHIES

Chris Myers Asch

A native of Washington, DC, **Chris Myers Asch** has taught DC history at the University of the District of Columbia and Colby College. He graduated from Duke University and earned a PhD in American history from the University of North Carolina. He is the author of *The Senator and the Sharecropper: The Freedom Struggles of James O. Eastland and Fannie Lou Hamer* and currently is at work with George Derek Musgrove on *Chocolate City: Race and Democracy in the Nation's Capital*.

Johanna Bockman

Professor Bockman is an associate professor of sociology and global affairs at George Mason University. Her book *Markets in the Name of Socialism: The Left-Wing Origins of Neoliberalism* was published by Stanford University Press and she is working on a project that explores globalization, neoliberalism, and gentrification in Southeast DC. She reports on this project on her blog *Sociology in My Neighborhood: DC Ward 6*, teaches urban sociology, is a founding member of the Cities and Globalization Working Group, and serves as president of the DC Sociological Society.

Ralph Buehler

Ralph Buehler is an associate professor of urban affairs and planning at Virginia Tech. His research interests fall into three areas: (1) the influence of transport policy, land use, and socio-demographics on travel behavior; (2) active travel and public health; and (3) public transport demand, supply, and financial efficiency. Most of his research has an international comparative perspective, contrasting transport and land-use policies, transport systems, and travel behavior in Western Europe and North America. He holds a PhD in planning and public policy and a master's of city and regional studies from Rutgers University, as well as a master's in politics and management from the University of Konstanz, Germany.

Bell Julian Clement

Bell Julian Clement, professorial lecturer, George Washington University, studies the public policies that have molded the nation's cities. She has participated in urban development efforts as a community organizer, as an economic development planner, and as a small business advocate. Her dissertation, "Creative Federalism and Urban Policy: Placing the City in the Great Society" (George Washington University, 2014), explores the Johnson administration's effort to restructure the American city in the context of the upheavals of the 1960s.

Michelle Coghill-Chatman

Michelle Coghill-Chatman, native Washingtonian, is an assistant professor in the Division of Social and Behavioral Sciences at the University of the District of Columbia (UDC). Her research interests are in urban life and well-being, African diasporic identity, global youth development, and contemplative pedagogy.

Margaret Cowell

Margaret Cowell is an assistant professor of urban affairs and planning at Virginia Tech. Her research and teaching interests include economic development, urban politics, regional development, and economic restructuring. Prior to her current position, she was an assistant regional economist at the Buffalo branch of the Federal Reserve Bank of New York. She received her BA in urban studies from Brown University, an MA in urban planning from the State University of New York at Buffalo, and a PhD in city and regional planning from Cornell University.

Natwar M. Gandhi

Natwar M. Gandhi was the chief financial officer for the District of Columbia from 2000 through 2013 and was responsible for the entirety of the city's finances, including its $12 billion operating budget and its bond obligations. During his tenure, Gandhi helped to restore the city's fiscal strength, led the District out of the congressionally mandated financial control period, and secured numerous bond rating upgrades for the city from the three major rating agencies, including the first "A" level rating for the District since 1995. Gandhi has received numerous awards, including the Achievement of the Year Award from the Association of Government Accountants, the President's Award from the Greater Washington Society of CPAs, and the inaugural Meritorious Leadership Award from the Morris & Gwendolyn Cafritz Foundation Awards for Distinguished DC Government Employees. He holds a doctorate in accounting from Louisiana State University, a master's degree in business administration from Atlanta University, and an LLB and a BCom in accounting from the University of Bombay.

Howard Gillette

A professor of history emeritus at Rutgers University-Camden, **Howard Gillette's** work in public history has included a role as a founder and first director of the Center for Washington Area Studies at the George Washington University and as editor of *Washington History*, the journal of the Historical Society of Washington, DC. He is the author *of Between Justice and Beauty: Race, Planning, and the Failure of Urban Policy in Washington, DC* (Johns Hopkins University Press, 1995) and *Camden After the Fall: Decline and Renewal in a Post-industrial City* (University of Pennsylvania Press, 2005), among other publications. He is a past president of the Society for American City and Regional Planning History, a founder and first director of the Mid-Atlantic Regional Center for the Humanities at Rutgers, and currently serves as coeditor of the on-line *Encyclopedia of Greater Philadelphia*.

Allison Heck

Allison Heck is a presidential management fellow with the US federal government specializing in policy related to resilience, social vulnerability, and the built environment. She received a BS in anthropology from James Madison University, MAs in anthropology and urban and regional planning from the University of Florida, and a PhD in planning, governance, and globalization from Virginia Tech. Her research and teaching interests include neighborhood change, equitable development, and cultural heritage preservation.

Kathryn Howell

Kathryn Howell is an assistant professor in urban and regional studies and planning at Virginia Commonwealth University. Her research focuses on affordable housing, community development, neighborhood change, and regional housing development. She received a bachelor's degree in political science from the University of Georgia in 2001 and a master's degree in public policy from Johns Hopkins University in 2005. After receiving her doctorate from the University of Texas in 2013, she served as a research associate at George Mason University's Center for Regional Analysis. Prior to coming to the University of Texas, she worked for the State of

Maryland and the District of Columbia Departments of Housing and Community Development, where she focused on policy development for local and state green building initiatives, affordable housing preservation, and inclusionary zoning.

Amanda Huron

Amanda Huron is an assistant professor of interdisciplinary social sciences in the Department of Political Science, History, and Global Studies at the University of the District of Columbia. Her research interests include affordable housing and the urban commons, and she is particularly interested in mapping as a tool for social change. She received a PhD in earth and environmental sciences/geography from the City University of New York Graduate Center, and taught for a year at CUNY's Hunter College. She worked for several years in community radio before earning a master's degree of city and regional planning from the University of North Carolina, Chapel Hill, after which she worked on local affordable housing policy and advocacy in Washington, DC.

Derek Hyra

Derek Hyra is an associate professor in the School of Public Affairs and founding director of the Metropolitan Policy Center at American University. His research focuses on processes of neighborhood change, with an emphasis on housing, urban politics, and race. Dr. Hyra is the author of *The New Urban Renewal: The Economic Transformation of Harlem and Bronzeville* (University of Chicago Press, 2008) and is completing his second book, *Making the Gilded Ghetto: Race, Class, and Politics in the Cappuccino City* (University of Chicago Press, forthcoming), which investigates the redevelopment of Washington, DC's Shaw/U Street neighborhood. He received his BA from Colgate University and his PhD from the University of Chicago.

Maurice Jackson

Maurice Jackson teaches history at Georgetown University. He is author of *Let This Voice Be Heard: Anthony Benezet, Father of Atlantic Abolitionism* (2009), coeditor of *African-Americans and the Haitian Revolution* (2010) and of "Jazz in Washington DC," special issue *Washington History* (April 2014). He is at work on *Halfway to Freedom: African Americans and the Struggle for Social Progress in Washington, DC.*

Christopher Klemek

Christopher Klemek, of George Washington University, traces the political and intellectual shifts affecting urban policy and city life. His first book, *The Transatlantic Collapse of Urban Renewal: Postwar Urbanism from New York to Berlin* (University of Chicago Press, 2011), compares the fate of older industrial cities in Europe and North America, including Berlin, London, Toronto, Boston, New York, and Philadelphia. He is currently working on a new book that compares the development trajectories of Paris and Washington, DC.

Heike Mayer

Heike Mayer is a professor of economic geography at the University of Bern in Switzerland and an adjunct professor in urban affairs and planning at Virginia Tech. Her research is in local and regional economic development with a particular focus on dynamics of innovation and entrepreneurship, place making, and sustainability. She is the author of *Entrepreneurship and Innovation in Second Tier Regions* (published by Edward Elgar, Cheltenham, 2011) and the coauthor of *Small Town Sustainability* (with Prof. Paul L. Knox, Birkhäuser Press, Basel, 2009). She has published articles in the field of economic geography and urban planning in various journals, including the journal of the American Planning Association, *Journal of Urban Affairs, Economic Development Quarterly, Regional Studies, Economic Development Journal, European Planning Studies*, and with the Brookings Institution.

Gordon McDonald

Gordon McDonald is a 30-year veteran of the Office of Budget and Planning (OBP) in the District government, serving as deputy CFO for OBP since January 2008 and providing overall management for the development and execution of the District's $12 billion operating budget and $6.2 billion Capital Improvements Plan. During his tenure with OBP, the District produced 20 consecutive balanced budgets and received 15 "Distinguished Budget Presentation" awards from the Government Finance Officers' Association for the District's annual budget document. McDonald has received numerous awards, including the CFO Award for "Sustained Budget Quality in the FY 2001 Budget," the CFO's "Special Act Award," the CFO's "Sustained Superior Performance Award," and the Morris & Gwendolyn Cafritz Foundation Award for Distinguished DC Government Employees in 2011; and he holds a bachelor's degree in business administration and an MBA degree in finance from Howard University in Washington, DC.

Gabriella Modan

Gabriella Modan is an associate professor of sociolinguistics in the English department at Ohio State University. Her research focuses on the intersection of language and urban identity, with an emphasis on ethnicity and the discursive construction of city neighborhoods. She is the author of *Turf Wars: Discourse, Diversity and the Politics of Place* (Blackwell, 2007), a study of gentrification in DC's Mount

Pleasant neighborhood, as well as articles in linguistics, anthropology, and urban studies journals.

George Derek Musgrove

Professor Musgrove is the author of *Rumor, Repression, and Racial Politics: How the Harassment of Black Elected Officials Shaped Post–Civil Rights America* (University of Georgia Press, 2012) and a number of popular and scholarly articles on post–civil rights era Black politics. He is currently working on a history of race and democracy in Washington, DC with his good friend Chris Myers Asch.

Sabiyha Prince

Native Washingtonian **Sabiyha Prince** is an anthropologist, author, researcher, and qualitative data analyst. Her work has focused on the ways class, race, and other aspects of status and identity overlap to shape the condition and experience of African Americans in cities, topics she has explored in her books *African Americans and Gentrification in Washington, DC: Race, Class, and Social Justice in the Nation's Capital* (2014) and *Constructing Belonging: Race, Class, and Harlem's Professional Workers* (2004). A proponent of an engaged anthropology, Prince has worked with community groups in Washington, DC and appeared on MSNBC, NPR, the Pacifica Radio Network, and Al Jazeera English as a key contributor to the award-winning documentary *There Goes the Neighborhood* (2010).

Blair A. Ruble

Blair A. Ruble is vice-president for programs at the Wilson Center, director of the Urban Sustainability Laboratory, and senior advisor to the Kennan Institute. Previously, he served as the long-time director of the Kennan Institute for Advanced Russian Studies (1989–2012), as well as of the Wilson Center's Comparative Urban Studies Program (1992–2012). He is the author of numerous books, including *Washington's U Street: A Biography* (2010), which explores the tentative mixing of classes in one of the nation's capital's most important neighborhoods, and *Creating Diversity Capital* (2005), which examines the recent arrival of large transnational communities in Montreal, Washington, DC, and Kyiv. Ruble received his MA and PhD degrees in political science from the University of Toronto (1973, 1977), and an AB degree with highest honors in political science from the University of North Carolina at Chapel Hill (1971).

Susanna F. Schaller

Susanna F. Schaller is an assistant professor at CCNY and a certified urban planner. Schaller's research focuses on the micropolitics of urban governance. Specifically, she examines processes of urban restructuring and place making through public-private partnership, homing in on questions of equity and on dynamics of inclusion and exclusion. She teaches courses in urban studies and planning.

James Spaulding

James Spaulding is the associate deputy CFO for budget and planning in the District of Columbia, and during his 14 years with the District's budget office he has worked to strengthen such areas as the District's long-term financial plan, labor cost estimation, the Capital Improvements Program, and the quality of public-facing financial data. Prior to his District government service, he worked for more than 10 years for the US General Accounting Office (now the Government Accountability Office), focusing primarily on higher education and labor issues. He earned his bachelor's degree from Haverford College and his master's degree and PhD, both in economics, from the University of Wisconsin-Madison.

John Stowe

John Stowe is a master's candidate in urban and regional planning at Virginia Tech. His primary area of interest is transportation, especially active transportation (bicycling and walking), and transit. Stowe's research projects at Virginia Tech have focused on transportation and planning projects in the Washington, DC region, including the local economic impacts and operational efficiency of Capital Bikeshare; school travel choices made by families in Arlington, VA; and economic considerations for the proposed 11th Street Bridge Park. Before attending Virginia Tech, Stowe graduated from Johns Hopkins University in 2006 with a BA in cognitive science.

Brandi Thompson Summers

Brandi Thompson Summers is an assistant professor of African American studies and Director of the Center for Research on Culture, Race, and Representation at Virginia Commonwealth University. Her research focuses on the intersection of race, aesthetics, and visual culture with an emphasis on the contemporary racialization of bodies and urban spaces. Summers received her MA and PhD in sociology from the University of California-Santa Cruz, an MA in social sciences from the University of Chicago, and a BA with honors in history from the University of Pennsylvania.

Katie Wells

Katie Wells is a postdoctoral associate at Virginia Tech's Metropolitan Institute, and a visiting scholar in the Department of Geography at George Washington

University. She completed her PhD in geography at Syracuse University's Maxwell School in 2013. Her research focuses on property conflict, especially disputes over housing, poverty, and urban planning in US cities. She has published work about DC's history of homelessness activism, real estate speculation, and short-lived radical housing laws.

Brett Williams

Brett Williams began her work as an anthropologist among migrant farm workers in Illinois, exploring how they coped with terrible poverty and helping them organize a lettuce boycott and raise money for a halfway house. Since coming to Washington in 1976, Williams has written about gentrification, displacement, and homelessness; urban renewal and public housing; race and poverty; environmental justice in the Anacostia Watershed; urban nature; illness and inequality; and the culture of credit and debt. She has published six books, including one on African American hero John Henry, *Upscaling Downtown* (Cornell University Press, 1988), on the pain and promise of integration in an urban neighborhood, and *Debt for Sale* (University of Pennsylvania Press, 2005), which explores the rise of the super-profitable credit industry, including credit cards, student loans, pawnshops, and other predatory lenders.

INDEX

Note: Page numbers in italic indicate figures or tables.